THE
CONTROVERSY
OF ZION

ALSO BY GEOFFREY WHEATCROFT

The Randlords

THE CONTROVERSY OF ZION

Jewish Nationalism,
the Jewish State, and
the Unresolved Jewish Dilemma

GEOFFREY WHEATCROFT

ADDISON-WESLEY
Reading, Massachusetts

Library of Congress Cataloging-in-Publication Data
Wheatcroft, Geoffrey.
    The Controversy of Zion : Jewish nationalism, the Jewish state, and the unresolved Jewish dilemma / Geoffrey Wheatcroft.
        p. cm.
    Includes bibliographical references and index.
    ISBN 0-201-56234-0
    ISBN 0-201-32801-1 (pbk)
    1. Zionism—History. 2. Israel—History. 3. Jewish nationalism.
    4. Jews—Politics and government—1948-   I. Title.
DS149.W49   1996
320.5'4'095694—dc20   96-22661
                                                              CIP

Addison-Wesley is an imprint of Addison Wesley Longman, Inc.

Published in Great Britian by Sinclair-Stevenson.

Cover design by Suzanne Heiser
Text design by Chris Holgate
Set in 11-point Baskerville by Deltatype Limited, Ellesmere Port, Cheshire

1 2 3 4 5 6 7 8 9-MA-0100999897
First printing, August 1996
First paperback printing, October 1997

Find us on the World Wide Web at
http://www.aw.com/gb/

To
Abigail
and
Gabriel

Contents

Preface   xi

Prologue: 1840   1

I
From 'the Jewish Question' to *The Jewish State*
1840–1896

1 The Jewish Question   21
2 People or nation?   34
3 At home in Europe   49
4 'I have the solution . . .'   61

II
From *The Jewish State* to a Jewish National Home
1896–1917

5 *Mauscheln*   81
6 Englishmen of Hebrew faith   98
7 'America is our Zion'   117
8 A national home   130

III
From a Jewish National Home to a Jewish State
1917–1948

9   A Seventh Dominion   151
10 Blood and fire   166
11 Fulfilling the American dream   187
12 To the gates of Hell   202

IV
From a Jewish State to a Jewish Solution?
1948–1996

13 Victors, not victims   235
14 They and we   254
15 Hebrew and Jewish   274
16 Fractured friendships   294

   Epilogue: 1996   325
   Bibliography   353
   References   362
   Index   383

Happy art thou, O Israel: who is like unto thee,
  O people saved by the Lord.

Deut.xxxiii.29

How can we make the Jews happier and more
useful?

debate in France, 1789

Wird einst die Zeit, die ew'ge Göttin, tilgen
Das dunkle Weh, das sich vererbt vom Vater
Herunter auf den Sohn – wird einst der Enkel
Genesen und vernünftig sein und glücklich?

Heinrich Heine,
'Das neue israelitische Hospital zu Hamburg'

'To Palestine?' Friedrich asked in amazement.
  'What do you want there?'
'It is our land. There we can be happy.'

Theodor Herzl, *Altneuland*, 1902

For two thousand years our people dreamed.
For two thousand years Jews remembered Zion
and prayed for deliverance. In song, in prose, in
their hearts and thoughts, Jews kept alive the
dream of the Return to Zion . . . It has
happened and is happening in our time . . . How
fortunate we all are! How happy we all are!

Habonim resolution, 1947

When Franz Rosenweig tried to convert the
philosopher Hermann Cohen to Zionism,
Cohen said scornfully, 'Aha! So now the gang
wants to be happy, does it?'

Preface

'Some people like Jews and some do not,' Winston Churchill once said. 'But no thoughtful man can deny the fact that they are beyond question the most formidable and the most remarkable race which has ever appeared in the world.' They have also had the most extraordinary story. After their return twice from exile in Antiquity and their generations of greatness in their own land, the destruction of their kingdom by the Romans led to a Third Exile which lasted nearly two thousand years. For most of that time they were spurned and all too often persecuted in the lands where they had been dispersed; they were despised outcasts, sometimes useful to the societies among whom they lived, but never granted equality, in law or of respect. Then, from the Enlightenment and the Revolutionary era onwards, they were slowly emancipated and many of them tried to become what they had never been allowed to be before, loyal citizens of the countries where they lived.

And yet, as the nineteenth century wore on, emancipation increasingly appeared an illusion. The Jew was still a stranger, contemned and disliked if not actually persecuted, his position the more false and humiliating for his attempt to try and shed his identity and change his colours. This was the 'Jewish Question', to which, at the end of the nineteenth century, a drastic solution was proposed: Jewish nationalism, or Zionism. In 1896, Theodor Herzl unveiled his plan for a Jewish state where the Jews could live as free men and take charge of their own destiny.

His idea startled Jewry, and shocked many Jews. Quite apart from its apparent impracticability, it seemed to threaten the position of Jews who considered themselves faithful Austrians, Frenchmen, Englishmen, Americans, and leave them open to the charge of disloyalty or dual allegiance. Jewry as a whole was converted to Zionism not by arguments but by events. Warnings about the increasing threat to the European Jews came unimaginably and appallingly true when what had appeared to be the most advanced of countries placed itself in the hands of a tyrant who conquered most of Europe and murdered most of its Jews. In the aftermath of that catastrophe, a Jewish state was born, and survived through a series of fierce wars. It attracted, and depended on, the support of those Jews – and they were much the larger part of the surviving Jewish population of the world – who chose to continue living outside its borders. In turn, Israel became a source of healing pride for Jews everywhere.

But this relationship could never remain painless or untroubled. The Balfour Declaration which created a Jewish homeland in Palestine thirty years before the Jewish state was born had optimistically denied that such a homeland, let alone a state, would prejudice either the rights of the existing non-Jewish communities in Palestine or the rights of Jews in other countries. That pious aspiration apart, Herzl had earlier hoped that a Jewish state would 'answer the Jewish Question'. A century earlier still, a debate had been held in revolutionary France on the topic, 'How can we make the Jews happier and more useful?' and it became the purpose of Zionism to answer that question also. It was a scheme to resolve the Jewish Question, and to make the Jews happy.

Did it? This book is prompted by that query. It is not a history of the Jews, or of antisemitism, or of Zionism, or of Israel, examples of all of which can be found in the bibliography. It is a discursive examination of the debates which were provoked by the Jewish Question and Zionism, and of the way in which the Jewish national movement and the creation of a Jewish state have affected Jews everywhere.

Of course I am conscious of my temerity or even impudence: both as a journalist entering a scholarly field and as an intruder trespassing on a Jewish debate. There are several omissions in my story, not through inadvertence. I hope I shall not be reproached with ignoring the impact of Zionism on the Arabs, as though I were unaware how great it was; but that is not my theme, which is the impact of Zionism on the Jews. Some omissions stem from modesty. There were important arguments about Jewish nationalism in terms of Judaic theology, which it would be more than impudent for me to judge. All in all, this is an amateur work, but in two senses: it is written by someone who is not a professional authority, but as well in the primary definition of an amateur as one who is fond of the subject; perhaps also in the sense of Groucho Marx's 'gifted amateur brain surgeon', though I hope not.

There might even be an advantage in looking at the story from a remove. Although I like to think that I come into Churchill's former category, I am not myself Jewish, Israeli, or a Zionist; nor for that matter an 'anti-Zionist': in the conflict between Jew and Arab in the Holy Land, I am a genuine neutral or agnostic, able to see right and wrong on both sides and wishing both sides well, a position which wins one no friends at all. But if agnosticism can be fatal to the politician or even the political journalist, it may help the historian. In the course of discussing nationalism and who is equipped to study it, E. J. Hobsbawm has suggested that, although a proud attachment to either the Irish-Catholic or Ulster-Protestant traditions might be compatible with the serious study of Irish history, 'to be a Fenian or Orangeman, I would judge, is not so compatible, any more than being a Zionist is compatible with writing a genuinely serious history of the Jews'. However that may be, Jewish writers, from Moses Hess and Theodor Herzl to Ahad Ha-am and Claude Montefiore to Martin Buber and Judah Magnes to Hillel Halkin and Bernard Avishai, Zionist or assimilationist, European, American or Israeli, all write inescapably from inside the argument; I, just as inescapably, from outside, and this at least allows a different perspective.

Even then, the subject is one which it is obviously, or notoriously, difficult to write about *sine ira et studio*; one where learning and lucidity may count for less than tone of voice. Before he began work on *The Decline and Fall of the Roman Empire*, Gibbon had considered writing a history of modern England, his own country in his own time. But he shrank with terror, as he put it in his memoirs, from a subject 'where every character is a problem, and every reader a friend or enemy; where a writer is supposed to hoist a flag of party, and is devoted to damnation by the adverse faction'; and anyone writing about the story of Zionism knows just what Gibbon meant. One colleague who read my manuscript suggested that my tone was sometimes too cool and detached. That may be so, but I hope it is a fault on the right side. Too many of the other books I have had to read while writing this one are, to quote Gibbon again, 'stained in every page by the disingenuous malevolence of party'. If I have had a conscious aim, it was to write without looking over my shoulder, neither slandering nor flattering any party; and, to conclude the absurd comparison, I should not at all mind the compliment which the author was paid by Hume after the first volume of *The Decline and Fall*: 'You have observed a very prudent temperament.'

Tone of voice apart, the subject presents other problems. It is – or so I have found – impossible to give a continuous narrative of historical events while discussing the controversies which they influenced, and which were influenced by them. The sound historical principle of chronology cannot always be reconciled with the sound journalistic principle of putting everything on the same subject in the same place. This is not a political or social history. It is a history of thoughts, of arguments, of feelings, I hesitate to say of *mentalités*, in which publication dates are often as important as the dates of battles or treaties. Which is to say that, although Gibbon (for the last time) advised historians 'never to pursue the curious', I have had to ignore this generally good advice, since 'the curious' is part of my subject.

One other piece of advice, however, I have tried to keep in mind. Another of the greatest of English historians, F. W. Maitland, told us always to remember that events now far in the past were once in the future, and, in his splendid book on Bleichröder, Bismarck's Jewish banker, Fritz Stern amplifies this: 'No one in 1880 could have imagined a Hitler any more than in 1933 people could have imagined an Auschwitz.' That is profoundly true, and profoundly important. Nothing in history is predestined. It was not inevitable that the Jews should be driven into exile, persecuted and reviled; that they should then have been emancipated; that emancipation should seem to have failed; that its failure should have produced the Jewish Question; that Zionism should have been proposed as an answer to this question; that a Jewish homeland should have been created as part of the outcome of one war; that Hitler should have come to power and murdered the European Jews during another war; that a Jewish state should have been created and survived; or that in the course of these other events the largest and richest Jewish community since Antiquity should have arisen in the New World which would succour that Jewish state, while enjoying a most complex relationship with it. And so the reader who wants a bare narrative, a partisan account, or a teleological drama should look elsewhere.

It is pleasing to thank those friends, acquaintances and strangers who in their generosity helped me while I was writing this book (and it is tempting to list those who conspicuously did not). An incomplete list must include the names of Bernard Faber, Jean Freas, Barry Gewen, Charles Glass, John Gross, Mickey Kaus, Mary Kenny, the late

Terence Kilmartin, Michael Kinsley, Susan Lynas, Diana Pinto, Jasper Ridley, Ian Thomson and Edward Timms, my father, Stephen Wheatcroft, and my father-in-law, Frank Muir. Rodney Blumer and Matthew Reisz both read versions of the manuscript, to my profit.

My greatest professional debt is to Gill Coleridge, literary agent, working mother and part-time psychiatric social worker, who has gently nursed me throughout. I am grateful also to her American colleague Kris Dahl, to Christopher Sinclair-Stevenson and Henning Gutmann for commissioning the British and American editions, and to Neil Taylor and Katie Green for their editorial care and attention. Julia Howard word-processed my inscrutable handwriting over and again with amazing speed and accuracy. Ilsa Yardley corrected my English, Gina Thomas corrected my German, and Hazel Bell corrected further errors in the proofs while making the index. This book was originally meant to be published in New York by Lee Goerner of Atheneum. It is sad to me that his list no longer exists, but infinitely sadder that Lee himself did not live to see the book in which he had shown faith.

The staffs of the British Library, the London Library, the New York Public Library, the Jewish Studies Library of University College, London, and the Wiener Library have all earned my gratitude. The last has been particularly helpful to me (and forbearing about overdue books), but is all too clearly run on limited resources. Since it and the Jewish Studies Library both duplicate and complement one another, and there is only a brisk ten-minute walk from Devonshire Street to Gower Street, could not a marriage usefully be arranged between the two, perhaps with the Jewish Historical Society as matchmaker? A word of thanks is also due to the greatest of the Hebrew prophets, for providing me with a title. Even if Isaiah did not have my subject in mind when he wrote 'For it is the day of the Lord's vengeance, and the year of recompenses for the controversy of Zion', he gave me a phrase which describes it very aptly.

Although I have never myself lived with someone who was writing a book, I have just enough imagination to realise that it cannot be easy. My dear wife has sustained me, for better for worse, for richer for poorer, in sickness and in health, through what have sometimes been trying and tiring times, though that partly for the happiest of reasons. It is enough to say that Sally helped to produce this book while also producing its two dedicatees.

Prologue: 1840

By the waters of Babylon we sat down and wept:
when we remembered thee, O Sion

Ps.cxxxvii.1

In August 1840, Lord Palmerston received a curious letter. The Foreign Secretary was absorbed at the time in the latest phase of the Eastern Question, as the Powers called the agonisingly protracted decline of the Ottoman Empire and its consequences for Europe. The letter touched on that topic, but only obliquely. It came from Lord Ashley, a younger Member of Parliament, and as it happened Palmerston's stepson-in-law. Palmerston had 'been chosen by God', Ashley wrote, 'to be an instrument of good to his chosen people; to do homage, as it were, to their inheritance'. Everywhere there had been a 'revival of zeal on behalf of God's chosen people'. Ashley was convinced that the Scriptures were soon to be literally fulfilled, and that the time was at hand 'for the return of the Jews to their inheritance in the Land of Promise'. Shortly afterwards, the letter was elaborated in a leading article in *The Times*, likewise inspired by Ashley. It proposed 'to plant the Jewish people in the land of their fathers' under the protection of a European power, presumably England.

Letter and leader must have puzzled Palmerston. He was certainly remote from the feeling which lay behind them. More than years separated him from Ashley. On the surface a flippant voluptuary, the Foreign Secretary was a sincere friend of liberty, a man who early in his career gave up office in support of Catholic emancipation and towards the end of it threatened to resign as prime minister if the campaign against the slave trade were relaxed. But even if he dimly recognised that remembrance of Zion inherited from God's chosen people which ran through Ashley's religion (and which inspired a hope on his part that, once restored to Palestine, the Jews would see the light of Christian truth), he was all the same a complete stranger to the younger man's brand of fervent evangelical Christianity and to what Carlyle called the 'universal syllabub of philanthropic twaddle' which it inspired. Although Palmerston understood and championed the cause of oppressed nationalities, it can scarcely have occurred to him that the Jews were such a nationality, 'a people struggling justly to be free' like the Greeks or the Italians. And he cannot possibly have guessed that, within eighty years, a British government would indeed have fostered the return of the Jews to the land of their fathers, or that, within little more than a century, his successors at the Foreign Office would be wrestling with another phase of the Eastern Question: the birth of a Jewish state in Palestine.

For God's chosen people themselves, remembrance was everything. Until the nineteenth century their history had been extraordinary enough, but divided into two utterly contrasting parts by one event. For more than two thousand years in Antiquity, the Jews had known every possible triumph and disaster. They had planted themselves in their land, with their Book and their God, pushing the Canaanites aside. They had been taken into Egyptian and then into Babylonian captivity. The Israelite and Judaean monarchies had risen and fallen. The Land of Israel had been conquered by Cyrus and Alexander the Great and by the Romans. But the Jews had always remained a nation, with a home to which they could return, once and again. They had a language, in which their sacred texts were written, and, even though Hebrew was scarcely spoken as an everyday tongue after the return from Babylonian captivity, there was never a time from then to the present when learned men could not read and write it.

And so the Jews' religion of one god, their sense of divine mission, their faith in messianic promise, had been fortified by memory: not of mythical heroes and deeds, like the religion of the ancient Greeks or the Hindus, but of real history, albeit in exalted form. 'We were slaves to Pharaoh in Egypt' when God's angel had passed over the Israelites' houses whose doorposts were marked with lambs' blood, and only the first-born of the godless were slain. Passover was followed by Purim, remembering Esther's defeat of Haman in his plan to destroy the Jews; by Hanukkah, remembering the purification of the Temple after its pollution by the Syrians; by remembrance of how Judith seduced Holofernes in order to kill him. These sanguinary memories of victory and deliverance sustained the Jews even when Pompey at last captured Jerusalem for Rome, killed many thousands of Jews, and made Palestine a Roman vassal.

For all their ancient sustaining faith, the end was now in sight for the Jews in their own land. Not only conquered, they were told to worship the Roman emperor as their new god, and refused. They were ordered to eat pork in humiliating defiance of their Law, and rebelled. Retribution followed swiftly. Jerusalem fell again, to Titus. And the Temple was destroyed. A group of fanatical Jewish nationalists or Zealots took refuge in the mountain fortress of Masada on the edge of the Judaean desert where they were besieged by the Romans. Rather than surrender, the remaining defenders took their own lives in a powerfully resonant gesture.

The Destruction of the Temple was an irreparable disaster and a great symbolic event, a caesura cutting Jewish history in two. Not only was the Jews' history disrupted: their religion and their own character changed. A sacrificing priesthood became a teaching rabbinate. A nation with a home became a people in exile. In the Greek sense of the words, the Jews had been drastic; they became pathetic. They had made their own story; now it was made for them. They had done; now they were done to.

Other peoples had known utter defeat before, or were to know it since. Seventeenth-century Europe saw the total eclipse of Czech Bohemia at the Battle of White Mountain and of Gaelic Ireland at the Battle of the Boyne, and it took either nation two or three centuries to get its own back. It took the Jews almost two thousand years. They had not been exterminated physically by a stronger empire, as happened later to simple indigenous peoples in large parts of America, Africa and Australia when Europe arrived. Instead they were scattered to the corners of the earth. Even by the time of Titus the greater part of the Jewish people probably lived outside the Holy Land.[1] There were already large Jewish colonies in Babylon and Hellenic Alexandria. Soon, the Jews were to live almost entirely in exile. A handful remained in their ancient homeland, but most now lived in the 'Diaspora' or Dispersion; in Hebrew, the Galut. The Roman Empire

[1] This name will often be used subsequently: it has the great convenience of evading the political implications of either 'Palestine' or 'Israel'.

which had destroyed Jewish sovereignty also made it easier for the Jews to migrate westwards and northwards. This Dispersion spread out from the eastern Mediterranean, to the Italian and Iberian peninsulas and northwards into Europe, as well as putting out shoots into Asia and Africa.

By the end of the first Christian millennium, the centre of the world, where Asia, Africa and Europe met and whence the Jews had sprung, was contested between two monotheistic religions and their cultures, both descended from Judaism. The Jews lived in both Christendom and Islam, but in both they lived as strangers. They were sometimes tolerated, sometimes not. There were rare places and brief times when Jews mixed freely and creatively with Christians and Muslims: Norman Sicily, or Moorish Granada. But these bright moments stand out in the darkness. Elsewhere the Jew was reviled and harassed and spurned. A long line of legal proscriptions across mediaeval Europe emphasised the Jews' abject and inferior position. Some Jewish communities were massacred, some were expelled, now from England, now from France. Even when they were allowed to settle, it was in humiliating conditions. Venice needed its Jewish colony for commercial purposes, but locked them in a kind of barracks or prison which, from the local dialect word for 'foundry', gave the name ghetto to all languages.

Two expulsions had historic consequences. By the late eleventh century a large Jewish community had formed in the Rhineland, but then massacres drove them out and eastwards, to settle slowly across eastern Europe from the Baltic to the Black Sea. Four hundred years later, Spain celebrated the union of the crowns of Aragon and Castile and the final conquest of the country from the Moors in 1492 by expelling the Jews, who fled, some of them to Portugal and the Low Countries, others eastwards along the Mediterranean, as far as Turkey. Those two branches of the Dispersion were dispersed again and became the groups of Jewry known as Ashkenazim and Sephardim respectively, though the terms are very imprecise. Wherever they had settled, the Jews had kept Hebrew, the language of the Torah, the Psalmist and the Prophets, as a sacred and sometimes as a literary language, but they also adopted and adapted local languages for everyday use. Two of these were taken with the harassed Jews on their travels: Yiddish, based on mediaeval Rhenish German, to eastern Europe; Ladino, based on mediaeval Castilian Spanish, to the eastern Mediterranean and the Balkans. It is a striking example of Jewish resilience and continuity that both these languages should still have been spoken in the early twentieth century, by hundreds of thousands in the case of Ladino, by millions in the case of Yiddish.

From the fifteenth century, Europe experienced a succession of intellectual and social revolutions. The 'rebirth' or Renaissance was followed by the Reformation in the sixteenth century and by the scientific revolution of the seventeenth. If the schoolbook theory of progress had been true, then each of these should have brought new freedoms and comforts for the Jews. In reality this period of Jewish history saw one false dawn after another, culminating at the end of the eighteenth century in the French Revolution. What indeed took place between 1492 and 1789 was the steady transmutation of the old Jew-hatred into something which would be called antisemitism. The distinction between the two can no doubt be exaggerated. There was a common thread, a dislike of the Jews' strangeness and otherness. But a difference does exist, which was to be thrown into highlight by the Jews' difficulty in being accepted as members of secular societies.

Jew-hatred had been based on religion, at least in appearance. The foes of the Church were the 'Jews, Turks, Infidels and Hereticks' for whom Christians prayed on Good Friday; but especially the Jews. All Christians believed that the Jews had killed Christ.[2] He might have been of the stem of Jesse, Son of an unimpeachably Jewish mother. The 'sacrifice of the Mass' by the Christian priesthood may have patently echoed the sacrificing religion of the old Hebrew priests. But that made all the worse the Jews' own pertinacity in error and refusal to recognise the Messiah.

Intolerant as Christianity so often was, it recognised at least in theory, as Islam also did, the possibility of contrition and conversion. Or did so until the period of the Renaissance: by no coincidence the years which saw the national state taking embryonic form saw also a plainly racial rather than religious Jew-hatred emerge. Like others before them, the Spanish Jews were offered the choice of conversion, expulsion or death. Some converted. Now, for the first time, these conversions were suspect, and not because of any objective evidence that they were in bad faith (the Catholic Church had always been happy enough with conversions under duress). The implication was clear: once a Jew, always a Jew. Even earlier, under the '*estatuto di limpieza de sangre*', the statute of purity of blood promulgated in Toledo

---

[2] And few Christians would have been impressed by Disraeli's ingenious argument: 'If the Jews had not prevailed upon the Romans to crucify our Lord, what would have become of the Atonement?'

in 1449, Jewish converts were forbidden to hold office, and these exclusions were intensified in the following century. Converted Jews became known as Marranos, a fighting word on both sides. To the Spaniards, they were untrustworthy or insincere, suspected, sometimes rightly, of keeping a secret attachment to their old faith; to the Jews, 'Marrano' became another word for apostate or trimmer.

Jews might have seen the Church of Rome as their special enemy, but the Protestant Reformation did not offer much improvement. Even before the Reformation began, the most enlightened Christian of his age, Erasmus the humanist, complained that the converted Jews among his opponents had not rid themselves of the spite which was their national instinct. Then came Martin Luther. In 1523 he published one tract with the unarguable title 'Jesus Christ was Born a Jew', in which he proposed the benevolent redemption of the Jews by conversion, and explained the Jews' bad character – on the existence of which so many writers, Jewish as well as gentile, were to agree for centuries to come – as a product of their unhappy history and centuries of Christian oppression. But this comparative benevolence was short-lived. Otherwise, Luther developed a novel and virulent strain of Jew-hatred. On a material level, he argued like many that the Jews were parasites bleeding the German nation white. On a moral level, Luther added with more originality that the Jews threatened to contaminate the spirituality of the German people, and of course the purity of Lutheran doctrine. This was the concept of *Verjudung*, 'Jewing' or 'Jewification', and it was something new. In 1539, Luther preached against the Jews and in 1543, he launched another diatribe, 'Against the Jews and their Lies'. 'They are our masters and we their servants,' he thundered; the princes should 'deal harshly with them . . . and drive them out like mad dogs'; the Jews 'are still our plague, our pestilence, our *misfortune!*'

Progress has never been linear. For the two-and-a-half centuries after Luther there were small improvements in the Jews' condition. The Dutch Republic offered them some shelter, Oliver Cromwell allowed them into England formally for the first time since they had been expelled by Edward I. As an English Puritan, Cromwell refracted a particular tradition, within the larger European tradition as it looked at the Jews. That attitude had almost always been hostile, but it was also ambiguous. The Church might pray for the conversion of the Jews who had killed Christ, Christians were taught to dislike and despise Jews. And yet Christianity itself was an offspring of Judaism, and resounded with Jewish echoes. Christians sang the Psalms of David, and the Nunc Dimittis, the Virgin's prayer 'to be a light unto the Gentiles: and to be the glory of thy people Israel'. For a thousand years the kings and queens of England have been crowned to the splendid words 'Zadok the Priest and Nathan the Prophet anointed Solomon king', made more splendid still from the eighteenth century by Handel's great setting. Different Christian factions invoked Jewish tradition for different purposes. A year after the Gunpowder Plot of 5 November 1605, when Roman Catholic conspirators tried to blow up Parliament, Lancelot Andrewes, bishop of Chichester (and one day to be T. S. Eliot's hero), preached a sermon on 'a day of God's making ... it is the Scripture fulfilled in our ears ... the destroyer passed over our dwellings this day. It is our Passover and our Purim.' And yet, his contemporary, the composer William Byrd, set the Lamentations of Jeremiah with an intensity which reflected his own feelings as a Catholic living in the shadow of persecution, while the Gaelic poets of Catholic Ireland wrote about their country's enslavement by Protestant England, using the imagery of Israel enchained by infidels.

Not only the European Christian religion, its churches and liturgy, were shot through with memories of Israel, from the Roman magnificence of Michelangelo's statues of Moses and David, to little Welsh chapels called 'Zion', or 'Ebenezer' (which Israel pitched beside, in the first book of Samuel). European culture, music and literature were shot through also. Handel wrote *Israel in Egypt*, Rossini wrote *Mosé*, Verdi wrote *Nabucco* with its haunting chorus for the Jews in Babylonian captivity, '*Va pensiero*'. When Dryden wanted to write a satire on English politics in 1681, it came naturally to call the Duke of Monmouth 'Absalom' and Lord Shaftesbury 'Achitophel' (after the story in the second book of Samuel). Even English socialists centuries later drew on their emotional roots in radical Protestantism, adopting as their own hymn Blake's 'Jerusalem'. The English were indeed a 'people of the Book', and so, notably, were their American offspring from the seventeenth century onwards. Their Book was, most of it, the Jews' Book. Much of what God's chosen people remembered, the English and the Americans also remembered. A later Lord Shaftesbury (as Ashley was to become) echoed that remembrance of Zion when he hoped for a return to the Land of Promise.

Against these was the steady climate of hostility and resentment, not only on the side of the Church and the *ancien régime* but, most ominously, of the self-styled philosophers of eighteenth-century

Enlightenment. On the one hand, an old-fashioned Jew-hater like
Johann Andreas Eisenmenger published *Entdecktes Judenthum* (*Jewry
Exposed*) in 1711, with Prussian royal patronage, detailing the barbarous
and murderous nature of the Jewish religion, denouncing the 'freedom
of trade' which made the Jews 'lords' over the Germans, relating tales
of ritual murder and poisoning of wells, and advocating the closing of
the synagogues and the conversion of the Jews. More ominous yet for
the future was Voltaire. The standard-bearer of philosophical reason
wrote of the Jews with unflagging hatred and contempt: 'this nation is
only an ignorant and barbarous people who have long united the most
sordid avarice with the most detestable superstition and the most
invincible hatred for every people by whom they are tolerated and
enriched.' The words are from the *Dictionnaire philosophique*, a book
which influenced a generation of the best minds in Europe. The
invocation of Jewish tradition was protean, but so was Jew-hatred. It
could be based on Catholicism or Protestantism, on Christianity or, in
Voltaire's case, on a dislike of Christianity.[3]

Most ominous of all for the Jews as the eighteenth century neared its
close was the emergence of what can now for the first time be called
nationalism: a newly formed ideology of nation based on history, on
language, and – though this did not emerge clearly until the nineteenth
century – on 'race'. As with Voltaire, this was not the work of vulgar
demagogues but of thinkers of the weight of Kant, Fichte and Herder.
None of these was a fully developed racist in the later sense. Herder in
particular condemned the 'animal' theory of purely hereditary national
type. And yet all three strongly believed in the doctrine of 'national
character'. Herder thought that the (it was almost superfluous to add
'bad') Jewish national character was so deeply entrenched as to be to
all intents hereditary; while Kant condemned Judaism as 'not really a
religion at all, but merely a community of a mass of men of one tribe'[4]
and thus without the 'pure moral belief' necessary to a true religion.
He attributed to the Jews' religion as well as their history their 'not
undeserved reputation for cheating', and despaired 'of vain plans to
make this people moral'.

[3] The prince de Ligne, who came to know him well, believed that 'the only reason
why M de Voltaire gave vent to such outbursts against Jesus Christ is that He was
born among a nation whom he detested'.
[4] This began from the correct observation that Judaism, unlike Christianity or
Islam, is not a proselytising faith, but is tied closely to the one people who handed
it down by inheritance.

These writers were not the only Europeans, nor even the only Germans. Their great contemporary Gottfried Lessing wrote his play *Nathan der Weise* (*Nathan the Wise*) in 1779, with three noble characters, a Christian, a Muslim, and in particular the eponymous Jew, making an eloquent plea for religious toleration. Three years later nature followed art. Joseph II of Austria's Edict of Toleration in 1782 was a landmark, a triumph of Enlightened statecraft, and also of far-seeing Habsburg policy. In A. J. P. Taylor's words, 'by freeing the Jews, Joseph II called into existence the most loyal of Austrians. The Jews alone were not troubled by the conflict between dynastic and national claims: they were Austrians without reserve.' Even this description carries a hidden sting. If the Jews were the most loyal subjects of the supra-national Habsburg monarchy, might they not also become the most hated target of those national movements which were to break up the empire?

At the time of the Edict, Joseph had just greatly enlarged the number of his Jewish subjects. By the middle of the eighteenth century, the Jewish Dispersion had been spread unevenly. Most Jews lived in Europe, of whom most lived in eastern Europe, of whom most lived in one vast country: the kingdom of Poland united with the grand duchy of Lithuania, which stretched almost from the Oder in the west to the Dnieper in the east, from the Gulf of Riga on the Baltic to within little more than a hundred miles of the Black Sea. Jews were still scattered throughout Islam from Persia to Morocco, tolerated rather than cosseted, and there were Jewish communities in most west European countries, though none of them numerous. There were at this time perhaps a little fewer than two million Jews in Europe, around four-fifths of the Jewish people as a whole; of the European Jews, five out of eight lived in eastern, one in four in central, and one in ten in western Europe; although it should be said that until the nineteenth century figures of Jewish population are largely conjectural.

There was even, by this time, a small Jewish settlement in that New World which Columbus had discovered just as his royal patrons were expelling the Jews from Spain. In 1654, a group of twenty-three Sephardic Jews who were fleeing the Inquisition landed in the Dutch colony of New Amsterdam, little knowing that it would one day be called New York, and become the greatest Jewish city on earth. For two hundred years this community very slowly expanded. As an offshoot of Puritan England, the American colonists had their own romantic memories of Zion. One preacher compared the rebellious Americans with the Jews, the thirteen colonies in revolt against George III with the ten tribes of Israel driven to rebellion by Reheboam. Thomas Jefferson, Benjamin Franklin and John Adams suggested that the seal of the United States should show the Jews crossing the parted Red Sea. And in 1823 another minister not only speculated whether the American Indians might not be descended from the lost tribes of Israel, but proposed their return, along with the other Jews, to the Holy Land.

But for all these far-flung outposts, in the middle of the eighteenth century much the greatest number of Jews still lived in Polish territory, whether Poland itself, or Lithuania, White Russia and Little Russia (Ukraine). Their numbers there may perhaps have been increased by conversion of the Khazar tribe in the Middle Ages, and had certainly been decreased by terrible massacres in the seventeenth century. Then in 1772, 1793 and 1795, three cynical and rapacious Partitions carved up Poland among its three neighbouring empires. As an overlooked consequence, Russia, Austria and Prussia acquired large Jewish populations for the first time, and from now on the story of the Jews was to be closely bound up with those countries. Across that huge territory this east European Jewry was largely homogeneous. Jews lived together in ghetto and shtetl ('little town' or village), dressed alike, practised the same religion with its intricate observances, spoke the same Yiddish language. In the nineteenth century, as soon as they could, many moved out of these small communities to cities and further afield. But old Poland-Lithuania remained the great reservoir of Jewry.

Before the Partitions were finished, Europe was shaken by the earthquake of the French Revolution. This had profound implications for the Jews, whose history was still being made for them from outside rather than by themselves. At first the Revolution brought emancipation: the ghetto doors were opened. It brought also a new questioning of the Jews' role in society. A debate was held in France on the subject 'How can we make the Jews of France happy and more useful?' It was a novel theme, and it divided the debaters on what were to become familiar lines. On the one hand were the foes of the Jews, who believed that their situation should never be changed, since 'their misery is a sign of the Christian Faith'; or that the best answer was to deport them *en masse* to the wastelands of Guiana. On the other were those who, while conceding the Jews' bad character, thought it was the product of environment rather than heredity: 'if someone wanted to produce such vices in the Jews', the best way would be to confine them in ghettos unable to play a full role in society; or, as Robespierre put it, 'the vices of the Jews spring from the degradation we have kept them in'. The enlightened conclusion to all these debates was summarised by the comte de Clermont-Tonnerre: 'We must grant everything to the Jews as individuals, but nothing to the Jewish nation ... There cannot be a separate nation within the nation.' He added minatorily that if the Jews wanted emancipation on those terms they should be welcomed, but if not they should be expelled.

In 1798, in the course of the career which would turn revolutionary and republican France into an empire, Napoleon Bonaparte landed in Egypt. From there he led his expeditionary army to Palestine, where suddenly and strangely he apostrophised the Jews: 'Thousands of years of conquest and tyranny have deprived you of your ancestral lands. Yet for all the time you have somehow continued to exist as a nation. Long ago when the prophets Joel and Isaiah saw the approaching destruction of their fatherland they also foretold the day it would be restored. Now at last that day has dawned. Arise with gladness ye heirs of Palestine. A great nation calls on you to take on what has been conquered and to remain as masters there, defending it against all comers. Hasten! Now is the moment which may not return for generations to claim back the rights you have been deprived of for thousands of years, to live again as a nation among nations.'

In France itself, the small Jewish community would have been puzzled by these words. French Jews were deeply grateful for the emancipation which the Revolution had brought, and anxious to hang on to it. As citizens and soldiers, they served Republic, Directory and then Napoleon's Empire as loyally as they were allowed to. For his part, Napoleon displayed a brilliant flair for publicity and opportunism. He conceded as much: 'It was as a Catholic that I won the war in the Vendée, as a Moslem that I established myself in Egypt, and as an Ultramontane that I won the confidence of the Italians. If I were governing the Jews, I should rebuild the Temple of Solomon.'

Unable to achieve quite that, he gathered instead an Assembly of Jewish Notables in 1806, and the next year a Sanhedrin, supposedly a revival of the supreme court of the ancient Hebrew commonwealth. This was a stunt. It was meant to appeal to Jewish feeling, which it did: the news was heard with joy as far away as Russia, whereas the speech in Palestine had been ignored even by the tiny Jewish community who lived there and who remained loyal to the Porte. It was also a political device equivalent to Napoleon's early concordat with the Papacy, and this too succeeded in the sense that the Sanhedrin adopted 'render unto Caesar': Jewish teaching, it proclaimed, was purely religious, the French Jews' political allegiance was purely to the Emperor. The Sanhedrin even condemned money-lending at high rates of interest though not usury itself. Above all, the offer of assimilation was met with a promise: the Jews 'no longer form a nation within a nation', said Abraham Furtado, a financier who had been head of the earlier Assembly. 'France is our country. Jews, such today is your status: your obligations are outlined, your happiness is waiting.'

Napoleon's motives throughout were calculated, not to say cynical. In 1798 his army was in the Levant, in 1806 his army was on the Vistula and needed the help of Jewish traders in Poland. His attitude to nationalism in general was ambiguous. Napoleon ostensibly embodied the new principle of national consciousness, as opposed to the Habsburgs' pre-revolutionary, anti-national dynasticism. In reality he exploited rather than embodied national feeling; and it might have been he rather than the Habsburg emperor Francis II who asked the famous question of a 'patriot', 'But is he a patriot for me?' That question was to be asked of the Jews, again and again, as their history continued to be made for them by others.

Whatever Napoleon's motives, his claim that the Jews were a nation presented them with a problem. The Revolutionary and Napoleonic era marked a decisive parting of the ways among European Jewry. Those in the east dug deeper into the burrow of their communal life. Neither emigration nor assimilation presented a dilemma for them, since neither was a practical possibility. Napoleon's vision of a nation among the nations was meaningless to them, if it meant a national state like France.

The Jews had never forgotten their Holy Land of Israel. They recited Psalm 137: 'By the waters of Babylon we sat down and wept: when we remembered thee, O Sion . . . How shall we sing the Lord's song: in a strange land? If I forget thee, O Jerusalem: let my right hand forget her cunning.' They prayed to 'next year in Jerusalem'. There was a touching custom among ghetto Jews of sending an invitation for a wedding, to be held in Jerusalem, unless the Lord in his wisdom had not by then restored the Land of Israel, in which case it would take place nearby. A great Jewish thinker like Spinoza believed that the Jews might once again become a nation in the full sense: 'unless the fundamentals of their religion have made them effeminate in mind, I would absolutely believe that at some time they, given the opportunity

– inasmuch as human affairs are mutable – may once again establish their state, that God may choose them anew.'

And yet: these speculations were not merely hypothetical, they were utopian in the full sense of More's coining, 'U-topia', 'no-place'. The Jews knew that Palestine existed, but there seemed absolutely no prospect of their returning thither. There had been earlier chiliastic movements of Jewish redemption. The *Anglo-Saxon Chronicle* tells what must have been a well-known story of a false Messiah who, in the sixth century, had persuaded the Jews of Rhodes that, as Moses had led his people through the Red Sea, they could walk to the Holy Land, with the result that numbers of them drowned. Other false Messiahs since had promised a return. Very rarely, pious Jews did manage to make their way to the Holy Land, though one of them, Rabbi Mendel of Vitebsk, worried in the 1770s that, if the Jews were to come, 'they would cover the whole land'.

There was, to be sure, an uninterrupted tradition of Jewish habitation of Palestine, despite conquest by Saracens, massacre by Crusaders and conquest again by Ottomans. Only a few years after Napoleon's expedition, another Frenchman visited Jerusalem. Chateaubriand found there a tiny community, despised and persecuted 'without complaint . . . It has seen Jerusalem destroyed seventeen times, yet there exists nothing in this world which can discourage it or prevent it from raising its eyes to Zion. He who beholds the Jews dispersed over the face of the earth, in keeping with the Word of God, lingers and marvels. But he will be struck with amazement, as at a miracle, who finds them still in Jerusalem and perceives even, who in law and justice are the masters of Judaea, to exist as slaves and strangers in their own land; how despite all abuses they await the king who is to deliver them.'

As a Catholic and conservative, Chateaubriand lamented the Jews' 'deplorable blindness, which merits our compassion'. And yet he was overwhelmed by the spectacle of this 'small nation' who had survived Persians, Greeks, Romans, now all vanished; 'If there is anything among the nations of the world marked with the stamp of the miraculous, this, in our opinion, is that miracle.' Jews everywhere had some sense of the same miracle. All the same, for almost all of them the Land of Israel was a place which existed in their hearts and imaginations, rather than a place to which they would go physically; still less one where they believed the old kingdom of David could be reborn.

For that tenth of European Jewry living in the western part of the

Continent, the idea that the Jews were a nation among nations
represented a different kind of challenge, and a threat. Before the
Revolution, there were signs of intellectual and social ferment
beginning in European Jewry, despite the fact that almost no careers
were open except finance and the rabbinate. The eighteenth century
had seen the fervent devotionalism of the Hasidic movement among
poor eastern Jews, and it had seen further west the contrary
phenomenon of the Maskilim, the men of the Jewish enlightenment
epitomised by Moses Mendelssohn, who much impressed German
learned society by his brilliance, and by his attempts to accommodate
the faith of his fathers to the Age of Reason. Then the Revolution and
the Napoleonic wars had together brought a wave of liberation. From
Atlantic to Baltic, ghettos were opened. Men who would have lived in
obscurity became famous writers, parochial money-lenders became
international bankers, like the Rothschilds of Frankfurt and the
Warburgs of Hamburg. There was indeed a bright moment, as
Hannah Arendt put it with a touch of exaggeration, when the old Jew-
hatred had died and the new antisemitism had not been born. That
was the age of the Berlin salons, of Rahel Levin, Amalie Beer and
Henriette Herz, brilliant and beguiling Jewish women (though almost
all of them became Christians). Either way, for the newly baptised or
for Jews who adhered to their religion, emancipation opened new
doors; and the idea of a 'Jewish nation' threatened to shut them.

Quite what this meant was not clear immediately. The Revolution
represented an idea, the Rights of Man, which Bonaparte took over
and adapted towards the realities of legal reform and efficient
administration. He also took over the notion of universal empire from
the Holy Roman Emperors with their shadowy legacy of Augustus and
Charlemagne. But the real bequest of Revolution and Empire was a
new sense of nation which was to transform Europe in the century
between Waterloo and the Great War. That century, and that new
nationalism, were to be crucial to the Jews' story.

As it was, Napoleon's fall seemed to dash Jewish hopes. Within five
years of Waterloo, Jew-baiting 'Hep! Hep!'[5] riots had swept Germany.
Jews could either return to cringe in ghetto or *Judengasse*; or, if they
wanted to retain the emancipated bourgeois status many had attained,
they could convert. On the face of things, conversion was an answer, at

---

[5] The old Jew-baiters' slogan which was supposedly an acronym of 'Hierosolyma
Est Perdita'.

least in practical terms. Christianised Jews could at last rise high. In Spain, of all countries, with its memories of the expulsion of the Jews and then of the persecution of the Marranos, it was now possible for a man of Jewish origin like Juan Mendizábal to become prime minister in 1835 (even if his enemies invariably caricatured him as a Jew with a devil's tail). In England, the country which all of enlightened Europe had admired since the seventeenth century, the Jews had had an easier time than on the Continent. Until the nineteenth century they could not enter Parliament or hold other offices, but then nor could Papists or Dissenters, and it was at those that the system of monopoly for the Church of England was aimed, with Jews almost as incidental casualties. Some restriction applied even to Jews who had become Christians. In 1785, the Courts of Aldermen of London passed a mean-spirited standing order that baptised Jews could not be admitted to the freedom of the City, which was not rescinded until 1828. But in Parliament there was no formal discrimination, and under the Georges several men of Jewish origin sat in the House of Commons.[6] There had even been romantic stories like Sampson Gideon's. He made an immense fortune in the City of London but could not be honoured since, despite his marriage to a Protestant Englishwoman and his severance of his connection with the Bevis Marks synagogue, he did not accept baptism. Instead, 'he breeds his children Christians', as Horace Walpole wrote. In 1759, a baronetcy was conferred on his son, a fifteen-year-old boy at Eton, who subsequently became Lord Eardley. One of Gideon's daughters married Lord Gage, one of his granddaughters married Lord Saye and Sele. When Gideon died, it was found that he had continued to pay a subscription to the synagogue under an assumed name. If I forget thee . . .

By the nineteenth century and the age of reform, with rational utilitarianism in the ascendant, full Jewish emancipation appeared among the political agenda. It had bitter enemies. Sir Robert Inglis, the extreme Tory Member for Oxford University, told the Commons in 1833 that 'the Jews are strangers among us. And strangers they must continue to be. They must ever remain a distinct and separate nation', a turn of phrase whose full implications Inglis himself may not have grasped. But emancipation had friends also. Its most eloquent parliamentary advocate was the statesman and historian Thomas Babington

[6] Among them Sir Mannaseh Lopes, Ralph Bernal and David Ricardo the great economist.

Macaulay. A century and a half later, his speeches on the Jews would still ring with life and honour, and his words remained the classic statement of the liberal position. He too accepted that the Jews had 'degenerated from the qualities of their fathers', that, 'bowed down under the yoke of slavery, they had contracted some of the vices of outlaws and slaves'. But this should be a matter of remorse and shame to those who had enslaved them. Until the Jews had been emancipated, 'let us not presume to say that there is no genius among the people of Isaiah, no heroism among the descendants of the Maccabees'.

Macaulay addressed the question in a way which was both humane and matter-of-fact. He was not so much concerned with the millions of Jews – the large majority of the Jewish people – living in eastern and south-eastern Europe under the old empires. He was concerned with the position of Jews in the West, in his case those – no more than a few score thousand – living in England. He was vaguely aware of the Jews' religious and millennarian traditions, but he was as untouched as Palmerston by Ashley's evangelical zeal, and did not begin to understand how that zeal could lead to an enthusiasm for restoring God's chosen people to the Land of Promise. In the same speech, Macaulay mentioned, as an objection which had been made to removing their disabilities, the fact that 'the Jews look forward to the coming of a great deliverer, to their return to Palestine, to the rebuilding of the Temple, to the revival of their ancient worship, and that, therefore, they will always consider England not their country, but merely as their place of exile'. But he dismissed this objection on the grounds that something which might (or might not) happen 'at some time altogether indefinite' could not 'occupy the minds of men to such a degree as to make them regardless of what is near and present and certain'.

This speech was all of Macaulay, showing his decency, and his complacency; his concern for the practical in the here and now, the present and certain, and his inability to understand anything romantic or irrationally inspiring. He was quite right in supposing that the restoration of Zion was something scarcely anyone, Jew or gentile, then seriously dreamed of. And yet in a passing phrase he had hit on the question which was to haunt the Jews, not less so as that fantastic dream became reality. Was England – or Germany, or France, or the United States – their home, or merely their temporary place of exile where they could only be strangers or guests, welcome at best, unwelcome at worst? Several years later the debate on whether Jews should sit in Parliament was about to be resolved; and as the first

Jewish MP took his seat, Thomas Carlyle expressed his venomous contempt: 'How can a real Jew try to be a senator, or even a citizen of any country except his own wretched Palestine, whither all his thoughts and steps and efforts tend – where, in the Devil's name, let him arrive as soon as possible and make us quit of him.' These words, too, brutal as they were, suggested a difficult but real question of identity.

For the moment, as Macaulay saw, the Jews' problems were practical. In the West they were despised rather than oppressed, in central Europe they were oppressed rather than persecuted, in the East they were still, from time to time, persecuted. The lot of the Jews who lived under the Tsar was heavy, and that of those who lived under the Sultan not always lighter. In the Ottoman empire the Jews constituted a 'millet' like the Greeks or Armenians, a community defined by religion rather than race and on the whole left alone as long as they did not make trouble. But persecution was always a real threat.

A reminder of how real it could be came in the same year in which Ashley wrote to Palmerston. Jewry everywhere was shaken by the Damascus affair. Torpid rather than tolerant, the Ottomans allowed Christian clergy to operate in most parts of their empire. One such was a Capuchin friar living in Damascus, where in February 1840 he was murdered. His colleagues claimed that he had been killed by Jews who wanted his blood for their Passover ceremonies. This was the ancient 'blood libel', which was to enjoy such a long and vigorous life: the belief that Jews killed Christians, often children, to use their blood for some ritualistic purpose. On this occasion, the libel was encouraged by both the local Ottoman governor and the French consul who was responsible for protecting Christians. Several Jews were interrogated under torture, two died, one 'confessed' and named other names, sixty-three Jewish children were taken hostage until their families revealed where the blood was kept.

Communication was slow, but when the story at last reached Europe it raised a storm. Maybe for the first time, but very far from the last, the prosperous free Jews of the West answered a call for help from their oppressed brethren in the east. The French Jew Isaac Adolph Cremieux, in his early thirties already a celebrated liberal lawyer, was enlisted in the affair (as, a quarter century later, and by then president of the Alliance Israélite Universelle, he was to intercede on behalf of the Romanian Jews by going to Bucharest), and went to Alexandria. The delegation was led by a British Jew, Sir Moses Montefiore, born in Leghorn but settled in London to become one of the twelve 'Jew brokers' of the City, president of the Board of Deputies and in the fullness of time the most venerated Jew of his age and place, a friend of Queen Victoria's whom he entertained when she was a girl. He knew the ways of the world and ensured Palmerston's support before he set off on his mission. In August, the month that Ashley wrote to Palmerston, Montefiore triumphed. The hostages were released and the Sultan officially prohibited the public circulation of blood libels, though he could not stop the credulous privately believing them.

This triumph warmed the hearts of those Jews who heard of it, but not before Jewish hearts had been chilled. It was a dreadful reminder, at what was in some ways a time of hope, of the precariousness of the Jews' position. They had a long way to go before they could emerge from helplessness, and the apparent difficulty of achieving true emancipation prompted much day-dreaming, on the part of Jews as well as of pious Christians like Ashley. Quite by coincidence, in the year of his letter also, a pamphlet was published in Berlin lamenting the Jews' fate in exile, and proposing a remedy: *Neu-Judäa: Entwurf zum Wiederaufbau eines selbständigen jüdischen Reiches* ('New-Judaea: outline for the rebuilding of an independent Jewish empire').

Although he did not reach the same conclusion, one other Jew was enraged. When the news of Damascus reached Germany a fifteen-year-old boy was overcome with shame as well as anger. 'Even the Christians marvel at our sluggish blood, that we do not rise, that we do not rather perish on the battlefield than by torture,' Ferdinand Lassalle wrote. 'Is there a revolution anywhere which could be more just than if the Jews were to rebel, set fire to every quarter in Damascus, blow up the powder magazine and meet death with their persecutors? Cowardly people, you deserve no better fate.' Written in a private diary, this was nevertheless an historic outburst. With his fantasies of physical force, Lassalle was rejecting the Jewish tradition of passivity and acceptance of injustice, adumbrating instead a new toughness and resistance. There is something new also – at least in the vehemence of its expression – in his sense of self-contempt and alienation. The Damascus affair in itself was no more than another episode in the long history of hatred and persecution of the Jews. Lassalle's response to it marks the early stages of something else: the Jewish Question.

I

From 'the Jewish Question' to *The Jewish State*

The Jewish Question

A faithless and stubborn generation.

Ps.lxxvii.9

Around the time of Ashley's letter, the Damascus incident, and the Berlin pamphlet, a new phrase appeared, as name and concept. In 1842, Bruno Bauer published *Die Judenfrage*, 'The Jewish Question', taking a hostile look at the Jews, but the name must have been in currency before then. Despite some continuity between the Jew-hatred of the old regime and more recent growths, this Jewish Question could not have existed before the French Revolution. It was a function not of traditional ostracism and oppression but of emancipation. And it scarcely affected, directly or to begin with, the traditional, unemancipated masses who were still the great majority of Jews in the East. 'There is a sense', as Isaiah Berlin puts it, 'in which no social problem arose for the Jews so long as rigid religious orthodoxy insulated them from the external world. Until then, poor, downtrodden and oppressed as they might be, and clinging to each other for warmth and shelter, the Jews of eastern Europe put all their faith in God and concentrated all their hope either upon individual salvation – immortality in the sight of God – or upon the coming of the Messiah whose approach no worldly force could accelerate or retard. It was when this great frozen mass began to melt that the social and political problem arose.'

The social and political problem was thus a paradoxical by-product of Enlightenment, of Revolution, of emancipation, of all the forces produced by and with the new industrialism which was gradually transforming Europe. It was the misbegotten offspring of liberalism, the doctrine which was spreading across Europe alongside economic change, with its programme of freedom of religion, of the press and of trade, of a rational rule of law, of constitutional representative government. This programme came often to be linked with nationalism, although there was no necessary connection: in the generation following Waterloo, there was an increasingly vigorous liberal movement in Italy, for example, but, whatever later nationalist historians asserted, before 1848 it had little to do with any demand for the unification of Italy as a national state.

Jewish emancipation was an instinctive part of the liberal programme. It came at different paces in different places: to Holland in 1796, to Belgium in 1833, to some German states in the 1830s, to Denmark and Piedmont in 1848. In England the barriers against unbaptised Jews participating in national life came in fits and starts as the old Anglican monopoly crumbled. Emancipation brought with it great opportunities for the Jews of the West not available to their kindred in the East, but it also brought agonies and dilemmas unknown in the ghetto. These were especially acute in Germany;[1] the Jewish story is intimately connected with German history. And the 'Jewish Question' is dominated in the middle of the nineteenth century by German Jews, though illuminated also by the career of an English Jew.

If you were born in 1786, as Löb Baruch was in Frankfurt, you were old enough to remember life before Napoleon, when a passing gentile could say 'Do your duty, Jew', and the Jew must doff his hat. Baruch described the good old days with the bitter irony which became a German-Jewish hallmark. By the loving care of the authorities the Jews were forbidden to leave their homes on Sundays, he said, lest drunkards molest them; they were forbidden to marry until twenty-five, so that their offspring were healthy; the promenades of the city were closed to them, so that they should walk in the countryside where their interests in agriculture could be kindled; and so sardonically on.

The young man was able to study medicine in Berlin, where he fell in love with Henriette Herz. Then in Hamburg, he was made a police actuary in 1811 under the liberal grand duchy which Napoleon had created. But in 1814, under the restoration, he lost his job. His first

---

[1] Germany here includes Austria: 'Germany' was not a political unit until 1871, except under the very notional Holy Roman Empire of 800–1806, and the German Confederation of 1815–66; and Austria belonged to both of those.

reaction was the obvious one: angered by the reborn oppression of German Jews, he took up the liberal cause as a journalist. As the nineteenth century wore on, radical or revolutionary politics and journalism were to be the paths taken by many men seeking a way out of their own Jewish problem.

Another way presented itself, and this course was also now taken by Löb Baruch when he became Ludwig Börne and converted to Lutheranism. Over the next century or more many other western Jews were to follow him into one Christian church or other, usually with the same motives. Some few converts, from Ezekiel Margoulioth, a rabbi who took Holy Orders in the Church of England and whose son was a clergyman, don and brilliant Orientalist, to the saintly Edith Stein, who became a Roman Catholic and a nun before she was murdered by the National Socialists, were devout Christians. More were not. Daniel Chlowson was born in 1819, the son of a poor melamed, or elementary Hebrew teacher, in a Lithuanian village called Eyishoshok. Since Russian universities were closed to Jews he went to study in Germany, but returned to Russia, was baptised into the Orthodox Church, and became a professor at St Petersburg university. According to a hallowed story, Chlowson was once asked if he had become a Christian from sincere conviction, and replied, 'Yes. I was sincerely convinced that it was better to be a professor in Petersburg than a melamed in Eyishoshok.'[2] It was the voice of thousands of others, in Russia, Germany and Austria.

If there was no sincere love of Christianity in Börne's conversion, there was something like a sincere dislike of Judaism, or even of the Jews. A year before Börne joined the church founded by a man who had called the Jews 'our plague', another Jewish family converted, this time into the Church of England. Isaac D'Israeli was an amateur scholar who compiled his engaging *Curiosities of Literature* while living on an independent income. He was also a pillar of his synagogue in London, until he quarrelled with it and left in dudgeon. All his children were taken to the Established Church to be baptised, including Benjamin, born in 1804. Isaac justified this momentous decision – which was to provide England with a prime minister – by saying that

---

[2] Not that this was a uniquely Jewish dilemma, or answer. In the previous century the heir to the Irish estate of Oranmore was brought up as a Roman Catholic, at a time when Catholics could not own land. He became a Protestant, and came into his inheritance. When the local Church of Ireland parson asked him one day what had brought him to the Light, he replied simply, 'Oranmore'.

Judaism cut the Jews off from the great family of mankind. This was an understandable sentiment, or at least one which many emancipated Jews were to feel. There were to be others, that is, like the English philosopher A. J. Ayer's Jewish grandfather, who 'had no liking for Judaism or indeed any form of religion [and] also believed that the Jews, throughout their history, had brought many of their troubles on themselves by their clannishness and religious obduracy'. This was an attitude which Zionists would later despise as a form of cringing subservience, but it seemed plausible enough to those who were trying to leave the ghetto emotionally as well as physically.

But Börne went further than his fellow converts. In an essay on *The Merchant of Venice* – he was a brilliant theatre critic as well as a political journalist – written in 1828, Börne saw Shylock both as an avenging angel for a 'despised, downtrodden race', and as a symbol of the incurable Jewish worship of the 'gold-devil'. From this, Börne moved on to a bitter attack on the Shylocks of his own day, bankers and speculators in whose world God is the great Finance Minister, the Fall of Man was the first stock-market crash, and the Day of Judgement is the close of the current account. Not all of these new Shylocks were Jews, he said, but the Christians scarcely deserved the name. Unconsciously echoing Luther, he said that all of European society was undergoing *Verjudung*: it was being 'judaised'.

This terrible passage had to be understood in terms of Börne's own story, his conflicts with his money-changer father, his resentment at his dismissal from his post, in which, by an all-too-familiar psychological process, righteous anger was turned into guilt, then self-contempt. Familiar among all people in one form or another, it became a dominant mode of feeling among emancipated European Jews, later to be given the name of Jewish self-hatred. That concept must be used with the greatest care; it cannot just be applied to any Jew critical of Judaism or Jewry. But it does mean something, in Börne's case for one.

Perhaps also in Heinrich Heine's case. The high priest of German-Jewish irony was just over ten years Börne's junior, but old enough to experience the same sequence of emancipation followed by its annulment, a process akin to a torturer's beatings, followed by soft words, followed by more beatings. At one moment Heine was able to study at university, at the next insulted so that he had to leave. He met the remnants of the emancipated society of Berlin; he continued to revere the memory of Napoleon; he travelled to England, where he admired Canning's political liberalism, but disliked the commercial materialism of the English; he converted. He became a Christian in name rather than spirit six years after Börne had, and from the same motives. In Heine's own phrase, conversion was the entrance ticket to European civilisation. It was not calculation or self-interest in the most cynical sense, rather an attempt to compromise with the society in which he lived, and to escape from the burden of the past. Heine shared Börne's dislike of financial money-grubbing, and of the Jews who practised it: 'Money is the God of our time, and Rothschild is his prophet.'

And yet, with all his savage indignation and his contempt for much about the Jews, Heine saw their predicament with tenderness as well as bitterness and irony. His overwhelmingly powerful poem about the Jewish hospital in Hamburg expressed this with a depth of feeling none had shown before. It describes 'a hospital for poor, sick Jews, for creatures thrice wretched, afflicted with the three gravest of ailments, poverty, illness and Jewishness! The worst of these three is the last, the thousand-year-old family malady, the plague from the Nile valley.' There is nothing modern medicine can do to alleviate this incurably deep sorrow. But

> *Wird einst die Zeit, die ew'ge Göttin, tilgen*
> *Das dunkle Weh, das sich vererbt vom Vater*
> *Herunter auf den Sohn – wird einst der Enkel*
> *Genesen und vernünftig sein und glücklich?*

'Will Time, the eternal goddess, one day wipe out the dark woe handed down from father to son – Will the grandson ever be cured and reasonable and happy?' This was not mere self-hatred, or contemptuous rejection of his people (though there are such overtones). And yet Heine had no remedy of his own to offer for 'the incurably grave illness of his brother'. He, and many like him, had left the physical ghetto, but were still trapped in a psychological and moral ghetto.

If irony was one means of escape, another was dandyish insolence. That was Disraeli's method, and it worked to an almost bizarre extent. Several of his first political associates in the Young England group like Lord George Bentinck were racing and betting men; when Disraeli entered the Commons in 1837 (heavily pursued by creditors: one of his strongest motives for becoming an MP was the immunity it gave him in regard to his enormous debts) and made his disastrous maiden speech, no gambler would have taken anything but the longest odds against his one day becoming prime minister. That is not to exaggerate the astonishing achievement of his career, in the way that he himself did. Certainly he triumphed over any number of obstacles, not least the racial hatred which pursued him throughout his career, and which his biographers have tended to underplay (Irish nationalists, from O'Connell in the 1830s to colleagues of Parnell's like Biggar in the 1870s, were particularly eloquent in this vein). But his ascent up the greasy pole was not quite as amazing as he liked to make it seem. Nor did all of his many bitter enemies have merely unworthy motives.

It is hard to fault what the high Tory, Lady Gwendolen Cecil, biographer of her father Lord Salisbury, said about Disraeli: 'He was always making use of convictions he did not share, pursuing objects which he could not own, manoeuvring his party into alliances which, though unobjectionable from his own standpoint, were discreditable and indefensible from theirs. It was an atmosphere of pervading falseness which involved his party as well as himself.' Or what the Whig Duke of Argyll said: 'It is really nonsense to talk of a man in such a position as a mere "Jew boy"[3] who by the force of nothing but extraordinary genius attained to the leadership of a great party. The only impediments in his way were not any want of external advantages but his own often grotesque and unintelligible opinions.' Disraeli was a romantic and a romancer; a chancer, a brilliant tactician and an opportunist; and there have been few more absurd projects than the attempt to construct a 'Disraelian' political philosophy since his death.

Far from denying his Jewishness (not that this was an option), Disraeli made much of it. He constructed a fanciful account of his origins, while relishing the incongruity of his position as a Jew who was a member of the Church of Hooker and Andrewes, sometimes with near-Heinean irony and relish: 'I am the blank paper between the Old and New Testament,' he is supposed to have told Queen Victoria. He wove the Jews into his own strange political theories, and projected his personal story on to English history. Some of what he said was shrewd. For more than a century, European and American conservatives instinctively saw the Jews as a radical and subversive group; the lesson of what Disraeli said – that 'the persecution of the Jewish race had deprived European society of an important conservative element and added to the destructive party an influential ally' – was not fully learned until the last part of the twentieth century. As Heine had said,

---

[3] Argyll was no bigot: his maiden speech in the Lords in 1848 had been in favour of removing Jewish disabilities.

Jews became more like the countries in which they lived, and they also reacted according to circumstances. Where they were oppressed, as by the Tsars, they became hostile and revolutionary. Often this hostility to existing society ,,as so ingrained that it lasted for a couple of generations after migration to the West. The latter shift of so many Jews away from revolutionism and radicalism was sometimes seen as the corrosive effects of prosperity, but it was really a reversion to type. Wherever Jews had been treated tolerably well, as by the Habsburgs, they had always been loyal and even conservative subjects. It was not just a question of 'an important conservative element'. Disraeli saw with almost frightening prescience that the Jews needed only the 'career open to the talents' to succeed and even excel. Once that was granted, they would be even more than they were, 'a living and most striking evidence of the falsity of that pernicious doctrine of modern times, the natural equality of man'.

Events had turned Börne and Heine towards liberalism; they turned Disraeli towards Toryism. But perhaps the three had more in common than this suggests. The crucial episode in Disraeli's career was the crucial episode in English history of the age: the destruction of Peel in the battle over the Corn Laws. Comically enough, Disraeli became the standard-bearer of the landed nobility and gentry, and thus the advocate of the cause of protection against the radical Cobdenites who wanted Free Trade. But Disraeli's romantic reaction was closely linked with a broader reaction against industrial society, materialism, progress. The age of Young England was also the age of neo-Gothic, of the Eglinton Tournament, of the Oxford Movement, of *Hard Times*.

Dickens's book was only one (though the best) of many: England in the 1840s saw a rash of didactic novels dealing with social, religious and political questions.[4] Disraeli joined in with *Coningsby*, *Sybil* and *Tancred*. These expounded his political philosophy, such as it was, condemning Whiggery, materialism, heartlessness towards the poor, and utilitarianism. In *Tancred*, part of the didactic purpose is philosemitic. The hero is an English lordling who reacts strongly against the social conditions of his country – the 'Two Nations', the rich and the poor, whose existence Disraeli evidently believed he was the first to have noticed – by travelling to the Holy Land. After an episode in which Tancred becomes involved in the struggle between Maronites and Druzes in

---

[4] By, among others, Kingsley, Newman, Mrs Gaskell, and – an extreme case – Mrs Frewing's 1849 novel, *The Inheritance of Evil or the Consequences of Marrying a Deceased Wife's Sister*.

Lebanon (maybe the one real case of precognition in the book), he falls in love with a Jewish girl and is vouchsafed a vision of the true doctrine of 'theocratic equality'.

All of his vaguely Judaic mumbo-jumbo, his half-remembered Hebrew phrases, maybe even his saying that 'Christianity is incomprehensible without Judaism as Judaism is incomplete without Christianity', might make Disraeli, in his eccentric way, a self-affirming Jew touched by that quality of *Ahabath Israel*, or 'love of the Jewish people', which German Jews so often seemed to lack. And yet there is a link between Disraeli and Börne. What was the utilitarianism, industrialism and money-grubbing which Disraeli condemned, but the corruption of society by the base and banausic values of commercial materialism which Börne also denounced – and saw as *Verjudung*? And, despite Disraeli's romantic vision of the Jews, there would be plenty of those on Left as well as Right who would be ready to make an explicit connection between greedy commercial society and the Jews. The French writer Toussenel put it succinctly in his book *Les juifs rois de l'époque*: 'the word [*juif*] is taken here in its popular meanings *juif, banquier, marchand d'espèce*.'

This connection only needed to be taken a step further. One other Rhineland Jew was born in 1818. Karl Marx's grandfather had been a rabbi, his father was a lawyer who in 1824, like Isaac D'Israeli a few years earlier, had his whole family baptised. If this was intended to make Karl an integrated and contented member of society, it was not a success. Marx studied law and philosophy, he met the young Hegelians of Berlin, and he began to formulate his own ideology which he correctly described as a mixture of German philosophy, French politics and English economics. He married a gentile woman of high birth.[5] He worked for a time as a journalist, but before long took up with the rich merchant Friedrich Engels, who supported him for most of his life. In 1848, Marx wrote *The Communist Manifesto*, a polemical call to arms, but it was not for nearly twenty years that he began to publish *Das Kapital*.

Although he was not a Jew by religion, although he is usually described as a 'non-Jewish Jew', and although he appears, like Börne, to be both radical and alienated, Marx was in many ways intensely Jewish: in his analytical cast of mind and also in his combativeness. But

[5] Descended from the Earl of Argyle who was beheaded under James II and thus a distant cousin of Disraeli's critic the Duke of Argyll.

he was most of all a Jew who hated Judaism, and even Jewry. In 1844 he published two essays 'On the Jewish Question'. He was replying to Bruno Bauer, who had urged the Jews to abandon their religion and join the rest of mankind. Marx agreed with Bauer, but went further. 'The Jew . . . and his money power . . . decide the destinies of Europe.' He warmed to his theme: 'Money is the jealous God of Israel, besides which no other god may exist. Money abases all the gods of mankind and changes them into commodities . . . The God of the Jews has been secularised and has become the god of this world.'

Much of this was the stock rhetoric of contemporary socialism. One of Marx's many left-wing foes (no man ever took less notice of the revolutionary slogan '*pas d'ennemi à gauche*') was the French socialist Pierre-Joseph Proudhon, and he had accused the Jews of corrupting the whole European bourgeoisie. They were the enemy of mankind, he said, unsociable, and infernal: 'We should send this race back to Asia or exterminate it.' It is striking, indeed, how protean Jew-hatred remained, how adaptable by people of all political outlooks, and how tenacious. There were not many Jews in western Europe in Marx's and Proudhon's day, they were mostly very poor, and most commerce and finance was controlled by gentiles. But 'the Jew' was an irrepressibly powerful idea, for Right as well as Left. From one side the Jew was attacked as the despised corrupter of aristocratic values, from the other, as the wicked exploiter of the proletariat.

Even by the standards of contemporary radical rhetoric in its mode of hostility to finance in general and Jewish financiers in particular, there is something extravagant about Marx's language. He saw clearly enough that the determining quality of Jews in central and western Europe was no longer their religion. In that case, emancipation would indeed have been the end of the 'Question', as it had been, for example, for the Roman Catholic minority in England or the Protestant minority in France. Marx distinguished between the 'Sabbath Jew', or religious Jew, and the 'everyday Jew', the profane basis of whose Judaism or Jewishness was his self-interest, his huckstering, his love of money. The only true emancipation of the Jews must be 'the emancipation of mankind from Jewry'.[6] Marx did not deny that he was Jewish; he even once referred to Disraeli as a man 'from our common stock'. But abuse of Jews ran through his public

[6] A continual ambiguity affects writers using German. That language has the one word – *Judentum* – for three in English, 'Judaism' (religion), 'Jewry' (people) and 'Jewishness' (characteristic). Judaism as a faith is not what Marx meant here.

and private writings, where he scorned the 'stock-exchange synagogue' and told the readers of the *New York Tribune* that, just as there was a Jesuit behind every pope, 'every tyrant is backed by a Jew'.

Marx's relations with his contemporaries were complex, and usually acrimonious. Of those other German Jews, Heine revered Marx, who inspired some of his poems, but Börne was denounced by Marx with extreme and inexplicable violence. Perhaps Marx unconsciously recognised a kinship with Börne; certainly his own attacks on the Jewish God of Money echoed Börne's hatred of *Verjudung*. As for Lassalle, he was the object of Marx's most venomous outpourings of hatred. Part of the motive for this was jealousy. Marx's own call to the barricades had gone unanswered. He preached his revolutionary doctrine to a devoted but tiny band of printers and tailors (skilled artisans, not even true proletarians) in London and Paris, while the masses ignored him. By contrast, short as it was, Lassalle's career as a socialist agitator was much more successful than Marx's. By the time of his abrupt death in 1864 he was the acknowledged leader of the working-class movement in Germany. Even Bismarck, though he was dismissive of Lassalle during his lifetime, spoke warmly of him after his death, and most people who knew Lassalle admired him for his courage and integrity, despite his absurdities.

These were obvious enough. Lassalle was not just a Jewish dandy, he was the original champagne socialist, the quintessence of radical chic. He combined his political career with an extravagant social life, entertaining splendidly in Berlin and indulging generally in a life of luxury and fashion. Lassalle devoted almost as much energy to the cause of an aristocratic woman friend, Countess Hatzfeldt, whom he believed to have been wronged by her husband, as to the cause of the workers. Years later he met another well-born young woman, and he died – of all ends for a populist and friend of the working man – fighting a duel for her honour. To that extent, Engels had some reason for writing to Marx that 'it is revolting to see how he tries to push his way in the aristocratic world'.

But the next sentence was even more riveting: 'He is a greasy Jew under his brilliantine and flashy jewels.' Incautious words to write to the grandson of a rabbi, it might be thought. But then Marx and Engels were, as the Germans say, one heart and one soul on the subjects of Lassalle, and the Jews. Marx described Lassalle as 'Baron Itzig', 'leprous', the 'Jewish nigger', speculating jocosely on whether he was not descending 'from the Negroes who joined in Moses' flight from

Egypt (unless his grandmother on his father's side was crossed with a nigger)'.

Despite this hatred, Marx and Lassalle had found the same way of escape from their origins, the same answer to their own Jewish problem. Disraeli sought another route. Compared with Marx he may seem lightweight, with Lassalle, insincere. And yet he saw something which eluded both of them. Marx's prophetic system had several great flaws. One was his belief in the immiseration of the proletariat, whom the bourgeois would be forced (whether they wanted to or no) to make poorer and poorer. Another was his claim that the proletariat would make a revolution and take power, when, according to his own theory, political power is a function of economic power, the former passing to those who control the latter, and the proletariat are by definition economically powerless.

But his greatest single error was his belief that class was all-important and class solidarity all-powerful. He quite failed to foresee that, for better or all too often for worse, it was kinship, race, nationality that men had always fought and died for, and would continue to fight and die for, in all parts of the globe, regardless of supposed common class interest. Though he was sometimes right, Marx was never more wrong than when he said that 'the proletariat have no fatherland' (that was often enough all the poor did have). And this blindness had a clear psychological explanation. Marx did not, deep down, ignore ethnicity; he projected it, into the terms of class oppression and class war. As Isaiah Berlin puts it, when Marx preaches uncompromising social conflict and revolution, 'it is the centuries-long oppression of a people of pariahs, not of a recently risen class, that seems to be speaking in him'; his voice is the voice of a 'proud and defiant pariah, not so much of a friend of the proletariat as of a member of a long humiliated race'.

For all his risible identification with the 'gentlemen of England', Disraeli did not need this act of transference. He understood better. Far from overlooking the ties of blood, he gloried in them. 'All is race – there is no other truth,' says Sidonia, the rich and mysterious Jewish banker in *Tancred*. And again, 'The influence of a great race *will* be felt . . . it is impossible to destroy the Jews.' Sometimes he dwelt on his ancestry gravely, sometimes gaily: 'Fancy calling a fellow an adventurer when his ancestors were probably on intimate terms with the Queen of Sheba.' The one thing he never did was to disavow his Jewishness, to apologise for supposed 'Jewish vices', or to turn on the

Jews as Börne and Marx had done. Neither of them would ever have boasted, like Disraeli, of belonging to a race which could do anything but fail.

More than that, he exalted feeling over reason in a way which rational men might find depressing, but whose truth they could not entirely deny. 'How limited is human reason,' Disraeli insisted. 'We are not indebted to the reason of men for any of the great achievements which are the landmarks of human action and human progress. It was not reason which sent the Saracens from the desert to conquer the world, that inspired the Crusades, that instituted the monastic orders'; and it was not reason which would send the Jews from the world to conquer the desert, would inspire a new Crusade in the Levant, or would create the monastic devotion of so many Zionists. 'Man is only truly great when he acts from the passions; never irresistible but when he appeals to the imagination. Even Mormon counts more votaries than Bentham.' The last flourish neatly avoided the fact that industrial society and the utilitarian principle of 'the greatest happiness of the greatest number' were indeed to have hundreds of millions of votaries, in the sense of those who enjoyed richer material progress thereby. But in another sense Disraeli was right. No one would ever fight and die for the dry principle of economic and social progress. Glib and unappealing as Disraeli's 'Race is all' might seem, the following century was to prove him terribly right.

Apart from undisguised racial insult, Disraeli's critics linked his mountebank falseness to his ancestry. Almost by his own admission he was a man without fundamental convictions. 'Damn your principles! Stick to your party' was not a joke; Disraeli's strongest political impulse was personal dislike, and this was directed at those – Peel at the beginning of his career, Gladstone at the end of it – who put conviction above ambition. The acerbic Duke of Argyll associated this with his birth: having as a Jew 'no opinion of his own', Disraeli 'was free to play with prejudices that he did not share, and to express passions which were not his own, except in so far as they were tinged with personal resentment'. Although not precisely antisemitic, this anticipated a pronounced strain in European antisemitism which saw Jews as rootless strangers, moral cyphers, national chameleons, taking on the coloration of their surrounding country. And it was a charge which Jewish nationalists themselves would in time face up to, accept, and deal with.

Disraeli was not a proto-Zionist. In *Tancred* he invoked the mysteries of Jewish history and the Holy Land, and in the earlier *Alroy* (his one completely overblown and unreadable book) he sent his hero off to restore the Holy Land to the Jews. But this was a conscious fantasy. The truth was that Disraeli knew little and cared less about the Jewish Question as a social and political problem. Marx may have known more, but in his apparent attempt to address it he evaded it. All emancipated Jews of this period were not only dealing with contempt and needling, they were by definition trying to be something which they, or their near ancestors, had not been. The more studiously they ignored their origins, or however fervently they denied them, they were always living with them. When they took up larger political causes or identified with classes to which they did not belong – whether the German proletariat in Lassalle's case or the English landed gentry in Disraeli's – they were projecting something of themselves. They had turned to public life in an attempt, as a character in Herbert Read's novel *The Green Child* puts it, 'to solve my personal problems in social terms'. They were not only looking for an entrance ticket to European civilisation, they were trying to shed the baggage of thousands of years of history.

Not all Jews joined in, not even in western Europe. In Italy there was a small Jewish community, still living until the middle of the nineteenth century under some degree of prescriptive exclusion from the surrounding society, and some of them had no wish to enter that society, certainly not on its own terms alone. Several Italian Jewish scholars devoted themselves to the study of Jewish tradition, emphasising their pride in it, prefiguring what was later called self-emancipation. One was Samuel David Luzzatto of Padua, an eminent Hebrew philologist from a distinguished family which had in the previous century produced Moses Chaim Luzzatto, who has been called the most eloquent Hebrew poet since the flowering of Spanish Jewry. The younger Luzzatto watched the endeavours of the partly emancipated and seemingly assimilated Jews, and did not like what he saw. Writing to a colleague in Germany, he hoped to see 'an end to the servility and spiritual degradation of those who say, "we are Germans, we are just like you, your culture is our culture, your morality is our morality!" It is not so!' His was a rare voice at the time, but he was a forerunner.

2

People or nation?

I am become a stranger to my brethren:
even an alien unto my mother's children

Ps.lxix.8

To speak of the social problems, anxieties and neuroses produced by emancipation is to see only one side of the coin. Insulated as the ghetto Jews were by religion and tradition, they were also inhibited by it. 'Jewish genius' is often spoken of, but that comes naturally only to those who have lived in the last two centuries. The truth is that for more than fifteen hundred years of the Third Exile there had indeed been little sign of that 'genius among the people of Isaiah' of Macaulay's eloquent flourish. There was Maimonides in the twelfth century and Spinoza in the seventeenth; and then who else? There might be a great writer of partly Jewish extraction like Montaigne, but he only proved the rule by living in gentile society and having ceased to be in any real sense Jewish. For all the difficulties which it was to create, for all of the 'Jewish Question', it was precisely emancipation which was to produce an astonishing new wave of achievement, as well as a bitter resentment of it.

Sometimes those who were most resentful were also those most conscious of the achievement, or at least of the potential for it. Ten years after Lassalle's outburst, there was another cry of rage, from another German. Richard Wagner's early career had been a struggle against obscurity and adversity, as no one was more conscious than he. His early operas had flopped, his career in Paris had been a failure, his third opera, *Rienzi*, designed to take that city by storm, had not even been performed there. This experience left deep scars, not properly healed when *Der fliegende Holländer* and *Tannhäuser* succeeded in Dresden. By 1850, Wagner had completed *Lohengrin*, and he had arrived. But his experiences in Paris had not merely soured him, they had provided him with a target for his resentment. Opera there had been dominated by the composers Fromental Halévy (born Lévy) and Giacomo Meyerbeer (born Jakob Liebmann Meyer Beer). At the time he was in Paris, Wagner had told a colleague that Meyerbeer had been untiringly loyal to his interests, which was indeed the case; as the saying is, no good deed goes unpunished. Out of resentment at kindly patronage, Wagner turned bitterly on Meyerbeer, Halévy, and the Jews in general.

He became one of the nineteenth century's bywords for Jew-hatred, a hatred which runs through both his public utterances and his private conversation as devotedly recorded by his wife Cosima, though this did not stop several Jews just as devotedly revering and serving him. His operas themselves may or may not have detectable antisemitic subtexts: informed opinion sharply differs, though it requires no paranoid hypersensitivity or overwrought imagination to suspect that the characters of Alberich, Mime and Beckmesser contain something of antisemitic caricature, and it is even possible that their very music may mimic what Wagner thought 'unmusical' synagogue chant. But what Wagner thought of the Jews is not in any doubt at all.

Plenty of other men disliked and feared Jews. Unlike them, Wagner was a genius. In 1850, he published *Das Judentum in der Musik* (*Jewry in Music*). It is an odious but penetrating essay. Wagner saw, unenthusiastically, of course, something that others missed, the imminent explosion of Jewish genius, which itself was a function of emancipation. Genius had been bottled up inside the Jews who were themselves bottled up in their ghettos. The ghettos were opened, and the genius began to flower, as Mendelssohn, Börne, Heine and Marx showed. They were only the beginning of what was to be an astonishing century or more of Jewish achievement in philosophy and science, letters and music, a century adorned with the names of Freud, Kafka, Svevo, Mahler, Schoenberg and Einstein, not to say in the arts of finance and commerce, where Rothschilds and Solomons, Seligmans and Loebs, Monds and Sieffs would give another form of expression to Jewish energy and creativity. But the circumstances which produced this outpouring of talent were the same as those which produced the 'Jewish Question': emancipation and emergence from the ghetto. And so the two – Jewish genius and Jewish problem – were to be inextricably bound up.

As he looked at the Jews through the prism of his hatred and disdain, Wagner advanced another thesis. He held that a true artist must be steeped not only in his mother tongue – this had been a familiar theme since Herder – but in a culture which sprang from its own history. This permeated the artist's whole being from his birth: a collective sense given expression through an individual personality. Jews did not belong in this intimate, unconscious, uncanny way to the nations among whom they lived. And so, however hard an emancipated Jew tried, he could not become a true artist. He was always speaking a language with a foreign accent (this was a metaphor which came naturally to Germans in this context; Yiddish was an offshoot of German, and Yiddish-speakers betrayed their origins when speaking the language of Goethe). That included the language of European music. Not only were Meyerbeer and Halévy hollow and artificial – a judgement which musical history has confirmed – but Wagner refused greatness even to Moses Mendelssohn's grandson, Felix Mendelssohn-Bartholdy, 'who has shown us that a Jew can have the richest abundance of specific talent, be a man of the broadest yet refined culture, of the loftiest, most impeccable integrity, and yet not be able – not even once, with the help of all these qualities – to produce in us that deep, heart-searching, soul-reaching experience that we desire from art'.

This was simply untrue. When Wagner wrote that 'of necessity what comes out of attempts by Jews to make art must have the property of coldness, of non-involvement, to the point of being trivial and absurd. We are forced to categorise the Jewish period in modern music as the period of consummate uncreativeness – stability run to seed', he was describing Halévy unkindly but not unfairly; he was not describing the composer of Mendelssohn's Octet – the greatest work ever written by an adolescent – or his Violin Concerto, perhaps the greatest example of its genre.[1] Mendelssohn's career was unsatisfactory in some ways, ways which may have been related to his own problem as an

---

[1] Oddly enough, a century and a quarter later another writer, a very conscious Jew, repeated Wagner's disparagement of Mendelssohn: in *To Jerusalem and Back* Saul Bellow makes abusive reference to the 'silvery' Violin Concerto. And E. J. Hobsbawm likewise dismissively places the genius among those 'not composers of the highest contemporary class'.

emancipated and baptised Jew; but to speak of a Jewish lack of true creativity is in his case absurd.

Elsewhere in his diatribe Wagner denounced his enemies in tones which sounded like psychological 'projection', or unconscious self-accusation. He sneered at Halévy for wanting 'to scale the heights of success' and for his obvious delight in material rewards. But few artists have ever been so keen as Wagner was on becoming rich and famous, or so ruthless in exploiting others to that end. There is another possible explanation of his rage: it was long suspected by some that Wagner was partly Jewish, or at least thought he was. This is probably not true – either descent or belief – but it is given some colour by the tone of what Wagner wrote, with something like the tender inwardness of self-hatred.

In private, Wagner's Jew-hatred was almost more venomous than in public; we have his wife's account of the time they heard about a disastrous fire at a theatre in which many Jews had died. Wagner 'playfully' said that 'all Jews ought to burn at a performance of *Nathan*' (Lessing's play). And yet, along with such psychopathic humour, Cosima Wagner records also the pathetic loyalty and devotion to the *Meister* displayed by several Jews. Heinrich Porges was a chief assistant at Bayreuth, Angelo Neumann spread Wagner's fame at home and abroad by touring his operas, Joseph Rubinstein was Wagner's long-standing guest and pianist in residence, Carl Tausig was a close friend who made a piano arrangement of *Die Meistersinger*, Hermann Levi – who was Wagner's 'court Jew' above all others – conducted the first performance of *Parsifal*, Wagner's most specifically Christian opera. These men may have been spared Wagner's jests about burning Jews, or his jocose remark to gentile friends that the Jews must have stolen a manuscript of his, or that 'a Jewish fanatic' must be responsible for some other mishap. They knew all the same what his views on the Jews were, and they took it almost happily.

'Some of my best friends are Jews' later became a nervous joke, a phrase which seemed to betray a certain lack of conviction. But the strange thing was and is how many people with antisemitic views did and do have Jewish friends. These are deep psychological waters, on both sides; and rarely have they been deeper than in the case of Wagner and his circle. Those Jews came to Wagner as penitents to a confessor, for reproach and pardon. Levi moved Wagner to pity, Cosima recorded, because as a Jew 'he regards himself as an anachronism'; Wagner was able to reassure him that 'the Jews were, after all, the oldest, most aristocratic race'. It might have been Disraeli speaking with all his bravado. There were those who knew Wagner who were not afraid to reproach him for his Jew-hatred, from his first wife Minna to his patron, the mad King Ludwig II of Bavaria, who in one of his saner moments wrote to his protégé on the subject, 'Whatever our religions may be, fundamentally we are all human beings and as such we are brothers, are we not?' That was not the voice of Levi. His father, the chief rabbi of Giessen, wondered out loud about his son's friendship with the great Jew-hater. Hermann replied that 'Wagner is the best and noblest of men . . . I thank God daily for the privilege of being close to such a man. It is the most beautiful experience of my life.'

In their adoration, none of Wagner's Jewish devotees seems to have studied the argument of *Jewry in Music* about the false position of the Jews in Europe, or thought through its implications. Its logical conclusion could have been either that the Jews should not only be emancipated but completely absorbed into gentile society (if they were not all burned, that is); or that they should seek out a national existence of their own, when they could become 'true Jews' as there were true Germans and true Frenchmen, in each case taking spiritual and cultural nourishment from the nation as a whole. Despite those day-dreams before the French Revolution, despite Napoleon's appeal to the Jews, despite the casual use of the phrase 'the Jewish nation', despite that pamphlet in 1840, this idea was still far-fetched when Wagner wrote his diatribe. It was not so much that Jews, or gentiles, rejected the idea that the Jews were actually a nation like the French or the Danes, as that it had occurred to almost no one.

Indeed, despite the way the national idea had seemed to conquer all in its path following 1789, despite the 'springtime of nations' which the next great revolutionary year of 1848 had supposedly seen, nationalism and national identity were by no means as securely established as nationalists wished to think. Often enough, the nationalist project was as much sociological and psychological as political: in a famous phrase, it was not enough to unite Italy, what was needed was to make Italians. And this was easier said than done, in almost every European country. Much of France had been more or less politically united since the sixteenth century, but the meaning of nationhood had not penetrated large parts of the country. An inspector of education on a tour of duty in the Lozère mountains in 1864 asked the children at a village school in what country was Lozère, and none knew, or could answer the question, 'Are you English or Russian?' At much the same time, after Garibaldi had so theatrically brought Sicily into a united Italian kingdom, the peasants of western Sicily were most of them aware that they had a new king; but so little did they know of what was now supposedly their country that 'La Talia' (l'Italia) was widely believed to be the name of their new king's queen. Before 'being made' Italians, they had quite simply to be told that they *were* Italians.

Elsewhere, the project in its psychological aspect took a different form. Unlike the peoples of Lozère and Sicily, who needed to be told that they were French or Italian, the people of Ireland had no need of being told that they were Irish. Few peoples in Europe were so conscious of their identity, even if that identity was more complicated than some Irish nationalists realised. The Irish had to be taught not to identify themselves, but to respect themselves. In the centuries of English rule, especially the period since the Battle of the Boyne, the Gaelic Irish had not only been defeated politically, they had been broken in spirit. They feared and hated their oppressor, but, like a kidnapper's victim, they were awed by him at the same time; they had become truculent and servile at once. And so a large part of the work of the national movement was to heal Ireland psychologically as well as to liberate it politically, to teach the Irish self-respect. This took expressions as different as the Gaelic language revival, the Gaelic Athletics Association, and the temperance movement.

With the Jews the question was comparable. Unlike the Sicilians or Languedocians, but like the Irish, the Jews knew exactly who they were, none better. Far from having any difficulty with their identity, they had never been allowed to forget it, and they – or those still living in their discrete unemancipated communities – were not ashamed of it. What was problematic was the meaning of their 'national' identity in social and political terms. Men had long spoken of a 'Jewish nation', and Napoleon had called on the Jews to live as a nation among nations, but the word 'nation' can obscure more than it illuminates. Its etymology is from 'birth', its primary dictionary definition is 'a community of people of mainly common history, descent, language'. This definition indeed fitted the bulk of Jews living in east Europe like a glove. As Amos Oz puts it, that great Jewry of many millions stretching from the Baltic to the Black Sea was in its way a true nation. Even if it may have had no government, army or stamps, 'even if it lacked the trappings of a state, it was splendidly civilised, with a religion, law and order, systems of education and welfare, a language, civilised manners, lullabies and fairy-stories, music, justice, literature, economics, politics, power struggles, and intellectual movements: everything you could find in more prosperous civilisations also existed in that Eastern-European Jewish shadow state. It was in no way inferior to "normal" nation states, and in some respects it was far superior to them and indeed to the present-day State of Israel. Despite the terrible poverty, no one ever starved to death, and there was not a man who could not at least read and write. There have been few "normal" states, either then or now, that could boast as much.'

Moving and accurate as this description is, the question remained of whether the whole of Jewry was in this sense a nation, whether it had even incipiently the makings of a formal nation-state, and whether nationalism on the burgeoning European pattern was an appropriate model for the Jewish people to emulate. It was also irrelevant to those who had left the ghetto. It was they who embodied the previously unknown Jewish anxieties and neuroses; they who were to express the new flowering of Jewish genius; they who were faced with a series of new questions: 'What am I? Do I like what I am? Do I like myself? Am I a member of the gentile nation among which I live, distinguished only by certain accidental characteristics? Or is there another people to which I really belong? Does a Jewish nation exist, and should I try to repudiate it, or to identify with it?'

With the question of Jewish nationhood unresolved, others had speculated that migration to the Holy Land might serve some millennarian purpose. The Jewish religion taught that the Messiah would come one day, no one could predict when, as an act of divine grace, to redeem his people. A pious Christian like Ashley had, of course, a contrary belief that the Messiah had already redeemed mankind, and his philosemitism was logically despite rather than in consequence of that belief. Logically also, some Jewish notions of Return were at variance with strict rabbinical teaching. Yehudah Alkalai was born in Sarajevo in 1798 but spent his boyhood in Jerusalem and returned to serve as rabbi in Semlin in Serbia. In 1834 he published a little book, *Shema Yisrael (Hear, O Israel)*, proposing the recolonisation of the Holy Land as a precondition of Redemption. Strictly speaking, this was an impious suggestion from a rabbi. Pure Torah Judaism had to some extent been clouded by other mystical and cabbalistic traditions, and Alkalai seems to have been influenced by these, with vague notions of a forerunner to the Messiah (as John the

Baptist is to Christians) who would lead the Jews in the war of Gog and Magog and reconquer the Holy Land.

Then, like so many others, Alkalai was revolutionised by the Damascus affair. This convinced him of something else: that what the Jewish people immediately needed was security and freedom, which they could only find if they took their destiny into their own hands. This would be not the long-promised Messianic Redemption, but self-redemption through their own efforts. In 'The Third Redemption' in 1843 he argued that 'we, as a people, are properly called Israel only in the Land of Israel'. The Jews should slowly return – 'the land must, by degrees, be built up and prepared' – to Palestine. The immigrants would be the poor at first, helped by the many Jews who remained in the Dispersion. A new assembly of elders should be chosen by 'our greatest magnates', to help the Jews regain their spiritual strength: 'We have certain bad habits among us and there are forces which are weakening our religion.' As for the settlement, 'the Sultan will not object, for His Majesty knows that the Jews are his loyal subjects. Differences of religion should not be an obstacle, for each nation will worship its own god and we will forever obey the Lord, our God.' Another rabbi, Zvi Hirsch Kalischer, born in 1795 in the newly acquired Prussian territory of Posen, addressed the same subject. In 1836 he besought the help of the Berlin Rothschilds, 'to gather the scattered of Israel into the Holy Land'. In 1860, a doctor called Hayyim Lurie organised a society at Frankfurt on the Oder to promote Jewish settlement in the Holy Land. Kalischer joined this group, and in 1862 published *Derishat Zion* (*Seeking Zion*), making the case for colonisation: 'without such a settlement, how can the ingathering begin?' These settlements would be farms and vineyards, one of the first hints of what was to become such an important Zionist theme, the healing virtue of physical labour and rural life. Very few Jews in the Dispersion lived directly on the land, but 'Jewish farming would be a spur to the ultimate Messianic Redemption'. Not only that, but working the land 'would also raise our dignity among the nations, for they would say that the children of Israel, too, have the will to redeem the land of their ancestors, which is now so barren and forsaken', a remarkably accurate prediction of how attitudes to the Jews would one day change.

This was read by others, especially by one man who saw the question with a new penetration. Of all the remarkable generation of German Jews which flourished between the 1820s and 1850s, Moses

Hess was the least regarded then and is the least known now. But it was he who grasped a truth about the 'Jewish Question' which Heine and Marx had missed. Like them, Hess came from the Rhineland. He was born in 1812 in Bonn, ancient seat of the Elector-Archbishops of Cologne and later to be the capital of the Federal German Republic. Like others, the Hess family experienced the manic joy of emancipation followed by profound depression after the restoration. Unlike the others, Hess's father did not convert. He went off to run his business in Cologne, leaving the small boy called Moritz with his grandfather, a pious old man who taught his grandson the Bible and the Talmud and whose tears as he described the Destruction of the Temple Hess remembered a lifetime later. Hess may briefly have attended university in Cologne, then he set off to wander Europe.

He was caught up first by the wave of patriotic fervour sweeping Germany, subsequently in exile by another tide of enthusiasm: for the brand of extreme revolutionary socialism already known as communism. This was the doctrine once preached by the violent French Revolutionary Babeuf, that society could only be properly transformed by the absolute equality of all which would follow the complete abolition of private property. Communist socialism had been rekindled in the turbulent years after Waterloo, along with new strains of nationalism and romanticism. In contrast to Lassalle, Hess at any rate preached what he practised. He spent a life of destitution, of self-abasement, and of quixotry, such as characteristically marrying a prostitute in order to rescue her (a gentile girl, with whom he lived happily ever after). Hess became a comrade of Marx and Engels, but they soon turned on him. He became an object of their deepest contempt, and, in what may have been the first example of Marxist rewriting of history, his contribution to the development of their policy was suppressed. This fact was that Hess made communists of both Engels and Marx. He met his hero – 'the only true philosopher now alive. Dr Marx – that is the name of my idol' – in August 1841, after which Marx drew on or even plagiarised Hess. It was this meeting which pushed Marx towards pure socialist collectivism, something Engels admitted in an article in an obscure journal in 1843, though Marx then turned on Hess contemptuously as a 'feeble echo of French socialism and communism with a slight philosophical flavour'.

Even with Marx's indebtedness, there remained indeed a great difference between them. Although extreme, Hess's own socialism was radically different from Marx's. Hess did not construct a scientific framework, he did not believe that men were driven inexorably by great impersonal forces, he did not think that class conflict was either inevitable or desirable: 'Hegelian historicism had evidently not struck so deep in him after all.' In other words, Hess's socialism was unashamedly ethical rather than 'scientific'. For that reason Marx and his henchmen sneered at the 'rose water' socialism preached by 'Rabbi Hess'; for that reason also, Hess's theses have not been falsified in their own terms as Marx's have. And in certain specific ways Hess has proved a better prophet than Marx, not that that is saying much.

Hess had not so much psychologically forsworn his Jewish heritage as been looking for other outlets for that inheritance. He then found his awakening, truly a Damascene conversion. He too heard about the Damascus incident of 1840, was shocked and, as he later said, began to wonder whether the abolition of private property and the universal egalitarian society which was to follow would in fact solve all the ills of humanity. In particular he began to wonder whether socialism would end the afflictions of his own people. A slap across one cheek when he heard about Damascus was followed by one across the other in the following year. Hess was still enough of a German patriot to be caught up in the hostility to France then sweeping Germany, and he was thrilled by a francophobic poem he read, written by a poet called Becker, so excited that he set it to music and sent it in the post for his approval. Becker replied with an icily polite letter, sent in an envelope on whose back was written, in his hand which he had barely tried to disguise, '*Du bist ein Jid*' ('You are a Yid' or 'a Kike').

Great consequences follow from trivial causes. In *The Psychopathology of Everyday Life*, Freud describes how he discovered the 'Freudian slip' when he fell into conversation on a train with another, younger Austrian Jew. In the course of railing against the antisemitism prevalent in their country, the young man tried to emphasise his argument with a quotation from Virgil, but misquoted it in a way which was unintentionally revealing. A discovery of similar magnitude came to Hess. He was not immediately transformed by Becker's insult. He tried to master his feelings, about Becker as also about the Damascus affair. For the time being he still clove to the socialist line that mankind was one family, that racial prejudice and persecution were morbid symptoms of a diseased and dying society, that the struggle of the proletariat was more important than any sectarian or national interest, and that the best thing the Jews could do would be to disappear not merely by assimilation but by the disappearance of their religion and their complete absorption into the gentile communities. All of this had been said before, and it would be said again: half a century later, before his own conversion to Jewish nationalism, Theodor Herzl would propose the mass baptism of the Austrian Jews as a solution to the Jewish problem; Karl Kraus would insist that social democracy was the answer; even after Hitler, Isaac Deutscher could still say that he wished the Jews had survived but that Jewry had vanished.

In the 1840s Hess remained a communist. Even after his hero turned on him, Hess remained loyal to Marx, and to Lassalle – 'the head of Goethe on Jewish shoulders' – who befriended him. He remained unsympathetic to most forms of nationalism, at least those which were allied with the forces of reaction. But one movement caught his imagination. The Italians were a people struggling rightly to be free, united in their determination to throw off the despotic yokes of Habsburgs, popes and Bourbons who divided the country between them.

More than two decades passed from when the first seeds had been sown in Hess's mind by Damascus and Becker. They were years of suffering and struggle, when he came to terms with himself as a man and a Jew. Then in 1862 he published a strange and haunting little book, *Rom und Jerusalem*. In his own words: 'Here I stand again in the midst of my people, after being estranged from it for twenty years, and actively participate in its feasts and fasts.' The title of *Rome and Jerusalem* is a bundle of allusions. It refers to the Italian national movement which had just conquered Lombardy, Sicily, Naples and Tuscany for the Sardinian throne; the unification was to be completed when Austria ceded Venetia in 1866 and when Rome itself fell in 1870 after a decade in which 'Rome!' was the simplest possible nationalist slogan.[2] This is an example to others, says Hess. He was not the last Jewish nationalist to be captivated by Italy, nor to glamorise and romanticise it. A later prime minister of Italy was to use a telling phrase about 'beautiful national legends'. These were the myths which bound a nation together, Giovanni Giolitti said (which is why he did not want them undermined by critical scholarship). Italy had plenty enough of these, notably connected with the 'revival' or Risorgimento. What was being 'revived' – an Italian national state – had never in fact previously existed, and the successes of Garibaldi gave an illusory impression of

---

[2] To this day a Naples daily paper is called *Roma* in commemoration of that slogan.

the enthusiasm for unification, and of the military zeal with which it was won. Venice and Rome both came to the Sardinians as by-blows of Prussian victories, and, as L. B. Namier once sharply observed, no Italian army ever defeated anything but another Italian army. Writing of Schwarzenberg's misplaced faith in the Austrian army after he had served with Radetzky in his reconquest of northern Italy in 1848, A. J. P. Taylor called him 'one of the first victims, in fact, of the great Italian illusion, which contributed a note of farcical light relief to a hundred years of European politics'. It is curious that a succession of Jewish nationalists from Hess onwards should have been susceptible to the same illusion.

There was more to the second allusion contained in the name of Rome: 'Ever since Innocent III conceived the diabolical plan to destroy the moral stamina of the Jews who at that time brought Spanish culture into Christendom by compelling them to sew a badge of shame on their clothes and down to the recent kidnapping of a Jewish child under the regime of Cardinal Antonelli, papal Rome was an unconquerable source of poison for the Jews.' Hess contrasted by implication the papal Rome of reaction and persecution with the ideal Rome of the Italian patriots, and took this liberation of Rome – unrealised as he wrote – as the model for another: 'The liberation of the Eternal City on the Tiber masks the emancipation of the Eternal City on Mount Moriah.' For Hess, the answer is clear. The Jews are more than merely a people; they must take their place as a nation among nations, they must resume life in their own land on the banks of the Jordan. More than sixty years after Napoleon's appeal to the Jews, Hess says that France will take up her Napoleonic role as liberator of peoples and help the Jews to find a home again in the Holy Land.

This might seem like day-dreaming, and early Zionist projects were plainly fanciful, dealing with states of mind rather than with nation-states. Hess was more practical than that. He looked to France as an ally; not only because of memories of Napoleon but because, under the great Napoleon's less great nephew Napoleon III, France had been fertile ground for speculation about a new Jewish homeland. Two years before Hess, Joseph Salvador had published *Paris, Rome, Jerusalem, ou la question religieuse au XIXme siècle*, a characteristic mid-nineteenth-century work of politico-philosophical speculation, not to say fantasy. Although Salvador was part-Jewish, he was dealing principally with the destiny of Europe and America; as a by-product of his rumination he advocated the creation of a new state in the Holy Land which should be populated by the Jews, despite what he considered as their degraded condition. And Ernest Laharanne had published *La nouvelle question d'Orient*. Laharanne was an official in the French government and a gentile who believed in the Jews' historic mission and 'mighty genius. You were strong in the days of Antiquity and strong in the Middle Ages.'

He was deeply impressed, as so many friends and even foes of the Jewish people have been, by their sheer capacity for survival in the face of the oppression of Greeks, Romans, kings and Jesuits. Now, he says, they must set forth with their French friends to rescue the Holy Land from the Turk (whom Laharanne detested as much as did English contemporaries like Cobden) and build the gates of Jerusalem. Although his belief in the need for a Jewish homeland was based on admiration for the Jews in their historic existence, Laharanne was clear-sighted enough to see the problem of Jewry as it actually was: the passivity of the poor Orthodox eastern Jews, and the indifference of rich emancipated western Jews.

As a friend, he reproached the Jews from the outside; Hess, from the inside. *Rome and Jerusalem* is a prescription for making the Jews happy. It proposes what before long began to happen: rich Jews should buy land in Palestine to be colonised by poor Jews. A Hungarian rabbi was ready to go to see the Sultan of Constantinople, with the encouragement of the Turkish ambassador in Vienna, to sell him this scheme. This belief that the Porte could be cajoled or bought was to be a persistent theme of Zionism for another sixty years, until the Ottoman empire finally staggered off the stage of history. It was characteristic of the high enthusiasm of these idealists, characteristic maybe also of their capacity for self-delusion. The Ottomans may have been decadent and corrupt (though the Turkophobia of a Laharanne or a Cobden took on a different colour in the light of what succeeded Ottoman rule: not universal peace and prosperity but mutually competitive and bloody nationalisms). But Hess's belief, or later Herzl's, that Jewish nationalism could be slipped into a supra-national Ottoman empire overlooked the intuitive sense of its own nature which even an embattled institution – perhaps embattled ones most of all – may possess. The Porte instinctively understood that it could tolerate on its own terms any number of religions, but that it could not compromise with the national principle.

Although *Rome and Jerusalem* presents itself as a practical blueprint, its real purpose is moral: an analysis and a reproach. It was not the first scheme for restoring the Jews to the Holy Land, but it was the first time in the nineteenth century that a Jewish writer had looked with real penetration at the Jewish Question as it had been created by emancipation, and at the emancipated Jew, for whom Hess feels undisguised contempt. 'The really dishonourable Jew is not the old-type, pious one, who would rather have cut his tongue out than utter a word in denial of his nationality, but the modern kind . . . ashamed of his nationality because the hand of fate is pressing heavily upon his people.'

These frightened, self-denying Jews mistake the problem when they are baptised or merely forsake their religion: 'The Germans hate the religion of the Jews less than they hate their race – they hate the peculiar faith of the Jews less than their peculiar noses.' In other words, Hess says that Jews have certain ineradicable characteristics, which they cannot shed. In trying to pretend otherwise they are 'in denial', as the modern phrase goes, and this can only make them neurotic and unhappy. Hess even makes the same point as Wagner about creativity, though in a different way: 'The holy spirit, the creative genius of the people, out of which Jewish life and teaching arose, deserted Israel when its children began to be ashamed of their nationality.' By reaffirming this nationality, therefore, creativity will return.

His project for rebuilding a Jewish homeland in Palestine is almost a metaphor or poetic image, as he comes close to admitting. He plainly concedes that the bulk of the Jewish people are not likely to migrate to the Holy Land even if the opportunity arose; they had not all returned thither after the Babylonian exile, after all, and 'we, therefore, need not expect such a miracle as a feature of a future restoration'. He has been commended for his prescience in seeing this, and in emphasising that 'when we speak of a Jewish settlement in the Orient, we do not mean to imply a total emigration of the western Jews to Palestine. Even after the establishment of a Jewish State the majority of the Jews who live at present in the civilised countries of the West will undoubtedly remain where they are.'

This was canny and prudential as well as far-sighted. Hess was the first true Zionist visionary, and he was the first to anticipate one problem: what if many or most of the Jews of the Dispersion did not wish to return to their 'homeland'? For one thing, Hess was implicitly looking for a solution to the material problems of the great Jewish population of central and eastern Europe, the 'uncivilised countries'. Even he did not foresee in the 1860s how much graver these problems

would become in his lifetime, but even more so soon after his death in
1875. For another, his clarion call to the emancipated Jews of the West
worked as an each-way bet. Even if they were not to become existential
Zionists by taking the physical road to Zion – even if no Jewish State or
even if no large-scale Jewish settlement in Palestine were ever realised
– these assimilated westerners could become better Jews and better
men by identifying themselves closely with the Zionist idea. In later
parlance from another context, they could 'come out' as Jews, and they
would be the happier for it.

In all of this, the poverty-stricken, unsuccessful Hess, spurned and
scorned even by some of his closest associates, showed insight of genius.
He was right: when a Jewish State was finally created, getting on for a
century after when he wrote, it would be a source of healing pride for
Jews everywhere, at a time when healing was needed as never before.
But there were other things he did not foresee. There is a faint hint of a
problem to come even in *Rome and Jerusalem.* He believed that the
European Power under whose aegis the Jewish State was to be
established would be 'France, beloved friend' of liberty, which turned
out to be wrong. An imperial power was to be necessary, all the same.
And when Hess went on to say that 'just as we' – even the pronoun was
significant, showing that he instinctively identified himself and his
people with imperial Europe – 'once searched in the West for a route
to India, and incidentally discovered a new world, so will our lost
fatherland be rediscovered on the road to India and China that is now
being built in the Orient'.

This was all too true. The power that would 'help the Jews to found
colonies which may extend from Suez to Jerusalem and from the banks
of the Jordan to the coast of the Mediterranean' turned out to be
England. But the imperial nature of the enterprise was to dog it,
morally as well as practically. Nor did Hess see something else; that the
great project might be accomplished, astonishingly enough within
ninety years; that it might indeed have a profound emotional and
social and political impact on Jews everywhere; but that in doing so it
might not so much finally resolve the Jewish Question as complicate it
further.

3

At home in Europe

The lot is fallen unto me in a fair ground:
Yea, I have a goodly heritage.

Ps.xii.2

Despite Hess's foreboding and his penetrating analysis of Jewish rejection, the middle years of the nineteenth century were in many ways a golden age for that minority of the Jewish people who lived in the West, for a fair number of them the best time since Antiquity. Even in Russia there were brief phases of comparative liberalism: between 1856, when Tsar Alexander II relaxed some of the heavier burdens imposed on the Jews, and the Polish rebellion of 1863 which brought renewed repression, and again in the 1870s. In the Pale of Settlement the Jews still huddled together for mutual comfort as the autocracy kept them in degraded conditions. They tried to move into cities, though these were sometimes closed to them; Warsaw nevertheless became one of the first European cities with a Jewish population of more than 100,000. To few did either the idea or the opportunity of emigration yet occur.

In central and western Europe Jews were flocking faster into cities, and a modest number of German Jews went further, sailing to America. In the United States, this still small Jewish community played its part in national life, despite the continuing cultural dominance of Protestantism; more than 7,000 Jews fought on one side or the other in the Civil War. But those who stayed behind had reason to think that good times had come. In numerous German novels of the 1850s and

1860s[1] the rapacious Jew still appeared as a stock figure. And yet in one of these books the narrator looks back to the 'vanished days' of the 1820s and 1830s, when in small towns and villages was found a distrust and dislike of Jews which 'happily one does not find so strongly emphasised today'. More strikingly still, in England one barrier after another fell. Sir David Salomons became the first Jewish Lord Mayor of London in 1855, Francis Goldsmid the first Queen's Counsel in 1858, Sir George Jessel the first High Court judge in 1873. Most astonishing of all, in 1868, six years after *Rome and Jerusalem* had proclaimed the failure of assimilation, Benjamin Disraeli became prime minister of the greatest power on earth. This was something beyond the dreams of any Jew, the richest merchant or the most trusted court Jew as much as the poorest artisan or pedlar, for centuries past. It could only have happened in that country and at that time, during that transition from aristocracy to democracy in which Disraeli played a not entirely willing part. It was freakish; but it was all the same, along with the triumph of financiers like the Warburgs, or Bleichröder whose services were so important to Bismarck's career, a symbol of hope and encouragement to Jews everywhere.

The Rothschilds' story was particularly inspiriting. Within a generation from the Frankfurt ghetto, they had become enormously rich and powerful, in Germany, Austria, France, for a time in Italy. Especially in England: Baron Lionel de Rothschild had become the first unbaptised Jew to take his place in the House of Commons, after being repeatedly elected until the parliamentary oath 'on the true faith of a Christian' was changed (his point made, he then sat for fifteen years without opening his mouth). It was he, as the story went, who lent Disraeli's government £4 million to buy the Suez canal while he peeled a grape. But the Rothschilds' ascendancy was quite as much social as financial. Baron Meyer de Rothschild was the first Jew to be elected to the Jockey Club, and in 'the Baron's Year' of 1871 his racehorses won four out of the five English Classic races. Three of them – One Thousand Guineas, Oaks, St Leger – were won by his filly Hannah, named after his daughter. Seven years later the human Hannah married the Earl of Rosebery, Whig grandee and a future prime minister (who himself owned two Derby winners). There could not have been a more dramatic display of the Jewish ascent or a more

---

[1] E.g. *Soll und Haben*, Gustav Freylag, 1855; *Der Hungerpastor*, Wilhelm Raabe, 1864; *Ein Kampf um Rom*, Felix Dahn, 1867.

potent cause for optimism. What did the worries of a Heine or a Hess mean set alongside the apotheosis of the Rothschilds? For the European Jews, the end of the 1860s could have seemed the greatest moment of the greatest century they had known. There was hope in Israel, and in 1869, Isidore Kaim could confidently say that 'There is no more Jewish Question'.

Hope can be turned off like a light. The 1870s proved to be a peculiarly ominous decade for the Jews. It began with a financial boom and then bust, the crash of 1873. The boom, which had seen 726 new speculative companies founded in Germany within the space of two years, was intimately associated with the Jewish railway promoter Baron Bethel Strousberg; the bust when it came was precipitated by another Jew, the great parliamentarian Eduard Lasker. His speech in the Reichstag denouncing the 'Strousberg system', its corrupt connection with high officials and its swindling of the small investor, led to a bear market on the Berlin Bourse which turned into a collapse. In another curious consequence, Gershon Bleichröder, Bismarck's Jewish banker, undertook to salvage what he could of the fortunes of numerous Junkers caught up in the disastrous toils of Strousberg's Romanian railway projects, and as a reward was ennobled by King William of Prussia, himself newly elevated as German Emperor. As the Jewish newspaper the *Allgemeine Zeitung des Judentums* proudly pointed out, 'It is the first time in Prussia that an Israelite who has direct descendants [as opposed to one who had no sons to inherit his title] had been ennobled.'

The paper's enthusiasm was not widely shared in Prussia. An unmistakable result of the 1873 crash was a new mood in Germany and Austria. It was a current of Jew-hatred. Or of 'antisemitism': the word itself seems to have been coined in 1879 by an otherwise forgotten journalist called Wilhelm Marr, to describe the policy he advocated. Four years earlier a very influential Prussian newspaper had found that 'the fiscal and economic policy of the German Empire gives one the impression of a Jewish policy . . . [three Jews are the] leaders of the so-called National Liberal majority in the Reichstag and in the Prussian parliament. Jewish banking houses influence the nomination of ministers . . .' Whether or not this was true, it was the case that by 1880, when there were barely 46,000 Jews in England and 51,000 in France, 80,000 lived in Berlin, and there was fertile ground there to be tilled. In the year of Marr's coining, Adolf Stoecker, Lutheran pastor and Court Preacher, set out 'Our Demands on Modern Jewry', and in

1879 also, Heinrich von Treitschke, one of the greatest historians of his age as well as a passionate nationalist and Anglophobe, published an article which famously concluded that 'the Jews are our national misfortune'.

Both men claimed that they had no racial animus against the Jews and were willing to accept them if they became Christians and good German patriots; as with other educated purveyors of prejudice before and since, they were both intelligent enough to know that this was a distinction which would be lost on their audience. As one historian says, just because of their eminence, 'Stoecker and Treitschke made antisemitism respectable, and this opened the door to every variety of the disease'. Even in England, Jew-hatred resurfaced. During the vehement controversy over the Bulgarian Horrors of 1876, Disraeli's refusal to intervene on the side of the oppressed Christian Bulgars was attributed by Gladstone, though in private, to his semitic affinity with the Turk, and the historian Edward Freeman publicly denounced him as 'the Jew in his drunken insolence'. In 1879, yet another Rothschild, Baron Lionel, won the Derby with his colt Sir Bevys; it was not much consolation to those Jews who felt the rising tide of hostility lapping around them.

Its causes were largely social and economic, quite apart from the 1873 crash. Large numbers of Jews had emigrated to Vienna and Berlin from the old heartlands, the Polish provinces of Galicia and Posen grabbed by Austria and Prussia at the partitions. If not immediately assimilated, these new city-dwellers were quickly *embourgeoisé*, more quickly than was to happen with Jewish immigrants to America a generation later. Only a handful of Jews had lived in Vienna before 1848, and almost none had attended the university; by 1880, 22.3 per cent of law students and 38.6 per cent of medical students there were Jews and within another ten years, almost half the faculty of medicine were Jewish. Jews prospered in trade, and in politics – so much so that the Austrian Prime Minister Taaffe suggested that the Jews should form a separate political party. He was effectively echoing an eminent Austrian physician, Theodor Billroth, who said that 'a Jew is as little able to become a German as can a Persian or a Frenchman, or a New Zealander, or an African'. A few years later, in 1881, Eugen Dühring published *Die Judenfrage, als Racen- Sitten- und Kulturfrage (The Jewish Question as a Question of Race, Morals and Culture)*. Dühring was a philosopher of distinction, and his book was one of the first expositions of the new antisemitism on an apparently elevated intellectual level. It advocated the *Entjudung* – 'dejudaising' – of the press, the law, medicine and other trades and professions into which the Jews had indeed made such advances. The book outraged but also impressed a young student in Vienna, Theodor Herzl. Dühring's genius, he wrote, was to see 'that religious attacks on the Jews no longer work. Now race must step forward!'

These misty Teutonic speculations little affected the poor Jews of the eastern ghettos, who were still living under the old regime with its quasi-religious hatreds and antique proscriptions. It was over these that the next great storm broke. Despite those intermittent remissions, the condition of the Jews in the Russian Empire had remained harsh. They were confined to the Pale, subject to brutal discrimination and savage military conscription, in general treated as a lesser breed. In the 1870s, repression eased. But then in March 1881 Alexander II was assassinated, and horror broke such as Jewry could scarcely remember. A wave of pogroms – beatings, rape, massacre – swept across the Pale. Acts had been committed, the American minister in St Petersburg reported to the State Department, 'more worthy of the Dark Ages than of the present century'. Those acts were openly encouraged by the controlled press, and almost openly by the government. The new Tsar, Alexander III, was advised by his old tutor, Constantin Petrovitch Pobedonostsev, an intelligent and able man, and an implacable Jew-hater. All Russian Jews were shocked and frightened, some took flight.

Even before the pogroms began, Russian Jewish writers had begun to re-examine their own Jewishness and what it meant. Peretz Smolenskin was born in the Pale, saw his brother 'snatched' for the dreaded twenty-five years' military service, was himself expelled from yeshiva or rabbinical seminary for impiety when he was found reading secular books, moved to Odessa and then settled in Vienna, writing and publishing in Hebrew. His monthly *Hashahar* played an important part in the language revival – a revival which foreshadowed Zionism. Hebrew had become the Jews' Latin, used for liturgical and limited literary purposes, but not a living, spoken tongue. To the pious, Hebrew remained a sacred language whose secular use was a form of profanity, and so its use by enthusiasts was a conscious statement that to be Jewish was to belong to a people rather than to adhere to a religion. *Hashahar* was read by younger writers like Eliezer Perlman who, in another symbolic gesture which was to be widely copied, Hebraised his name as Ben-Yehudah. Twenty-four years after *Hashahar* was launched, the Gaelic League was founded to promote the revival of the Irish Gaelic language, though this, in contrast to Hebrew, had been spoken as an everyday language by millions early in the century and was still the native language of hundreds of thousands. Irish language enthusiasts likewise Gaelicised their names and founded journals. What happened to the two languages over the next century was hard to foresee: the dark horse won.

In the mid-1870s, Smolenskin insisted that the secret of the Jews' survival was that they had always regarded themselves as a people, 'a spiritual nation'. Like Hess, he addressed himself in reproach to all those who tried to evade or deny their Jewishness. He longed instead for 'a national sentiment which makes everyone born a Jew declare: "I am a son of this people . . . *every Jew belongs to his people so long as he does not betray it*" '. And in case that seemed to beg a question, he ringingly asserted, '*Yes, we are a people.*'

This was some way short of a call for a national state or even a national home. It was only a reaffirmation of Hess's rediscovery of his own people. And it was written before a new horror was visited on the Russian Jews. The shock of the 1881 pogroms not only shook all Jews out of any complacent optimism; it suggested a new course, 'new remedies, new ways', in the words of Leo Pinsker. He was notably assimilated, brought up by a father in the spirit of the Haskalah, the German-Jewish enlightenment of the eighteenth century, whose programme Smolenskin had called 'quite different and quite simple: "Imitate the gentiles" '. Pinsker went to a Russian high school, studied law in Odessa and medicine in Moscow, and had been honoured by the Tsar for his services as a physician during the typhus epidemic which accompanied the Crimean War. He did not convert, but went further than most enlightened Jews in his country by saying that the Jews could be in effect completely Russicised – as some English Jews wanted to be Anglicised or French Jews Gallicised – and adopt the Russian language and culture as their own. Pogroms in Odessa in 1871 did not dent Smolenskin's optimism; it could not survive the disaster of 1881. He completely changed spiritual course, and in 1882 wrote *Self-Emancipation; An Appeal to His People by a Russian Jew*. With a different emphasis from Smolenskin's, Pinsker concluded that 'the Jews are not a living nation; they are everywhere aliens; therefore they are despised.

'The proper and the only remedy would be the creation of a Jewish nationality, of a people living upon its own soil, the self-emancipation of the Jews; their emancipation as a nation among nations by acquisition of a home of their own.'

Only a few years before Pinsker wrote, a great English novelist had played with the same dream. George Eliot's *Daniel Deronda* was published in serial parts in 1875–6. The heroine, Gwendolen Harleth, has made a calculating and unhappy marriage but falls, spiritually at least, for Daniel Deronda. It transpires that Daniel is Jewish and he in turn falls under the spell of a noble Jew, Mordecai, and his sister Mirah. Mordecai was modelled on George Eliot's friend Emmanuel Deutsch who had taught her some Hebrew and had become fervently attached to the idea of 'Return': 'all my wild yearnings fulfilled at last,' he wrote to her from Jerusalem, and he infected her with this enthusiasm, which was added to her already strong philosemitism.

She may also have known the theme of *Rome and Jerusalem*, since George Henry Lewes, her husband in all but legal form, had met Hess. Mordecai expresses Deutsch's and Hess's yearning with George Eliot's own eloquence. When the Jews return to the Land of Israel, 'the world will gain as Israel gains. For there will be a community in the van of the East which carries the culture and sympathies of every great nation in its bosom; there will be a land set for a halting-place of enmities, a neutral ground for the East as Belgium is for the West.' And when at the end of the novel Daniel marries Mirah (to Gwendolen's disappointment) and sets off for the Holy Land, it is to create again 'a political existence in my people, making them a nation again, giving them a national centre, such as the English have, though they too are scattered over the face of the earth'.

This remained one of the most touching and powerful pleas for what was not as yet called Zionism, even if the reference to Belgium was not only somewhat bathetic but was to seem ill-chosen with hindsight of a century in which two bloody wars were fought on Belgian soil. But George Eliot skated lightly over any possible conflict between the idea of 'a nation again' in merely cultural terms, and 'a political existence'.

This was to be a peculiarly contentious issue among Jews for generations to come. Pinsker had argued that the Jews were not a nation, because they lacked 'a distinctive national character, possessed by every other nation, a character which is determined by living together in one country, under one rule'. Such a national character could clearly not be developed in the Dispersion where 'the Jews seem rather to have lost all remembrance of their former home. Thanks to their ready adaptability, they have all the more easily acquired the alien traits of the peoples among whom they have been cast by fate.'

To say this might seem obvious enough but – especially when

coupled with the proposed remedy of *Self-Emancipation* – it cut many emancipated Jews to the quick. So Pinsker soon discovered. Having written his great polemic and founded the Hibbat Zion to promote emigration to Palestine, Pinsker visited Vienna in 1882. The Jewish community there was acutely aware of the sufferings of their co-religionists under the Tsar, who had begun to escape from his rule. It was a curiosity of the great emigration of Jews from Russia which began in 1881 and accelerated for a third of a century until war interrupted it in 1914 that it took place, in its initial stages, largely overland. Many of the Tsar's Jewish subjects lived near seaports like Riga on the Baltic or Odessa on the Black Sea. But there were few modern, cheap shipping services sailing thence across the Atlantic and, in any case, to take ship there meant doing so under the eyes of the Tsarist authorities, who were as keen to harass Jews trying to leave the country as those who stayed behind. The alternative, taken by hundreds of thousands, was to cross the long, permeable frontier with Austrian Galicia and then continue to the German ports. So this huge human traffic passed not far from the Jews living in Vienna, whether in the poor, cramped Leopoldstadt or the more spacious suburbs into which the prosperous Jewish middle classes were moving.

If emancipated Viennese Jewry had a leader in these years it was Adolf Jellinek,[2] who was called to Vienna as preacher in 1856 at the Leopoldstadt Temple, where he became known as the greatest Jewish preacher of his age, and a standard-bearer of Jewish liberalism. In a famous Passover sermon in 1865 he fervently welcomed enlightened measures just passed by the government, and two years later he acclaimed an Austrian monarchy which had thrown off the shackles of the Middle Ages. But before very long Jellinek had cause to repent this rosy optimism. He was one of the first to see that the racial theories propounded by writers like the Frenchman Ernst Renan, distinguishing between 'Aryan' and 'Semite', carried a graver danger for the Jews than the old religious hatreds, and he was as conscious as any of the new tides of prejudice which were rising round the German and Austrian Jews.

But he refused to concede that emancipation had been premature, or the Jews unready for it: 'It is not the Jews but certain individual

---

[2] Unusually enough for any Jew, let alone a great rabbi, Jellinek was not Jewish by ethnic descent: his ancestors were Czech peasants who had converted to Judaism in the eighteenth century.

peoples, especially German and Slav, who are not yet ripe for so-called emancipation, they are not sufficiently advanced in their culture or feeling, their intellectual education and their ethical thinking to be capable of unprejudiced and just behaviour towards the Jews.' And yet, for all this, Jellinek abhorred the idea that assimilation was doomed to failure and that the only answer was a new Jewish nationalism. When he met Pinsker that May of 1882, he told him so: Pinsker must be in a state of emotional shock to propound the theories he did, Jellinek said; he needed medical attention.

When he had recovered his own composure, Jellinek went on to give a classic defence of the assimilationist position. Pinsker said unarguably that something had to be done for the suffering Russian Jews, and Jellinek naturally agreed; it was his and other fortunate Jews' charitable duty to do what they could to alleviate the sad situation of their co-religionists in Russia. Almost as plausibly, Pinsker claimed that the rising tide of antisemitism in central Europe, notably Germany, was if anything more ominous for the Jews as aliens when 'a nation as highly civilised as the Germans can tolerate antisemitic scenes in the capital of the German Reich – if a court chaplain[3] agitates and rages against those who profess Judaism and arouses the most brutal hatred against equal citizens of the same Reich'? Antisemitism could no longer be explained away as a transient aberration. It was endemic, rooted deep in gentile society, an inevitable consequence of the Jews' homelessness.

Here Jellinek differed emphatically. The plan for an independent territorial home for the Jews was absurd and impossible, he said. He deplored the creation of what he called with prescient acuity 'a small state like Serbia or Romania outside Europe, which would most likely become the plaything of one Great Power against another, and whose future would be very uncertain'. But this was not the nub of his opposition. The real objection to a Jewish territorial home would be that it threatened the position of western Jews, and would thus be rejected by them: 'almost all Jews in Europe' would vote against the scheme if they were given the opportunity. This was because they were not, as both Pinsker and the antisemites seemed to think, transient vagrants in the countries where they lived.

'We are at home [*heimisch*] in Europe, and feel ourselves to be children of the lands in which we were born, raised and educated,

---

[3] i.e. Stoecker in Berlin.

whose languages we speak and whose cultures constitute our intellectual substance. We are Germans, Frenchmen, Englishmen, Hungarians, Italians, etc. with every fibre of our being. We long ago ceased to be genuine, full-blooded Semites and the sense of a Hebrew nationality has long since been lost.'

Perhaps Jellinek was right in claiming that this was the view of most European Jews, though it would have been more accurate to say of almost all assimilated, bourgeois Jews in central and western Europe, and it remained true of them for years to come. They saw Jewish nationalism as a threat to their position, and they opposed it for as long as they could whenever the opportunity arose. The poor Jews of Russia might have been sympathetic to the scheme of migration to the Holy Land if it had existed in reality. A very few did at this time undertake the journey, or 'make *aliyah*', the Hebrew for 'going up'[4] which became the exalted term for migration to the Land of Israel. Jellinek himself admitted that he had been deeply moved by the sight of a group of Jewish children from Russia passing through Vienna on their way to Jaffa. This was the beginning of the First Ascent, conventionally dated as 1882–1903, which brought some 25,000 people to the Holy Land. They came largely as beneficiaries of the charity of rich western Jews, especially Baron Edmond de Rothschild; more important, they were, after twenty years, and as the twentieth century began, still only a tiny minority in Palestine; most important of all, they were only a tiny fraction of the Jews who uprooted themselves from east Europe in this period and crossed the seas.

There was indeed a great Jewish adventure afoot as Jellinek and Pinsker debated, but it was not the Ascent. Writing as the pogroms burst upon Russian Jewry, Smolenskin said that it was best for 'people who are leaving one country to migrate together to the same new land, for they could then understand and help one another'. This is what the Russian Jews did. He had also insisted that 'if the wave of emigration is to direct itself to one place, surely no other country in the world is conceivable except Erez Israel'. Here he was quite wrong. Jellinek got it right when he said that the best solution to the Russian Jews' plight was large-scale emigration to a democratic country like the United States.

Thither the Jews went, in a trickle which became a stream which

---

[4] Or 'ascent'; it implies, as the *Encyclopaedia Judaica* says, not only personal participation in the rebuilding of a Jewish homeland but 'the elevation of the individual to a higher plane of self-fulfilment'.

became a torrent. The figures speak for themselves. In 1880, three-quarters of the nearly eight million then living Jews lived in eastern Europe. During the 1880s, some 200,000 of them migrated to the United States; in the 1890s, 600,000; in the 1900s almost a million; and the rate of migration continued to accelerate until it was cut off by events. By 1914, a full third of the Jewish population of east Europe had crossed the Atlantic in a little more than thirty years.

In their new country they encountered hardship and prejudice. Like all immigrants, they formed a pool of cheap labour fuelling the new American industrial economy, and for years to come many of them knew only gruelling toil and indigence. As the Jews already living in the United States before 1881 could have told them, Jew-hatred was far from unknown in the Land of the Free. New York finance was dominated by a small group of German-Jewish bankers who also set the heavily Germanic tone for New York culture at the time. But even these magnates had sometimes to endure humiliating rebuffs. There had been a notorious episode in 1877 when Joseph Seligman, an enormously rich member of the financial élite, went to stay in the holiday resort of Saratoga Springs, at the Grand Union Hotel, owned by Judge Hilton, which he had often patronised before, but now found himself refused admission because he was a Jew. Jewish merchants took revenge by boycotting Hilton's wholesale company and forcing it into bankruptcy, but the current of social antisemitism continued to flow strongly. The *Elite Directory* in San Francisco included Jews on a separate list, the New York *Social Register* did not include them at all. By 1893, the Union League Club in New York, founded partly by Jews, barred Jews as members. In southern states, antisemitism took violent form, with Jewish stores sacked and Jewish houses burned down. The arrival of a flood of poor new immigrants added to these tensions and inflamed further hostility. Or so it certainly seemed to those German Jews of uptown Manhattan who viewed the arrival of hordes of their co-religionists with if anything even more apprehension than that shown by the assimilated bourgeois of Berlin and Vienna when the *Ostjuden* poured into their cities.

But when all this was said, the immigrant Jews of New York and other American cities really had found a golden land. For all of nativism and bigotry, the country's very size and diversity formed a huge advantage for any newcomers. So did the fact that these Jews were easily outnumbered by other immigrants, from Ireland, Italy, Poland, elsewhere in eastern and southern Europe, who drew a good deal of nativist and specifically anti-Catholic hostility of their own. So (a more cynical reflection still) did the existence of blacks, freed legally more than economically and spiritually from slavery, and who ensured that, however lowly and ill-regarded any newcomers were, they would never be quite at the bottom of the social ladder.

And so, despite everything, these new Americans had good grounds to face the future with optimism, much better grounds than their cousins who had stayed behind in Russia. Many Jews in western Europe also faced the 1890s cheerfully, despite the reversals of the 1880s. In England, the Jewish community was increased by new arrivals from the East who came to a country which was comparatively speaking tolerant and assimilationist. In France, a smaller Jewish community even more passionately identified with what they believed was their country. They echoed Jellinek: they were French with every fibre of their being. As one rabbi put it in 1889, 'We have adopted the custom and traditions of a country which has so generously adopted us and today, thanks to God, everyone in France is considered French.'

4

'I have the solution . . .'

Let us break their bonds asunder:
and cast away their cords from us.

Ps.ii.3

Five years after the rabbi spoke those optimistic words, on 29 October 1894, the readers of the reactionary French paper the *Libre Parole* were asked tantalisingly, 'Is it true that military authorities have made a very important arrest? The charge brought against the man who has been arrested is said to be spying.' It was true. Before long all of France knew what Commandant Henry of French military intelligence had told Edouard Drumont of the *Libre Parole*, that Captain Alfred Dreyfus had been arrested; Henry had added that 'they want to hush the business up. All Israel is on the job.' Within weeks, Dreyfus had been charged with treason and convicted by a military court. Drumont was a captive audience, a journalist who had published *La France Juive* (*Jewish France*) in 1886, to explain the conspiracy which was undermining the country and in particular thwarting the careers of talented men such as himself.

The son of a prosperous Alsatian merchant family, Dreyfus was an able if not particularly amiable man, and the first Jew to serve on the general staff of the French army. In its small way his career had been a tribute to the ideals of Republic and Revolution, and he was the very type of Jew who had 'adopted the customs and traditions' of his country. He had no possible motive for treason. With a substantial independent income, he scarcely needed the *pourboires* which the Germans were offering for information; equally, he could have made far more in business if he had not patriotically joined the army. Dreyfus's enemies alleged a Jewish conspiracy; there was none. For that matter there was no deep-seated conspiracy to destroy Dreyfus, merely an improvisation among various narrow-minded, stupid and bigoted officers whose own motives ranged from the classic framer's belief that any conviction is better than none to a determination that under no circumstances should the 'honour' of the army be impugned and its enemies vindicated.

On 5 January 1895, Dreyfus was formally degraded at the Ecole Militaire in Paris, his epaulettes stripped and his sword broken, while a mob cried '*A mort les juifs!*', and he was transported to his life imprisonment on Devil's Island. One of those who had borne false witness against him claimed that while he was under interrogation Dreyfus had shouted, 'My race will take vengeance on yours.' This claim was preposterous; the truth was more poignant. As he stood on the barracks square, destroyed and utterly humiliated in the name of France, Dreyfus protested his innocence, and cried, '*Vive la France!*' All of this was witnessed by the young correspondent for the *Neue Freie Presse* of Vienna, Theodor Herzl.

At the time of his conviction Dreyfus was friendless. The clerical Right crowed over his treason, which seemed to justify everything they believed about the Jews. And on the other hand – the Left hand – there was little more sympathy for him. The first, instinctive reaction of the great socialist leader Jean Jaurès was to complain about the class justice which merely imprisoned an officer when common soldiers were shot for disobedience. Not least, most bourgeois French Jews decided that the best thing was to keep quiet and hope that the sorry business would be forgotten as soon as possible. It was only thanks to the obvious flaws in the case against Dreyfus, to the persistence and brotherly loyalty of Mathieu Dreyfus, and to the sense of justice of Colonel Georges Picquart – a conservative Catholic officer with the usual prejudices of his class, including pronounced antisemitism, who nevertheless recognised that wrong had been done – that the truth slowly emerged.

As it did so, *l'Affaire Dreyfus* became the central episode which shaped the Third Republic between 1871 and 1914. Although the *Affaire* had profound implications for Jews everywhere, it was not in origin part of the 'Jewish Question': Jewish history was still being made from the outside. The fact that Dreyfus became, most unwillingly, the great Jewish hero of his age was, despite the ranting Jew-hatred of his enemies in the *Libre Parole*, really peripheral to the issue. Two sides had been spoiling for a fight, and they got it. It was a decisive *Kulturkampf*, pitching the Republic against its unreconciled enemies, anti-clericalism against the Church, radicalism against militarism, and they happened to pick a battlefield named after a Jew. It became the great cause of a generation. Clemenceau and Zola led the charge for the Dreyfusards, supported by most of literary France. But there were many eminent names on the other side. The *Affaire* rent French society. It divided friend from friend, brother from brother, the Dreyfusard Claude Monet from the anti-Dreyfusard Paul Cézanne, the duc de Guermantes from the prince de Guermantes. At its height, the witty Parisian caricaturist Caran d'Ache published a cartoon which would have been understood by later generations who lived through Munich or Suez or Vietnam. It showed a drawing-room, completely wrecked, furniture smashed, paintings knocked down, curtains ripped. Underneath the caption read simply, '*Quelqu'un en a parlé*': Someone mentioned it.

And yet in another sense, the *Affaire* was a vital part of the Jews' story, as their enemies were quick to see. Dreyfus had so much wanted to be French, did indeed see himself not as a Jew but a Frenchman *tout court*. His '*Vive la France!*' during the degradation was echoed almost louder when he was returned to France for a retrial, falsely convicted again, and responded by shouting from the dock, '*Vive l'Armée!*' It was assimilationism taken to its extreme, not to say reduced to absurdity. It did not satisfy the Jews' enemies and never would. For them, although they persuaded themselves to believe passionately that Dreyfus was guilty as charged, his innocence or guilt were neither here nor there. He was a Jew, '*the* Jew'; he must be at least a potential agent of outside powers, since he was not French; he did not belong.

This was put with brutal wit by a fictional character. Marcel Proust was part-Jewish and was profoundly exercised by – not to say hung-up about – his part-Jewishness. He became a Dreyfusard, but he mixed in circles where anti-Dreyfusards were prominent and vociferous. This was reflected in his epic novel-sequence *A la recherche du temps perdu*. One man, the monstrous and fascinating Baron de Charlus, looms large and long over the book. On one occasion when he is in conversation with Proust's narrator, he commends Bloch, whom they both know, saying that it is not a bad idea 'to have a few foreigners among your friends'; and then, to the reply that Bloch is French: 'Indeed,' said M. de Charlus, 'I took him to be a Jew.' His assertion of this incompatibility made the narrator suppose that M. de Charlus 'was more anti-Dreyfusard than anyone I had met'. Charlus goes on to protest against the charge of treason levelled at Dreyfus, but only in sourly sarcastic terms.

'I believe the newspapers say that Dreyfus had committed a crime against his country – so I understand; I pay no attention to the newspapers . . . In any case, the crime is non-existent. This compatriot of your friend would have committed a crime if he had betrayed Judaea, but what has he to do with France?' Reminded that French Jews could be drafted into the army, Charlus compares them with troops from the French African empire: 'I hardly suppose that their hearts will be in the task of defending France, and that is only natural.' Proust may have known Drumont's contemptuous words about Dreyfus: '*Pour trahir sa Patrie, il faut en avoir une*' ('To betray one's country, one must first have one'); Charlus puts it more cruelly still: 'Your Dreyfus might rather be convicted of a breach of the laws of hospitality.' These stinging words were to echo over the next hundred years. They returned to haunt some Jews when there really was a 'Judaea' – a Jewish state – which could command loyalty, and raise in new form the question of the Jews' position in the countries of the West.

From the point of view of the European Jews themselves, the *Affaire* could be interpreted in two ways. After a fierce struggle, Dreyfus was cleared, reinstated and lived to a ripe old age (when he could be heard muttering of some scandal, 'There's no smoke without fire') but a new and venomous Jew-hatred had been inflamed, with Drumont forming a Ligue Antisémite in 1898 and with the reactionary, monarchist and, of course, antisemitic Action Française established in this same year. Dreyfus's conviction was finally quashed in 1906, but by then he was already free, and it was possible to interpret the course of the *Affaire* as a vindication not of one man only but of French society and of liberal European civilisation as a whole, in which the Jews could live happily enough, albeit with occasional and inevitable upsets. That was just how many Jews across Europe did interpret the Dreyfus Affair. In Vienna, the *Neuzeit*, leading organ of Austrian Jewry, saluted France as Jews had a century earlier during the great Revolution: in the title of one article, there had been '*Der Triumph der Gerechtigkeit*', the triumph of justice.

But there was another interpretation. Herzl, who had earlier witnessed his degradation, formed his own view of what Dreyfus epitomised: 'The Jew who tries to adapt himself to his environment, to speak its languages, to think its thoughts, to sew its insignia on his sleeve – only to have them ruthlessly ripped away.' He might have been speaking of himself. Maybe he was.

Theodor Herzl was the creator of political Zionism. He was also – could only have been – a product of the Austro-Hungarian Empire. In its final phase, the Habsburg monarchy lasted just over a century, from reconstruction after the Napoleonic wars to disintegration at the end of the Great War. It could be seen as an absurdity, or a noble failure, or something in between: an attempt to maintain a multinational empire in the heart of Europe during the crescent triumph of the national principle. In practice, this meant that Austria-Hungary was, in Karl Kraus's phrase, at the sharp edge of modern Europe.

The Jews played a central part in its conflicts and turmoils, and it was no accident that new types of Jewish creativity, new sorts of Jewish neuroses, a new Jew-hatred, and a new Jewish nationalism, all sprang from Vienna at the turn of the century. Herzl himself came from Budapest, born there in 1860, seventeen years before it became the capital of the other half of the joint monarchy. Like Vienna, though even more so, Budapest had acquired a Jewish population very rapidly. There had always been Jewish communities scattered through disparate territories which were gathered under the Habsburgs, but it was the partition of Poland which had hugely increased the Jewish population of the monarchy, and it was an influx of Jews from Galicia which revolutionised the character of Vienna.

In the years immediately after 1848 the number of Jews in the capital only slowly increased, but then the Jewish migration suddenly accelerated; there were 40,227 Jews in Vienna in 1869, 99,441 in 1890, and by 1910 175,318, or nearly a tenth of the population of the city. By the same time, Budapest had been even more dramatically transformed. Immigration must also have explained the huge rise in the numbers of Jews in Hungary as a whole, from 75,000 in 1785 to 552,000 in 1870. By 1910, 240,000 of the citizens of Budapest were Jewish, or almost one in four, and these two were, after Warsaw, the largest Jewish cities in Europe. Herzl was a man of this world: an emancipated Jew who grew up fluent in Hungarian but equally at home in German, which was still the language of culture and commerce throughout the empire, not least in Budapest.[1] In Hungary,

[1] Less than thirty years before Herzl was born, German-speakers had easily outnumbered Hungarian-speakers in Budapest, which had two daily papers in German and none in Hungarian; and the city council conducted business in German until the 1880s.

as in Bohemia, antipathy for the Jews was made sharper still by the fact that so many of them were German-speaking.

By the time Herzl entered his *Gymnasium* or high school in 1875, a branch of the new antisemitism had sprouted in Hungary. Gyözö von Istóczy made a violent speech in the Hungarian parliament denouncing the Jews in terms which combined the old and the new: the Jews were an exclusive tribe who had defied absorption into the outside world for thousands of years and who aimed at economic conquest of their gentile neighbours under cover of 'liberalism'. Three years later, in 1878, the year of the Congress of Berlin, Istóczy made a still more remarkable speech. He supposed that 'in no other land in Europe does the Jewish Question necessitate a more urgently radical solution than in our monarchy and especially in Hungary', and went on to propose just such a radical solution: the restoration of a state for the Jews in the Holy Land, 'from which they have remained expelled for 1800 years'. He appealed to the great statesman of Europe who were Jewish 'by race' – Disraeli in England, Lasker in Germany, Gambetta in France, Glaser and Unger in Austria – to take up his plan. It is unlikely that Istóczy had heard of Napoleon's appeal eighty years earlier, inconceivable that he had read either Moses Hess or George Eliot. His proposal came from nowhere, a strange flash of lightning, casting weird shadows. The Jews had always prayed to spend next year in Jerusalem. Here was someone who wanted them to do just that: the man who organised the first self-styled antisemitic political movement in Europe.

In 1882, these Antisemites had won five seats in the Hungarian parliament, which within five years had become seventeen, or one tenth of seats. In that same year, Istóczy helped to organise an Antisemitic Congress in Dresden, and that year also he played a part in the Tisza-Eszlar affair, when the age-old charge that the Jews practised ritual murder of Christians resurfaced. Istóczy's participation in that blood-libel was natural enough, as were his demands that any Jews who remained in Europe should cease to be a 'state within a state' and instead make 'an honest peace with Christian civilisation'. Far more startling that he should favour the return of the Jews to their own land: it was the first time that a connection appeared between antisemite and Zionist.

By the time of the Tisza-Eszlar case, the Herzl family had moved to Vienna. Despite recent events, one eminent member of the Viennese Jewish community even used events in Hungary to illustrate the way in which the Jews were at home in the dual monarchy. What struck Josef Ritter von Wertheimer was not the crudescence of old hatreds, but 'the moral earnestness with which the Jew-baiter was repelled and reprimanded in the Hungarian House of Deputies'. This could only 'increase still further the ardent patriotic feelings manifested at every opportunity by Hungarian Israelites. But on this Austrian side of the Leitha, too, antisemitism finds no soil.' This was sadly over-optimistic. Following defeat by Prussia in 1866 and the *Ausgleich* or 'Compromise' in 1867 which established the Austro-Hungarian Dual Monarchy, the political character of the Habsburg monarchy, the national question, and the position of the Jews, had taken complex and sometimes bizarre courses. Reacting against the restless pressure of the Slav nationalists, the Germans of Austria had developed a new political consciousness. Were they Germans or 'Austrians'? What indeed was 'Austria'? Did it have any emotional meaning, rather than a technical description of an area?

This Austria – the 'cisleithine' half of Austria-Hungary in distinction from Hungary on the east of the Leitha river – included several million Czechs and Poles as well as Slovenes and Croats, and of course Jews. As the Jews moved physically from shtetl and ghetto and rose socially, they identified more and more closely with the Austrian monarchy. Joseph II had 'called into existence the most loyal of subjects' when he emancipated the Jews; Francis I had asked, 'But is he a patriot for me?' Now Joseph's work was done; Francis's question was answered. And as Dr Joseph Bloch said in 1886, 'If one could constitute a specifically Austrian nationality, then the Jews would constitute its foundation.'

In an old phrase, 'the thanks of the House of Habsburg' meant no thanks at all. That was what those patriotic Austrian Jews had received, not from the dynasty itself but from their fellow-citizens. In a novel published in 1907, *Der Weg ins Freie* (*The Road to the Open*), Arthur Schnitzler put an eloquent outburst in the mouth of one of his characters. The elderly businessman Ehrenberg warns a younger Jewish friend who is flirting with socialism: 'Exactly the same thing will happen to you Jewish Social Democrats as happened to the Jewish Liberals and German Nationalists . . .

'Who created the Liberal movement in Austria? . . . the Jews. By whom have the Jews been deserted and betrayed? By the Liberals. Who created the German-National movement in Austria? The Jews. By whom were the Jews left in the lurch? . . . what – left in the lurch!

... Spat upon like dogs! ... By the National-Germans, and precisely the same thing will happen in the case of Socialism and Communism. As soon as you've drawn the chestnuts out of the fire they'll start driving you away from the table. It always has been so and always will be.'

This was an accurate history lecture. Strange or bitter as it might later seem, the Jews had indeed been closely involved in the creation of a German national party in Austria. For some of them, it was not enough to identify with the supra-national empire which survived under the Habsburgs; they wanted to identify with the national German empire which Bismarck had just created under the Hohenzollerns. In the years after 1867 many of the Austrian Jews were 'the most ardent representatives of the *Anschluss* idea',[2] the socialist leader Karl Kautsky later wrote. One such, who later followed Kautsky into Social Democracy, was Viktor Adler. He was joined by another Jew, the great historian Heinrich Friedjung, in propounding the '*grossdeutsch*' or pan-German idea in the 1870s. In 1882, they joined with the German nationalist Georg von Schönerer to draft the Linz programme for reconstruction of the Austro-Hungarian empire on '*deutschnational*' lines. The fact that two of three men who created this pan-German nationalist programme should have been Jews – in troika with an incipient antisemite – is the surpassing irony even of this episode in European, and Jewish, history.

The three soon parted company. Adler forsook nationalism for socialism. Friedjung remained a *grossdeutsch* nationalist even though he was driven out of the nationalist party by Jew-hatred. As for Schönerer, he dropped the social radicalism of Linz (which had also demanded an expanded suffrage and taxation), and replaced it with vehement antisemitism. In 1885 he founded the German Nationalist party, and by 1897 he had his greatest success, though a sterile one, when German riots brought down the government. Schönerer insisted, once his new campaign was in motion, that 'our antisemitism is not directed against the religion but against the racial traits of the Jews'. He combined the rhetoric of Right and Left: straightforward racism in which antisemitism was 'a basic pillar of the national idea ... the principal means of promoting genuine national [*volkstümlich*] convictions, and therefore as the greatest national achievement this century', and the denunciation

---

[2] *Anschluss*, 'connection' or 'joining', meaning here the merging of Austria into the German Reich which was indeed accomplished by an Austrian-born politician, in 1938, with appalling consequences for the Austrian Jews.

of the Jew as a 'sucking vampire' who preyed on the poor. This was what a German radical called antisemitism, the socialism of fools.

To talk about 'Left' and 'Right' is misleading in this context, perhaps in any. The very concept – the metaphor which arose when the bourgeois radicals of the French Revolution took their seats to the left of the aristocratic conservatives – had bedevilled and confused European politics in the succeeding century, up to the age of Schönerer, and has bedevilled them since. The Jewish Question illustrates this vividly. It is not the case that antisemitism was a movement or passion of the 'Right' alone. Quite apart from Marx with his self-tormenting Jew-hatred, there were Proudhon, Kropotkin and Bakunin, unarguably men of the Left, Jew-haters all. Even in the more torpid air of England there were contemporaries of Schönerer's like the radical anti-imperialist J. A. Hobson, who saw Jews as 'almost devoid of social morality', infesting society in 'true parasitic fashion'; or the Labour leader John Burns who saw 'the financial Jew operating' behind imperial intrigues; or the libertarian socialist Edward Carpenter who claimed that British politicians were 'being led by the nose by the Jews'. For that matter, Hilaire Belloc, often taken as a 'right-wing' antisemite, might more properly be seen as a representative of 'the Radicalism of fools', with his hatred of the rich in general and rich Jews in particular.

At any rate, the concept of Left and Right scarcely describes Schönerer's move from liberalism to populist anti-liberalism, in which process he became a fully developed political antisemite. So did his colleague, and then rival, Karl Lueger. Although they used some of the same language, Dr Lueger's Christian Socialist movement was quite different from Schönerer's pan-German – and anti-clerical – nationalism. Lueger drew on the Austrian Catholic tradition, deliberately calling his party Christian, and following the teaching of the Roman Church set out in the 1890 papal encyclical *Rerum Novarum*, with its hostility to Marxist Social Democracy but also to the Manchester free-enterprise capitalism which socialism opposed. Christian Socialism was anti-Marxist but also anti-capitalist, anti-liberal, and antisemitic.

Part of Lueger was cynical manipulator. He played on a deep undercurrent of hostility to the Jews in Vienna, itself a product of large Jewish immigration and large Jewish success. It could be traced back as far as the 1848 revolution, 'the springtime of nations', and the hostility to Jews which ran through all too many nationalisms; it had received a powerful stimulus with the stock market crash of 1873 which destroyed so many, obscure and famous, from small businessmen to field marshals. The resentment caught hold of the huge lower-middle class of artisans and tradesmen, who became Lueger's particular constituency, and also students at the university which was such a notable focus of Jewish endeavour.

A form of social revenge was open to the gentile majority among the students. One fraternity or student union after another excluded Jews from membership, an example followed by sporting clubs throughout Austria. And in 1896, a convention of fraternities declared that in view of the 'lack of honour and character' the Jews had shown, 'no Jew is to be given satisfaction with any weapon'. This was an insult, but also a back-handed compliment. For years past, Jewish students had tried to beat their Christian contemporaries at their own game. A Jewish-nationalist fraternity, the Akademischer Verein Kadimah, had been founded at Vienna university in 1882. Jewish students refused to grovel before their tormentors but instead took part with gusto in the ritual of duelling, until the point when, as the Vienna correspondent of *The Times* put it, the best fencers of the fighting German corps found that Zionist students could gash cheeks quite as effectively as any Teuton and that 'the Jews were in a fair way to become the best swordsmen in the university'. Those Jewish sabreurs were among the first to set a new pattern. They had tried assimilation, and been rejected. Their new motto was, as it were: if you can't join them, beat them. It was an historic departure for Jews.

When Herzl first arrived at the university, so far from taking up the Jewish cause he had identified with the German nationalists. He was conscious of his double problem of identity, as a Jew and as a Hungarian (not to say as a Hungarian Jew, the particular group which Lueger said he most cordially disliked). And so he joined the nationalist duelling fraternity Albia, took as his *nom de combat* Tancred – Disraeli's fictional hero – and fought a duel. But he was swimming against the tide, the rising tide of the new Jew-hatred which finally re-awoke his Jewish identity. His first decisive moment came in 1883. The death of Richard Wagner that February inspired a great wave of sentimental commemorations which took on, among the Viennese students, a strongly pro-German and antisemitic colour. Herzl resigned from Albia, as a 'lover of freedom'. He did not renounce German *Kultur* in general, however, or Wagner in particular. It is a strange example of Wagner's protean appeal – not to say on the intimate symbiosis of Jewish and German which lasted for so long – that years later Herzl could describe how he had written *The Jewish State*, working in a frenzy: 'My only relaxation in the evening took the form of listening to Wagner's music, especially *Tannhäuser*, an opera which I heard as often as it was performed. It was only on the evenings when no opera was given that I felt doubts about the rightness of my ideas.'

For all the continuing spell cast by Wagner's music, those demonstrations in 1883 helped Herzl snap out of it. He had suffered from his own relatively mild infection of self-hatred. Herzl was an imposing and elegant figure, with a leonine personality but also an hauteur which did not always win friends; even more than most educated Austrian and German Jews, he was acutely conscious of the displeasing appearance and manner of the *Ostjuden*, seemingly mis-shapen by inbreeding, whose 'gloomy ghetto' still cast a shadow across their emancipated brethren, 'like a tight ring tormenting and paralysing the fingers, preventing creative activity, initiative and free movement in Jewish life'. With the vision of genius, Herzl saw the psychological root of the problem, and the shape the new antisemitism was taking, racial and national rather than religious.

Despite that, Herzl remained aloof in the 1880s from the Jewish renewal movement and from Jewish nationalism. He took his law degree but instead of practising as a lawyer travelled across Europe and went into literary journalism, became a master of the '*Feuilleton*', the literary or general essay which, as word or genre, has no exact English equivalent. With these gifts Herzl soon made a large name for himself, writing first for the *Wiener Allgemeine Zeitung*. Then in 1891 he became Paris correspondent of the *Neue Freie Presse*. And it was there, thanks to Dreyfus, that he discovered afresh what forms Jew-hatred could take. The *Affaire* was one of several dramatic evidences of the mood throughout Europe.

For an adoptive Viennese like Herzl, events in France, even though he witnessed them in person, may have been less frightening than the rising success of the Christian Socialist Party in Vienna, where Lueger was thrice elected mayor, but where the emperor, shocked by his demagogy, thrice refused to confirm him. Here, at the heart of the great empire, was a triumphant political party with hostility to Jews as a principal plank in its platform. Lueger was himself a man of remarkable character, personally honest and even generous, whose own antisemitism was directed, as he saw it, against the rich and the corrupt rather than at poor Jews. When reproached by a tougher-minded colleague for showing kindness to individual Jews, Lueger replied, in words quoted for years after in Vienna (and in Viennese), '*Wer e Jud' is', döss bestimm' i*'': I decide who's a Jew. But by the same token, an individual Jew was not to be allowed to decide for himself whether he was a Jew. The choice was made for him, by his enemies.

All of this came to Herzl. His first look at the Jewish Question was indeed 'feuilletonistic' or literary. *Das neue Ghetto* was a play, written in three weeks in 1894, although not performed until 1898. Its hero is a Jewish lawyer who is confronted by antisemitism in vivid form – at the end of the play he is killed in a duel by a Jew-hating titled former officer – but is also at odds with his own society, the emancipated and prosperous Jewish bourgeoisie, whose very rapid economic rise and apparent assimilation has corrupted them. One character, a worldly and materialistic rabbi, points out that the old physical ghetto had gone, but that the Jews were 'still rigidly confined to a moral ghetto', the new ghetto of the title, though he thinks that they should be content to remain there. The hero himself says that, on the contrary, the 'moral ghetto' is one built of the bad character which the Jews had acquired with emancipation, 'a ghetto we must clear away ourselves, we ourselves, on our own'. And when he falls, mortally wounded at the hand of a foe who despises his people, he apostrophises that people: 'My brethren, they won't let you live again', before expiring on the words, 'I want to . . . get . . . out! Out . . . of . . . the . . . Ghetto!'

When he wrote the play, Herzl was not yet a Jewish nationalist, only a highly intelligent and perceptive man who had tried to evade the Jewish Question, and had run into it as if into a wall. His play deliberately portrayed affluent assimilated Jews in a poor light. Antisemites had insisted for centuries that there was a bad Jewish character; Herzl, and other Jews like him, agreed, only suggesting that the bad character now took the form of emotional falseness and emptiness rather than treachery and rapacity, and that it was a product of environment rather than heredity. Although he saw the need to escape from his spiritual ghetto, Herzl was at a loss to see how this should be done. His first schemes were wonderfully chimerical. Weirdest of all was his plan to apply the old remedy of baptism, but on a universal scale. The Jews of the Habsburg monarchy would accept Christian baptism *en masse*, voluntarily and honourably assembled in Vienna: 'at twelve o'clock of a Sunday, the exchange of faith would take place in St Stephen's Cathedral, with solemn parade and peal of bells'.

It was as well for Herzl's reputation in his own time that this proposal (which would have made a grand canvas for some Victorian epic painter) remained in the privacy of his diaries. Maybe not too much should be made of it. Herzl was a man of his age, an age when the energies of bourgeois Europe were bursting out in all directions and when speculation and fancy were taking quaint shapes. The quaintest could go hand-in-hand with practical achievement: Herzl was a contemporary of Cecil Rhodes, who, when he was not amassing a colossal fortune from diamonds and gold and expanding his brutal sway over numberless Africans, was dreaming puerile dreams of 'a Secret Society, the one aim and object whereof shall be the extension of British rule throughout the world', a project which included 'the ultimate recovery of the United States of America', as well as the conquest of the Holy Land. For that matter he was a contemporary of Oscar Wilde, and there is a touch of dandyish flamboyance in Herzl's schemes.

What woke Herzl from his own reveries was the pattern of events. In May 1895, a few months after Dreyfus's conviction, Herzl went to see Baron Maurice de Hirsch, a leading Jewish financier and a leading Jewish philanthropist. Hirsch came from a family of Bavarian 'court Jews', and had himself become a multimillionaire from sugar, copper and especially railways. Now settled in Vienna, he stood as high as the Rothschilds among the plutocracy of late-Victorian Europe; a race-horse-owner whose filly La Flèche had started favourite for the 1892 Derby (though she was beaten); a social figure on friendly terms with the Prince of Wales and the ill-fated Crown Prince Rudolf of Austria.[3]

Aside from accumulating a fortune, Hirsch had devoted himself tirelessly to the welfare of his own people. He wished to rescue the eastern Jews from destitution and degradation, to help them regenerate themselves physically and psychologically by making farmers of them. His Jewish Colonisation Association was founded in 1891 and worked in harness with the Baron Hirsch Fund in New York: its object was to settle poor Jews in the Americas, North and South, especially in the Argentine. The one place of settlement towards which he was cool was the Holy Land. But although Hirsch wanted to rescue the Jews from poverty, he did not want to turn them all into bourgeois. They should become farmers and artisans; but 'No, no, no,' he told Herzl at their

---

[3] Whose suicide at Mayerling in 1889 had been such a blow for the Austrian Jews: Rudolf was an outspoken liberal who had condemned antisemitism as 'the disgrace of the century' and had been denounced in turn by the antisemites as a paid tool of the 'Golden International'.

meeting, 'I do not want to raise the general level. All our misfortunes come from the fact that the Jews want to climb too high. We have too much brains. My intention is to restrain the Jews from pushing ahead. They shouldn't make such great progress.' This closely anticipated the way Labour Zionists later hoped that hard toil and husbandry would transform the Jews from a class into a society.

There were other grave and comic moments in the interview – as when Herzl suggested that the Argentine colony would be a failure and thus 'furnish a dreadful argument against all Jews', or when in reply to Herzl's, 'You talk like a socialist,' the millionaire Hirsch replied, 'I am one.' And yet this was the moment when a vision came to Herzl. He wrote a memorandum to Hirsch, then wrote down a long pamphlet, at high speed. In his own words in his diary, 'I have the solution to the Jewish Question. I know it sounds mad; and at the beginning I shall be called mad more than once – until the truth of what I am saying is recognised in all its shattering force.' This solution was presented to the public in February 1896 as *Der Judenstaat* (*The Jewish State*).[4] It revolutionised the argument. It sounded mad. It had indeed a shattering force for some – far from all or even most – Jews, but that force produced radically different effects.

Herzl's first and essential premiss was that antisemitism was now an insoluble problem. 'No one can deny the gravity of the Jewish situation. Wherever they live in appreciable number, Jews are persecuted in greater or lesser measure.' Although 'oppression and persecution cannot exterminate us', the Jews were not going to be left in peace. Emancipated Jews longed for assimilation, but this was an illusion; or, rather, true assimilation could be achieved only by intermarriage. The only answer was to recognise that the Jewish question was not a social or religious one but a national question, which must have a national answer: 'We are a people – one people.' And as a people they needed a homeland of their own. It might be Palestine or the Argentine: he would take whatever was offered and whatever Jewish public opinion favoured, though 'Palestine is our unforgettable historic homeland'. Years later, Chaim Weizmann, by then the leader of Zionism, was to say that Herzl evidently had somewhere like the Argentine in mind while he was writing *The Jewish*

---

[4] This translation is too well-known to discard, but is misleading. The words 'Jewish State' have an exact German equivalent, *jüdischer Staat*; Herzl seems to have intended 'The Jews' State', a state of, or for, Jews.

State and had only added the emphasis on the Holy Land as an afterthought.

Wherever it was to be, once established in a land of their own, 'a wondrous breed of Jews will spring up from the earth. The Maccabees will rise again ... The Jews who will it shall achieve their State ...

'We shall live at least as free men on our own soil, and in our own homes peacefully die.'

Herzl's real audience were those like himself, emancipated intellectual Jews for whom emancipation had brought as much anguish as happiness. He himself admitted as much. In 1897, the first Zionist Congress was held at Basle. The Stadt Casino concert hall was decorated with a flag, the blue stripes outside white, and a Star of David hung over the hall: the symbols which would one day fly over the State of Israel. Some enthusiasts claimed that the flag was the banner of the ancient Hebrews; it had in fact been devised by David Wolffsohn, one of Herzl's associates, a nice example of the way Zionism, like so many European nationalisms, relied on invented tradition.

Addressing the congress, Herzl was frank in explaining its emotional background:

'Our adversaries may be unaware of how deeply they have wounded the sensibility of the very people among us who perhaps were not even the primary targets of their attack. That part of Jewry which is modern and cultured, which has outgrown the ghetto and weaned itself away from petty trading, was hurt to the quick.' And Max Nordau amplified the theme: a moral distress more bitter than physical distress 'because it afflicts the sophisticated, prouder, more sensitive human beings. The emancipated Jew is unstable, insecure in his relationship with his neighbours, timorous in contacts with the unknown, suspicious even of the secret feelings of his friends.' That could almost have been one definition of the Jewish Question: the hurt feelings of sensitive educated Jews. In every country with a sizeable Jewish population, Herzl said 'the position of Jewish lawyers, doctors, technicians, teachers and employers of every description becomes daily more intolerable'. Everywhere the mob was incited against prosperous Jews, including those who had bettered themselves by their own efforts as a consequence of living in an open, liberal society. Not that Herzl thought those who taunted the Jews always without reason: a large cause of antisemitism is 'our excessive production of mediocre intellectuals, who have no outlet downward or upward'.

It would be unfair and too paradoxical to say that Herzl's scheme was a product of his obvious unease about the Jews and his highly ambiguous attitude towards Jewishness. But as those words show, along with much else he wrote, including some of the characters in *The New Ghetto*, he plainly disliked, not merely the persecution of his people, but what that people had become. His feelings about the poor eastern Jews were very ambivalent, and far from merely loyal and affectionate; but then so, though in a different way, were his feelings about the class to which he belonged, too many of whose members seemed emotionally and intellectually mediocre. These people, who now spent their lives in the liberal professions, the arts, science, commerce, journalism, far from the ghetto, the product of modern society, weaned away from Jewish tradition, as he put it, and obliged to find both their bread and their self-respect outside Jewish society, were at once notably cut off from their Jewish roots, with few spiritual links to Judaism, and notably vulnerable to the new mood of Jew-hatred.

This may have been a penetrating analysis, if a chilly one. And yet Herzl's 'answer to the Jewish Question' contained its own ambiguities and contradictions. Just whose problem was he trying to solve? Like Hess before him, Herzl recognised that a large part of Dispersion Jewry was not likely to uproot itself and live in this Jewish state he dreamed of, particularly the prosperous bourgeois whose false position he perceived. He sometimes spoke as though these people were the indirect targets, or innocent bystanders; that the rise of antisemitism was caused by the mass of poor Jews as they flooded westwards and embarrassed those already in residence (a view silently shared by some of those assimilated Jews in their well-to-do quarters, from Döbling in Vienna to Charlottenburg in Berlin to Bayswater in London to the Upper East Side of New York). If the masses had somewhere to go, a land of their own, Herzl suggested, it would ease the pressure on middle-class Jewry: Zionism would, in an indirect way, facilitate the successful absorption into their societies of those who stayed behind.

This then raised another question, as Herzl was aware. On a visit to London, the Jewish audiences he addressed put several objections to his scheme, 'the most important of them: English patriotism'. If there ever were to be a Jewish state, where would English – or German, Austrian, French, American – Jews owe their loyalty? Would they not be open to the antisemite's accusation that they belonged to an international tribe and not truly to the country of their residence; that, just as Charlus said, anything they did there could only be judged in terms of the laws of hospitality? Herzl listened to these objections from his English audience, 'which I refute', he said with his usual breezy confidence. But they were not so easily refuted as he supposed.

Nor was another charge: that Zionism was not only an admission of defeat, not to say that it was the other side of the same coin of antisemitism. Herzl came close to admitting this himself. Why else did he say that the antisemites 'will be our most reliable friends, the antisemitic countries our allies'? Why was he, in his proclaimed mission of rescuing Jewry, rejecting so much of Jewish tradition? Sixty years after *The Jewish State* appeared, Hans Kohn observed that it was an outgrowth of the European nationalism which had brought such sorrow to the Jews, and that the whole tenor of this nationalism not only 'had nothing to do with Jewish traditions; it was in many ways opposed to them'. Not merely nationalism in general, but one nationalism in particular, inspired Herzl. In Thomas Mann's novel *Doctor Faustus*, Herr Fitelberg muses on the comparison between German and Jewish nationalism: *'une analogie frappante!'* As Hannah Arendt put it, Herzl thought in terms of nationalism inspired from German sources. In the German theory, people of common descent or speaking a common language formed a nation and ought to form a state. As Kohn said, this was an idea which ran counter to the western political ideal that a country could consist of peoples of various and even unknown ethnic origin who owed a common allegiance: an ideal exemplified, Kohn said, by the United States above all, though he might have pointed out that it had also described the Habsburg monarchy.

These problems apart, Herzl cannot have understood all that he was doing. With all his brilliant literary gifts, he remained an intellectual dandy rather than a logician. His plan was not only an acceptance of the reality of antisemitism and nationalism, it was an almost conscious mirror-image of European nationalism based on a belief in the failure of assimilation and liberalism. At the same time, it was a radical break with Jewish tradition. It was from the beginning consciously secular – and was to become steadily more so, until the day would come when Zionist zealots picnicked off ham sandwiches on Yom Kippur. Herzl did not go so far, but he dreamed of a Jewish state which was both secular and unmilitaristic: 'We shall know how to keep the rabbis in their synagogues, and our generals in their barracks', not as it turned out part of his prophecy which would come true.

Nor did he see how Zionism, like so many doctrines, might develop.

He did not grasp the audacity of a project which would like to be seen in mighty terms, as nothing less than a plan for ending the Jews' 'chosenness' and for 'normalising' them, turning them from a class into a society, reinventing them as a nation, making them 'like other peoples'. And he did not see that his dream might come true, that a Jewish state might become reality, but that this would have quite different consequences for Jewry than he envisaged.

II

From
The Jewish State to
a Jewish National Home

5

Mauscheln

Yea, their own tongues shall make them fall.

Ps.lxiv.8

As the young Zionist movement got under way, Herzl decided that congresses should be held annually to keep up the momentum. By the fourth congress, in London in 1900, it was reported that there were more than 1,000 local organisations in Russia, with 100,000 people paying 'the shekel', the fund-raising equivalent of O'Connell's 'Catholic rent' eighty years earlier which had gathered pence by the million from the poverty-stricken Irish masses. But as that very comparison shows, Zionism was still only a small affair. Although it had touched the hearts of fair numbers of the poor eastern Jews, it had the flavour of so many political or religious movements in their early stages. It would be an exaggeration to say that early Zionism was all leaders and no followers, but officers often seemed to outnumber the other ranks.

It was from the Russian heartland that some of the doughtier young enthusiasts came. Chaim Weizmann was born in 1874 in Motol, David Ben-Gurion in Plonsk in 1886. Both men were, not assimilated Jews, in the western sense, but heirs of the Maskilim, the Jewish enlightenment which had been drawing away from Orthodoxy and Yiddishkeit towards modernity and the prevailing culture of the country. Zionism both drew on and reacted against the Maskil tradition: it was a form of secularism, and bitterly resisted for that reason by many rabbis, but it was also an assertion of Jewishness against the false hopes of assimilation. Those two men took different courses. Weizmann, unable to study at Russian universities, went to Germany and Switzerland before settling in England in 1904. He had become an ardent devotee of Hibbath Zion and had attended the second Zionist congress, though he later admitted that he had not been immediately bowled over by Herzl personally. But he did not migrate to Palestine, spending instead several decades at Manchester university, though continually visiting London, and moving from one western capital to another to persuade politicians and cajole commentators.

By contrast, Ben-Gurion helped to found Poale Zion. This was a Zionist Labour group which had not then developed into a political party. It was inspired by the ideals which had earlier been expressed in England by Ruskin, with his hatred of industrial materialism, and in Russia by Tolstoy, with his sometimes sentimental belief in the virtues of the peasantry and the worth of honest toil. These themselves were transfused into Zionism by A. D. Gordon, 'the Tolstoy of Palestine', and were of huge importance to the movement. Gordon was to be sceptical about political Zionism, the Balfour Declaration, and the goal of a Jewish state. His own concerns were different. Along with other forms of Jewish alienation, he abhorred the way 'the Jewish people has been completely cut off from nature and imprisoned within city walls these two thousand years. We have become accustomed to every form of life, except to a life of labour – of labour done at our own behest and for its own sake. It will require the greatest effort of will for such a people to become normal again.' So it did, but the will was found, producing agricultural settlements and the collective kibbutzim. He practised what he preached. Born in the province of Padolia in 1856, Gordon lived in Russia until the age of forty-seven, when he took his family to Palestine and insisted on becoming an agricultural labourer, ending in one of the earliest kibbutzim before his death in 1922.

Gordon's brand of Zionism enjoyed a remarkable success in changing the Jews, or many of them, from pedlars and money-changers to farmers and artisans. The deeper social and psychological project was, in the words of Amos Oz, one of Gordon's later followers, 'the gradual improvements in human nature through a purification that must come through intimacy between individuals, through a renewal of links with the old elements: the soil, the cycle of the seasons, tilling the soil, "mother nature", inner rest'. This was a project so far-reaching as to be almost impudent, and was perhaps unrealisable, but the attempt at least inspired many people.

In the Second Ascent of 1904–14 about 40,000 settled in Palestine.

Ben-Gurion migrated in 1906 and worked as a farm hand, but was also an activist and polemicist, who attended the 1913 Congress, and at the same time laid the foundations for the union organisation which was to expand until, in the Yishuv or Jewish settlement in Palestine between the Balfour Declaration and Israel's statehood, and still more in Israel itself once the state was born, it was to become far more than the labour movements of western countries, a central estate of the realm.

Zionism did not kindle such passion everywhere, and it was not only rabbis who vehemently opposed it. For the rest of his brief life Herzl remained with the *Neue Freie Presse*, but his relationship with the paper was oblique. Moritz Benedikt, the famous editor of the *Presse*, used to say with a smile that when Herzl came into his office to talk about submissions, 'I never know whether it is my literary editor or the Messiah after all'. The paper itself was editorially less affable. It kept up an unremitting hostility to Zionism, whose very name was not even mentioned in its pages. Benedikt tried to dissuade Herzl from publishing the *Judenstaat*, he tried to make him sever his links with the Zionist weekly, the *Welt*, which Herzl himself had founded, he tried to prevent him from playing a leading part in the Zionist congresses, he tried in short to strangle Herzl's new idea at birth. He told Herzl that his Zionist project was like 'setting this avalanche in motion – endangering so many interests', and again that it was 'a powerful machine-gun and it may go off backwards'.

As those lurid metaphors suggest, Benedikt now regarded Herzl as a dangerous man and his idea a terrifying one. The *Presse* epitomised the new Jewish grand *Bürgertum* of Vienna, who had achieved an astonishingly quick ascent to power and position, and were at the same time acutely conscious of the fragility of that power and position. And the paper now came to epitomise the intense hostility of most emancipated Jews to Herzl's scheme of political Zionism. Benedikt's antipathy was partly prudential: he warned Herzl that 'we shall no longer have our present fatherland and shall not yet have the Jewish state', which indeed was to be the case in the hour of the Jewish people's greatest catastrophe.

For years before Herzl's confrontation with Benedikt, the Zionist idea had been mocked by Jewish critics for pragmatic reasons, because it was so absurd, so impossible of attainment. But this vehemence said something about the critics. Few of the early critics of Zionism were concerned with what later became the most widely voiced objection, the dispossession of the Arabs who were a large majority of the population of the Holy Land in the time of *Rome and Jerusalem*, or of *The Jewish State*, or indeed of the Balfour Declaration. In 1902, Herzl published *Altneuland* (*Old-Newland*), a utopian fantasy about the future Jewish state. Its epigraph was the words, '*Wenn ihr wollt, ist es kein Märchen*': If you wish, it's no fairy-tale. In this spirit, he optimistically foresaw warm gratitude on the part of the Palestinian Arabs. An Arab character, Rashid Bey, asks, ' "The Jews have enriched us, why should we be angry with them? They live with us like brothers, why should we not love them?" '

This somewhat implausible scene was dented by Herzl's colleague, Max Nordau, when he pointed out that Palestine was not an empty wilderness but had a substantial indigenous population: 'We are committing an injustice.' But Nordau was unusual in seeing this, though Herzl did, in fact, have an inkling of the problem without quite knowing that he did. He only ever visited the Holy Land once and briefly, and that was not to make contact either with the Arabs or with the Jewish settlers already there, but to meet the German Kaiser who was visiting Turkey and whose support Herzl sought, with his faith in diplomatic intrigue at the highest level. But while passing through Egypt he was impressed by the ability and intelligence of young Egyptians, writing in the privacy of his diary, though still with unconscious irony, 'They are the coming rulers of the country; and it is a wonder that the British don't see this.'

It later became the fashion to denounce the whole Zionist idea as a form of colonialism, and to call all the Zionists imperial conquerors from the beginning. This was little more than a truism; as a judgement, it was not so much wrong as prochronistic. Herzl and his colleagues were not rapacious or brutal men, only men of their time. Once it became a serious enterprise and not simply a day-dream – *kein Märchen* – Zionism became patently a colonial enterprise. But then the time of Herzl's dream was the 1890s, the heyday of European imperialism. At the beginning of that decade, Africa had finally been partitioned, at the end of it Kipling would urge the Americans to 'take up the White Man's burden' in the newly acquired Philippines.

Later generations came to see imperialism as a reactionary cause. To its proponents at the time it was the opposite. As A. J. P. Taylor once put it, imperialists believed that Europe 'had achieved the highest form of civilisation ever known and that it was her duty to take this civilisation to "the lesser breeds without the law" '; and he added just as

correctly that 'these were Radical beliefs'. Marx himself was notoriously contemptuous of non-European societies, making an exception
only for Turkey as a country which might pass directly to socialism
without first becoming capitalist. He objectively favoured European
imperialism in Asia, on the grounds that 'the British were the first
conquerors superior, and therefore inaccessible, to Hindu civilisation',
a civilisation which he openly despised. It was the most enlightened
and progressive of Englishmen, Frenchmen and Dutchmen who
wanted to serve the 'sullen peoples, half devil and half child' over
whom Providence had appointed them to rule. Macaulay was in his
own eyes and those of his contemporaries unquestionably a voice of
progress, the man who had so eloquently preached justice and
emancipation for the Jews; and he had sincerely believed that the
Indians would be raised up by studying Shakespeare and the history of
the Glorious Revolution. Nor did his countrymen see anything
incongruous about building churches in the Decorated mediaeval style
in West Africa or Ceylon, or teaching the children of West Indian
slaves and Bengali coolies to play cricket.

By that standard there was nothing uniquely odd in Herzl's dream
of transplanting the culture of the central European Jewish bourgeoisie
to the Levant, down to the most comical and touching detail: 'I shall
transport over there genuine Viennese cafés. With these small
expedients I ensure the desirable illusion of the old environment.' He
also believed that German would be the official language of the Jewish
state, but, 'I have nothing, however, against French or English. I shall
incline the *jeunesse dorée* towards English sports, and in this way prepare
them for the army.'

Along with cafés, football and cricket, Herzl wanted to transport the
very idea of Europe to the Levant, just as the Crusaders once had. But
why not? The Crusades seemed to later generations a curious way of
promulgating a gospel which promised the meek the inheritance of the
earth and called the peacemakers the children of God. That was not
how it seemed to men at the time, any more than most former societies
had felt the need to apologise for brutal subjugation of other peoples.
Herzl proposed no massacre or military conquest; but he did not give a
second's thought to colonising a country which then had few Jewish
inhabitants. Quite apart from the historic claim of the Jews on the
Land of Israel, even as Herzl wrote, millions of men were swarming
across the world to settle in the Americas, southern Africa, Australia,

all of them places which had not known a single European inhabitant four hundred years earlier when Isabella expelled the Jews from Spain.

In another sense also Herzl mirrored his own age. The nineteenth century may have seen the 'springtime of nations' across Europe, but this flowering of nationalism had led to an uncomfortable discovery. Nationalities and nationalisms were not clear-cut, black and white: peoples overlapped, competing for the same territory, and any national action tended to produce an equal and opposite reaction. At the time of Herzl's campaign, and Lueger's triumph, the conflict between Jew and gentile in Vienna was only one of the national struggles gnawing at the Habsburg monarchy, and not the most violent. The conflict between Czechs and Germans in Bohemia had brought government to a standstill, the South Slav question ticked away like a bomb which might – and finally did – blow up the empire.

In all this, the awkward discovery was again and again made, that good and enlightened nationalism turned out to have a darker side. The two national movements which had caught the hearts of liberal Europe, Italian and German, went wrong. One became a joke, the other a nightmare. Germans and Italians proved just as much capable of national oppression as they had once claimed to be victims of national injustice. Even Irish nationalism, struggling against centuries of English oppression, made its own inconvenient discovery that in the north-east of the island were a million Scotch-Irish Protestants who did not want to be part of an independent Irish nation.

Apart from their Hungarian gusto and imagination, there was a certain aptness in the fact that Herzl and several of his Zionist colleagues came from Budapest. Hungary had turned out to be the archetype of two-sided nationalism. The Hungarians had claimed that they were oppressed by their Habsburg rulers and that they were a people struggling rightly to be free. But, even before the Compromise of 1867 made Hungary an equal partner in the Dual Monarchy, it had become clear to those who wanted to see that the Hungarians were themselves a master race within the borders of historic Hungary, borders which contained millions of Slovaks, Ukrainians, Romanians, Serbs, 'the victims' victims'. An enlightened Magyar landlord might have hoped that these people would enjoy the benefits of Hungarian rule, just as Herzl foresaw the Arabs giving thanks for a Jewish state; in neither case did things work out like that.

Much more audible at the time than any worries about the colonial nature of Zionism and its threat to the Arabs were the protests of Jews who regarded the Zionist idea as a threat to themselves. On the one hand were the devoutly religious. Reform as well as Orthodox Jews thought that Zionism attacked and degraded Judaism and the Jews as a religious community, quite apart from impiously anticipating Messianic Redemption and the restoration of God's People by the Messiah, in God's time. Orthodox and Reform Judaism had been strongly hostile to one another, and the precise flavour of their anti-Zionism differed. For the Orthodox, Zionism blasphemed Torah Judaism; for the Reform synagogue it represented, as Robert Wistrich puts it, 'a parochial retreat from the universalist Jewish "mission" of *Weltbürgertum* [citizenship of the world] to an anachronistic mode of tribal nationalism'. Such people bitterly resented being lectured by Zionists about what it meant to be a Jew; they did not relish having their faith impugned – or their patriotism. One devout Jew went further, acutely discerning – and lamenting – what he called the 'evil craving' on the Zionists' part 'to remould us on the European model, to "make men of us"'. That was just what Herzl and his associates did want to do, and that was why they could afford politely to ignore religious objectors.

Practical objectors were harder to deal with. Despite the reality of the small Jewish settlements in the Holy Land which had taken place (with mixed results) by the time *The Jewish State* was published, the idea of transporting a large portion of the Jewish population of Europe to the shores and hills of the Holy Land was on the face of it fantastic in a high degree. These objections shaded into another: that even if Dr Herzl's scheme were practicable it would be undesirable. Gentile hostility to Zionism was more damaging practically; Jewish hostility more dangerous morally. It came 'from many directions, religious and atheist, assimilationist and autonomist, from conservatives, liberals, and socialists'. An increasing number of Jews had been beguiled by another dream, of socialism. At the turn of the century, this movement, inspired by the Jewish prophet Marx and usually called social democracy, still presented something like a united front. It had not yet been broken into majority and minority (in Russian, 'bolshevik' and 'menshevik') factions, irreparably split between revolutionary communism and constitutional socialism.

To the downtrodden Jews of the Tsarist empire especially, socialism spoke powerfully, and Jews played a part out of all proportion to their number in the Russian revolutionary movement, some of them carrying the torch into American exile. Among the Russian Jews' cousins in the poverty-stricken townships of Austrian Galicia, socialism also caught fire, fanned by the largely Jewish Social Democratic Party. Its leaders, like Hermann Diamand and Hermann Liebermann, saw Zionism not only as a rival but as a delusion. Their colleague, Max Zetterbaum, denounced *Der Judenstaat* in the most violent terms. He called it the work of a man quite cut off from his Jewish roots, certainly from religion; it was a product of Viennese café society, of an essayistic, *fin-de-siècle* literary decadence which had to be understood in terms of personal frustration rather than genuine social forces.

The Zionists had their own riposte to critics on the Left. Why suppose that socialism would be any different from any movement before in Christendom? There had been enough false dawns before, from Reformation to Enlightenment to Revolution, each with a sting in its tail for the Jews. Nor would the fact that Marx and Lassalle and Adler were Jews be any help. As Nordau said, 'the founder of Christianity was a Jew too, but to the best of my knowledge Christianity does not think it owes a debt of gratitude to the Jews.' In Schnitzler's *Der Weg ins Freie* the Jewish Question and the Zionist response are discussed at length. Schnitzler's plays and tales had already caught better than anyone else's the mood of Vienna at the turn of the century, a place and society where 'the situation is hopeless but not serious'. But there was more to them than Nineties decadence and manic frivolity. Schnitzler sensed the impending doom of Habsburg Austria, and that its demise might be followed by something far nastier. Especially, he understood what it was to be a Jew in that strange, gay, cruel society. A man could never ignore the fact that he was a Jew, Schnitzler said: 'Nobody else was doing so, not the Gentiles and even less the Jews. You had the choice of being counted as insensitive, obtrusive, fresh; or of being over-sensitive, shy, and suffering from feelings of persecution.'

'I myself have only succeeded up to the present in making the acquaintance of one genuine antisemite,' says the young dandy Nürnburger sneeringly in Schnitzler's novel. 'I am afraid I am bound to admit, dear Herr Ehrenberg, that it was a well-known Zionist leader.' By now the equation of Zionism and antisemitism was a commonplace among those who opposed the movement for a Jewish homeland. Those who made it could produce a good deal of plausible evidence. The fact that Istóczy, the Hungarian antisemite, was also a proponent of Jewish settlement in Palestine had not gone unnoticed.

No one made the equation with as much bitterness as Karl Kraus. Writing in September 1898, he described how he had been asked to contribute to a movement 'which is known as Zionist or by the good old word antisemitic'. This was written at the beginning of his ferocious polemic *Eine Krone für Zion* (*A Crown for Zion*). At the time, Kraus himself was not yet twenty-five but already a famous figure in Vienna. He was precocious enough to have appeared in a reference book of intellectual and cultural Vienna in the year he left his *Gymnasium*. Like many Viennese Jews, among them his great enemy, Sigmund Freud, Kraus was not born in Vienna, but moved there as a child. His father was a successful paper-manufacturer, and Kraus was able to spend the rest of his life without earning a living (his career thus illustrating Lady Bracknell's theme, 'the influence of a permanent income on Thought'). The *Neue Freie Presse* would have liked him to work for them, but he refused, and the *Presse* became one of the lifelong objects of his invective and abuse, though only one. In 1899, at the age of twenty-five and the year he decided not to write for the *Presse*, Kraus founded his own magazine, the *Fackel* (*Torch*), which he published on and off for the rest of his life, or the best part of forty years. In it he set about him at the official Viennese culture of his day in its falseness and corruption, not least in the corruption of humane values and of language itself.

Kraus's relationship with his Jewishness was unusually complicated. His greatest hostility as a satirical commentator was reserved not so much for the ostensible ruling order of Austria – the dynasty, court, army, 'first society' of old aristocrats, bureaucracy – as for the new commercial and cultural élite who increasingly exercised real power. And this élite was largely Jewish. It wasn't Kraus who coined the line about Moritz Benedikt of the *Presse* – that 'next to him, the emperor is the most important man in the country' – but it might have been. The press on the whole, and the *Presse* in particular, were largely Jewish in ownership and staff. Wickham Steed of *The Times* claimed that 'some clear-sighted Jews attribute, albeit with conscious exaggeration, the growth of political antisemitism in Austria to detestation of the *Neue Freie Presse*, a journal that embodies in concentrated form and, at times, with demonic force, the least laudable characteristics of Austro-Hungarian Jewry'. He regretted that more Jews were deterred 'by fear of playing into the enemy's hands, from public criticism or rebuke of their co-religionists' indiscretions'; Kraus was not deterred. The *Presse* replied by ignoring him, exactly the same '*Totschweigtaktik*' – death by silence – that it had practised with Zionism. Kraus continued his barrage of withering scorn, against old targets in the press, against new ones in the psychoanalytic movement and, in between those, against

Zionism. Now long forgotten, *Eine Krone für Zion* is an historic document in the moral struggle for the Jewish soul.

In it, he describes how 'one of the gentlemen who now set themselves up as advocates for the Jewish people and, with their eyes strangely narrowed against the dawn, agitate for the return of the rest of the Jews to the ancestral land of Palestine', had recently visited him to ask for his support and to solicit a contribution for the great new enterprise (the 'crown for Zion' of the title is a coin). Kraus mistook his friendly collector at first for a representative of Lueger's Christian Socialists, come to gather a '*Schussgeld*' or bounty on Jews. But, no, he is a Zionist. The common interest and mutual sympathy of Zionists and antisemites is rubbed in over and again by Kraus: Zionism had been greeted with sincere good will by Ernest Schneider, a parliamentary deputy and, in a strongly contested field, perhaps the most remorseless and repellent Jew-hater among contemporary Viennese demagogues.[1]

The first Zionist congress had recently been held in Basle the year before, and Kraus pours a torrent of mockery on its proceedings, as reported with starry-eyed rhapsody by an enthusiast, who described his own intense emotion at seeing the blue-and-white flag with its Star of David flying from the balcony of the congress hall. The stilted innocence with which all this was written was to Kraus the scent of the fox to hounds – and polemical journalism was for him a form of blood sport. Yet again he returns to the comparison: the 'new theory that the Jews only linger in Europe to improve it as a tourist resort' was advocated both by a gifted literary journalist (as Kraus calls Herzl without irony), and by Ernst Vergani (another rabble-rousing Jew-baiter, editor of the muck-raking *Deutsches Volksblatt*, and a man who had stood trial for embezzlement). Herzl is proud of the goodwill 'with which the indigenous inhabitants view his scheme for segregation', and his own words – 'Many Christians say themselves that they are delighted with our work' – are contemptuously and sardonically flung back at him. For Kraus the impossibility of the enterprise was obvious: the idea of settling so many Jews in Palestine is one absurdity, but another is the pretence that there is a true nationality shared by the caftan-wearing tradesman in the Galician shtetl and the literary poseur of the Viennese cafés. 'What common bond ought to hold together the

[1] Schneider once told parliament that the Jewish Question could be solved by baptism for all Jews – 'but I should immerse them for the duration of five minutes'.

interests of German, English, French, Slavonic and Turkish Jews? Is the faith in Dr Herzl's literary gifts so strong that it can bring about a union in spite of all linguistic differences? Or does the King of Zion think that he can satisfy the Czech Jews at the expense of the German Jews by granting language ordinances?'[2] As for the 'King of Zion', this derisive nickname stuck, and Herzl was labelled thus thereafter.

Constructive criticism was something Kraus could rarely be accused of. *Eine Krone für Zion* is a fine specimen of his early style. Everything is there: the ludic brilliance, the verbal fireworks, the savagery, the relentless sarcasm which can all make Kraus a trial as well as a pleasure to read. When he did try to answer the Zionist case constructively he could only manage the wan conclusions that broader social developments would take care of the problem of antisemitism, and that political radicalism would thwart the false prophets of Zion: 'It is almost unimaginable that this time the Jews will reach the Promised Land with dry feet; another Red Sea, Social Democracy, will bar their way.' In other words, socialism and not Zionism would be the solution to the anguish of the poor Galician Jews: a proposition which would be more convincing if it had been related to what had gone before in the diatribe or if indeed Kraus had been a sincere socialist.

The real interest of *Eine Krone für Zion* lies elsewhere. More than thirty years after the pamphlet was published, Theodor Lessing published another disturbing book, *Der jüdische Selbsthass*. 'Jewish self-hatred' was far older than 1890s Vienna, but Lessing took Krause as an egregious and tragic example of the phenomenon. It was a charge on the face of things easily made against Kraus. Was it true? The facts undisputed by either side are that Kraus stood at an angle to his Jewish inheritance. In 1907 he formally left the Jewish fold (a step available in Austrian law) and in 1911 he became a Roman Catholic (though later he left that fold as well). His lifelong polemical engagement with all that he found rotten in Vienna, under the empire and then under the republic, took him into battle with the press and the *Presse*, with posturing café literatteurs, with the psychoanalytical movement; in other words, over and again, with Jews. Besides, everything which Kraus stood for was a rejection of nationalism, chauvinism, group loyalty, team spirit. That applied to his country and his class, so why

---

[2] A reference to the ordinance of April 1897, by which Badeni, the Austrian prime minister, had tried to grant equality between Czech and German in Bohemia, but which had only provoked a great upsurge of German rage, directed by Schönerer, and had thus brought down Badeni.

not also his people? He represented also a type, who out of moral and intellectual honesty often finds it necessary to denigrate those who instinct says are his friends and praise those who should be his foes. In Jews, notably, this can take acute forms.[3] When all that is said, the case for the prosecution is strong.

In his own time, Kraus divided opinion, his chosen enemies on one side, on the other the '*Krausianer*', the devoted fans who hung on his every word in the *Fackel* and every word of Shakespeare's he spoke at his famous readings, and he has divided it since, with partisans who sing his praises and insist that he was free of 'Jewish antisemitism'. Someone whose mission was to expose falseness and shallowness was obliged to criticise many of the 'mediocre' Jewish intellectuals of whom Herzl had also complained. Wickham Steed complained that among many Jewish writers in Austria the number of really good writers of German was 'singularly small', attributing this to the fact that for so many of them their mother tongue was Yiddish (as was 'frequently discernible in their work'), that they suffered from a glib facility so that 'their easy knack of turning out readable "copy" on any subject seems a positive obstacle to the attainment of excellence', and that these characteristics combined to lead such journalists into pomposity and artificiality; the mordant satire and brilliant style of Kraus – 'a Viennese product', Steed said, 'scarcely intelligible save in relation to the Viennese press' – was refreshment and relief.

But there is more to it, more to it even than the patent cruelty with which Kraus pursued his quarry. Despite his protestation of socialist fraternal feelings for the Galician Jews, few assimilated Jews have been so ambiguous in their attitude towards the poor Jews of the East. He wrote not long after *Eine Krone für Zion* that, with all respect for the principle of religious equality, 'oriental enclaves in European civilisation are a nonsense'. Kraus hoped that they would soon outgrow these degraded, or at least backward, tribal marks and customs, the sidelocks, the caftans, the Yiddish – all of them worn and spoken by Kraus's forebears not very long before, of course.

The hostility which kept breaking through when Kraus wrote about the eastern Jews disturbed some of his readers. Years later, Max Brod

---

[3] Hans Keller, a brilliant musical writer born in Kraus's Vienna (though he disliked him) and who had experienced National Socialism at first hand before he escaped in 1938, once wrote that Richard Wagner was not only a great genius but also 'a thoroughly nice man', a claim which cannot be sustained by any evidence whatever.

(Kafka's friend and executor) deplored these attacks, and George Clare (born Klaar in Vienna, where as a boy he was taken to hear Kraus reading) saw how this bitter feeling infected what some see as Kraus's masterpiece. *Die letzten Tage der Menschheit* (*The Last Days of Mankind*) is an enormous drama, more than 700 pages of text and virtually unperformable on the stage, inspired by the physical and moral catastrophe of the Great War and foreshadowing even worse catastrophes to come. It is an apocalyptic denunciation of militarism and political oppression and journalistic mendacity. And yet as Clare noticed, it is only 'when Jewish figures bestride Kraus's panoramic stage [that] the attack becomes really vicious [and] he fills his pen not with the acid of satire but with the cyanide of deadly hatred'. It is not so much that these Jewish characters (several of them unmistakably Moritz Benedikt in different guises) are corrupt or avaricious. They were all grovelling, fawning parasites, facets of the oldest stereotypes of the Jew. To make the point clear (in the unlikely case that a Viennese audience would not take it), they all of them speak a familiar brand of broken German; that is, they *mauscheln.*

The word has no English equivalent or easy translation. In origin Yiddish, it had taken on layers of further meaning, always derogatory, and usually antisemitic. The noun *ein Mauschel* could mean 'a Jewish trader' or 'a cheat'; the verb *mauscheln*, 'to make deals', 'to act in an underhand way', but also 'to talk Yiddish', 'to talk German with a Yiddish accent' or even 'to behave in a Jewy way'. In Vienna it was a fighting word.[4] Herzl had published an attack on his Jewish critics in the *Welt* in 1897, under the title '*Mauschel*', and clearly aimed at Baron Edmond de Rothschild. '*Mauschel*' is the cringing, fawning Jewboy; and '*Mauschel* is an anti-Zionist'.

At the beginning of *Eine Krone für Zion* Kraus mentions this piece of Herzl's, before proceeding to lay about him in a tone which for all its vehemence seems to justify Herzl's strictures. Any ambiguity about the eastern Jews is nothing compared to the savagery with which he assaults the gilded youth of '*Jung Wien*', the Young Vienna literary group, most of whom were Jewish and several of whom were drawn to

[4] Arnold Schoenberg, the great composer who was Kraus's exact contemporary, was the revered master of younger composers, Alban Berg and Anton von Webern. Schoenberg was a Jew and might have suspected, though he could not know, the germ of prejudice which Berg harboured. Then, after Berg's death in 1935, his widow asked Schoenberg to complete Berg's unfinished opera *Lulu*; one of the reasons why Schoenberg declined seems to have been that word *mauscheln*, used as a stage direction in Berg's libretto.

Zionism. Until now these boulevardiers had devoted themselves to
their clothes and their nail-care; now they wanted to become a nation
of farmers. They had chased bits of fluff from downtown; now the bit
of fluff was transformed into a Miriam. There ought to be room for
hope: 'the most stubborn Zionist should be easily civilised as a
European in a few years.' But no, the Zionists insist on answering a
drunkard's shout of 'Away with you Jews!' in their own more refined
tones, 'Yes, away with us Jews.'

Then, after a blistering attack on rich, propertied 'feudal Jews',
Kraus's invective runs away with him. He is writing from the resort of
Ischl, he says, where the only Zionist is a dentist, who lives brooding on
the thousand-year-old toothache of Jewry. But Kraus himself, as he
wanders, 'heard a brook speaking Jewish, and, astonished as I was, I
called out to the wood and Echo answered me with a question . . .'[5]
This characteristic passage managed to combine a literary echo (of
Muller's, and Schubert's, *Schöne Müllerin*); an inside-outing of an
everyday German phrase; and an antisemitic sneer. It was not only the
wood which echoed: echoing in Kraus's remarkable mind was the
lisping speech of his ancestors.

His refusal to play for any Jewish team took him to absurd extremes.
The *Fackel* was published from 1899 to Kraus's death in 1936. From
1911 onwards it was entirely written by Kraus, but before then others
contributed. They included distinguished names of the age, Strindberg,
Wedekind, Werfel, Schoenberg – and Houston Stewart Chamberlain.
This strange figure, born into an English naval and military family,
had settled first in Dresden, and came entirely to shed his upbringing:
he wrote three books about Wagner, one in French, then two in
German, and later married Eva Wagner, the composer's daughter,
spending his last twenty years living in Bayreuth at the heart of the
'*Bayreuther Kreis*', the gruesome cultic circle which worshipped the
memory of the *Meister*, and being naturalised as a German during the
Great War. Before then, from 1899 to 1908, he had lived in Vienna,
and in the same year as the *Fackel* was launched he had published his
Die Grundlagen des Neunzehnten Jahrhunderts (*The Foundations of the Nineteenth
Century*). It is an extraordinary work of amateur scholarship, learned,
diffuse, cranky, and racist. Chamberlain took the ethnic obsession of
Herder a degree further, seeing the creation of European culture as the

---

[5] '*Ich hört' ein Bächlein mauscheln, und da ich, darob erstaunt, in den Wald hineinrief, hat mir
das Echo mit einer Frage geantwortet . . .*'

work of 'Germanen', or Aryans, and holding that the Jews were 'an element foreign to everything that Europe had hitherto been, and achieved, and had a call to achieve'.

Kraus was well aware of what Chamberlain stood for, and by publishing him – not to say the odd anti-Dreyfusard piece – he was dissociating himself as clearly as he could from the Jews and Jewish liberalism. An essay he wrote in 1913, under the title '*Er ist doch e Jud*' ('But he's still a Jew': a phrase used in a reader's letter in a previous issue), gave an even sadder leper's squint into Kraus's own 'Jewish problem'. Another reader wrote to complain about the phrase, and to ask Kraus bluntly if he agreed with the thesis of racial antisemitism, and whether he believed that any Jewish qualities adhered to him. In reply, Kraus contemptuously dismissed his critics, and insisted, for once without a tincture of irony: 'I feel with the overwhelming force of revelation that I am entirely free of what we may at present identify by cgeneral consent as Jewish characteristics' (before adding a Krausian joke: 'I go along with the development of Jewry as far as Exodus, but leave where the dance round the golden calf begins').

Could Jewish self-rejection go further? The answer to that was given by Otto Weininger, another brilliant young Jew who appeared like a shooting star in the Viennese firmament at the turn of the century. As a student, he became obsessively interested in psychology. Like Kraus he renounced Judaism (though in favour of Protestantism, itself a rejection of Catholic Austria), and then wrote a book. *Geschlecht und Charakter* (*Sex and Character*) is a strange, dazzling, warped work. It develops, as contemporary psychological writers were doing, a theory of the duality of Masculinity and Femininity. Woman was the lower part of human nature, negative and guilty: 'Woman is the sin of man.' This theory had ethnic implications. Weininger saw Jews, like women, as the expression of negativity, incapable of grasping either the meaning of individual freedom, or of the ethical character of the State. The Jew lacked personal nobility, could not distinguish good and evil. His arrogance was another side of the coin of his servility, deriving in turn from the Ten Commandments, 'the most immoral book of laws in the universe'. Not only was Richard Wagner (but of course) the greatest of all geniuses; his was a truly Aryan genius which no Jew could understand, let alone emulate.

It is eerie and frightening to read anyone, let alone a Jew, propounding in 1903 theories which would be made flesh unimaginably a generation later. But, however tormented or malformed he may have been, Weininger was not stupid. Ludwig Wittgenstein, Hermann Brosch, Robert Musil and Arnold Schoenberg all admired him and saluted his intellectual honesty. Kraus promoted him in his lifetime, and defended him after his death, which came soon. In October 1903, shortly after his book was published, Weininger took his self-hatred to its logical conclusions and killed himself, at the age of twenty-three. It was the first of the twentieth century's 'Jewish suicides', setting a pattern among writers and savants which was to become an epidemic as the century grew darker.

There was nothing unique in this self-hatred, least of all in central Europe at the turn of the century. A reliable witness quotes a half-Jewish Hungarian describing the Jewish race, which 'battens so upon the land it has fastened its tentacles on that, whether the race be comparable with orchid or spider, nothing remains but the dead trunk or bloodless corpse . . . Remember I am half Jew by blood . . . I admire their strength, their constancy, their intelligence, but I hate the Jew because of his nature he is evil.' Weininger was unusual only in the ferocity of his self-hatred and in the brilliance with which he expressed it. He, too, sneered at the Zionist idea. It was doomed to failure, he said, by the Diasporic nature of Judaism which meant that the Jews could not be mobilised for the project of building a State, an accusation which was to be repeated by many Jew-haters, notably National Socialists, until it was experimentally confuted. Like other antisemites, gentile or Jewish, he confused two kinds of *Judentum*, the Jewish people and the Jewish religion. He did not foresee that Zionism was to take shape largely as a secular and even irreligious movement, made by Jews for whom the new Zion was not an extension of traditional faith, but a replacement of it. In any case, as Weininger and Kraus railed against the Jewish people and *The Jewish State*, they were patients as well as agents. With all their sparkle and sarcasm and brilliance, their self-hatred and inability to reconcile themselves to what they were made their criticisms of Jewish nationalism and Jewish pride circular.

Other Jews might be making aliyah (though not many), more might be paying their shekels to the movement, many more might be ignoring Zionism altogether, and seeking other practical solutions. The vehement opponents of Zionism were another matter. They had of course a good case to make, though it inevitably involved a degree of 'denial', of pretence, of deliberately ignoring the humiliations and rejections which they, like all Jews in western society, had to deal with, or at least were always lurking, potentially if not actually. Kraus could pour all his scorn on Herzl's idea, and he could score palpable hits. All the same, the very tone and violence of that scorn said as much about him as his target. He was the problem Herzl wanted to solve.

6

Englishmen of Hebrew faith

And yet they think that their houses
shall continue for ever.

Ps.xcix.11

In the early stages of his agitation, Herzl had written that 'the campaign's centre of gravity has shifted to England'. This was a fanciful exaggeration: in the 1890s and for decades to come the centre of gravity of the Zionist movement rested somewhere between Austria and Germany on the one hand and the great reservoir of eastern European Jewry on the other; as it were between Vienna and Berlin, and Warsaw and Vilna. It was not until after the Great War that the movement's balance did indeed shift from the German-speaking to the English-speaking countries. But England played a particular part in the consciousness of Zionists, as of so many other Jews. It was 'a land of freedom and justice', where Jews had lived from the seventeenth century without physical constraint and where in the nineteenth century they had been granted full civil rights, before most other countries. Speaking at the first Zionist congress in Basle, Nordau had gloomily reviewed the condition of the Jews throughout Europe, and then added that 'There is only one country, England, which is an exception to what I have said above. The English people does not allow its progress to be fixed upon from without; it develops from its inner self. In England, emancipation is a reality. It is not merely in the books; it is lived. It had already long been realised in sentiment before legislation expressly confirmed it ... Naturally, a great nation, with a more intense spiritual life, must be somewhat affected by every spiritual current, or even blunder of the age, and so England, too, has its few instances of antisemitism, but those are important only as imitations of Continental fashion.'

There was something in the last words, and there was to be more in them over the next twenty years, when the nearest thing England saw to an open antisemitic movement was a direct Continental import. Otherwise, Nordau reflected a sentimental Anglophilia which was to be characteristic of almost all Zionists, of Herzl himself, of Weizmann, even of Ben-Gurion, up until, or even after, the point where Zionists were fighting British troops in Palestine. It was inspired by genuine admiration for the English traditions of constitutional government and personal freedom, as well as by an exaggerated notion of English fair play, open-mindedness, and philosemitism (an idea which might not have entirely survived a more intimate acquaintance with English upper-class society).

Then and later, Anglo-Jewry knew that the truth was more complicated. They had many slights and rebuffs to endure and, although they were enjoying in many ways a financial and social triumph as the twentieth century began, the leaders of that community knew that their position was, if not perilous, then ambiguous. Small numbers of Jews had settled in England once Cromwell and Charles II had readmitted them. They had prospered in London, building the beautiful Bevis Marks synagogue in the City in 1701. The architect and builder was the Quaker Joseph Avis, who returned his fee to the congregation. This was a touching example of English philosemitism, but as such it has to be set against a whinny of Jew-baiting. There was no English Luther, Herder or Wagner to write full-blown antisemitic treatises (if only because England was the land without philosophy as well as *ohne Musik*). But the glory of England was her imaginative writers; and through their pages the whinny runs, from *The Merchant of Venice* onwards. The only English writers George Orwell could think of who, 'before the days of Hitler, made a definite effort to stick up for Jews are Dickens and Charles Reade'.[1] From Chaucer and Shakespeare, the writers on the other hand who dealt more or less contemptuously with Jews included Smollett, Thackeray, Shaw, Wells, T. S. Eliot and Aldous Huxley. Orwell could have added to his list his own contemporaries Evelyn Waugh and Graham Greene. The wittiest, most genial, in many ways most 'modern' and in many ways

---

[1] Apart from the obvious exception of Disraeli, Orwell had forgotten George Eliot.

most likeable of Victorian novelists was Thackeray, and he ceaselessly lampooned 'Ikey Solomons', 'Nathan Hounsditch' and 'Moss Abrams', with their gross manners, their outlandish accents (*mauscheln* again, even without an English word for it) and their hook noses, to say nothing of his journalistic treatment of such living personages as Nathan Rothschild, 'a greasy-faced compound of donkey and pig'. Thackeray set the tone for *Punch*, which other contributors took up in the heyday of that unlamented weekly magazine. And Thackeray was by most counts a liberal, certainly a friend of religious toleration.

So, for all that the nineteenth century brought the English Jews emancipation, allowing them at last to sit in Parliament, enter the professions, rise to the highest in business, their own pursuit of happiness was uneasy. By almost any contemporary standards England was a tolerant country: there was no Anti-Semite party, no Christian Socials (English 'Christian Socialism' was a very different and more tepid kettle of fish from the Austrian kind), no *Libre Parole*, no Lueger, Drumont, no Pobedonostsev. The distinction is crucial: just as English Jew-baiting on the printed page came from novelists and not philosophers, so everyday antisemitism was social and not political. As everywhere, antipathy to Jews was increased by immigration: the exodus from Tsarist rule substantially increased the numbers of Jews in Great Britain, but on a much smaller scale than in the United States, producing in the end a community in the hundred thousands rather than the millions.

For those who did come, the groundwork had been laid: by 1880, British Jewry numbered around 65,000, and they were mostly secure, if not all prosperous. To the extent that this community was led, its leaders were those whom Herzl met; above all the Rothschild family. Having made a great fortune in their first generation, the Rothschilds had taken root in several European countries, and had given a nice demonstration of Heine's saying that the Jews became like the peoples of the countries they lived in, only more so. The Austrian Rothschilds were very Austrian, the French Rothschilds very French, and the English Rothschilds had come to occupy a special position in their adoptive country. By the reign of Victoria their head had assumed among English Jews something like the position held among English Roman Catholics by the Duke of Norfolk. When Jewry needed to be spoken for, the Rothschilds spoke.

With all these triumphs, not even the Rothschilds could imagine that their position was impregnable. The free institutions which England had built over the centuries and which had made it the object of reverence for liberals, not least Jewish liberals, all over Europe, meant that a religious or ethnic minority could live free of persecution, but not free of tension. The poor Jews who arrived in Whitechapel in the East End of London from the 1880s were not confronted by a mass antisemitic political movement on the Continental scale, but their welcome was muted. A trade unionist expressed a widespread feeling when he said, 'We sympathise with you, we have a feeling of solidarity with you, but we should have been thankful if you had never come.' If they wanted to get out of the ghetto, it would be a steep and tricky climb. At every step, the question would still be: where did they belong?

Hostility took different forms, plebeian or patrician, Left or Right. With the Church of England never truly the church of the English people, and with Roman Catholics always a minority and still an unpopular one, there could be no religious-reactionary antisemitism. But the 'socialism of fools', as a German politician had famously called antisemitism, was on the march in England and quickened its pace thanks to an accident of imperial history. In the 1870s and 1880s first diamonds and later gold were found in South Africa, a remote and impoverished land, part of which was, more by accident than design, under British rule. Within a few years the country was transformed, and a handful of men had taken control of this new mining industry to become hugely rich and powerful. These 'Randlords' caught the public imagination, as a pure type of entrepreneur in the heyday of capitalist expansion. Most of those men had come from Europe to South Africa, most of them were Jewish, and the South African mines were – like Viennese culture at the time, or Hollywood later – in their way a great Jewish achievement.

The origins of Barney Barnato, Alfred Beit, George Albu and Sigismund Neumann did not escape their critics' notice, critics who were themselves on the anti-imperialist Left. In 1895 the larger mine-owners conspired with the British authorities to overturn Kruger's Boer republic in the Transvaal and replace it with a more pliant regime. This conspiracy ended in the fiasco of the Jameson Raid. There were plenty (some already encountered) who knew who the culprits were. John Dillon, the Irish Nationalist and old agrarian rebel, told the House of Commons that the villains were mostly of 'the German Jew extraction'; John Burns, the great Labour leader and hero of the London dockers, said that the British army 'has become in Africa a janissary of the Jews'; J. A. Hobson, socialist economist and foe of imperialism, explained to readers of the *Manchester Guardian*, the leading Liberal newspaper in England, that the approaching Boer War had to be understood in terms of those whom it would benefit: 'Johannesburg is essentially a Jewish town ... [although many of the Jews] have Anglicised their names in true parasitic fashion ... the directory of Johannesburg shows sixty-eight Cohens against twenty-one Joneses'; and so forth.

The Boer War traumatised England. It was opposed by a group of radical 'pro-Boers', among them G. K. Chesterton and Hilaire Belloc. Along with their hostility to imperial expansion and the rule of the rich, and their enthusiasm for populist 'redistribution', 'Chesterbelloc' also did their best to infect England with the new religious-racist antisemitism from the Continent (Belloc was a Roman Catholic by birth, Chesterton became one later). Belloc lampooned Jews in prose and poetry, in his entertaining political novels and in his even more entertaining light verse. In one poem he ironically saluted the gallant men who had fought the Boer War: 'the little empty homes forlorn, | The ruined synagogues that mourn | In Frankfurt and Berlin . . .'

A further irony seems to have escaped Chesterton and Belloc. They were importing the new European crusade, in which the Jew was reviled not only because he had denied and crucified Christ but because he did not belong, was an alien and a potentially treacherous element in the body politic. And yet this very accusation had for centuries been used in England – and given English circumstances with more justification – against Roman Catholics rather than Jews. In any case Chesterbelloc failed. The failure of political as opposed to social antisemitism to take root was epitomised by Belloc's career. He entered Parliament in the Liberal landslide of 1906 and campaigned as bitterly inside the Commons as outside against the corruption of the party system. But in a speech on the Address in February 1910 he reverted to his colours and spoke of 'the modern Anglo-Judaic plutocracy under which we live'. The phrase did him immense harm, and he did not stand again in the second general election of that year.

As a result he missed from inside the Commons the opportunity for what might have been his greatest triumph. In 1912 the Marconi scandal broke. A contract had been granted by the Post Office to the British Marconi Company, who specialised in the new technique of wireless telegraph or radio transmission, to build a network of stations girdling the global Empire. Before long it was rumoured that the deal was corrupt: that the Postmaster General, Herbert Samuel, had granted the contract for pecuniary advantage and that other ministers of the Crown – Rufus Isaacs, Lloyd George, the Master of Elibank, in 1912 respectively Attorney General, Chancellor of the Exchequer and Chief Whip – had used prior knowledge to the contract to buy Marconi shares and enrich themselves. Best of all, Samuel and Isaacs were the first two unbaptised Jews to sit in a British Cabinet.

As Algernon Moncrieff says, the truth is rarely pure, and never simple. Godfrey Isaacs, brother of Rufus, was managing director of the British Marconi Company; shares had not been bought in that company; but shares had been bought in the American Marconi Company, by Rufus Isaacs, Lloyd George and Elibank. Thus the Attorney General was able to tell the Commons that 'never from the very beginning . . . have I had one single transaction with the shares of that company', 'that' being British Marconi. It was this which inspired Kipling's savage poem 'Gehazi', written when Rufus Isaacs later became Lord Chief Justice and a peer: 'In scarlet and in ermines | And chain of England's gold . . . Whereby my zeal hath made me | A Judge in Israel.' Kipling intended that parliamentary denial when he sourly and memorably described 'the truthful, well-weighed answer | That tells the blacker lie'. This poem had been called antisemitic, but Kipling was not an antisemite in the Chesterbellocian sense: at the other pole to these Little Englanders, he was the great bard of Imperialism, and on friendly terms with those men, Jewish Randlords among them, who practised what he preached. As for the central allusion to Gehazi, servant to the Syrian captain Naaman (in 2 Kings v), that merely showed how intimately familiar with Scripture were English Protestants of Kipling's age. And his scorn was not without reason: the Marconi affair was fishy even by the standards of what was the most corrupt period in English public life between the ages of Walpole and Thatcher, and Isaacs's Commons statement had been a shameless cocktail of *suggestio falsi* and *suppresio veri*.

More important than the affair itself was what the Marconi scandal – almost a British Panama scandal, though never a Dreyfus Affair – said about the place of Jews in England. Even if Rufus Isaacs had been as culpable as his enemies said, he was only one of three principal culprits, along with Lloyd George and Elibank: a Jew, a Welshman and a Scotchman in dubious league together proved no more than that, as Mark Twain said, the trouble with the Jews is that they are no better than the rest of us. And yet those concerned saw it differently. Herbert Samuel knew himself to be blameless in the matter. He was a high-minded Balliol prig, who despised Lloyd George as much for his financial as for his sexual improprieties. But when the scandal broke he wrote to Rufus Isaacs, cautioning against legal action to silence their calumniators, since 'it would not be a good thing for the Jewish community for the first two Jews who have entered a British Cabinet to be enmeshed in an affair of this kind'. It was the age-old Jewish response: keep your heads down, don't make trouble.

Most of Samuel's contemporaries would have agreed. None of them can possibly have gone through life ignorant of sneering prejudice and bigotry, but, although their response was not to deny themselves, nor was it to proclaim themselves. They knew the rules. English Society had (and has) always had its own version of Lueger: we decide who are the Jews. Society decided, that is, whom it would accept on its own terms. There was a Jewish *zweite Gesellschaft*, of which Herbert Samuel was a notable example, living a life of dignified opulence in the large houses of Bayswater and St John's Wood. King Edward VII himself was notably friendly towards numerous Jewish financiers and merchant princes who baled him out financially when he came to the throne. At the time of the king's accession, Max Beerbohm drew a gently malicious cartoon of these Cassels and Sassoons with the caption, 'Are we still welcome?' But of course they were. In any case, there was no magic inner circle of Society from which Jews, as Jews, were excluded: in that respect, a Rothschild's election to the Jockey Club had been as important a milestone in the history of English Jewry as a Rothschild's election to Parliament, and the family had fully entered the English pantheon when the first Lord Rothschild could deathlessly observe that 'Every garden, however small, should include at least two acres of rough woodland'.

Some Jews did take assimilation to its full conclusion of Anglicising and Anglicanising themselves. Baptism and the deed-poll were powerful devices, like Siegfried's Tarnhelm, for changing identity. Families were so successfully absorbed that most people forgot that any Hambro or Sainsbury had ever been Jewish, and only the quickest sleight of hand was needed to turn a Sigismund Neumann to a Sir Gerard Newman; German-born mining magnate to English country gentleman in a couple of generations. For those who did not undergo this social equivalent of plastic surgery, the haunting question remained: whom did they think they were kidding? To their faces,

England might smile a cheery smile, but what did she say behind their backs? Less worrying than the public abuse of demagogues was the fear of whispered contempt and rejection.

The fear was not groundless. English attitudes towards the Jews were characterised always by ambiguity, not to say by deceit and hypocrisy, or alternate affection and disaffection. The politician and connoisseur Lord Crawford and Balcarres is a case in point. In 1900 that highly intelligent and civilised man found himself bidden to Hertford House in Manchester Square (now home to the Wallace collection) where a large party had been assembled by Alfred Rothschild and Rosebery to meet the Prince of Wales. 'The number of Jews in this palace was past belief,' Crawford wrote. 'I have studied the anti-semite question with some attention, always hoping to stem an ignoble movement: but when confronted by the herd of Ickleheimers and Puppenbergs, Raphaels, Sassoons, and the rest of the breed, my emotions got the better of logic and justice, while I feel some sympathy for Lueger and Drumont.'[2]

Even those whose own family were Jews might have mixed feelings about them. Rosebery used to find the evenings tedious at Mentmore, the house in Buckinghamshire he later inherited from his father-in-law, and would dismiss his family as he went to bed with the words, 'To your tents, O Israel.' In years to come he would treat his elder son Henry cruelly, not least because he took after his mother's heavier Jewish features, rather than Rosebery's own looks which were inherited by his younger son, Neil. And yet Rosebery, a man who had married Hannah – and to an extent loved her, even if her dowry helped – could not be called an antisemite in the *Libre Parole* sense. The mood of many Englishmen remained complicated, and was to be unimprovably expressed years later by Harold Nicolson: 'Although I loathe antisemitism, I do dislike Jews.'

For their part, the mood of the English Jews was thus alternately confident and apprehensive, a feeling beautifully captured by John Singer Sargent's portraits of the London *haute juiverie* at this time. These were the people Herzl had met when he had come to London. The question was, whether the tensions and dissatisfactions of their lives were sufficient to make them receptive to his scheme. Were they alienated enough from the country they lived in to take to the rebirth

---

[2] To show cross-party support, this Tory added that 'John Burns, by the way, says the Jew is the tapeworm of civilisation'.

of the Jews as a political nation? The politeness of those whom Herzl met undoubtedly misled him. He made contact with the *Jewish Chronicle*, the long-established organ of English Jewry, which gave him at any rate a friendlier hearing than his own paper. He visited Israel Zangwill at his 'rather dingy' house in Kilburn, noting its disorder, describing his host as of 'the long-nosed Negro type', and writing with characteristic confidence that 'I have read none of his writings but I think I know him'. Zangwill gave him the names of those whom he should meet in London: Colonel Goldsmid, Claude Montefiore, Lucien Wolf, the Chief Rabbi, 'a smart officer, Captain Nathan', and from another introduction he met Sir Samuel Montagu MP. These men were the élite of Anglo-Jewry; their reaction to Herzl, to the alternating moods of acceptance and rejection in England, and to the Zionist scheme, tells the story.

Zangwill himself seemed the best catch. He was a member of the English Hovevei Zion Association, a pre-political-Zionist group dedicated, as he put it, to 'slowly and prosaically colonising Palestine with Jews'. After his meeting with Herzl, he visited the Holy Land and attended the first Zionist congress where despite his scepticism he was carried away on the tide of emotion and was seen at the final session cheering and waving his old handkerchief. He had already shown his intense sympathy for his own people (despite discarding Judaism) in *The Children of the Ghetto*; now he wrote *Dreamer of the Ghetto*, which includes a description of the congress.

Perhaps because he was conscious that he seemed to many an impractical dreamer, Herzl was keen to show how hard-headed he could be. He was ready to do business with anyone, even bitter enemies of the Jews; he was open to any suggestion for Jewish settlement. Demonstrating the former, he would meet Grand Vizier, or Pope, or Russian Minister of the Interior. Then at Easter 1903 an appalling pogrom broke out in Kishinev. Not as bad as some the Tsarist empire had seen in the past, it was all the same a bad start to the twentieth century, and it was more widely condemned in the West than the pogroms of twenty years earlier.

Herzl's response was to go to St Petersburg to see V. K. Plehve, the Tsar's interior minister and the man many, including the London *Times*, held directly responsible for the massacre. He was acting on his principle that the antisemitic countries would be his allies, and that he would deal with anyone at all in pursuit of his vision, not to say on Bismarck's principle, *à corsaire, corsaire et demi*. In Herzl's case this could only be applied morally rather than diplomatically or militarily; but, if the enemies of the Jews were tough, he would show the Jews how to be ruthless. He managed to shrug off the character of the regime which Plehve served. In objective terms, Russia was a country with a huge Jewish population, and it was a Great Power in traditional rivalry with Turkey on whom the Russians might yet exert pressure to grant a Jewish settlement. Although very few Russian Jews had left for the Holy Land, Zionism had become a lively movement inside Russia, combining practical Jewish self-help and messianic fervour. Plehve had mixed feelings about Zionism. He was all in favour of anything which reduced the number of Jews in Russia but he deplored anything which 'directed itself towards strengthening the Jewish national idea' or which encouraged 'the organisation of Jews in closed societies'. It was the old objection to granting the Jews any rights as a group rather than as individuals (not that Plehve had any wish to grant those either). He consented to see Herzl, though in the telling words that he 'would heartily support a movement for Jewish emigration without the right of re-entry'.

On his way to St Petersburg, Herzl had passed through Warsaw and Vilna with their enormous Jewish communities. Although the news of Herzl's journey had been kept secret, it got out and he received a fervent welcome: 'They are in such miserable straits that I, poor devil, appear to them as a deliverer.' When they met, Plehve insisted that his Jews of Russia must be loyal to the Tsar, 'that they look patriotically upon the Russian State as an integral part of their life'. He conceded that the empire could not do away with all differences of language or creed – 'the old Scandinavian culture has become permanently rooted in Finland' – but that it insisted on a certain homogeneity among its population. He wanted to assimilate the Jews, through education and economic improvement, but this was a very slow process. At the same time, the number of Jews admitted to the benefits of higher education needed to be limited, 'otherwise we should have no positions left to give the Christians'. This was a significant admission: underlying much hatred and suspicion of Jews was a fear that if allowed equal opportunities they would – implicitly through their superior energy – swamp the gentiles.

He admitted also that conditions of life for many Jews were bad, but complained that the Jews themselves had taken the wrong course: 'Of late their situation has grown worse, as a consequence of their joining the revolutionary parties.' This was perfectly true. If politically unaware Jews in eastern Europe had tried to escape as far away as possible, the politically aware Jews had gravitated towards varieties of revolutionary socialism: by the beginning of the century almost a third of political exiles in Siberia were Jewish, when the Jews were fewer than one twentieth of the Russian population. Plehve would far rather, he implied, that Jews turn to Zionism in its original, emigratory form, which Herzl did not need to expound: '*Vous prêchez à un converti.*' But he was disturbed at the way Zionism was developing: 'There is less talk about Palestinian Zionism, and more about culture, organisation, and Jewish nationalism. That doesn't suit us.' Plehve was referring to the Zionist conference held at Minsk in September 1902. It had been publicly sanctioned by the government, which was, however, dismayed at the amount of time devoted to Hebrew culture and the spirit of Jewish nationhood, and no other Zionist conference was ever sanctioned in Tsarist Russia.

Herzl's meeting with Plehve ended in misunderstanding; at least, Plehve later appeared to have forgotten any encouragement he had given to a Jewish state in Palestine, which Herzl had believed him to favour. This may have been dishonesty on Plehve's part but Herzl always had the enthusiast's knack of believing what he wanted to believe. This bolstered his spirits, but it was also dangerous. Amateur diplomatists notoriously tend to misrepresent the position to both sides; in his elated state, Herzl sometimes misrepresented it to himself, as can be inferred by reading – or decrypting – his own diaries. He had expected Lord Rothschild to provide him with an introduction to Witte, the Russian finance minister, but Rothschild demurred because of 'present circumstances' ('Is it opportunism or cowardice?' Herzl privately wondered).

All the same, he managed to see Witte, who was uncompromising and brutally insulting. He distinguished first between honest and dishonest prejudices against the Jews. The Tsar's were of the former character, being essentially religious. Others had baser material motives. And then there were those – especially journalists – who had turned Jew-baiting into a business. One of the filthiest such specimens was called Grund, and he, Witte added no doubt with glee, 'is a baptised Jew, but he has retained all the Jewish traits'. He agreed that the enthusiasm of Jews for revolution was the fault of the government and its policy of oppression, but went on with still more chilling geniality to recall how he used to say to the late Tsar Alexander III: 'If it were possible, Your Majesty, to drown six or seven million Jews in the Black Sea, I should be perfectly satisfied. But, if it isn't possible, we must let them live.' When Herzl said that he needed some encouragement from the Russians, Witte replied with words at which Herzl's icy politeness almost snapped, 'But we do give the Jews encouragement to leave. *Par exemple les coups de pied*' (a good kicking).

Witte did not confine himself to these pleasantries. He had practical objections also. The Russians sincerely believed that they had a duty to watch over the Holy Places in Jerusalem – one of the causes of the Crimean War – and 'it would create alarm, if people knew there were Jews close by'. Of course, there were Jews there already and always had been, but Witte made himself clearer when Herzl pointed out that the Holy Sepulchre was at present guarded by Turkish soldiers: 'This is less intolerable than if the guards were Jews. If a few hundred thousand Jews were to go there, we would at once have Jewish hotels, Jewish businesses – and that might wound Christian sensibilities.'

With appalling historical irony, Herzl agreed that the Jews could not be destroyed physically: 'As Your Excellency rightly observed, it is impossible to drown them in the Black Sea.' But they both agreed on the urgency of the Jewish Question and they both thought that emigration was the answer. When Plehve said that America was the right destination for this migration, his answer was the one which east European Jews preferred when they were given the choice. Neither Herzl nor Witte foresaw that the real problem about Jewish settlement in Palestine would not concern the Holy Places, or in general 'Christian sensibilities'.

It was to flee such Russian rulers that tens of thousands of Jews came to England in the last decades of the nineteenth century, until the British government brought in an Aliens Bill to control immigration. The prime minister who introduced the Bill was A. J. Balfour, who insisted that it was not a specifically anti-Jewish measure and that he would deplore it if it was: 'The treatment of the race has been a disgrace to Christendom, a disgrace which tarnishes the fair name of Christianity even at this moment.' All the same, Jewish immigration was the only kind England had recently experienced and still was experiencing, apart from the Irish who came from what was still the United Kingdom.

But England was also the centre of the greatest empire the world had ever seen, with vast territories at its disposal. The Colonial Secretary, Joseph Chamberlain, had visited some of these and had been struck by the aptness of the highlands of the recently acquired

British East Africa for white settlement. On the same day in August 1903 when Herzl was talking to Plehve in St Petersburg, the Foreign Secretary, Lord Lansdowne, told the Zionists that the British were prepared to discuss a suitable site in East Africa 'for the establishment of a Jewish colony or settlement, on terms which will enable the members to observe their national customs'.

This was the 'Uganda Offer'.[3] Even at the time there was something comical about the project. The idea of a colony of Jews with synagogues and seders, perhaps in caftans and fur hats, or perhaps elegantly dressed men and women sitting in the old Viennese cafés of which Herzl was so enamoured, all gathered on the hillsides of the Equator, is at the least quaint. The Uganda Offer split the Zionist movement. At the sixth Zionist congress in 1903, a proposal by Herzl to send an expedition to East Africa at least to investigate conditions was passed, a minority being bitterly opposed even to contemplating or discussing an alternative Zion other than the Holy Land itself. The idea of rescue was designed for the persecuting Jews in Russia and it was they who most passionately rejected Uganda, the delegates from Kishinev among them. As Herzl said, 'These people have a rope round their necks and still they refuse.'

Although the Russian enthusiasts in the movement rejected Uganda with disdain – and the Argentine, or any other alternative homeland – it was built up enthusiastically by numerous writers, notably English Jews. Uganda was not formally turned down until after Herzl's death In the event no synagogues or cafés were built on the African hillsides, but the 'Territorialist' movement continued. The Territorialists had an ulterior though scarcely disguised motive. Territorial Zionism was designed to find a settlement outside of Europe for poor or persecuted Jews, but in doing so it was also designed to thwart the political Zionists' aim of a Jewish state. No Jew could object to Jewish emigration from eastern Europe or to philanthropic schemes to settle the migrants; as the meaning and seriousness of Herzl's plan sank in, more and more Jews could and did object to it with intense feeling.

This was not immediately obvious to Herzl and his successors. They saw, in England for one country, numbers of emancipated Jews who still chose to affirm themselves as Jews. They took part in the activities of the Anglo-Jewish Association, the Hovevei Zion (Lover of Zion),

---

[3] The colonial, later to be post-colonial, borders of East Africa had not yet been fixed, and the territory concerned was in fact in modern Kenya.

which organised philanthropic settlement in the Holy Land, the Maccabeans. The last named was an intellectual dining club which met to promote an interest in Jewish culture. Among them Herzl had met that 'smart officer', Captain Mathew Nathan. He was a man who epitomised the gradual success of English Jews, but also the limits of that success, and perhaps most of all the way in which their personal happiness could be checked by their ambiguous social position.

Born in 1862, the son of a London merchant, he went to the Royal Military Academy and was commissioned to the Royal Engineers in 1880. The numbers of Jews in the British Army at the time could be numbered on the fingers of not many hands, and they did not have an easy time of it. Herzl noted in 1895 that Captain Nathan was to have gone to Vienna as military attaché but had been unacceptable there because he was Jewish; and in the British Army itself there were earlier episodes of Jewish officers who had been hounded out of fashionable cavalry regiments by their 'brother' officers. The Sappers were more open to the talents, and Nathan made rapid progress: in the heyday of imperial expansion there were ever more colonial campaigns to serve in and colonial territories to be governed. He fought in the Sudan in his twenties, administered Sierra Leone in his thirties, was knighted at forty and made governor of Natal at forty-seven.

Then he returned to domestic administration, as secretary to the Post Office where he was quite by coincidence involved in the Marconi business at an early stage. He advised that the new service 'should be provided by the State as a national undertaking rather than by a Private Company for the purposes of profit', and warned that 'the grant of a concession to the Marconi Company would place a virtual monopoly of Imperial wireless communication in the hands of a Private Company', advice and warning which if taken and heeded would have saved much trouble. His career suffered scarcely a setback, until he found himself under-secretary for Ireland, and in charge at Dublin Castle, at Easter 1916. But for his last five years in public life he served as governor of Queensland, before retiring to his country house in Somerset. It was a story which all British Jews could take pride in, a tribute to Jewish ability and to British openness as a society. And yet there was another side to it. What sort of man was Nathan, and what sort did he become? It would be good to think that he was entirely at his ease in military and political society, but he was intelligent enough to be aware of the miasma of hostility through which he strode. He succeeded, but maybe at a cost to his character. He was one of a type of Jew common at his time, who needed enormous self-mastery and self-control – repression even – to surmount barriers and overcome or ignore prejudice. The cost could be something like emotional maiming. In Nathan's case there is evidence of this.

In the same year that he met Herzl, Nathan also met Mary Kingsley. She was slightly younger than he, in her early thirties, and one of the most remarkable Englishwomen of her age. Two years earlier she had begun to make her name exploring tropical Africa, on whose peoples she became an authority. Back in London, she was lionised and asked everywhere. Dining at the house of Sir Samuel Montagu, banker and Member of Parliament, she was taken in to dinner by Nathan, at this time serving as chairman of the Colonial Defence Committee. Mary Kingsley was smitten. She wrote to a friend: 'I dote on the military and have a weakness for the nation Israel,' adding that what she liked about Jews was, 'their dreamy minds, their hard common sense and their love for material objects – it is just the same thing that makes me love African society'.

If only Nathan had had a dreamy mind there might have been a romantic ending to the story. In fact, he noted only that he had met Miss Kingsley, 'a cheerful person who advocates no direct taxation in Sierra Leone but government monopolies on salt and tobacco'. After she next departed for West Africa, Mary wrote a twenty-four-page letter beginning 'I shall keep that letter of yours until the day I leave for the coast [of Africa] again and then I shall burn it', before pouring out her heart, gambling everything on a response in kind. Nathan never replied. He merely and laconically noted in his diary that Miss Kingsley had written 'her open soul'. Too long a sacrifice can make a stone of the heart: Nathan was far from being the only Jew of his generation for whom the uphill struggle for social and professional success in a none-too-friendly world had been achieved at the expense of emotional atrophy.

Another military man whom Herzl had met and characteristically been taken by was Colonel Albert Goldsmid. The Goldsmids were a burgeoning clan of higher Anglo-Jewry, connected through business, marriage, and charitable work among the Jewish poor of the East End with Montefiores, Mocattas, Montagus and Henriques. One branch of the family had produced an officer of the 19th Dragoon Guards and his son, Major-General Sir Frederic Goldsmid, who had fought in the Crimea and the Indian Mutiny. Colonel Albert himself had risen to command the Welsh regimental district at Cardiff by 1894. In 1883 and

1891 he had visited Palestine and had joined the Hovevei Zion movement, before organising the Lovers of Zion Association on military principles. When Herzl went to visit him in Cardiff, Goldsmid with his 'Anglicised Jewish face' listened to the great scheme expounded, said 'That is the idea of my life', and added, 'I am Daniel Deronda'.

Many of them were Daniel Deronda in their dreams; not always when they woke up. When Herzl had met the Chief Rabbi, Dr Adler had also exclaimed: 'That is the idea of Daniel Deronda.' And yet: although not English by birth, Adler had found a niche in English society well beyond his pastoral connection with his own community. His defence of his people against the well-worn charge of lack of civic responsibility won praise from Gladstone; he became a worthy consulted by sundry parliamentary committees; he was made Doctor of Civil Law by Oxford, a Commander of the Royal Victorian Order by King Edward VII, and a member of the Athenaeum on the proposal of the Bishop of London. He had made it, he was at home. Did this comfortable adoptive Englishman really want to follow Daniel's footsteps to the mystic East? Adler answered the question himself: having given Herzl a polite welcome on his first visit, he waited no longer than the first Basle congress to pronounce political Zionism 'an egregious blunder'.

Others likewise showed an initial interest, and then changed their minds. The banker Sir Samuel Montagu, at whose house Mary Kingsley had met Mathew Nathan, now entertained Herzl ('Kosher food, served by three liveried footmen') and airily spoke of buying Palestine for £2 million. He was a Lover of Zion, but not a political Zionist. Having first distanced himself from Herzl, telling him that it would be premature for him to speak in Montagu's East End constituency, Montagu became in the end a vigorous opponent of the idea of Jewish statehood. This son of a Liverpool watchmaker (who had reversed his son's original name of Montagu Samuel to Samuel Montagu), had from small beginnings become one of the grandees of the City, the greatest foreign exchange operator of his age, a staunch Liberal MP; a baronet in 1894 and finally, in 1907, a decade after his flirtation with Zionism, Lord Swaythling. He had married Ellen Cohen, whose brother also became a baronet. She had borne him four sons and six daughters; the eldest son inherited the peerage, the second, Edwin Montagu, followed his father into the Commons in 1906. The family was another remarkable tribute to what Jews could achieve in England, and how high they could rise. Montagu was deeply proud of and attached to his religion, and his will disinherited his children who abandoned Judaism or married out of it. But as 'an Englishman of Hebrew faith' he had no wish to compromise his position.

Montagu through marriage was related to yet another of the grand Anglo-Jewish dynasties, the Montefiores. Ellen's great-aunt Judith was married to Sir Moses Montefiore, he who had devoted most of his immensely long life to charity on behalf of his fellow Jews, beginning with the Damascus affair in 1840. Sir Moses's great-nephew Claude was born in 1858 and received a Jewish education as well as a secular one. At Balliol, the Oxford college then at the height of its reputation, Benjamin Jowett encouraged Claude to devote himself to Judaism, to make it 'a most living religion, and investigate its relation with other religions', which he did. He almost became a rabbi but instead devoted himself as a layman to the 'rational religion' so beloved of Victorians: an attempt to reconcile the new age of scepticism and scientific discovery with some form of revealed religion.

A branch of reformed Judaism, the English Reform congregation, had been established in 1841. It was initially placed under a *herem* or excommunication by the Orthodox, and was bitterly opposed by Sir Moses Montefiore. But Reform made some headway among emancipated Jews who found Orthodoxy socially restricting and intellectually frustrating. By 1890, a Saturday afternoon service had been started at West Hampstead Town Hall, 'to attract those who found no spiritual satisfaction in the existing services'. There, Claude Montefiore was a regular lay preacher. By 1901 this had become a new organisation, the Jewish Religious Union, with sermons in English (and no longer than seventy-five minutes), hymns also in English, men and women sitting together and the men allowed to attend bare-headed if they wished, all in defiance of Jewish tradition. And by 1909, with Montefiore's help, a Liberal Jewish congregation was established.

It was characteristic of Claude Montefiore that he occupied himself with the question of whether Shabat, the Jewish Sabbath, should be moved to Sunday: living in a society which was not merely gentile but more and more secular had put severe pressures on Jewish life, notably by making it almost impossible to keep the Sabbath-day holy as commanded. In this, Montefiore was the Jewish equivalent to those Christians – or at any rate gentiles – who thought of moving Christmas to a Sunday and Easter to a fixed date in the year.[4] Montefiore was much concerned with Christianity and its Jewish roots, and believed, in a characteristic phrase, that 'the achievements of Jesus and Paul (in spite of some sad retrogressions) are great achievements'. He believed that it was time for Jews to read the New Testament and to study Jesus as a Jewish teacher and hinted that he was looking for a way of reconciling the two faiths. All of this caused much offence among the devout; they might not have been utterly surprised that a later scion of the Montefiore dynasty would not only join the Church of England but become a bishop.

Although Zionism was a secular movement much disliked by many pious Jews, it was in its own terms an affirmation of Jewish tradition and of Jewish differentness. Rejecting the separateness of old ghetto Orthodoxy, Montefiore also emphatically rejected Zionism. A Jewish state would be either secular, or theocratic, he said (Montefiore did not foresee that it might be a bit of both). If it was a secular state, it would include people of all religions and could not be a Jewish state in any real sense. If on the other hand it was to be a religious state, would citizenship depend on faith, and what would be the position of a Jew who chose to become a Christian? Herzl, the self-proclaimed free-thinker, dismissed all these objections, but events proved that Montefiore, with all his crankiness, was the more far-seeing.

His antipathy to political Zionism was almost temperate alongside Lucien Wolf's. In 1895, Wolf's had been yet another of the names Herzl collected in London and the following year Wolf interviewed Herzl for the *Daily Graphic*, expressing some interest of his own in the scheme. It was short-lived. By the time of the Uganda Offer he was one of the most eloquent of all Jewish opponents of a Jewish state. He was well aware – how could he not be? – of the rise of a new antisemitism on the Continent which coincided with his tenure as foreign editor of the *Daily Graphic* from 1890 to 1909. In 1911, he wrote the article on 'Antisemitism' for the eleventh (and best) edition of the *Encyclopaedia Britannica*. He concluded it on a note of guarded optimism, while admitting that a 'Jewish Question' would continue in Europe as long as six million Jews in Russia and Romania were systematically degraded and overflowed the frontiers: 'Though antisemitism has been unmasked and discredited, it is to be feared that its history is not yet at

---

[4] Later in the twentieth century, one notably *déraciné* member of the German-American Warburg banking family was convinced that Yom Kippur did in fact fall every year on a Sunday.

an end.' Two practical responses to it had been made by Jews: the cultural revival of groups 'who seek to unite the Jewish people in an effort to raise the Jewish character and to promote a higher consciousness of the dignity of the race'. By this he intended the Maccabeans, the very people whom Herzl had met, and dismissed as ineffectual 'Pickwickians' – not an inaccurate phrase for English Jews, many of whom were, or at least wanted to be, more at home in Dingley Dell than either the ghetto or Judaea.

The other Jewish response was Zionism, Wolf wrote, 'a kind of Jewish nationalism, vitiated by the same errors that distinguish its antisemitic analogue'. Which was to say, the belief that antisemitism was unconquerable. A few years earlier, Wolf had summarised his feelings in a pamphlet with the uncompromising title, 'The Zionist Peril'. Despite a flowering of interest in Zionism among some assimilated western Jews, for years to come Wolf spoke for more.

7

'America is our Zion'

Wherefore my heart was glad, and my glory rejoiced:
my flesh also shall rest in hope.

Ps.xvi.10

Like so many other new-born creeds or revolutionary movements, the young Zionist movement was soon riven by disputes and rifts. Even Herzl's own legacy seemed dubious. When it was proposed to publish his diaries posthumously, his closest collegue Nordau vehemently denounced the idea, which would portray the founder of Zionism, he said, as a fool and a swindler. Annual Zionist congresses came and went, distinguished by ever more hot-tempered arguments. The seventh annual congress of 1905, in Basle like the first, finally rejected the Uganda proposal, and by implication a Jewish homeland anywhere but in the Holy Land. As a result, one faction departed, the 'Territorialists' led by Zangwill and supported by Lucien Wolf and Lord Rothschild. Although (again, as is so common, from the early churches, to the psychoanalytic movement, to Trotskyism) the ramifications of doctrinal difference were endless, and were exacerbated by bitter personal animosities. The broad outlines of disagreement were that Territorialists had proposed Uganda or the Argentine, less because of their inherent attractions than precisely because they were not Palestine, the implication of making which the Jewish homeland was that it would become a Jewish state. 'Practical' Zionists encouraged Jewish settlements in Palestine, as a way of relieving the suffering of Jews in east Europe, and of rebuilding dented Jewish pride, but they were just as chary as the Territorialists of the notion of Jewish political sovereignty.

Herzl's immediate successor as head of the movement was David Wolffsohn, a successful Lithuanian-born Cologne timber merchant, but a man whose business abilities were not translated into political leadership. Negotiations continued with the Porte on and off, but came to little. It was quite obvious that the Muslim Ottoman empire, for all its tradition of tolerating other religious communities on its own terms, was never likely to foster the Jewish state of Herzl's dreams. And yet it was to be part of Zionism's misfortune that its homeland was established not by consent on the territory of a decaying empire, but by conquest under the auspices of another empire at its zenith; and, at the same time, that a Jewish state was to be founded not in the popular heyday of imperialism and colonialism, but when they had begun to go severely out of fashion. Zionism got its timing wrong.

When Wolffsohn reluctantly took over the leadership, he was one of seven members of the newly elected action committee. The seven came from Cologne, the Hague, London, Paris, Berlin, Odessa and Yekatrinoslav, a geographical list which gives a fair idea of where the balance of the movement – though not of the Jewish people – lay. In western Europe, Zionism continued to gain a number of enthusiasts, many of them highly educated. Arthur Ruppin, himself an activist in Germany, pointed out that the keenest Zionists then tended to be university men since it was at universities in Germany and Austria that the virulent and insulting flavour of the newly vigorous antisemitism was most keenly felt. As Herzl had said, it was precisely the most educated, emancipated and – as they had hoped – assimilated of Jews who had been most shocked and depressed by the rapid recrudescence of antisemitism. But for all that, few sophisticated and sensitive Germans followed Herzl and Nordau into Jewish nationalism, and by 1914 there were little more than 8,000 shekel-payers or subscribing Zionists in Germany. For all of much unmistakable hostility, insult and threat, most German Jews continued to believe in Germany and in their part in it.

It was almost impossible for Jews to feel the same about Russia. The Zionist movement put down roots there, but, after the revolution of 1905 all Jewish groups were repressed and harassed by the Tsarist regime with renewed vigour, while more and more able and energetic Jews turned from Jewish sectional movements to revolutionary socialism. As for the Jewish masses, their own remedy was physical escape from Russia. Some made their way to Palestine, but not many. The 65,000 settlers of the First and Second Ascents had some impressive achievements to their name, but the most striking thing was how exiguous their numbers were, and how enormously they were dwarfed by another much greater Jewish migration, itself a kind of aliyah or ascent: to the west, and across the Atlantic.

This migration between 1881 and 1914 was one of the greatest adventures in Jewish history. By 1890 the Jewish population of the United States was 450,000; by 1900, more than a million; by 1910, more than two million; by 1920, thanks to natural increase but also the great crescendo of immigration just before it was cut off, 3.6 million. In the space of fifty years, Jews had risen from 0.52 to 3.41 per cent of the American population. Almost more to the point, while in the mid-nineteenth century barely one Jew in a hundred lived in North America, by the third decade of the twentieth century one Jew in four did. These American Jews were overwhelmingly townsmen, and their arrival, as well as other immigrants', helped change the balance between town and country, so that only a quarter of the American work-force was in agriculture in 1920, as against half forty years earlier. In city after city, the Jews formed new districts of their own, in Boston, in Philadelphia, in Chicago, but above all in New York. There, in the Lower East Side, but gradually spreading from it, the immigrants created a great new Jewish city, outstripping Vilna, or Budapest or Vienna. They also created a new Jewish society.

That was just what some had feared. Rabbis regarded east Europe as the natural *heimat*, the homeland where God in His wisdom had placed the Jews, and they suspected America as a source of impiety and corruption. America was a *treyfene medine*, an impure or non-kosher land. And from their own points of view the rabbis were right. From the moment the immigrants arrived at Castle Garden or Ellis Island, they began to shed their old life, however slowly and imperceptibly. At first the new arrivals preserved many of their traditions, speaking Yiddish and observing the faith. But soon the pressures of life in the New World began to exert themselves. Even if the migrants had wanted to preserve shtetl life intact, four thousand miles from home it was impossible. Many soon found that they had to work on Saturday: the six-day week was then universal in industrial countries, and, since American industry was run by those who were Christians in name at least, they could choose their own Sabbath as the day of rest, and the new arrivals could no longer create the world within a world they had enjoyed (or at least known) in the backward, time-lost fastness of the Pale.

For the pious, and not only for them, there was natural nostalgia for the world they had lost; but for most of those millions drawbacks and misgivings were enormously outweighed by what the new-found land gave them. There was great poverty in the tenements and sweatshops of the Lower East Side, there was prejudice and resentment against which the Jews struggled for decades. At first the more energetic and capable of them made their way in small business, though only in business: the professions did not welcome them to begin with, nor did the universities. But, however hard the struggle, there was a new hope. Many years later a gentile friend asked one of those who had come to New York as a boy at the turn of the century, and who was by then an elderly and prosperous citizen, if they had not been disappointed by America when they arrived; hadn't they been told that the streets there would be paved with gold?

'But there *was* gold to us,' the old man said. There was no institutionalised persecution, there were no Cossacks, there were no pogroms; as a character in Anzia Yezierska's story 'How I Found America' said, 'There is no Tsar in America.' Having escaped from the Pale itself, the American Jews – as they had become – could escape from poverty and from the ghetto, which they could not in Russia. In the Pale, the Jews had been at the very bottom of the heap, literally as well as figuratively spat upon by the poorest Polish, Ukrainian or Lithuanian peasant. Now they found themselves part of a kaleidoscope of peoples and classes being shaken into new patterns. In a more familiar image, they were part of 'the Melting Pot': not by accident, it was a Jewish author, Israel Zangwill, who coined the phrase as the title of a play. *The Melting Pot* was written in 1908, sixteen years after Zangwill's previous play *The Children of the Ghetto*, and it was a huge success in the United States where it was set, running for years.

In these circumstances, the incipient Zionist movement was never likely to make much headway among immigrant American Jews. It did not. The small, august and prosperous society of German Jews who had been in New York before the great influx began in the 1880s were horrified by Zionism for the same reason that it horrified people like them from Vienna to Paris to London. As for the immigrants, Herzl's plan for making the Jews happy left them cold. Many dreamed their own dreams of liberation, but this was to be through socialism, which played a very important part in the life of Jewish America for many years. Its high point came in the second decade of the twentieth century, when Meyer London, running as a socialist, was three times elected to the United States Congress for a mostly Jewish district of Manhattan, and when London's close contemporary, Morris Hillquist, born like him in the Pale, won nearly a quarter of the vote in the New York mayoral elections.

This gave little pleasure to those Jews who were already – or were doing their best to become – good, assimilated participants in the American way of life. The conservative *American Hebrew* complained about 'the short-sighted policy of making the Jew the scapegoat for all radical movements'. In return *Vorvarts (Forward)*, the leading Jewish socialist – in fact the leading Yiddish – daily paper in the country, lambasted the propertied Jew who 'in today's free, proud, democratic America comes and tells us to be afraid, to conceal our feelings, not to do what we consider decent and honest. From what mediaeval cellar come these words? From what terrified, broken Jew, with wobbly knees and bent back? Is this the voice of an old-time innkeeper who kissed the whip with which the Polish nobleman slashed him across the face? No, it is the voice of an American Jewish millionaire.' It is unlikely that London or Hillquist had heard of Karl Kraus; they would have agreed, all the same, with the peroration of *Eine Krone für Zion*: socialism was the new Red Sea which would keep the Jews from Herzl's Zion.

For American Jewry as a whole, in its first great generation from 1881 to 1914, Zionism remained, in the words of one Zionist historian, 'a small and feeble enterprise ... [meeting] like votaries of some bizarre cult'. The Federation of American Zionists was founded in 1898, but seven years later it could only count a notional 25,000 supporters. The Zionists used the arguments of Hess and Herzl. There was no peace for the Jews in a gentile world. Assimilation was self-delusion. Even in the land of the free, the greatest secular republic the world had ever seen, Joseph Zeff insisted, they must not 'fool yourselves that you are Americans. You are not counted as Americans and never will be.' Others might be assimilated, 'but not the Jews. The Jew will always be alone. Against his own wishes he will remain loyal to his race and his past.'

Most American Jews had indeed no wish to betray past or race at this time. They stayed true to both, at least for as long as they could; even if they abandoned strict Orthodox observance along with sidelocks and caftans, they were still self-affirming Jews. There was a very strong sense of community among the million or more Jews of

New York in the first years of the century, who were paid a notable compliment by a European Jew and Zionist. 'It was in America that I first discovered the Jewish people,' Albert Einstein later wrote, meaning that most American Jews still possessed 'a healthy national identity'.

Self-affirmation largely took a cultural form. Yiddish culture flowered brightly in New York and other American cities for many decades, with a lively press and theatre. This affirmation through culture and tongue was in extreme contrast to the Irish-Americans. A very large number of the nearly three million Irish who migrated to America in the quarter century after the Great Famine were native, and sometimes monoglot, speakers of Irish Gaelic. But the moment the exiles reached Boston and New York, Gaelic was entirely abandoned apart from a few sentimental tags. On the other hand, unlike the Jews forced by circumstances into a latitudinarian attitude to their traditional religion, for the Irish in America the Roman Catholic church in a triumphalist guise was the central expression of their ethnic heritage.

There were other comparisons between different hyphenated Americans. Each developed a distinctive and Americanised species of its own culture: Italian-American, Irish-American, Jewish-American. It was effortless to call these cultures bastardised, because that was self-evident, but the hyphens did pose real psychological problems. These could be seen in vaudeville, the great popular entertainment of the time. Before the turn of the century, Frank Bush the 'Jew comic' sang, in a little hat and a long beard, 'Oh my name is Solomon Moses | I'm a bully sheeny man.' David Warfield played 'Sigmund Cohenski', a Jewish millionaire, who, when asked whether the pen is mightier than the sword, says, 'You bet my life. Could you sign checks with a sword?' Eddie Cantor sang 'Cohen Owes Me Ninety-Seven Dollars' and 'Sadie Salome Go Home'. And the young Irving Berlin wrote screeds of 'Jew songs'. 'Sadie Salome' was one; another was 'Yiddle on Your Fiddle'; another, 'Goodbye Becky Cohen', in which Becky tells her boyfriend not to go off to war: 'Where's the percentage in that? | No, you better mind your store | Let McCarthy go to war'; and yet another, 'Yiddish Eyes': 'Oy, oy, oy, those Yiddishe eyes, Benny had those Yiddishe eyes, | He took a look in her bankbook with his Yiddishe eyes.'

Too much can be made of this. It was part of the bubbling, seething melting pot, to whose rumbustious humour stereotypes came naturally, the grasping or go-getting Yid[1] along with the garrulous Wop, the bibulous Mick and the happy-go-lucky Darkie. Too little can also be made of this. Ethnic stereotypes were harmless up to a limited point. But in another light, they were part of just that falseness and humiliation from which Zionists wanted to break free.

Although many of these new American Jews kept their traditional faith, language and culture, they mostly had little interest in the new Jewish nationalism. Their whole life was, as it were, existentially anti-Zionist. As Irving Howe says, 'Hundreds of thousands of people had uprooted themselves at great cost from their ancestral life in eastern Europe; they had suffered in the new world; they were still – by, say, 1905 or 1910 – finding it hard to establish themselves in the American cities. And then came a band of Zionists, *luftmenshen* of ideas, who told them in effect that they had journeyed in the wrong direction, America was not the answer to their problems, they must look elsewhere, to a land that seemed very distant and inhospitable. Not surprisingly, most newly American Jews had little time for those *luftmenshen*.

There were important and interesting exceptions, both among the new immigrants of the teeming city slums and among educated American-born Jews. Judah Magnes was a particularly illustrious example. He was born in San Francisco in 1877, grew up across the bay in Oakland, and was the first student from west of the Mississippi to attend the Hebrew Union College in Cincinnati, intellectual centre of assimilated, advanced Reform Judaism. He became a rabbi, studying first in Germany, but also became a Zionist. His Zionism was based, as for so many others like him, on self-affirmation and self-respect. 'We Jews shall be able to accomplish something only when we have left off imitating the rest of the world,' he told his family in a letter written from Berlin when he was twenty-four. 'Why can we not live our own lives? Why must we ever be on the look-out lest we offend the sensibilities of this one or that? Why do we make it our first business to wipe out everything that marks us out as Jews? Why should not a Jewish nose be as beautiful to us, aye more beautiful than another nose?' And he looked towards the day 'when the Jewish state comes into existence'. Then, each Jew would be asked a question by Zionism: 'are you ready to regard yourself as a citizen of the Jewish state, and a foreigner, a Jew, in the land in which you live?'

[1] As late as the 1960s, in the author's memory, Bud Flanagan (né Chaim Weintrop) was still making jokes about Jewish tight-fistedness on the London variety stage.

In 1904 Magnes went to New York to serve a synagogue in Brooklyn and two years later, still in his twenties, he crossed the East River to become an associate rabbi at Temple Emanu-El. This was the religious and, perhaps even more, the social centre of rich, German-Jewish Reform Judaism in Manhattan, where Seligmans, Schiffs, Guggenheims and Warburgs worshipped. Magnes had mixed feelings about this Upper East Side *haute juiverie*, and much of his energies were taken up with the interests of the poor immigrants downtown, and with the cause of the persecuted Jews of Russia. He was active in launching a new Yiddish newspaper in New York, as a challenge to the existing Yiddish press, yellow, power-hungry and corrupt; he tried to establish a Kehillah, a communal Jewish body; he corresponded with Chaim Weizmann about the project to found a Hebrew university in Jerusalem.

But, especially as the Great War approached and then in 1914 broke out, Magnes became embroiled in controversy with his fellow Jewish-Americans and his fellow Zionists. One of these was among the most distinguished American Jews of his time, who had taken up the Zionist cause, but in a curiously ambiguous way. Louis Brandeis was a great jurist, who in 1916 became the first Jew to be appointed to the Supreme Court. By then he was a convert to the cause; he became leader of the American Zionist movement the year before he joined the Court. He himself was born in Kentucky years before the great migration began, was in other words a true-born as well as assimilated American, against whom the nativist charge of alien otherness could not easily be levelled. And he almost consciously collected as fellow leaders of the movement men like himself, 'so that the movement escaped the "stigma" of the East Side'. With true American pragmatism and ingenuity, he consciously pitched his appeal so that Zionism could be combined with Americanism.

In 1915 he told the American Zionists, 'Let us Americans . . . lead earnestly, courageously, and joyously in the struggle for the liberation of the Jewish People! . . . American Jews have not only the right but the duty to act. We are free from political or civil disability, and are relatively prosperous . . . Whether the Jewish problem shall be solved depends primarily, not upon others, but upon us.' These were significant and also prophetic words. No less significant was his constant evocation of American themes. Zionism was no more than 'the Pilgrim's inspiration and impulse over again . . . the fundamentals of American law, namely, life, liberty, and the pursuit of happiness are all essentially Judaistic and have been taught by them for thousands of years'. There had been American Zionist leaders before Brandeis who were better qualified than he in terms of their roots in the east European Jewish traditions, imbued with Yiddish and Hebrew culture as Brandeis was not. Indeed he was not only an assimilated but a somewhat accultured Jew, who had little connection with and knowledge of Jewish life and custom. But this very drawback was his selling proposition. Precisely because he was so sophisticated and 'evolved', Brandeis could speak to the American political establishment on equal terms in a way in which the most gifted immigrant from east Europe could not.

Brandeis had great advantages. One was general. For all the tide of prejudice sometimes lapping about him and his fellow Jews, the United States was different in one crucial respect. In reply to Jellinek's claim that the European Jews were 'Germans, Frenchmen, Englishmen' with every fibre of their being, antisemites had asserted that they were nothing of the kind, that they were Charlus's 'foreigners', that they could never truly belong. This assertion was empty in a country founded not on ethnicity but on an abstract proposition; where even those who considered themselves indigenous and illustrious were (as Franklin D. Roosevelt once reminded the Daughters of the American Revolution) descended from immigrants and revolutionaries; whose basic principles were immigration and assimilation.

Another advantage was personal. Precisely because he was an American by birth, Brandeis could appeal without an immigrant's self-consciousness to the American way, and without absurdity to Zionism as an extension of it. 'My approach to Zionism was through Americanism,' he wrote. 'In time, practical experience and observation convinced me that Jews were by reason of their traditions and their character peculiarly fitted for the attainment of American ideals. Gradually, it became clear to me that to be good Americans we must be better Jews, and to be better Jews we must become Zionists. Jewish life cannot be preserved and developed, assimilation cannot be averted, unless there be established in the fatherland a centre from which the Jewish spirit may radiate and give to the Jews scattered throughout the world that inspiration which springs from memories of a great past and the hope of a great future.'

More than that, Brandeis played a new variation on a theme first heard in *Rome and Jerusalem*. Moses Hess had hoped that large numbers of poor Jews from the East would go to the Holy Land, a hope which was even at the time far-fetched; but he foresaw that most assimilated Jews in the West would not go. Herzl addressed himself to both assimilated and ghetto Jews, with the implied hope that the latter would be raised to the level of the former through his beloved cafés and the other appurtenances of Viennese culture; Brandeis was addressing American Jews who were most of them still on the road from ghetto to assimilation, and who had no wish to be side-tracked from that route. And so Brandeis told them that they did not need to be: they could be good Zionists without themselves actually taking the path to Zion. They might wish to pray a Jewish version of St Augustine's prayer for chastity: Lord, let us make aliyah, but not yet. Or, to take another phrase from Christian history, for the American Zionist there could be justification by faith rather than works. As Brandeis said, 'the place is made ready; legal right of habitation is secured; and any who wish are free to go. But it is of the essence of Zionism that there shall be no compulsion.'

To some rigorous Zionists, this was nonsense. Zionism must mean a commitment not to live in Vilna, Vienna – or New York. It was in this light as absurd to say that you could be a good Zionist without making aliyah as to say that you could be a good Catholic without ever going to Mass. The logical Zionists agreed objectively with assimilationists: you were one or the other, you either stayed in the Galut and rejected Zionism, or left it and rejected assimilation. But Brandeis's argument was of immense importance for the future: fifty years later his principle would underlie the development of American Jewry into Israel's lifeline and mainstay.

When Brandeis spoke, and even after, what he said laid him open to the charge of hypocrisy: how could a Jew of the Dispersion sincerely call himself a Zionist when he had no intention of putting Zionism into personal practice? But the Brandeis version had certain things going for it, apart from its immense potential appeal to contented American Jews. For one thing, there was nothing unique about the compound in 'Jewish-American'. When Woodrow Wilson first used the phrase 'hyphenated Americans' he was describing numerous different groups, several of whose concerns echoed the Jews'. That is, each hyphenate took an interest in its own people across the sea – and each for that matter was open to the accusation of dual loyalty, which was to be such a bugbear for Zionism.

Earlier in the year that the Balfour Declaration was to be issued, the United States had entered the Great War. This war directly affected several hyphenates. German-Americans were the group who would be written out of the script of American history, to the extent that many Americans would later be ignorant of the enormous German contribution to American culture and society; in 1917, they found themselves agonisingly torn between their new country, and the country of their fathers with which it was now at war. Meanwhile the Irish-Americans found themselves fighting alongside England, their ancestral oppressor, but took the opportunity to try and exert American pressure on the British to grant self-government for Ireland. Equally, the Czech-Americans used their political influence to impose another policy on Washington: the establishment of a Czech state, which spelled the end of the Austro-Hungarian empire.

In each case, the hyphenates were acting as a group, pushing a policy in the supposed interests of that group, and doing so – it could easily be argued – in disregard of broader American interests. It was by no means obviously an American interest to destroy the Habsburg monarchy and turn central Europe into a patchwork of authoritarian and corrupt national states with whose bloody rivalries the Americans still found themselves dealing in the 1990s; or to create an independent Irish state whose neutrality was to cost American lives during the war against Hitler. In view of all this, why should the Jewish-Americans feel bashful?

But for all the ingenuity of Brandeis's case, most American Jews continued to reject Zionism actively or passively. This rejection was neither precisely effect nor cause of assimilation, but symbiotically linked with it. Orthodox rabbis condemned the Zionists, but then the American Jews had already silently defied those rabbis by migrating, and were doing so again by dropping out of Orthodox practice thanks to the social and economic exigencies of American life. The small but powerful German-Jewish community already in the United States before 1881 had already turned its back on Orthodoxy in favour of Reform Judaism, the emancipated or 'protestant' version of the faith which had begun life in eighteenth-century Germany. And from the beginning the American Reform rabbinate was even more hostile to Zionism than the Orthodox. The hostility had several sources. Reform Judaism had anyway put aside the ancient and profound belief that the Jews were a people with a Messianic mission, or even a 'people' at all. Moses Hess insisted that the Jews were a race; Reformism insisted not. The Jews, it said, were not a racial or ethnic group but a religious faith, scarcely different from Roman Catholics or Episcopalians or Unitarians. They were no more than 'Americans of Mosaic faith'.

This became the cry of assimilated Jews. The official voice of Reform Judaism was the *Reform Advocate*, which adopted an anti-Zionist tone almost as strident as Karl Kraus's, if not quite so bitter. When a gentile enthusiast presented a petition to the President proposing 'Palestine for the Jews', Rabbi Emil E. Hirsch of Chicago had denounced this 'fool's errand'. He deplored the fact 'that such a memorial ever was composed and laid before the Executive head of our government'. He believed that the movement was inspired by 'sympathy with the unfortunate Jews of Russia' which was in itself creditable, especially on the part of gentile sympathisers. 'That so many Jewish signatures should have been gotten to the petition is . . . less gratifying to us.' And he insisted that 'we modern Jews do not want to be restored to Palestine . . . we will not go back . . . to form a nationality of our own'. Chicago was something of a centre of resistance. The *Chicago Israelite* called the scheme proposed in *The Jewish State* 'a pretty good joke', given that Herzl and his immediate colleagues were agnostics, 'but not half so good as the spectacle of a crowd of followers composed of ritualistic Jews, who have staked their whole existence on the letter of the law and on traditional Judaism'. After the first Zionist congress the *American Hebrew* said that 'the entire Jewish press of the world with less than half-a-dozen exceptions has been opposed to the Congress'. Certainly, the American-Jewish press was close to unanimity. One paper saw 'no good things' in Zionism, another mocked the idea of 'a little State in Palestine somewhat weaker than Greece and somewhat stronger than Monaco'. And the *Menorah Monthly* presciently reminded Jews that the Holy Land was holy to Christians and Muslims as well as Jews.

Not surprisingly, the more successfully assimilated – or simply the more successful – American Jews were, the more hostile they were to Zionism. Nowhere was this more strikingly true than with what had already established itself as the most famous newspaper in the United States. The *New York Times* resembled the *Neue Freie Presse* in more ways than one. In the very year of the *Judenstaat*, the *Times* was acquired by Adolph Ochs and his rich, assimilated family of German-Jewish origin. Its stance towards Zionism then, and for decades afterwards, was one of hostility as unremitting as the *Presse*'s. A year later, in 1897, the *Times* sneered that Herzl's proposal to buy Palestine from the Porte had 'the flavour of the Stock Exchange', and referred to 'the Zionist scheme that has been so coldly received by those [to] whose attention it had been called in this country'. When it came to pronounce directly on Herzl's book, the *Times* spoke for those Jews who believed that any Jewish state must be a 'small, weak state, existing by suffrance', and that in any case 'Israel's mission is no longer political but purely and simply religious'. In case the point was not made clearly enough, the *Times* brought on Rabbi Isaac Mayer Wise, leader of Reform Judaism and father-in-law of Adolph Ochs, to write an article called 'A Jewish State Impossible'.

And so, 'Speaking as an American', the banker and philanthropist Jacob H. Schiff said, 'I cannot for one moment concede that one can be at the same time a true American and an honest adherent to the Zionist movement.' He insisted that Zionism could find no justification whatever in Jewish scripture or religious teaching. And, most emphatic and important of all, he said that 'the agitation for a Jewish state is apt to retard the Americanisation of thousands who, in recent years, have come among us, and whose success and happiness [must] depend upon the readiness with which the newcomers shall be able in their civic condition – as separate from their faith – to become absorbed into the American People'. He was echoed by Henry Morgenthau Sr: 'We Jews of America have found America to be our Zion. Therefore I refuse to allow myself to be called a Zionist. I am an American.'

This was the heart of the matter. American Jews might not have heard Schiff's or Morgenthau's words. But for the moment most of them instinctively sympathised with what they said. They might not have heard either of the Reform rabbinate's resolution which declared itself 'inalterably opposed to political Zionism', but silently they rejected Herzl's solutions to the 'Jewish Question'. Why should they need it? They had made their decision, that heroic generation, voted with their feet, two million of them, in crossing the Atlantic to a land founded on the very principles of life, liberty and the pursuit of happiness. They had no need of any other way to pursue it. They had found in America much prejudice and hardship, but they had also found something unknown to them before: a land where a poor Jew could live freely without fear, and a rich Jew could live openly without evasion. They had solved their own Jewish Question by becoming Americans. From the bottom of their hearts, they spoke the same words: 'America is our Zion.'

8

A national home

O be favourable and gracious unto Sion:
build thou the walls of Jerusalem.

Ps.li.16

For a generation after *The Jewish State* a polemical battle raged. This war of words between Zionists and assimilationists produced a huge number of books and pamphlets, some in English, more in German. As Walter Laqueur has observed, since the arguments which can be made on either side are strictly limited, this dialectical literature is notably repetitious. And yet, tedious as they sometimes were, these debates were of huge importance for the future. It was important also that the debates shifted westward all the time, from the Jewish heartland in the Pale, to the German-speaking central Europe and finally to the English-speaking West.

Pinsker had come from Russian Poland, Asher Zvi Ginsburg was born in Russian Ukraine thirty-five years later, in 1856. His family was rich but strictly pious; as he progressed through reading enlightened and sceptical authors he had slowly but surely lost his own faith. He moved to Odessa, adopted the name 'one of the people' – in Hebrew, Ahad Ha-am – and became a journalist and pamphleteer. For a time he edited a Hebrew monthly, before going into business with a tea company. This took him, like so many Zionists of this generation, to London, where he lived from 1907 until at last in 1921 he settled in the Holy Land. But, although he was a practical Zionist in that sense, he stood at a distance from Herzl's political Zionism; he became an intimate and adviser of Weizmann's but he never attended a Zionist congress or took any part in the movement.

Instead Ahad Ha-am became the most penetrating critic of Zionism from the inside. He was not an assimilationist who opposed the whole concept of a Jewish people: he longed for Jewish renewal, for the rescue of that people, and believed that Zionism of the spirit could play a vital part in renewal and rescue. But he was acutely sceptical of the plans for a Jewish state. Like Kraus, Ahad Ha-am observed the euphoria attending the first congress in Basle and reacted against it, but in an entirely different spirit; and his 'The Jewish State and the Jewish Problem' written in 1897 is a fascinating contrast to *Eine Krone für Zion*.

The majority of Jews could not be settled in Palestine, and did not want to be settled there, Ahad Ha-am said. A Jewish state could not of itself resolve the economic misery of eastern Jews, and nor would it necessarily resolve the broader Jewish Question. He saw with remarkable penetration that Zionism could become an enthusiasm and an exalting occupation for western Jews even if they never left their present homes in the Dispersion: 'the very existence of a Jewish state will raise the prestige of those who remain in exile, and their fellow citizens will no more despise them and keep them at arm's length as though they were ignoble slaves, dependent entirely on the hospitality of others. As [the Western Jew] contemplates this fascinating vision, it suddenly dawns on his inner consciousness that even now, before the Jewish state is established, the mere idea of it gives him almost complete relief. He has an opportunity for organised work, for political excitement; he finds a suitable field of activity without having to become subservient to non-Jews; and he feels that thanks to this idea he stands once more spiritually erect, and has regained human dignity, without overmuch trouble and purely by his own efforts.'

As Ahad Ha-am saw it, Herzl had put the cart before the horse, thinking purely – not to say tritely – of political structures, to be secured by diplomatic intrigue, rather than of a new Jewish society growing from the roots up. Even Herzl's title is unconsciously accurate, Ahad Ha-am notices. His proposed state may well be literally a *Judenstaat*, a state of Jews; what is needed is a true *jüdischer Staat*, a Jewish state. He saw, that is, the need for a centre of Jewish life which would radiate outwards to Jews throughout the Dispersion. It was a Jewish vision of Palestine comparable to Evelyn Waugh's Roman Catholic vision of Dublin as it might have been: not a mere capital city of a mundane national state, but 'one of the great religious capitals of the world', where Catholics from across the world 'resorted for education and leadership'.

Just as penetratingly, Ahad Ha'am saw something which other enthusiasts for Palestine as a Jewish homeland or state had missed. It was singularly ill-placed to be that other neutral Belgium of George Eliot's dream, or the 'Switzerland of the Middle East' of Lilienblum's phrase. 'A comparison between Palestine and small countries like Switzerland overlooks the geographical position of Palestine and its religious importance for all nations,' Ahad Ha-am pointed out. 'These two facts make it impossible for its "powerful neighbours" . . . to leave it alone altogether; and when it becomes a Jewish state, they will still keep an eye on it, and each Power will try to influence its policy in a direction favourable to itself, just as we see happening in the case of other weak states (like Turkey) in which the great European nations have "interests".' Again, he saw that, just because the Jews were so singular and so unique, they could not become another little country, like one of the newly created Balkan states. Others used just the same comparison in derogation of the Zionist idea. Tolstoy had condemned Zionism as a retrogressive and implicitly militaristic movement which was contrary to the highest Jewish spirit; did the Jews of all people want to be nothing more than a national – and nationalistic – statelet like Serbia or Romania? Ahad Ha-am saw further still: that it was not only ignoble for Jewry to become another Serbia or Romania, puffed up with fatuous nationalism and power hunger, but that this would not even work. The Jewish people could not turn themselves into a bit-part on the stage of history; the Jewish Question could not be wound up like a trivial sub-plot.

In 1891, not long before Herzl wrote *The Jewish State*, Ahad Ha-am had visited the Holy Land for the first time, and his description of his visit, 'Truth from the Land of Israel', is astonishingly far-seeing also. Max Nordau had supposedly discovered the 'Arab question', and told Herzl that they were committing an injustice. But it was not true that the early Zionists had been ignorant of the existence of an Arab population in Palestine. They had merely, in one way or another, wished it away. Moses Hess had hoped for an independent Arab Syria and Egypt on either side of his Jewish commonwealth, Herzl had vaguely hoped that the Arabs would welcome a Jewish state for the material benefits it would bring. Not only were these Zionists Europeans of the age of imperialism; they supposed, without formulating the thought, that the Arabs were malleable and quite without national consciousness. And this was indeed the case at that time. In the 1890s, and for some time after, most of those living in Palestine were even less conscious of their national identity than those French or Sicilian peasants earlier in the century. A dweller in the Holy Land, if asked what he was, would have given the traditional answer, 'I am a Muslim from here.' Few were conscious of being Arabs, none of being a 'Palestinian'.

But this is not to say that they never will be, Ahad Ha-am points out. 'We tend to believe that Palestine is nowadays almost completely deserted, a non-cultivated wilderness, and anyone can come there and buy as much land as his heart desires. But in reality this is not the case. It is difficult to find anywhere in the country Arab land which lies fallow.' It is not only a question of the Arabs' existence: 'We tend to believe abroad that all Arabs are desert barbarians, an asinine people which does not see or understand what is going on around them. This is a cardinal mistake. The Arab, like all Semites, has a sharp mind and is full of cunning ... The Arabs, and especially city dwellers, understand very well what we want and what we do in the country; but they behave as if they do not notice it because at present they do not see any danger for themselves ...

'But when the day will come in which the life of our people in the Land of Israel will develop to such a degree that they will push aside the local population by little or by much, then it will not easily give up its place.' And with haunting foresight, he insisted, 'We have to treat the local population with love and respect, justly and rightly. And what do our brethren in the Land of Israel do? Exactly the opposite! Slaves they were in the country of exile, and suddenly they find themselves in a boundless and anarchic freedom, as is always the case with a slave that has become king; and they behave towards the Arabs with hostility and cruelty.' Twenty-five years after this was written, Ahad Ha'am was in London and saw much of Weizmann; it was not his cautionary words Weizmann acted on.

Indeed, for all his growing influence among parts of the east European intelligentsia and despite his long residence in London, Ahad Ha-am remained very little known in the English-speaking and German-speaking countries, where the debate over Zionism continued and where, although many assimilated Jews continued to regard it with aversion, it became a passion for others. Martin Buber was born in Vienna in 1878, but grew up in Lemburg in Galicia, where his family were distinguished rabbis and scholars. Buber touched on all the different and sometimes mutually hostile aspects of central European Jewish life: German *Bildung* and *Kultur* at universities in Vienna, Leipzig, Zurich and Berlin; traditional piety in the form of Hasidism, with which he formed strong and permanent ties in Galicia; and Zionism. He joined the movement in 1898 and founded a Zionist students' club at Leipzig, then worked on the *Welt* with Herzl for some months, but broke with him and founded with Weizmann a 'democratic faction' of the movement, emphasising cultural as opposed to political Zionism.

Buber often talked and wrote about Zion in the misty language of German philosophy, and he seemed before 1914 to toy with the thoroughly Germanic concept of *völkisch* nationalism, and with the general current of anti-liberal irrationalism running through Europe. In fact, Buber was a humanist (in the older sense, before it became a genteelism for 'atheist') and a near-pacifist. He believed passionately that the Jews as a people had an historic role, but that their role was not mere assertive nationalism. This was a difficult doctrine to preach in mass political terms, as Buber recognised by withdrawing from active public affairs. He spent the 1920s translating the Bible into German in collaboration with Franz Rosenzweig, himself a keen spiritual Zionist.

A few years earlier Buber had engaged in debate with a much older man. The neo-Kantian philosopher Hermann Cohen had expressed the classic assimilationist line, which took its strongest – and, in hindsight, most poignant – form among German Jews. There was no Jewish nation as there was a German nation, Cohen said, because there was no Jewish state. This was a poor argument from a logician: the Zionists wanted a Jewish state precisely in order to make a Jewish nation, and in any case there had patently been a German nation before a German state was created in 1871. 'I do not read *Faust* just as a beautiful poem,' Cohen said, 'I love it as a revelation of the German spirit. I feel in a similar way even about Luther, about Mozart and Beethoven, Stein and Bismarck.' But the German spirit as expressed by Luther and Beethoven predated the creation of a German state by Bismarck. Behind all this reverence for German lay something else: a contempt for the idea of a Jewish nation as a way of rescuing the Jews from their 'problem' and their neuroses. It was Cohen who put this with memorable sarcasm when Rosenzweig was explaining the merits of Zionism: 'Aha, so now the gang wants to be happy, does it?'

That was just what Buber did want, but he remained dubious about the political project. He stayed in Frankfurt even after Hitler came to power, bravely helping to organise the Jewish community in the face of persecution. In 1938 he left for Palestine where with the same courage he advocated co-operation with the Arabs and a binational state.

The exchange between Buber and Cohen took place in Germany during the Great War, and was echoed – or mirrored, back to front – by a debate among Jews taking place in wartime England. In 1914, many Jews sympathised with Germany, not only in Germany itself: in the United States, the old German Jewry naturally sided with the land of Goethe and Beethoven, and the mass of Russian Jews warmed to Germany as the country which was fighting Tsarist Russia, the country they had fled but had not forgotten or forgiven. But French Jews and Italian Jews were equally keen to show their loyalty to their own countries. And British Jews also; not only were they eager to demonstrate their hostility to Germany, many of them remained bitterly opposed to a Jewish state. In England as in Germany, a war of words was fought between Zionists and assimilationists before and during the Great War, and in England the anti-Zionists marshalled even more of the heavy weapons.

The Jewish population of Great Britain had expanded rapidly, from 65,000 in 1880 to 300,000 in 1914. One of the great centres of Anglo-Jewry was Manchester, with its trade and industry and with the radical political and economic tradition of the free market known to the world as the 'Manchester school', *das Manchestertum*. In Manchester as in London there was a small but enthusiastic Zionist movement, ignored by many Jews and vehemently opposed by some. Having settled there, Weizmann became a prominent activist, though as yet not one of the leaders of the Zionist Organisation. In Manchester during the 1906 general election, he met A. J. Balfour, the Tory leader, and much impressed him with his presentation of the Zionist case.

Others were less impressed, among them the Jewish anti-Zionists like Lucien Wolf and Claude Montefiore who opposed the project with unflagging energy. Two titles of essays speak for themselves. Wolf wrote 'The Zionist Peril', Montefiore, 'The Dangers of Zionism'. Montefiore harped on the by now familiar theme that 'those who have no love for the Jews, and those who are pronounced antisemites, all seem to welcome the Zionist proposals and aspirations'. Why should this be, unless 'Zionism fits in with antisemitic presumptions and with antisemitic aims'? Although in many ways a peculiarly conscious and pious Jew, he did not begin to share Weizmann's concept of Jewish nationality; Montefiore was an 'Englishman of Jewish faith'. As such, he foresaw the gravest threat from the Jewish State. Imagine what the antisemites would make of it. 'Why should all other countries suffer these Asiatic foreigners gladly, when they now have their own shelter, their own country, their own National Home? It seems as clear as noonday that the establishment of a Jewish State will, on account of this alone, and on this argument alone, enormously increase the volume of antisemitic activities. In every country, but especially in Austria, Germany, Poland, Romania and Russia, the position of the Jews will tend to become worse rather than better.'

But Montefiore lost the argument in the gale of war. Horrible as it is, war is also the great motor of history. Again and again, the story of the Jews was drastically changed by wars which did not ostensibly concern them. The war which broke out in 1914 had nothing to do with the Jews, at least not to begin with. It was a war between Austria and Serbia, between Germany and Russia, and then between the Central Powers and the Allies: a struggle for the mastery of Europe. Almost by accident, the Ottoman empire joined in on the side of the Hohenzollern and Habsburg empires, and all three empires were doomed to destruction when defeat came, along with the Romanoff empire which the war had already destroyed before its end.

For the Zionists, this was the great opportunity. With all Herzl's faith in intrigue and plain bribery, it had become plain that a Jewish homeland was never going to be established under the Ottoman empire. But what if that empire were to disappear? Then what the Zionists needed was a sympathetic successor government; ideally for Palestine to pass under British control; maybe to have a voice within the British government. When Weizmann had met C. P. Scott, the famous editor of the *Manchester Guardian* showed enthusiasm for the cause and offered to introduce Weizmann to Lloyd George. He added, 'You know, you have a Jew in the government, Mr Herbert Samuel,' to which Weizmann replied, 'For God's sake, Mr Scott, let us have nothing to do with this man.' He explained later that he had assumed from afar that Samuel was 'the type of Jew who is by his very nature opposed to us'. This was not so. When the two finally met in December 1914 Weizmann was surprised and delighted to find how wrong he had been. Samuel had long been familiar with the Zionist idea, and sympathetic to it. If anything, he thought that Weizmann's plans were too modest. At that point the Jewish settlement in the Holy Land was still insignificant and powerless, and it was essential that the

Jews should build railways, harbours, a university and a network of schools; 'the University seems to make a special appeal to him,' Weizmann recorded, a seat of learning 'where the Jews can work freely on a free soil of their own. He also thinks that perhaps the Temple may be rebuilt, as a symbol of Jewish unity, of course, in a modernised form.'

Weizmann's surprise was understandable. He could scarcely have known that the innocent victim of the Marconi affair had undergone a prolonged spiritual crisis about his Jewish identity. Intellectually Samuel had lost the strict religious faith of his fathers – in this he was no different from so many other Balliol men of his generation, who had come from devout Christian homes – but at the same time he consciously adhered to Judaism. This was not as paradoxical as it might seem. Religion was to be for him, in a formal sense, an affirmation of identity, as it might be for, say, a spiritually emancipated Irish Catholic who, even while privately disbelieving in a literal sense in what the Church taught, could not publicly reject the Church, the one institution which still gave his 'little platoon' an identity. Religion was the more important as a badge of identity since the Anglo-Jewish commercial élite from which Samuel came were in general very hostile to political Zionism. In the case of Samuel Montagu, the first Lord Swaythling, this hostility was ambiguous. He had visited the Holy Land in 1875 and 1905, had chaired meetings of the Hovevei Zion, at least he had before Herzl exploded on the scene. Even then, he had met Herzl in 1895 and told him that he thought of settling in Palestine with his family, he had spoken in a newspaper interview of settling two million Jews there, he had sent a copy of *Der Judenstaat* to Gladstone.

His own objections to Herzl's scheme was pragmatic: 'How is it practicable?' The Jewish state could only come into being 'under the sanction and guarantee of the Great Powers and utmost good will would be needed in the whole matter'. This was half-prescient. The sanction of the Great Powers would be necessary and forthcoming when the Jewish state was born; the utmost goodwill was unnecessary, and not forthcoming. Answering his own question, Montagu had come to the conclusion that it was not practicable as long as the Turks ruled Palestine, and in 1905 he and other Anglo-Jewish eminences had written to *The Times* with almost audible relief to say that with the death of 'the noble-hearted Herzl' it had to be accepted that his great dream had 'faded into a vision of the distant future'; another version of the Augustinian plea: Lord, give us Zion, but not yet. It conveniently deflected Zionist accusations of faint-heartedness, while postponing to infinity the threatening reality of a Jewish state. Indeed, this anticipated the attitude of a large part of Dispersion Jewry after the Jewish state came into existence: let us support Zion, but not go there.

This polite passivity might have been inherited by Samuel Montagu's nephew, Herbert Samuel. As a young man he was not a passionate Zionist, or indeed a passionate anything: Samuel was a clever, charmless cold fish of the kind who 'has no enemies but none of his friends like him'. He took up with the reformist New Liberalism, not far off from Fabian Socialism, but nothing ever inflamed him. A curiosity is found among his papers. An acquaintance of his was an English lady in her eighties living in Florence, Lucie Alexander. In 1900 she was sent a letter by Samuel's son Edwin (though more accurately, no doubt, by his parents, since he was a small child and it was the first letter he had ever signed). In reply, Miss Alexander said that she would treasure the letter until bequeathing it back to his family so that as an old man he could enjoy showing it to his grandchildren. 'Perhaps by that time', she added, 'he may have been Governor of the Holy Land, for I believe in the prophecies as much as you do that the country shall be restored to its owners.' In fact, this strange prophecy came true quicker than she could have realised: within twenty years, Herbert Samuel himself was to be ruler of the Holy Land, where Edwin was to serve for many years as an official. But there is nothing to suggest that when this exchange took place Samuel was in any sense a Zionist.

By 1914 he was a member of the Cabinet, and by then everything was changed. In November, three months after war began, that Cabinet finally accepted that the hallowed principle of 'Ottoman integrity' – the holding together of the Turkish empire at all cost which had been the central premiss of British policy for a century – must at last be abandoned. The implication of this for Zionism was crucial and obvious. Samuel told Sir Edward Grey, the Foreign Secretary, that he had never been a Zionist until then. 'But now conditions are profoundly altered. If a Jewish State were established in Palestine it might become the centre of a new culture.' He also talked to Lloyd George. The two had uneasy relations in the course of their long careers. Uneasier than Samuel realised: he did not know that Lloyd George called him 'an ambitious and grasping Jew, with all the worst characteristics of his race' (and is also supposed to have said once in exasperation that 'when they circumcised Samuel they threw away the wrong bit'). For all that, in 1914 he spoke in Cabinet of 'the ultimate destiny of Palestine', and told Samuel that he was 'very keen to see a Jewish state established there', emphasising – maybe even sincerely as a man from little Wales, overshadowed by England but seeking solace in its Chapels called Zion and Emanuel – the fellow feeling of small nations.

Now Samuel took up the cause with great energy. He met Russian Zionists, he lobbied Lord Rothschild at Tring, he tried to enlist Sir Philip Magnus MP, a past president of the Anglo-Jewish Association, he met Weizmann several more times, he drafted a Cabinet memorandum on 'the Future of Palestine'. It was written with an exaltation no one who knew Samuel would ever have expected. 'A stirring among the twelve million Jews scattered throughout the countries of the world' had been set off by the feeling that 'now, at last, some advance may be made, in some way, towards the fulfilment of the hope and desire, held with unshakeable tenacity for eighteen hundred years, for the restoration of the Jews to the land to which they are attached by ties as ancient as history itself'. Samuel's characteristic caution took over when he said that the time was not ripe for the establishment of an independent Jewish state, and he recognised the practical difficulty which remained when Turkish rule ended: at that moment the Jews were only a small minority of the population of Palestine and, as he added with parliamentary understatement but also prophetic acuity, if it were attempted 'to place the 400,000 or 500,000 Mahommedans of Arab race under a government which rested on the support of 90,000 or 100,000 Jewish inhabitants, there can be no assurance that such a Government, even if established by the Powers, would be able to command obedience. The dream of a Jewish State, prosperous, progressive and the home of a brilliant civilisation, might vanish in a series of squalid conflicts with the Arab population.' He proposed therefore British annexation of the Holy Land; thereafter, 'Jewish immigration, carefully registered, would be given preference' so that in the course of time a Jewish majority would be obtained and granted self rule.

There were obvious imperial and strategic advantages for the British in acquiring control of Palestine, most of all by ensuring that no rival Power – France rather than decadent Turkey – had a foothold so near the Suez canal. But Samuel knew English politics well enough not to present a proposal in purely cynical terms. He spoke also of England's long sympathy with national struggles, of the Protestant emotional link with the people of the Book, of the need to redeem the Holy Places, almost as though this were to be the last Crusade (as perhaps it was). In his peroration he eloquently returned to the old theme of making the Jews happy by rescuing them from their psychological and spiritual plight: a Jewish centre in Palestine could achieve 'a spiritual and intellectual greatness', whereby 'the character of the individual Jew, wherever he might be, would be enabled. The sordid associations which have attached to the Jewish name would be sloughed off . . . For fifteen centuries the race produced in Palestine a constant succession of great men – statesmen and prophets, judges and soldiers. If a body can again be given in which soul can lodge, it may again convince the world.' And he echoed Macaulay's great exhortation: until Jewish nationhood had been restored, 'let us not presume to say that there is no genius among the countrymen of Isaiah, no heroism among the descendants of the Maccabean'.

Not all of his colleagues were moved by this. Writing to Venetia Stanley, the young woman with whom he had a long *amitié amoureuse* and to whom he confided every Cabinet secret, Asquith said that the memorandum 'reads almost like a new edition of *Tancred* brought up to date. I confess I am not attracted by this proposed addition to our responsibilities. But it is a curious illustration of Dizzy's favourite maxim that "race is everything" to find this almost lyrical outburst proceeding from the well-ordered and methodical brain of H.S.' And again he mentioned with amusement that, although Lloyd George did not care a damn for the Jews, he was insistent that 'agnostic atheistic France' should not control the Holy Places, and so favoured this scheme under which 'the scattered Jews could in time swarm back from all quarters of the globe, and in due course obtain Home Rule. (What an attractive community!)' That last parenthesis said a good deal about the prejudice which tinged the outlook even of a famous Liberal statesman.

As he wrote to his young friend, Asquith did not know that within a year his beloved Venetia would desert him for a Jewish colleague, that within two years he would have been supplanted by Lloyd George as Prime Minister, and that within three years Samuel's 'almost dithyrambic memorandum' would have become the basis of British policy. By then also A. J. Balfour had returned to the Cabinet. Prime Minister from 1902 to 1905, he had resigned not quite voluntarily as the Tories' leader in 1910 after a 'BMG' – Balfour Must Go – campaign in his party. Following the revolution of December 1916 in which Lloyd George replaced Asquith, Balfour returned to office as Foreign Secretary, destined to become a famous name in Jewish as well as British history.

Balfour was no instinctive philosemite. He once described a 'long, hot and pompous dinner' at Reuben Sassoon's house in Brighton and had reacted much like Lord Crawford: 'I believe that Hebrews were in an actual majority – and tho' I have no prejudice against the race (quite the contrary) I began to understand the point of view of those who object to alien immigration.' Putting this understanding into practice, he had introduced an Aliens Bill in 1905 to control immigration. As Jews flooded into England from the East, he told the Commons that unless this were checked there would be 'an immense body of persons who, however patriotic, able and industrious, however much they throw themselves into the national life, remained a people, and not merely held a religion differing from the vast majority of their fellow countrymen but only intermarrying among themselves'. And when he first met Weizmann, he told him that he had earlier visited Bayreuth and met Cosima Wagner, and had told her (of all people) that he 'shared many of her antisemitic postulates'.[1] This was the man chosen by fate to proclaim the first Jewish homeland for nearly two millenniums.

After their first meeting, Balfour and Weizmann had kept in distant touch: Balfour appointed Weizmann to a position at the Admiralty laboratories, where he made a small but significant contribution to the war effort when he discovered a means by which an explosive could be extracted from horse chestnuts: although not a great theoretical scientist, Weizmann was a brilliant inventor. In the same way, the philosophical underpinning of Zionism concerned him less than the practical realities, and it was to these he applied himself. When they met again, Balfour first told Weizmann, 'You may get your things done much more quickly after the war.' In the early stages of the war, there was little Weizmann could do to get his things done. What he did in 1915 and 1916 was to try to form a common front in the Allied countries, and in what was still the most important neutral country, the United States. The ground there was fertile: in late 1915 Lucien Wolf had reported from America, with dismay, that the Zionist organisation had lately captured Jewish opinion. This was an exaggeration; but it

---

[1] The pompous phrase a reminder that Balfour was an amateur philosopher, the author of a *Defence of Philosophic Doubt*.

was true that American Zionism had in Brandeis a leader who was not only a more formidable personage but who had access to President Wilson.

The hostility for the Allied cause felt by Jewish-Americans ceased with the February Revolution of 1917 which overturned Tsarist autocracy; 'the Jews seem to have changed their mind to a considerable extent,' the British Ambassador in Washington reported four months later. By April, the United States was in the war, and Balfour was in the United States. He met Brandeis who, urged in turn by the London Zionists, pressed the case for a national home for the Jews in Palestine under British protection. Balfour was in an awkward position, since he knew that his country had devious plans for partitioning the Ottoman empire in its own interests rather than anyone else's. Vague promises had already been made to Arab chieftains, whose rebellion was encouraged by an English adventurer, T. E. Lawrence. At the same time, the London government was keen to interpose something between the French, who were planning to take over Syria, and the Suez canal. In this respect, the idea of a Jewish Palestine was tempting.

Whatever Weizmann or Brandeis said to him, Balfour was well aware of the unremitting and bitter opposition of anti-Zionist Jews, on both sides of the Atlantic. In June the *New York Times* published an article, 'Zionism no Remedy', by Henry Moskowitz. He described the curse of nationalism which hung over the world as its most terrible war raged, 'in which the idea of domination has given certain nations a form of megalomania', and he had no wish for the Jews to join in this game. The whole nature of Jewish nationalism was reactionary and an unsatisfactory philosophy of life he argued; what the Jews needed rather was a revival of the Hebraic spirit which gave birth to Israel's vision, to David's Psalms, to Spinoza's God.

Across the Atlantic Lucien Wolf fired another salvo, explaining that Zionism was a product of Austro-German Jewry and its problems, and was inapplicable to the Jews of the western democracies. Philip Magnus, for all that Weizmann had tried to bring him on board, remained unconvinced: 'The time has not yet come, nor is it likely in the near future to arrive, for any re-establishment of Israel's political nationality or restitution of Palestine to the Jews.' A Jewish state would do spiritual harm to Judaism and practical harm to the Jewish people 'by compromising the position of the Jews in other lands'. His namesake Laurie Magnus was more contemptuous still of the Zionists, or neo-Zionists as he liked to call them: 'We used to hear about Little Englanders. Surely Little Jews is the right term for the neo-Zionists.' The duty of Jews was to remain where they were, in the case of the Russian Jews to help Russia become a modern state, while 'German Jews will teach semitic virtues to the disciples of Herren Stoecker and Houston Chamberlain'. That was the mission of the Dispersion, and that was the way to find, he concluded, 'a final solution of the Jewish question'.

In May, David Alexander and Claude Montefiore, presidents respectively of the Board of Deputies of British Jews and of the Anglo-Jewish Association, published a statement in *The Times*; it was seconded a few days later by a letter from several eminent British Jews. Any proposal 'to invest the Jewish settlers' in Palestine, Alexander and Montefiore wrote, 'with certain special rights in excess of those enjoyed by the rest of the population [would] prove a veritable calamity for the whole Jewish people'. Wherever they lived, the principle of equal religious rights was vital for the Jews. And 'the establishment of a Jewish nationality in Palestine, founded on this theory of Jewish homelessness, must have the effect throughout the world of stamping the Jews as strangers in their native lands, and of undermining their hard-won position as citizens and nationals of those lands'.

This was an admirably succinct statement of the Jewish anti-Zionist position: quite apart from injustice in Palestine itself, Jewish national-ism was a direct threat to assimilated Jews everywhere. Asked by the British government to comment on a draft of what became the Balfour Declaration, Montefiore expanded his view: 'I deprecate the expres-sion "a national home". For it assumes that the Jewish race constitutes a "nation", or might profitably become a nation, both of which propositions I deny. The phrase "a national home for the Jewish race" appears to assume and imply that the Jews generally constitute a nationality. Such an implication is extremely prejudicial to Jewish interests, as it is intensely obnoxious to an enormous number of Jews. There can be no objection to Jews who *want* to form themselves into a nationality going to Palestine and forming themselves into a nationality in that country, but it must be effected without any prejudice to the character and position of the Jews as nationals of other countries.'

And yet all these pamphleteers and polemicists were wasting their ink. None of them carried real weight inside the British government – and even someone who did was powerless to stop the current of events. In 1917 there was only one Jew in the Cabinet. Herbert Samuel had chosen not to join the Coalition government which Lloyd George had formed the previous winter, inaccurately predicting that it would not last long. But there was another, young rising star in the Liberal Party: Edwin Montagu, younger son of the first Lord Swaythling. He had entered Parliament in the 1906 Liberal landslide, aged twenty-six. He was private secretary to Asquith before becoming an under-secretary and then entering the Cabinet in 1915 as Chancellor of the Duchy of Lancaster, still only thirty-six. In December 1916 he resigned in sympathy with Asquith, whom he admitted to hero-worshipping, and whose worship Asquith repaid by gently mocking him behind his back as 'the Assyrian'. There had been a deep personal bond, and then rift, between them: Asquith doted pitifully on Venetia Stanley, and was heart-broken and outraged when she married Montagu. By June 1917 Montagu was back in the Cabinet as Secretary of State for India.

This was a very important job, but it left him with energy to spare for one other task: opposing Zionism with all his might, and doing everything he could to thwart Weizmann's plan for a Jewish homeland. He was convinced that Zionism was a Teutonic plot against England, 'to bolster up German influence in Palestine, most Zionists being of German origin'. As the negotiations and intrigue proceeded, Montagu became ever more angry, but his anger was impotent. By now, Weizmann had secured the support of Lloyd George as well as Balfour, and *The Times* had expressed friendly interest in the project for a Jewish homeland. The shift in the mood of Anglo-Jewry was epitomised by the Rothschild family. Lionel Walter Rothschild was the son of the first baron, 'Milord' who had offered Herzl little encouragement. Walter succeeded his father on his death in 1915. He had worked in the family bank and been an MP, but his real interests – characteristic of the family in the twentieth century – were intellectual and scientific. He was also more sympathetic than his father to Zionism, and he dissociated himself from Alexander's and Montefiore's letter. In midsummer a letter of support for their cause was drafted by the Zionist leadership in London. The Foreign Office wanted to describe Palestine as an 'asylum' or 'sanctuary' for persecuted Jews, but this was just what the political Zionists did not want. A compromise was proposed: not Jewish state or sanctuary but 'National Home'. The compromise was reached just as Montagu rejoined the Cabinet, where he fought a fierce rearguard action. He bitterly denounced the Zionists and – not only in Whitehall but in London clubs and drawing-rooms – asked friends just as bitterly why they wanted to send him back to the ghetto, to 'repatriate' him as an oriental alien. Nor did he eschew emotional personal argument in Cabinet. He was Indian Secretary; how could he go to India on behalf of the British government when the same government had said that his own national home was somewhere in Turkey? He was supported by Curzon, who shared his antipathy to Zionism, who thought that the Holy Land was too small and dependent on agriculture to support a large Jewish settlement, who objected that the existing Moslem population could not be expelled, and who in any case could not conceive, as he told Montagu, 'a worse bondage to which to relegate an advanced and intellectual community than to exile in Palestine'.

But the tide was now flowing so strongly that Montagu and Curzon could not stem it. More and more important Jewish leaders in England were induced to give their blessing; American support was prayed in aid; the Germans were said to be wooing the Zionists also. And so at the Cabinet meeting of 31 October a letter was approved, to be dated 2 November addressed to Lord Rothschild, and signed by Balfour.

'I have much pleasure in conveying to you, on behalf of His Majesty's government, the following declaration of sympathy with Jewish Zionist aspirations, which has been submitted to, and approved by, the Cabinet.

'His Majesty's government views with favour the establishment in Palestine of a national home for the Jewish people, and will use their best endeavours to facilitate the achievement of this object, it being clearly understood that nothing shall be done which may prejudice the civil and religious rights of existing non-Jewish communities in Palestine, or the rights and political status enjoyed by Jews in other countries.'

Sir Mark Sykes, a diplomatist and Member of Parliament who had become a keen Zionist even though he was also an enthusiast for Arab nationalism,[2] brought the letter out to Weizmann who was waiting outside the Cabinet room, with the words, 'Dr Weizmann, it's a boy!' Weizmann replied that it was not the boy he expected and that he did not like it. This sullen response meant that the Declaration did not propose a Jewish state, only 'a national home' – and even the indefinite article was an important textual amendment; Montefiore in particular had insisted that it should not be '*the* national home'.

Such was the Balfour Declaration. It was the product of bitter in-

---

[2] And also 'in spite of his fervent Catholicism', as his biographer says.

fighting, it was inspired by high idealism and by cynical calculation. As Winston Churchill put it twenty years later, 'We did not adopt Zionism entirely out of altruistic love of starting a Zionist colony: it was a matter of great importance for this country. It was a potent factor in public opinion in America.' It was also a time bomb. The Declaration was signed by a man who admitted to 'sharing antisemitic postulates' while opposing Jewish immigration to his own country, and it was opposed with unswerving resolution by many thoughtful Jews, including the only Jew in the Cabinet which approved it. Above all, its last two clauses – which Weizmann may have disliked as too hedging – were fraught with potential difficulties. Could a Jewish home really be established in the Holy Land without compromising the rights of others? Despite that phrase, most of those concerned with the Declaration seem to have been almost wilfully blind about the reality of those 'existing non-Jewish communities'. One historian wondered whether 'Lloyd George and Balfour merely took their knowledge of Palestine from the Bible, which in this respect happened to be out of date', but even such irony may be misplaced. A few weeks after the Declaration, Lord Robert Cecil, Parliamentary Under-Secretary for Foreign Affairs, said that the government's 'wish is that Arabian countries shall be for the Arabs, Armenia for the Armenians and Judaea for the Jews', which indeed suggested the early pages of an historical atlas. In any case, a taste for political prestidigitation in the form of incompatible promises was nothing new in British history, and Lloyd George was the most prestigious of statesmen in this respect. Three years after the Declaration, he attempted to resolve another problem, or find an answer to another unanswerable 'question', in his 1920 Government of Ireland Act. This gave something to everyone, an autonomous government at Dublin but a separate Ulster, partition but potential unity, Ireland autonomous but Ireland under the Crown. At the time it seemed to help perform the necessary conjuring trick; in reality it stored up trouble for the future, and so did the mutually exclusive promises made to Arabs and Zionists in 1916–17.

Not everyone was deluded by these sleights of hand. Apart from his other objections, Curzon pointed out that there were in fact half a million Arabs in this proposed home, who 'will not be content either to be expropriated for Jewish immigrants or to act merely as hewers of wood and drawers of water for the latter'. These words were not heeded. Nor were other warnings. If the idea that a national home could be created without prejudicing the rights of existing communities was in retrospect to seem far-fetched, to put it no more strongly, so was the idea that it could be achieved without compromising in any way the position of Jews in other countries. Herzl's dream might yet come true; it might seem to solve the Jewish Question, and even, for a time, to 'make the Jews happy'; but it might also, in the end, prove to be a further development in the Jewish Question rather than just an answer to it.

III

From a
Jewish National Home
to a Jewish State

9

A Seventh Dominion

O put not your trust in princes.

Ps.cxlvi.2

Five weeks after the Balfour Declaration, Jerusalem fell to the British Army. Arriving at the gateway, General Allenby dismounted and entered the holy city on foot. It was a gesture which caught the public imagination, in England at least, implying as it did a contrast between the brutish Turk, with his arrogant Prussian ally, from whom the city had been taken, and the true humility of those who were now the rulers of Jerusalem: Right had triumphed over Might. This would have been misleading in the general context of British imperialism; it was even more misleading in the particular context of what was soon to become British Mandatory Palestine.

Under the *ancien régime*, princes had rarely felt the need to claim that morality was on their side. In the age of nationalism, that claim was made more and more; wars had to be justified in terms of a higher good. After the Austro-Prussian War of 1866, zealots in Berlin wanted in some manner to punish Austria for having had the temerity to fight the war at all, and to introduce the concept of 'war guilt'. Bismarck knocked the suggestion on the head with his usual common sense when he said, 'Austria was no more in the wrong to resist our demands than we were to make them.' But he spoke for an age and an outlook which were passing. By the time the Great War was over, the new spirit had triumphed. The Western allies had gone to war for plausible reasons, France to defend her own territory, England to protect the neutrality of

Belgium. When the war ended, it had accomplished quite different goals which were earlier unforeseen. Four empires had been destroyed; and this needed to be justified. So it was, in terms of national self-determination. Once the Americans entered the war, the principle was enshrined in Woodrow Wilson's Fourteen Points, demanding national freedom for the sundry European peoples.

Even at the time, this was part illusion and part fraud. One of Wilson's Points demanded the cession to France of Alsace, a province which was historically, geographically and culturally German. Another said that Italy should have frontiers 'along clearly recognisable lines of nationality', when Italy had already been promised, and was to receive, lands in the South Tirol and Istria most of whose inhabitants were not Italian. An Irish historian has lamented that the border between the new Free State and Northern Ireland was drawn in a way unfair to the former, at a time when 'borders were revised in central and eastern Europe in favour of small states'. But nothing of the kind happened after 1918. Borders were everywhere revised in favour of the winners in the war, and at the expense of the losers. Italy acquired the South Tirol with its German-speaking majority from a smaller Austrian state, Romania acquired the Banat and Transylvania with their large Magyar and Saxon minorities from the smaller Hungary, and those territories were transferred because Italy and Romania had both (as much by luck as judgement) backed the winning side in the war.

So had Zionism. The Balfour Declaration might have been Wilson's Fifteenth Point. Another national home was to be established, like the national home for the Czechs which Wilson adumbrated. That 'Czechoslovak' state included more Germans than Slovaks, Germans who did not want to be Czechs; but then the Czechs had 'won' the war, the Germans had lost. The Zionists had likewise 'had a good war'. It had been the need for Jewish support, along with British strategic considerations, which produced the Mandate; at the same time, it was defended in terms of abstract justice, and this, along with the pattern of making conflicting promises to Jew and Arab on which the British had embarked, prepared the ground for terrible conflict.

A taste for mutually contradictory promises was not confined to the British. One of Wilson's Points had indeed been addressed to 'the nationalities which are now under Turkish rule', who were to be 'assured an undoubted security of life and an absolutely unmolested opportunity of autonomous development'. This periphrastic and ambiguous wording reflected the fact that it was published two years after a vague promise of the Arab lands of the Turkish empire had been made to Sherif Hussein, Emir of Mecca, by the British agent, Sir Henry McMahon, and two months after the Balfour Declaration had claimed that nothing would be done to prejudice the civil and religious rights of existing non-Jewish communities in Palestine. This seemed from the beginning an empty and hypocritical promise and it might have been better if it had never been made. But then the British were not making these reservations to calm Arab anxieties so much as to salve their own conscience. For the same reason, the notion of the 'mandate' was invented. After 1918, the victorious European Powers acquired new territories from the losers in Africa and Asia.[1] So as to distinguish these from old-fashioned, colonial conquests, they were dressed up as mandates from the newly formed League of Nations, with the implication that these territories were to be held in trust and administered for the good of their peoples. In the case of Palestine, this sleight of hand begged a question: in the interest of which people? It was a question unanswered for the unhappy and ignoble quarter-century the mandate lasted.

A congruence of the Balfour Declaration with the rest of the post-war settlements struck even some Zionists. In New York, Judah Magnes explained why he could not regard the proclaimed national home under the British Mandate as a reason for rejoicing: 'Not that I have lost my faith or hope that Zion will welcome back her children, as the Confuters of our People have always predicted.' But the war which he had so hated 'has given me a horror and mistrust of all governments, quite in line with the traditional Jewish suspicion and loathing of the *al titvadda larashut*: "become not too intimate with government"'. Jerusalem was the Holy City of three great religions, Magnes said, and the fact that it should have been conquered by force of arms 'is a paradox worthy of a smile of derision'; this conquest, and the way Palestine had been 'made "Jewish" by the iniquitous Peace Conference' reminded him of the old Jewish phrase, 'Conceived and born in uncleanness'; while the Jewish people 'with its complex "Jewish Problem" and its scattered and precarious status in the world cannot be redeemed by a vague political decree'.

The peace conference Magnes had in mind was San Remo, one of the innumerable subsidiary conferences of the great Versailles meeting.

---

[1] Not only the European Powers: in Washington in 1919, it was seriously discussed whether the United States should accept mandatory control over Turkey, Albania, Armenia or Mexico.

The San Remo conference was to decide on the succession to the Ottoman empire which had collapsed at last, ending the old Eastern Question but beginning a new one. At the conference, and in the Treaty of Sèvres which ratified its work, the British Mandate was confirmed, to the dismay of some of those present as well as others. The Foreign Secretary was now Curzon, the grave and reverend signior who had earlier been Viceroy of India, a profound believer in England's imperial mission but also in even-handed justice between peoples. Knowing that Curzon had been hostile to the proposed Jewish homeland, Balfour had tried to convert his successor, arguing that Zionism, 'be it right or wrong, good or bad, is rooted in age-long traditions, in present needs, in future hopes, of far profounder import than the desires and prejudices of the 700,000 Arabs who now inhabit that ancient land' – a perfectly fair summary of the argument in its own terms, but one which then and later could never be used publicly. Curzon was unconvinced. He was quite sure, he told Balfour, that while Weizmann might say one thing to the British about the meaning of a national home 'he is out for something quite different. He contemplates a Jewish state, a Jewish nation, a subordinate population of Arabs etc. ruled by the Jews; the Jews in possession of the fat of the land', which goal Weizmann was 'trying to effect . . . behind a screen and under a shelter of British trusteeship'. What Curzon did not realise was that he was preaching against the converted. Two years later, Balfour admitted to Winston Churchill that, in his and Lloyd George's view, the Declaration had 'always meant a Jewish State'.

For his part, Magnes detested San Remo, a worthy heir to Versailles as 'a denial of almost every principle of democracy, of self-determination, of reconciliation'. The principle of self-determination had been shamefully disregarded in the Holy Land, he said. There were five or six times as many Arabs as Jews there, and the argument of 'historic rights' was contemptible if those rights were to be exercised by brute strength. 'I, too, believe in the "historic right" of the Jewish people to the Land of Israel, meaning thereby the right to make their historic land their own not by major force but, if they can, by labour, by work of brain and hand, by collaboration with and education of the present majority . . . In other words, "historic right" means for me: equal opportunities for Jews, Arabs, Syrians, Moslems, Christians to live their lives freely and in proportion to their labour of hand and brain.'

A year later, Magnes analysed his faith: Zionism for him meant 'helping the Jewish people to preserve its identity and deepen its spirit.'

He wrote this just as he was sailing with the family to spend a year of study and self-exploration in Palestine. In fact, he spent the rest of his life there; thanks to the generosity of Felix Warburg, the Hebrew university had become a reality, and Magnes became its first president, and a great figure of the Yishuv, the Jewish settlement in Palestine. And yet his position there was complicated and uneasy. He intensely admired the spirit of the young men and women, practical Zionists in every sense, who were digging fields and breaking rocks, and at the same time making themselves Jews again by learning Hebrew. When he saw them 'talking Hebrew – vocabulary limited, hard as *k'riat yam suf* [parting the Red Sea] – I ask myself, why do they do this? Have they not enough hardships to overcome? Then I think each time that this is *ham 'haddesh b'kohl yom ma'ase v'reshit* ['who renews every day the work of creation', echoing the Hebrew morning service]. But for all his love of Zion in these tangible and audible ways, Magnes stood more and more of a distance from political Zionism with its own increasing reliance on physical force, at first defensive and then offensive. He posed questions which others left unanswered. Could a Jewish state really be created except by violence and dispossession? What sort of state would it be? And what would it say about – and do to – those who created it?

At all events, the practical creation of a Jewish settlement in Palestine continued, as Magnes said, under imperial auspices. Only weeks after the Balfour Declaration, a memorandum had been sent to the French Foreign Ministry by Sylvain Levi, an anti-Zionist French Jew, reporting that Herbert Samuel had been tempted by the Zionists with the offer of becoming 'His Britannic Majesty's first proconsul in the Zionist State'. This was untrue at the time, and yet an uncannily precognitive piece of rumour-mongering. Samuel lost his parliamentary seat in the general election which followed the Armistice in 1918 and found himself out of politics; in 1920 Lloyd George indeed asked him to become the first High Commissioner, or proconsul, for Palestine. Samuel was in two minds. He had written to his son from Jerusalem that 'the more I see of conditions here the more I think it would be inadvisable for any Jew to be the first Governor. It would render more difficult, I am inclined to think, and not more easy, the fulfilment of that Zionist programme. Arab Nationalist and Anti-Zionist feeling is a very real thing . . . With a Jew as Governor, many measures would be viewed with suspicion and would provoke antagonism . . .' But he overcame these misgivings, and in June he returned to Jaffa to take up his new post. The departing Chief Administrator facetiously handed him a form to sign: 'Received from Major General Sir Louis Bols, one Palestine, complete.' Samuel signed, adding in the same jocose spirit, 'E. & O.E.', the businessman's catch-all: 'Errors and omissions excepted'. Many a true word is spoken in jest.

The 'first Jewish ruler in the Holy Land since Agrippa II' found the country under his charge 'almost derelict, politically and materially'. He went out of his way to govern justly and even-handedly in the English Liberal tradition; as he soon found, that tradition did not apply in a divided community. Jewish immigration increased. At the end of 1918, the population of Palestine comprised 512,000 Muslims, 61,000 Christians, 66,000 Jews (the last representing a decline from 85,000 in 1914). The Third Ascent of 1919–23 brought more than 20,000 Jews to the Holy Land, most of them educated, and most of them socialists. A Fourth Ascent in 1924–8 increased in numbers, to a peak of 33,000 in 1925. Apart from 1934 and 1935, this last was the highest figure for Jewish immigrants for any year before the creation of the Israeli state. These immigrants came from Poland and Russia. The reborn Polish state was strongly antisemitic in character. Thanks to the fortunes of war, it had acquired a huge area of White Russian and Ukrainian territory and thus an even larger Jewish population to harass. The harassment was mainly economic, and large numbers of traders were driven out of business. This was the largest of the Ascents to date, and it was also the first composed not for the most part of zealous Zionists but of people who, as even an historian sympathetic to Zionism admits, 'might have chosen America, had that option been still open'.

The British authorities maintained a policy, set out in a 1922 White Paper, of promoting a multinational commonwealth, and Samuel himself, while acknowledging that 'some thought that a national home for the Jews must mean subordination, possibly spoliation, for the Arabs', added that 'I did not share that view'. He recognised Arab opposition to the sequestration of their lands, to heavy Jewish immigration, and to the establishment of a Jewish state, but insisted that 'none of these things' was part of the British government's programme, or 'contemplated by responsible Zionist leaders'. This was not how it looked to the Arabs; there had been riots between Jews and Arabs not long before his arrival, and they flared up again after it giving Zionism new martyrs. Chief of these was Joseph Trumpeldor, at one time a Tolstoyan pacifist but who became supposedly the only Jew to have been commissioned as an officer in the Tsarist army, after he had lost part of an arm fighting in the Russo-Japanese War. He had then settled in Palestine, and had served in the British army with the Jewish unit which he helped to raise, before returning to his settlement in Galilee. It was there that he was killed in an Arab attack in March 1920. As the story went, Trumpeldor fell with the words 'It is good to die for our country' on his lips. He had certainly been caught up in an exalted mood, and the former pacifist came to celebrate the new Jewish militancy. Writers like Gogol and Dostoievsky would have changed their tune and their antisemitic prejudices, he wrote a few months before his death, if only they could have seen the new Jew, 'forty brave lads standing fearlessly at their post, facing an angry sea' of Arabs.

But others saw the conflict in a wholly different light. Magnes was one, Ahad Ha-am was another, now settled in the Holy Land but deeply troubled by events. In 1922, young Jewish zealots killed an Arab boy. This brought a cry of rage from Ahad Ha'am. 'Jews and blood – are there two greater opposites than these?' he asked in a letter to the Hebrew paper *Ha'aretz*. 'Is this the goal for which our ancestors longed and for which they suffered all those tribulations? Is this the dream of the return to Zion which our people dreamt of for thousands of years: that we should come to Zion and pollute its soil with the spilling of innocent blood?' Little noticed at the time, least of all by western Jews, there was a profound moral conflict in the making, which would become more painful still as more blood was shed in Zion.

The same post-war period saw a recrudescence also of antisemitism in the West, unconnected with Zionism and the Holy Land. It was partly stimulated by that other 'aliyah', the continuing economic and social ascent of the Jews. In England the Great War had produced a new mood of jingoism and xenophobia, directed not only against foreigners but the enemy within. There had been anti-Jewish riots in Leeds only months before the Balfour Declaration, and the 'war profiteer' became a standard figure of satire and obloquy, his Jewish origin usually made clear by satirists. He was the profiteer who had changed his name to Fitzwarren, to be buried 'in some corner of an English field which is forever foreign'; he was caricatured in the ever-unfunny *Punch* with blue jowls and hook nose and, in one cartoon, driving a car whose number plate – hazy but legible, like the sneer on the back of Hess's envelope – read 'Yid'.

The openness of antisemitism, unimaginable a generation later, was exemplified in 1923 when the Tory MP Sir George Hamilton shouted 'Jew' at Emanuel Shinwell across the floor of the House of Commons. And this casual Jew-baiting was given a more bitter edge by Catholic polemicists. Soon after the Balfour Declaration, that old war horse – or pantomime horse – Chesterbelloc rode into action again. In 1920, G. K. Chesterton published *The New Jerusalem* and in 1922 Hilaire Belloc, *The Jews*.[2] Each returned in their comparable, different ways – Chesterton mellower and more reflective, Belloc cleverer and sharper – to the 'Jewish Question'. Each assumed that the Jews remained an alien and unassimilable element in Christian Europe. Both were fascinated by Zionism, and by the way it seemed to reflect their own thesis.

Chesterton described his visit to Palestine, 'where everybody recognises the Jew as something quite distinct from the Englishman or the Europeans; and where his unpopularity even moved one in the direction of his defence'. He poured scorn on the idea that the Jews were always the oppressed and never the oppressors, and he wondered whether 'the Jews shall continue to control other nations as well as their own'. After some fairly good-natured rambling about Jerusalem and its varied peoples, he came up short at the appointment of Samuel as High Commissioner, at which Chesterton affected astonishment, Belloc disgust.

In his book, Belloc asserts emphatically that the Jewish problem – 'friction between the two races – the Jews in their dispersion and those among whom they live' – not only exists but is growing and may soon lead 'to the most fearful consequences, terrible for the Jew but evil also for us'. In flat contradiction to Jellinek and other assimilationists, and in the best tradition of the antisemitism which had flourished for a half-century past, Belloc was contemptuous of any idea that Jews could become Englishmen, Frenchmen or Italians – or that 'the Jew' even wanted this: 'what he wanted was *security*'. He harps continually on the rootlessness and chameleon-like adaptability of the Jews, some of them adopting three or more national colourings in a single lifetime (a psychologically revealing argument, coming from a writer who made much of Englishry but whose name attested his French birth and descent).

Belloc was afflicted to a peculiar degree by the professional Jew-

---

[2] Belloc's book, antisemitic by the standards of its own age as well as later, is dedicated to 'Miss Ruby Goldsmith, the best and most intimate of our Jewish friends', taking 'some of my best friends . . .' beyond parody.

baiter's flair for detecting Jews everywhere, disguised under assumed names or otherwise: he believed for example that Matthew Arnold and Robert Browning were both Jewish, something few Jewish enthusiasts for English letters have claimed. He saw Jewish influence spread by 'an anonymous Press' and by Freemasonry, 'with which they are so closely allied and all the ritual of which is Jewish in character'. He assumed that the Bolshevist movement was Jewish. He believed, like Charlus, that the Jew 'can only be charged with treason when he acts against the interests of Israel'. He claims, perhaps with some truth, that most better-off Jews in England mixing with the better-off classes there, had no true idea of their real position in the eyes of those gentiles, which was to say of how much dislike and resentment was expressed behind their backs. And he even, in a bravura performance, writes a chapter on 'the Anti-Semite', from whom he carefully distinguishes himself, and whom he condemns.

They are strangers, they don't belong, they cannot be true members of any other nation – they are a nation in themselves. This is the Jewish Question, which Zionism was designed to resolve. But would it? Will 'the Zionist experiment ... tend to increase or to relax the strain created by the presence of the Jew in the non-Jewish world'?

Venomous as Belloc is, he addressed here a real question which Zionist enthusiasts had brushed aside. If Mandatory Palestine ever became a Jewish state, would Jews throughout the world be allowed to regard themselves as citizens of that state, or even be regarded as citizens of it whether they wanted or not? And would it lessen or increase the hostility to Jews which was already rising elsewhere (even in 'the countries where Jewish finance controls the politicians', as Belloc puts it)? These questions are posed by Chesterbelloc in the deliberately minatory way which those hostile to the Jews had come to adopt: if the Jews didn't watch out they were in for a nasty shock. 'I would like to add a few words to the Jews,' Chesterton had said a few years earlier. 'If they continue to indulge in stupid talk about pacifism, inciting people against the soldiers and their wives and widows, they will learn for the first time what the word antisemitism really means.' Needless to say, Belloc rose to heights of vehemence in denouncing 'the strange selection made by the Jews for their first ruler of the Arabs and Christians in Palestine': not one of the blameless and upright Jews in public life but the man who had declared in the House of Commons that no politician had touched Marconi shares (a travesty of Samuel's position).

Less cruel and malicious than Belloc, Chesterton also made a shrewder point. Samuel's appointment was neither a concession to Zionism nor an experiment in Zionism, it was 'a flat and violent contradiction to Zionism'. For 'where is Sir Herbert Samuel's natural home? If it is in Palestine he cannot go there as a representative of England. If it is in England, he is so far a living proof that a Jew does not need a national home in Palestine.' This was near the knuckle for assimilationist Jews. They knew (if they knew Chesterton at all) that he believed 'Jews are Jews; and as a logical consequence that they are not Russians or Romanians or Italians'. He had always hoped that 'Jews should be represented by Jews, should live in a society of Jews, should be judged by Jews and ruled by Jews. I am an Anti-Semite if that is Anti-Semitism. It would seem more rational to call it Semitism.' He saw in Zionism two advantages, 'for if the advantage to the Jews is to gain the promised land the advantage to the Gentiles is to get rid of the Jewish problem.'

Above all, he saw a vindication of what he had long said about that problem: 'It was always called Anti-Semitism; but it was much more true to call it Zionism.' That was what Kraus had said twenty years earlier; that was what Montefiore, Wolfe and Montagu had feared: the antisemites were linking hands with the Zionists. Even some of Chesterton's sneers had Zionist echoes. We have all known many industrious Jewish scholars, Jewish lawyers, Jewish doctors, Jewish pianists, he said, but 'we have not known personally many patient Jewish ploughmen, many laborious Jewish blacksmiths, many active Jewish hedgers and ditchers, or even many energetic Jewish hunters and fishermen'. This was just what Gordon and the Labour Zionists also disliked about their own people, and were trying to put right in practice by forming their settlements in Palestine. A Jewish state will not be a success, Chesterton said, until 'the Jews in it are scavengers, when the Jews in it are sweeps, when they are dockers and ditchers and porters and hodmen'; the very project was already under way.

The anxieties of Jewish anti-Zionists did not trouble the small but growing and influential group of Zionists in the West. Isaiah Berlin described how as an Oxford undergraduate in the 1920s he came across an article on Zionism by L. B. Namier, written with 'a combination of intellectual power, historical sweep and capacity for writing clear and vigorous prose' never normally encountered on the subject. Namier's career and abilities were indeed as extraordinary as his personality. His father was born Bernstein, or Bernsztajn, had become the administrator of a large estate in Austrian Poland, and had been converted to Roman Catholicism as a matter of form. Although brought up as a 'gentile', Ludwik Bernsztajn had come, like Hess and Herzl before him, to see the position of people like his parents as false and humiliating. Jews like his parents 'had abandoned the traditional misery of their ancestors only to find themselves in a no-man's land between the two camps, welcome to neither'. Those who most longed to be accepted as nothing more than Poles (or Englishmen), he once wrote, 'are the more unhappy among the Jews. For the desire to be "assimilated" is a confession of inferiority, an attempt to divest oneself of one's inheritance in order to share in that of others.' He had set off for the England admired by him as by so many European Jews, studied at Balliol, but failed to get a Fellowship at All Souls, a ludicrously inferior candidate being preferred.

Namier was a Jewish problem all of his own. His relations with his adoptive England were always to be awkward and angular. He saw the attempts of his fellow Jews 'to assume protective colouring and disappear into the Gentile world' as a degrading and pitiful form of self-deception, just as Chesterbelloc did. He soon found that most English Jews were either uninterested in or hostile to Zionism, and he thus chose to see them as deluded fools. As opposed to English Jews, the English won his continuing admiration; or at least a number of the upper class did, especially those who were both sympathetic to Zionism and hostile to Germany. His Anglophilia was founded on a mixture of acute understanding, and of complete incomprehension. His scholarly books on politics and society in the late eighteenth century show a deep knowledge of how England ticked then, and still did in the twentieth century. He notoriously discounted serious political belief in favour of interest and connection, oblivious of the way that he himself existentially disproved this. As his colleague, friend and then enemy A. J. P. Taylor remarked, it was odd that a man who so despised ideas as an historical force should have become so wedded to Zionism, an idea in history if ever there was one.

Even so, although he admired the English upper classes as much as he despised most assimilated Jews (not to mention most Zionist leaders), Namier never fully understood the English. Grasping in theory how much they valued people who were charming and amusing (to the detriment sometimes of more serious qualities), he quite failed in practice to see that in their eyes he himself was charmless and overbearing. With his extraordinary personality, leonine or unbearable according to taste, he was, in Taylor's words, 'an intolerable bore unless you were fascinated by the subject he talked about'.

There was a relentlessness also about his approach to the Jews and to Zionism. On paper he analysed the problem with real penetration. He saw as others before him had that the 'Jewish Question' was a consequence of emancipation; that 'Orthodoxy is a melting glacier and Zionism is the river which springs from it'. He saw that Jewry itself was tending to disappear in Europe west of Poland: by the late 1920s in Hamburg and Berlin, for every two Jews who married other Jews one Jew married a gentile; and he concluded too soon that there was therefore no longer a real Jewish Question in Germany. He saw that there were two numerically important Jewries, the Yiddish-speaking Easterners, and the Americans, children of the great migration. He saw that this last, combined with the Palestine Mandate, had meant that the leadership of Jewry had passed from the German-speaking to the English-speaking world. He saw that 'with the loss of the Messianic hope the passivity of orthodox Jewry breaks down'. And he insisted that 'we have to find our own place on earth and live as other people do . . . every nation must somewhere have its own territorial centre'.

Namier may have been as much a burden and a trial to the Zionist movement as an adornment. His relations with the movement were always ambivalent. Other Zionists must have found him at times as exhausting and monological as non-Zionists did. His effect on the latter was notorious; as Isaiah Berlin put it, he would corner someone from the Foreign Office or Colonial Office at the Athenaeum and 'treat him to a terrifying homily which the victim would not soon forget, and which would probably increase his already violent antipathy to Zionism in general and Namier in particular . . . If he came across latent antisemitism he stirred it into a flame.' At the same time his undisguised contempt for most Zionists did not endear him to them either.

But there was more to it than that. Zionism was meant to be a cure for Jewish self-contempt; in Namier's case, it came close to being an expression of self-contempt. As his wife said, 'he didn't basically like Jews . . . he didn't like what had become of the Jewish character.' Asked once why he wrote English and not Jewish history, he said, 'There *is* no modern Jewish history, only a Jewish martyrology, and that is not amusing enough for me.' And the outcome of this psychic conflict was extreme pugnacity. It was directed not only towards British officials and 'the rabbis' or the 'O.T.I.' – the Order of Trembling

Israelites, as he called other Zionists – but the Arabs. Sometimes, like so many Zionists, he imagined this problem away. 'What more can we Jews offer the Palestinian Arabs than complete equality . . . ? If the Arabs sincerely and unreservedly accept such a symbiosis, all serious difficulties between us are at an end – even the question of which side is in the majority becomes unimportant . . . What "grievance" then remains?'

This was the politically approved – and psychologically necessary – Zionist line. It deftly avoided the question of whether the Jewish homeland was a colonial scheme. But then it could have been said by other European settlers across the globe if they had pretended to offer equality to those in whose lands they were settling.

At this point, in the 1920s, the nature and image of imperialism was changing perceptibly. A generation or more earlier, imperialism was still widely seen as an enlightened force, but a reaction had by now begun. In 1902, the radical English economist J. A. Hobson had published his book *Imperialism*. It explained European lust for conquest in novel terms: 'the modern foreign policy of Great Britain has been primarily a struggle for profitable markets of investment', a theory previous moral critics of empire had not advanced, nor Marx and other socialists.

Now Lenin annexed Hobson and made him the basis of Communist policy. This was despite the fact that Hobson had formed his theory from observation of one great imperial episode, the Boer War (his description of which was far from free of antisemitic abuse of the gold-mining capitalists of Johannesburg who, he thought, had engineered the war), and as a general analysis this specific case did not apply: in material terms, South Africa was a prize well worth fighting for, which the rest of Africa was not. Not that Hobson discarded the ethical condemnation: the peroration of his book announced that 'Imperialism is a depraved choice of national life, imposed by self-seeking interests which appeal to the lusts of quantitative acquisition and of forceful domination surviving in a nation from early centuries of animal struggle for existence.'

After this it was difficult for anyone who called himself a radical, liberal or socialist to call himself an imperialist also. Or if he did, he was obliged to use conscious irony, as Josiah Wedgwood did when he published *The Seventh Dominion*. Wedgwood was a member of two interesting groups: the upper-class radicals, and the gentile Zionists (his book is dedicated to one of the most admirable of the latter, Mrs Edgar

– Blanche 'Baffy' – Dugdale, Balfour's niece and biographer, a tireless campaigner for her friend Weizmann and his cause). Wedgwood was a scion of the famous Staffordshire family of pottery manufacturers, a brave soldier in both the Boer and Great Wars, and an MP for nearly forty years, first as a Liberal and then, from 1919, Labour.

His book was a plea for the establishment in Palestine of a Jewish state which could be a member of what had recently come to be called the British Commonwealth. As he admits, some will call him an imperialist, and 'if it be Imperialism to be convinced that the race that spread out from, and came to, these islands is the finest on earth and in history, then I am an Imperialist, though I hardly think that my reasons for this faith would appeal to the fascist, fox-hunting, nigger-kicking people who too often annex that name and tarnish the lustre'. Wedgwood ingeniously, and plausibly, argued that British imperialism had taken a new and more benevolent direction, especially in the Mediterranean now that 'fear of Signor Mussolini and the Roman fasces lies heavily on all'. He argued, also plausibly, that Zionism was bringing material progress to the Holy Land ('the fact is that the Arabs had obviously benefited by the arrival of the Jews'). Most of the resistance to the Jews there was led by Christian Arabs: 'Jerusalem seems populated by innumerable repetitions of Mr Hilaire Belloc in sweeping black robes – less clever, of course, but also with less to distract them from the supreme issue: "Who crucified Jesus Christ".'

Wedgwood wanted Palestine to become the Seventh Dominion. His title has a gnomically religious ring, but merely borrows the name recently adopted for the former British colonies. Even without hindsight, this was unintentionally revealing. Apart from the Irish Free State, with its own complicated and unhappy history, the other six dominions as they were then numbered were all places of European settlement outside Europe. In three, Australia, New Zealand and Canada, the indigenous population had been dispossessed and largely destroyed. In another, Newfoundland (then a dominion of its own independent from Canada), the original inhabitants had been not only expropriated but entirely exterminated. And in the last dominion, South Africa, the Europeans had remained a small minority which held the non-European majority down as a toiling helotry without rights. None of these was a happy precedent for Palestine.

Wedgwood touched on one other contemporary theme: transfer of population. This was to be one of the potent ideas of the century. Following the Great War, and yet another savage bout of fighting between Greece and Turkey, there had been huge forcible migrations of population: 1.4 million Greeks had been moved from Turkish rule to settle in Macedonia, and 350,000 Turks from Grecian Thrace had moved to Turkey. The former, at least, seemed to Wedgwood a hopeful example of how such large-scale settlements could take place and prosper. But he admitted that 'this transplanting of peoples, according to their tongue or religion, is a wretched business. It exposes the dirty side of religion and nationalism.' What he did not foresee was how large a part this transplanting of peoples, involuntarily as well as voluntarily, was to play in the creation of a Jewish state. In his last word, he hoped that 'Zionism will give peace and justice as well as pride to the Jews, both of Palestine and the Diaspora'; he did not see how fraught this might all the same be.

Neither Wedgwood nor Namier could be sure how the new dominion or commonwealth was to be achieved, and they begged the question of physical force. Neither was a pacifist: not Wedgwood the holder of the DSO, nor Namier who had exulted in the destruction of Germany and Austria-Hungary in 1918. Namier remained fiercely anti-German even before Hitler, and became a bitter critic of appeasement in the 1930s. A German nationalist who was visiting Oxford at that time dined at All Souls and held forth about Germany's right to regain tropical colonies, until he was silenced by Namier with the words, '*Wir Juden und die anderen Farbigen denken anders*' – 'We Jews and other coloured people think differently.' It was a ferocious shaft of irony; and it was destined one day to backfire. So was Namier's bellicosity towards the Arabs, concealed behind the phrases of 'complete equality' and 'symbiosis'. Interviewing for appointments at the University of Jerusalem, he would fix a timid lecturer with his baleful, annihilating glare and say, 'Mr Levy, can you shoot?' and, after something was muttered, 'Because if you take this post, you will have to shoot. You will have to shoot our Arab cousins. Because if you do not shoot them, they will shoot you.' Mr Levi was not appointed, but a point had been made. It was to be made far more forcefully by Vladimir Jabotinsky, whose influence on the story of Zionism and whose part in the controversy of Zion would be enormously greater than Wedgwood's or Namier's.

10

Blood and fire

He smote divers nations: and slew mighty kings.

Ps.cxxxv.10

In one other respect the Zionists were in agreement with Jew-baiters like Belloc. They both foresaw a new flood tide of antisemitism after the Great War. Not that this was easy to miss. Apart from the old centres of reaction in Poland and Romania, newly aggrandised and inflamed by nationalism, a fresh mood was unmistakable in Europe. It came to be known universally as fascism; but the country where it was first given that name played a curious part in the story of Zionism. Moses Hess had already seen in the new Italy a model for a Jewish Risorgimento, as much as he had seen the Roman Church as the deadliest of the Jews' foes; or so he thought, unable to see that modern nationalism might be deadlier still. Theodor Herzl had visited Italy to be told that the Church would welcome the Jews if they accepted conversion, by the Pope that the only answer to Herzl's idea of a Jewish state was '*Non possumus!*' and by the king that no distinction was made in Italy between Jew and Christian.

This was true, to a degree which made Italy under its bourgeois monarchy almost unique in Europe. The Jews of Italy had flourished wonderfully after emancipation. Oppressed more than in almost any European country as late as 1848, the small Jewish community had benefited dramatically from the unification of Italy under the Piedmontese monarchy. King Victor Emmanuel III told Herzl, 'everything is open to them . . . Jews for us are full-blown Italians', and

Weizmann later agreed that the Italian Jews 'were to all intents and purposes indistinguishable from their fellow-citizens, except that they went to synagogue instead of to Mass'. Antonio Gramsci, the leading theoretician of the Italian Communist party and creator of intelligent neo-Marxism, attributed this tolerance and integration to the Italian traditions of municipal particularism and cosmopolitanism. However that may be, given that they were fewer than 50,000, the Jews of Italy enjoyed an astonishing success not only in politics but also – quite unparalleled in any other country – in the army. Sidney Sonnino, a baptised Jew, became prime minister in 1906, Luigi Luzzatti, unbaptised, followed him in 1910, while General Ottolenghi became war minister (the king showed his familiarity with Jewish matters by telling Herzl how Ottolenghi had once tried unsuccessfully to muster a minyan – a quorum for religious service – in Naples).

This philosemitism was linked not only to the cosmopolitanism and the underlying decency of the Italian people but to the specific circumstances of the Italian state created by the Risorgimento. That state was bitterly opposed by the Roman Catholic Church, which also remained hostile to the Jews; thus, an Italy which was anti-clerical and secular was – objectively, existentially, and on the principle of 'my enemy's enemy . . .' – philosemitic. Equally, the Italian state's sympathy for the Jews only increased the Church's antipathy to them, and not least to the Zionist scheme. With his '*Non possumus*', Pius X had also told Herzl, '*C'est une honte*': It – this idea of a Jewish state – is a shame or a disgrace. And this remained the Vatican's policy.

It was supposedly justified by theology and history. The Jews had rejected their Messiah; the Church was not the 'true Israel' and exclusive heir to all that God had wrought in the Bible. In 1897, the year of the first Zionist congress, the Jesuit journal *Civiltà Cattolica* harked back to Jesus' own prediction 'that Jerusalem would be destroyed . . . that the Jews would be led away to be slaves among all the nations, and that they would remain in the dispersion till the end of the world . . . According to the Sacred Scriptures, the Jewish people must always live dispersed and wandering among the other nations, so that they may render witness to Christ not only by the Scriptures . . . but by their very existence. As for a rebuilt Jerusalem, which could become the centre of a reconstituted state of Israel, we must add that this is contrary to the predictions of Christ himself.' With or without this baroque language, the Vatican opposed Zionism implacably. Herzl had ingratiatingly suggested that restoration would resolve a problem for Christendom, since the Holy Land ought never to be the possession of one great Power: 'The return of the Jews to Palestine would solve this problem for the world and for the Turks.' This cut no ice with the Curia, for whom even the continued possession of the Holy Places by the Turk was preferable to their possession by the Jews.

Dogmatic and bigoted, perhaps, Roman opposition to the project was not ignorant. Pius X was well enough informed to see that Zionism was a secular movement: the Jews might go to Palestine with their Christ-denying faith, which was bad enough, 'or else they will go there without any religion, and then we can be even less favourable to them'. And Cardinal Merry del Val grasped the distinction between merely humanitarian settlements in Palestine – 'the Holy Church is apostolic; it will never oppose an undertaking that alleviates human misery' – and political Zionism, which the Church would always oppose.

For twenty years this opposition was merely tacit. Then came the Balfour Declaration, and the Vatican was appalled. 'The undefined British "home" is to become a political and independent state,' the clerical Roman paper *Tempo* said, adding that the plan for a Jewish state was supported by French and Italian Freemasons. And in March 1919, Pope Benedict XV delivered a fierce denunciation. After all 'the efforts of Our predecessors to free them [the Holy Places] from the dominion of infidels, the heroic deeds and the blood shed by the Christian of the West throughout the centuries', the Church now found 'that non-Catholic foreigners, furnished with abundant means and profiting by the great misery and ruin that thus has been brought upon Palestine, are thence spreading their errors. Truly harrowing indeed is the thought that souls should be losing their faith and hastening to damnation on that very spot where Jesus Christ Our Lord gained for them life eternal at the cost of His Blood.' And yet the Church found itself powerless to stop the developing Jewish homeland.

Nor could it affect the rapidly changing course of Italian history, though many in the Church at least quietly welcomed the collapse of bourgeois democracy in 1922 and its replacement by a new ideology called fascism. Benito Mussolini had taken his name from the Italian *fascio*, for a bundle or group, and taken as a symbol the fasces, the bundle of rods and axe which had been the Roman lictors' emblem of power. The first 'fasci' had been organised by socialists in Sicily at the turn of the century; Mussolini began his political career as an extreme socialist; and fascism was a heresy of socialism, retaining its populist and to an extent its equalitarian rhetoric, but adding on a new nationalistic rhetoric, along with a mixture of glamour and terror. Like socialism itself, fascism was a product of the mass age, a strange flower growing on the decay of nineteenth-century liberalism.

Although intensely nationalistic and authoritarian, fascism was not to begin with racist, certainly not antisemitic. Mussolini was virulently anti-German, on political grounds: during the Great War he said that only when the machine of German militarism was smashed 'will the pillaging and murderous Germans reacquire the right of citizenship in humanity'. Like so many orators of his age, not least on the Left, he took swipes at the Jews. But when in the late 1930s fascist toadies looked for early evidence of his Jew-hatred to please Hitler, they could only adduce an attack he had written on 'Judaeo-German Bolshevism' which saw the October Revolution as the worst of the German High Command acting in collusion with 'the synagogue'; and in 1938 the rulers in Berlin were not pleased to be told that Pan-German nationalism and militarism were really Jewish forces. At the same time, Mussolini was influenced by several Jews, and the founders of the *fasci di combattimento*, the Fighting Fasces, in 1919 – the equivalent of Hitler's *alte Kämpfer* a few years later – included five Jews. Those apart, one of his closest women friends, Angelica Balabanoff, and one of his mistresses, Margherita Sarfatti, were Jewish.

In 1918 Mussolini expressed some enthusiasm for Zionism, but he soon reversed that line. This was partly to curry favour with the Vatican, and in any case Italian Jews like Sonnino and the sometime foreign minister, Carlo Schanzer, shared the acute distaste for Zionism of so many assimilated Jews elsewhere. But Mussolini remained for long untouched by antisemitism. In March 1922, six months before he took power, he visited Berlin. He condemned the German extreme Right (though without mentioning Hitler, of whom, before the Munich putsch, he may not even have heard), and he greatly admired Walther Rathenau, the brilliant Jewish businessman who played a vital part in running Germany during the Great War, became foreign minister of the Weimar Republic in 1920, and was assassinated in 1922 by right-wing extremists. Mussolini met Rathenau, and after his death said that it had been intolerable for the fanatics who killed him 'that a Jew should lead and represent Germany before the world . . . It makes no difference that the German Jews conducted themselves with gallantry in the War.' He even renounced his earlier charge, saying that: 'Bolshevism is not, as people believe, a Jewish phenomenon. The truth is that Bolshevism is leading to the utter ruin of the Jews in Eastern

Europe.' And in eloquently assimilationist terms he explained that Zionism was unnecessary. The Italian Jews had no need of a national home: their New Zion could only be 'right here, in this adorable Italy of ours which, for the rest, many of them have heroically defended with their blood'.

Soon after he came to power, Mussolini received a delegation of Italian Zionists, and explained that his hostility to their cause was not anti-Jewish but anti-British: Zionism had become a ploy of British imperialism. And he repeated this to Weizmann when he met him only a few weeks later. The Zionists were trying to *'faire le jeu d'Angleterre'*, the object of the game being to weaken the Moslem states (Weizmann replied with serpentine ingenuity that this was not true but that, even if it were, Italy stood to gain as much from such weakness as England). Within a decade Mussolini had changed his tune on both Zionism and Jews. Throughout the 1920s, the official line remained that 'the Jewish problem does not exist in Italy'; but the fascist paper *Tevere* began to attack the Jews in 1933. The date was scarcely an accident: Hitler had just come to power. In the next few months a huge number of Germans joined the National Socialist party, and a Berlin wit called them the ' *'33er Spätlese'*; in its new-found animus against the Jews, Italian fascism also belonged to this late-gathered vintage.

At the same time, Mussolini privately told Jewish representatives of his 'cordial sympathy' for the Jews in general and for the National Home in particular. And in 1935, Mussolini sent Corrado Tedeschi, one of his trusted Jewish colleagues in the Fascist party, to Palestine with the task of wooing Zionist leaders. He met Meir Dizengoff, mayor of Tel Aviv, and Ittamar Ben Avi, a senior colleague of Jabotinsky's in the Revisionist party and editor of the Revisionist organ *Doar Hayom*, and several members of the Jewish Agency including Dr Leo Kohn and Moshe Shertock, later Sharett and prime minister of Israel. This charm offensive was connected to Mussolini's Abyssinian adventure: other Italian Jews were despatched at the same time to London, to try to persuade British Jews to use their influence (which Mussolini exaggerated) to help his adventure. There was even talk of a Jewish settlement in Italy's new Abyssinian empire, and as late as this point articles sympathetic to Zionism appeared in Italian fascist papers, reciprocated by pro-Italian pieces in Zionist papers in Palestine.

Nowhere did this connection between Italian and Jewish nationalism take more remarkable form than in the extraordinary career of Vladimir Jabotinsky, who transformed the story of Zionism, and began a new struggle for its soul. He was born in 1880 in Odessa, which ranked with Warsaw, Vilna and Salonika as one of the great Jewish cities of Europe. Like Herzl, he was less of a ghetto Jew than a literary cosmopolitan. He was raised on Russian culture and became a polyglot newspaperman who (also like Herzl) wrote didactic novels. Zionism was not merely an 'idea in history'; the idea was largely the creation of feuilletonists, literary journalists.

Jabotinsky went straight from school to travelling as a foreign correspondent, in Bern and then in Rome where he also attended the university, before returning to work on a daily paper in Odessa. He was a brilliant orator, an agitator of genius, a man of parts, a skilful writer in several languages. Jabotinsky was in fact one of those who defined the linguistic culture war within Jewry. Pious eastern Jews continued to speak Yiddish, and then English if they migrated to America, while regarding the secular use of Hebrew as impious; secularised, not to say agnostic, Jews like Jabotinsky made Hebrew into a twentieth-century language, into which the rest of the world's major and minor classics could be rendered.[1]

By his early twenties he was a committed Zionist, and a committed advocate of physical force. The Jews' problem was their passivity, he thought, their traditional acceptance of suffering. As pogroms rolled over Odessa, he organised self-defence units to fight the persecutors. They were the precursors of militant Jews to come, from the Jewish corps Jabotinsky raised for the British army in 1917 to the uniformed Revisionist youth movement Betar (a name echoing one of the ancient Hebrew revolts against alien rule), whose members would fight National Socialists in 1930s Vienna, to the Irgun underground in Palestine which would fight British and Arabs in Palestine. Was there still heroism among the descendants of the Maccabees? Jabotinsky's life's work was to answer that rhetorical question. Labour Zionists wanted to recreate the Jew as farmer and artisan; let us recreate him as soldier also, Jabotinsky might have added. He put it with his usual pithy bluntness. In their contemptible exile, the Jews had become Yids; they must now become Hebrews. 'Because the Yid is ugly, sickly, and lacks decorum, we shall endow the ideal image of the Hebrew with masculine beauty. The Yid is trodden upon and easily frightened and, therefore, the Hebrew ought to be proud and independent. The Yid is

---

[1] Even now, when there are many Israelis who are followers of Jabotinsky through the Likud, few of those could name him as the man who translated the Sherlock Holmes stories into Hebrew.

despised by all and, therefore, the Hebrew ought to charm all. The Yid has accepted submission and, therefore, the Hebrew ought to learn to command. The Yid wants to conceal his identity from strangers and, therefore, the Hebrew should look the world in the eye and declare: "I am a Hebrew."' These words became in effect a text for even those Zionists and Israelis who were not political followers of Jabotinsky's.

He continued to travel widely before the Great War, and in the process began to re-examine the Zionist project. For one thing, he not only rejected the pieties of assimilationism, to the extent that he did not care about the charge that Zionism was a form of antisemitism, he almost welcomed it. In his autobiography, he describes how he first came into contact with the Zionist movement, when he was studying in Bern. He announced on the spot his adherence to the cause, in strange terms: 'I am a Zionist, because the Jewish people are a very nasty people, and its neighbours hate it, and they are right; its end in the Dispersion will be a general Bartholomew's Night, and the only rescue is general immigration to Palestine.'

This was to be his consistent theme until his death more than thirty years later: forget about spiritual regeneration through Zion, concentrate on what Jabotinsky called 'the objective Jewish question', the practical problem of the European Jews living in an alien world which was becoming more and not less hostile. Zion meant first of all rescue, a haven. This was what he preached in the early years of the century, and this is what he was still preaching to the British Royal Commission in Palestine in 1937.

In the same way, he did not think Zionists should be squeamish about their methods, or choosy about their allies. He would be happy to collaborate with the Jews' worst enemies if it could help the Jews, and his own plans for them. This was a theme which was to recur. He was never dogmatic in the sense of allowing fixed principles to get in the way of pragmatic experiment. He did not, for one thing, suppose that the long-term Zionist goal should compromise the pursuit of national rights for Jews in the Dispersion. In Vilna in 1906, he met several colleagues, among them Avraham Idelson, editor of a Zionist weekly in St Petersburg, and Yizhak Gruenbaum, who was about to become editor of a Polish-language Zionist paper. They laid down a policy: 'Zionism, which seeks the Return of the nation to its historic homeland and its Redemption as a self-governing people, proclaims . . . its refusal . . . its refusal to be denied a national life [for Jewry] in its Exile so far as that might be obtainable.' Behind this lay a fear that those who should be fighting for Zion were being seduced into practical politics as an alternative which did not challenge their Yiddishkeit.

Jabotinsky's next move had been to Constantinople where the Ottoman empire twisted and writhed in its death throes. In 1908, the Young Turks' revolution imposed a form of constitutional government on the old autocracy of the Sublime Porte. This made little immediate difference to the small Jewish settlement in Palestine, or not directly. One development was unforeseen, and ominous, for the Zionists. A free press emerged on Ottoman lands for the first time, and the Arabic free press in Palestine – mostly written by Christian Arabs – was violently anti-Zionist. Bizarrely enough, Jabotinsky became deputy editor of the revolutionary *Jeune Turc* in Constantinople. He then moved to Vienna, and covered northern and western Europe for a liberal Moscow daily when the Great War broke out. As soon as Turkey entered the war on the side of the Central Powers, Jabotinsky recognised immediately what the opportunity was and what needed to be done: Zionism must place itself whole-heartedly on the Allied side.

In much of his personal social and economic outlook he was, or at least began as, a nineteenth-century liberal. But, like the socialists and the fascists, he quickly recognised that classical liberalism was doomed as a political force once the masses entered politics. And he had a truly Marxian grasp of objective force. Previous Zionists had appealed to the better nature of Jews and gentiles alike: the cause was a high and moral one, they believed, and higher morality would ensure its success. To Jabotinsky this was self-deluding humbug. The Allies would not support Zionism without Jewish support in return. Hence the three Jewish battalions in the British army, beginning with the 38th Royal Fusiliers in which Jabotinsky himself served as private and subsequently lieutenant. But then, even after the Balfour Declaration, and despite it, he perceived with rare acuity that any sincere will on the British part to support the rapid development of a Jewish homeland would soon evaporate.

He grasped something more important still. Even when they did not go so far as to pretend that Palestine was 'a land without people for a people without land', all previous Zionists had wished away the fact of the large Arab majority. Herzl had set the tone when he naively supposed that the Arabs would welcome Jewish immigrants creating a new land of milk and honey, its prosperity shared in some measure by all. He was no doubt sincere in this vague benevolence towards the

Arabs, but there is no doubt either that he saw the question – unconsciously more than consciously – in imperial terms. Others went further. A few early Zionists had dreamed of voluntary collaboration between Jew and Arab, with their common semitic origins. In 1914 the Zionist writer Nahum Sokolov gave an interview in the Cairo newspaper *Al Ahram* in which he looked to an Arab-Jewish partnership which would build a great new Palestinian civilisation, and his idea was expounded in practical terms after the war by the Viennese writer, Eugen Hoeflich, who settled in Jerusalem and wrote as M. Ben Gavriel. His book *Die Pforte des Ostens* (*The Gateway to the East*) published in 1924 advocated a binational Jewish-Arab state, an idea which continued to beguile other liberal Zionists.

In Jabotinsky's view, this was all nonsense. He was one of those uncomfortable men whose brutal honesty follows through the logic of circumstances to disconcerting conclusions. Of course the Arabs would not welcome a Jewish colonisation of the Holy Land, he said. Why should they? He recognised as much as any Arab the illogic of the Balfour Declaration's claim that the homeland should be established without prejudicing the civil or religious rights of the existing inhabitants. That could not be. The Arabs themselves must recognise this. And, since they were not likely to hand over their land without a fight, they must be fought for it. Even after the Balfour Declaration, not only did more Zionists still hesitate publicly to advocate an independent Jewish state, most did not even publicly advocate a Jewish majority in Palestine. To Jabotinsky this too was nonsense. The vision of Zion could only be realised with a Jewish majority, as soon as possible. And he recognised that this meant the use of force.

He presented a fascinating contrast with an earlier Jewish militant. Lassalle the left-wing socialist had once penetratingly said of himself that if he had not been a Jew he might have become a right-wing nationalist; Jabotinsky was a Jew, and he became a right-wing nationalist. As it happens he was fascinated by Lassalle, whose voluminous writings (forgotten even by admiring German socialists) he knew intimately. When a Polish politician asked him once whether reason or force rules human destiny, Jabotinsky replied with a quotation from Lassalle's *Franz von Sickingen*: all that is great owes its triumph to the sword. He certainly used other language which echoed the European apostles of totalitarianism: 'It is the highest achievement of a multitude of free human beings to be able to act together with the absolute precision of a machine.' And in his ruthlessness he was ready to form tactical alliances with those who might appear his bitter enemies, advocating an agreement, for example, with the murderously antisemitic Ukrainian nationalist Petliura after the Great War.

In the same spirit, he thought it was sentimental delusion even to speak of the Arabs as the Jews' brothers. When he had helped to raise a Jewish legion to fight with the British against the Ottoman army, it was as much a symbolic as a practical event: the first time since Antiquity that a Jewish army, however small, was fighting as such, and a demonstration of Jabotinsky's personal vision of remaking the Jew in a new, martial image. Nordau questioned whether they should be fighting the Turks at all: 'The Muslims are kin to the Jews, Ishmael was our uncle.' Jabotinsky replied, 'Ishmael is not an uncle. We belong, thank God, to Europe and for two thousand years have helped to create the culture of the west.' This spelt out with painful clarity the colonial nature of the project. It was not what many Zionists wanted to hear.

Although he was fanatically wedded to his people's cause, there was something which struck others as un-Jewish about Jabotinsky. His Zionist opponents emphasised this, not necessarily in a denigratory way. To Weizmann, 'the inner life of Jewry had left no trace on him . . . he was rather ugly, immensely attractive, warm-hearted, generous, always ready to help a comrade in distress; all of these qualities were however overlaid with a certain touch of the rather theatrically chivalresque, a certain queer and irrelevant knightliness, which was not at all Jewish.' And Ben-Gurion, his bitter enemy, conceded in a similar back-handed way that Jabotinsky had 'in him complete internal spiritual freedom; he had nothing in him of the Galut Jew and he was never embarrassed in the presence of a Gentile'. Even if they were back-handed, Jabotinsky would have taken these posthumous descriptions as compliments. More than any other Zionist before him, he did not want to be 'a Jew' – not a Galut Jew, defensive, passive, unhappy in himself. He specifically repudiated the mystical or cultural Zionism of Ahad Ha-am, but his Zionism still had a psychological content. For him it meant not re-creating a place of resort where the Jews could find some vague inner rebirth, but all or nothing, the hope of some day seeing in Palestine a new Jewish national life, 'Otherwise I would have only an archaeological interest in that country.'

Jabotinsky's single-mindedness drove him down a path of his own. He had hoped that the Jewish legion (whose significance he exaggerated) would continue after the war as the nucleus of a Jewish army; but the British did not in the least want a Jewish army and disbanded it. He nevertheless organised units of Haganah, which called itself the Jewish Defence Force and indeed became the nucleus of a Jewish army. Imprisoned by the British and amnestied by Samuel when he arrived as High Commissioner, he joined the Zionist executive in 1921, but soon quarrelled with the Labour Zionists who dominated it: he wanted a Jewish armed force as soon as possible to protect the settlement. He quarrelled with pacific Zionists who hoped for peace and co-operation with the Arabs. His ally, Richard Lichtheim, said before the war, 'The Arabs are and will remain our opponents. They do not care a straw for the "joint semitic spirit" . . . The Jew for them is a competitor who threatens their predominance in Palestine.' Jabotinsky agreed. He quarrelled with Brandeis and the other leaders of American Zionism, who remained 'minimalists', perfectly content with the Jewish homeland granted by Balfour and nothing more, a settlement which was not a Jewish state and need not even contain a Jewish majority. For Jabotinsky the Balfour homeland was no more than a starting point. Finally he quarrelled with the executive itself and resigned in January 1923. By then he had come to regard Weizmann as a trimmer and compromiser, and Weizmann and his colleagues had come to regard Jabotinsky in turn as a dangerous extremist: 'fantast' was their charge against him; his reply, crueller still, was that Weizmann was guilty of 'subconscious Marranism', that is, the cringing subservience of the forced convert.

Before long there were other words to describe Jabotinsky. Later in 1923 he founded Betar, the youth movement of the larger movement that was to be known as Revisionism. Its end was simple. It had been defined as 'the gradual transformation of Palestine (including Trans-Jordan[2]) into a self-governing commonwealth under the auspices of an established Jewish majority'. These were the words – surprisingly and, if the Palestinian Arabs had known, alarmingly – of Sir Herbert Samuel, speaking in London before he left to take up the High Commissionship of Palestine. Jabotinsky publicly proclaimed his first goal as the establishment of a Jewish majority on either side of the Jordan: 'trans-Jordan' had always been part of Jewish Palestine, he said. This would mean immigration at a rate of 40,000 a year for

---

[2] The easterly part of the Mandatory territory; what later became the Kingdom of Jordan.

twenty-five years, or half as many again if, better still, both banks were to be colonised.

This was a deliberate challenge to Weizmann who still insisted that 'I have no understanding of or sympathy for a Jewish majority in Palestine'[3] and who as late as 1930 told the Zionist General Council that a Jewish state was impossible 'because we could not expel the Arabs'. But then Revisionism was a challenge in every sense to mainstream Zionism, and there was a compelling simplicity about Jabotinsky. He did not pretend. He thought that, if a majority and a state were the goals, they should be loudly proclaimed instead of kept hidden like some slightly discreditable secret. He did not expect that the Arabs would welcome this, or that it could be justified to them on moral terms; its justification was that the Arabs had many states and much land, while the Jews had none, and nowhere to go, while they faced what emerged more and more clearly as a catastrophe of incalculable magnitude. He did not deny the Arab claim to Palestine in its own terms; he only said, unforgettably, in 1937, that 'when the Arab claim is confronted with our Jewish demand to be saved, it is like the claim of appetite versus the claim of starvation'.

Here was another question on which Jabotinsky was brutally honest: what to do with the Arabs of the Holy Land. To him, it was clear that, however many Jews immigrated, even when they became a majority in Palestine (which seemed very remote in the 1920s), there would still be many Arabs; perhaps too many. Zionists had already begun to talk of the 'Arab problem' or the 'Arab question'. The irony of this was painful. Zionism was itself a response to antisemitism, to gentile contempt, and to the concept of the *Judenfrage*, the Jewish Question. It had always been a begged question: Christendom persecuted and despised the Jews, and then called this a problem. Were not the Jews now doing the same: trying to settle a land against the wishes of most of its inhabitants, and then calling these people a problem?

Once the problem was proclaimed, an answer suggested itself: the 'transfer' or removal of many or most of these problematic Arabs. Generations later, long after the successful establishment of the Jewish state, the importance of 'transfer' in Zionist thought and practice became one of the strongest themes of the anti-Zionist case. From the beginning, it was argued, the Zionist project had implied some degree

---

[3] Though Weizmann later said that he had been misquoted, and that what he objected to was cheap rhetoric about a Jewish majority.

of – to some degree coercive – removal of the Arab population, to make room for Jewish settlers and to allow a homeland and then state to be established securely in terms of population. By the 1980s, Israeli scholars took the subject up and examined the creation of the state in this light, and with devastating effect.

And yet their discoveries, and the anti-Zionists' polemics, were little more than another truism. Not only all imperial ventures but all migrations – arguably all progress – have involved some measure of 'transfer'. In the seventeenth and eighteenth centuries the English had tried to solve their 'Irish Question' by extermination of the population or its expulsion to the West, though without success except in one province of Ulster. Even there, transfer was only partial, so that the descendants of Scotch Protestant settlers formed a bare majority by the twentieth century. Once an independent Irish state was created out of the three and a third provinces with Catholic majorities, a new problem emerged, to baffle Irish as well as English politicians. Eamon de Valera, leader of Ireland for nearly thirty years, proposed to solve the 'Ulster Question' by transfer: the partition of Ireland could be ended by the return of all those in Ulster who did not consider themselves Irish to the mainland of Great Britain. De Valera dressed up this proposal as an exchange of populations: movement in one direction would be balanced by the return of Irish emigrants from Great Britain to Ireland.

That plan prefigured what happened later in the Holy Land. But, in any case, it was much in accord with the spirit of the age. After 1918, the conflict between Greeks and Turks seemed insoluble, with the fall of the Ottoman empire and the establishment of a Turkish national state, and with the two peoples still mixed up together all around the Aegean. Not only Wedgwood but Curzon saw transfer as the answer. The Foreign Secretary, who was not a despot or brutal racist, advocated a simple solution to the problem, by transferring all Greeks out of Asia and all Turks out of Europe. Part of the equation came true in 1922 when Turkey rigorously expelled scores of thousands of Greeks from Smyrna, where they had lived for centuries past, amid scenes of rape and massacre. Not that wrong was on one side only. Ten years earlier, the Greek national state (fewer than a hundred years old) had acquired Crete, and had transferred all its numerous Muslim inhabitants, most of them of Greek origin, to Anatolia, where their fair, blue-eyed descendants still live. 'Transfer' was indeed one of the great political ideas of the twentieth century, one on which Zionists could claim no copyright.

If Jabotinsky was a threat and challenge to Weizmann, they were both of them challenged by Magnes. He was increasingly critical even of the mainstream Zionist movement. When Maxim Gorky had told him that he – like many other Jews of his age – disapproved of the Zionist scheme to take Jews 'away from the larger world where, particularly in these days of stress, they had so important a part to play', Magnes had replied that his conception of Zionism did not mean an ingathering of the whole Jewish people: 'If it were physically possible to bring all Jews here – which of course, it is not – the world would be a poorer place and the Jewish people would deprive itself of a large part of its opportunity to be of service to mankind.' Zionism for Magnes continued to mean something else, a means of strengthening the Jewish people, of making them 'cleaner, better, truer'.

This was not an end he saw Weizmann's means as likely to achieve. Their estrangement could be followed in their correspondence, even in the superscription of the letters. In 1913 Magnes wrote to 'Dear Chaimchik', in 1916, to 'Dear Weizmann', by 1926 to 'Dear Dr Weizmann': in a warming friendship, the changes in a mode of address would have been the other way round. By the late 1920s Magnes was very critical of the conduct of the Zionist organisation and Weizmann's addiction, like Herzl's before him, to backstairs negotiation and intrigue with the powerful and mighty. Their relationship was soured by the affairs of the Hebrew university, and the intervention of another great Jew.

Albert Einstein had been converted to Jewish nationalism, as his admirer Leon Simon put it, 'because without it the survival of the Jew is neither worthwhile nor ultimately possible'. He deplored the domination of Jew over Arab, thought that a permanent state of mutual hostility between them would mean the failure of Zionism, and sought to promote Jewish-Arab co-operation, without any marked success. Einstein addressed some of the familiar topics and problems. An economically independent existence for Palestine was essential. The rebirth of Hebrew was a great boon for the spiritual and moral growth of the Jews. And yet it was not necessary for all Jews to emigrate or forswear their existing national identities: 'The German Jew who works for the Jewish people in Palestine no more ceases to be a German than the Jew who becomes baptised and changes his name ceases to be a Jew,' a rather curious comparison.

Like so many others, he emphasised the sociological character of the project: the Jews of Palestine must not 'repeat the old mistake of one-sided devotion to the professions and intellectual pursuit. On the contrary, the thing to aim at is a normal distribution of the Jewish population among the various occupations. The notorious one-sided-ness of the occupational distribution of the Jews in the Diaspora must not be reproduced in Palestine . . . it is not our aim to create another people of city-dwellers, leading the same life as in the European cities, and governed by the standards and conceptions of the European bourgeoisie. We aim at creating a people of workers . . .'

He also aimed at creating an educated Hebrew culture through the university, and did not believe that Magnes was qualified to be president. Einstein told Weizmann so, who told Magnes, whose attitude to both men may have been affected thereby. Deep down, as he confided in his own journal, Magnes distrusted Weizmann and, although that may have been unfair, his larger verdict was less so: along with his many high qualities, his intellectual ability, his courage, vision and dignity, 'it is his moral quality that is questionable. He is through and through the politician. He is constantly playing a game, very cleverly, and one does not know what he is after.' That was something which could never be said of Jabotinsky: what you saw was what you got.

In August 1929, a long-simmering dispute over the Holy Places in Jerusalem came to the boil and produced the worst communal violence yet witnessed in Mandatory Palestine. Arab gangs killed 133 Jews, six Arabs were killed in a Jewish counter-attack and another 110 by the police. Apart from depressing many Zionists inside and outside the Yishuv, the events of 1929 further polarised the movement. Those who had hoped for understanding with the Arabs seemed discredited and demoralised. Only four years earlier Arthur Ruppin, a leading German Zionist, had founded the Berit Shalom (Covenant of Peace) society, with Magnes among others, to promote Jewish-Arab understanding and perhaps in the long run to create a binational state. He now admitted defeat. At the very most the Arabs were prepared to give the Jews of Palestine rights as a minority: 'But we have already had enough experience of the situation in eastern Europe.' Einstein continued to hope for a *modus vivendi* with the Arabs; but his hopes seemed more and more forlorn. He insisted that 'Zionism is not a movement inspired by chauvinism or *sacro egoismo*' and did not 'aspire to divest anyone in

Palestine of any rights or possessions he may enjoy'; but could it survive otherwise?

Although Magnes stuck to his own pacific and anti-chauvinist policy, he recognised that the equivocation of mainstream Zionism could no longer be sustained. Immediately after the 1929 violence, and putting aside the embarrassing disagreement over his fitness to lead the Hebrew university, he wrote to Weizmann. What was to be done? Where were they to go? What did they want? Magnes had been removed from the Zionist Organisation of America in 1915 because of his insistence that the Jews should ask for no special privileges in Palestine, and had publicly criticised Balfour Declaration and Mandate. He did not pretend that true co-operation with the Arabs was easy or even possible: 'The Palestine Arabs are unhappily still half savage, and their leaders are almost all small men' (the second clause, if not the first, was true enough). What was clear was that there were now only two policies possible: either the policy which Jabotinsky had just spelled out again in a letter to the press, 'basing our Jewish life in Palestine on militarism and imperialism; or a pacific policy which treats as entirely secondary such things as a "Jewish State" or a Jewish majority; or even "The Jewish National Home", and as primary the development of a Jewish spiritual, educational, moral and religious centre in Palestine . . . The question is do we want to conquer Palestine now as Joshua did in his day – with fire and sword?'

Less than a year after this was written, Weizmann told the Zionist General Council that a Jewish state was impossible 'because we could not and would not expel the Arabs'. The Arabs loved their country too, and would not be persuaded to hand it over to others, especially as their own national awakening was under way; and even to speak of a Jewish state was to encourage the 'calumnies' being spread that Zionism intended the expulsion of the Arabs. Perhaps Weizmann was entirely sincere when he said this, though Magnes was right when he said that Weizmann had the instinct of so many politicians to try and please his audience and flatter his interlocutors. But he, too, was running into an insoluble dilemma, and he was not alone.

A matter of months before the 1929 killings, a British general election had taken place, the second Labour government had taken office, and the new Colonial Secretary was Sidney Webb, translated improbably into Lord Passfield. He was a desiccated economist and bureaucrat who with his imperious and even more inhuman wife Beatrice had been cruelly lampooned by their Fabian colleague H. G.

Wells in his novel *The New Machiavelli*, though a couple who could spend their honeymoon attending the Trades Union Congress in Glasgow were in truth beyond satire. The Webbs were no Zionists, or philosemites. In an early Fabian pamphlet, written in 1907 (that is, just over ten years before he drafted the Labour party's constitution) Sidney had advocated eugenics, or scientific breeding, as a remedy against 'national deterioration', which he saw as 'this country gradually falling to the Irish and the Jews'. And Beatrice had once wondered why it was 'that everyone who had had dealings with Jewry ends by being prejudiced against the Jew'.

In his new office, Passfield looked into the Palestine problem in a dispassionate and dry way. He decided that faster Jewish immigration could only displace the Arabs, who would resist it by further force, and in October 1930 he published a White Paper restricting Jewish immigration. Passfield was bitterly denounced by the Zionists, all the more when, within a few years, persecution produced a new flood of refugees. All the same, as an historian later wrote, the unfortunate Passfield had made an awkward discovery by stumbling unwittingly on a question where the governing assumption of all English progressives and *bien-pensants*, even of the whole European liberal tradition since the Enlightenment, did not work: 'there was irreconcilable conflict between Arabs and Jews, not a community of interest which the two peoples merely failed to recognise by mistake.'

One of the Webbs' most eminent colleagues on the joyless Left was himself Jewish. Harold Laski came from a well-known Manchester merchant family. His father Nathan had been connected with the early Zionist movement but had strongly backed Zangwill's Territorials and opposed Jewish statehood; he might have been one of the provincial commercial Jews whose materialism Weizmann came to dislike when he lived in Manchester, 'who consider themselves better than "our poor ghetto brothers" [but] are in fact worse. Their Zionism is empty, a mere amusement.' At the age of eighteen, Harold wrote an unpublished essay on 'The Chosen People'. Not only was the young man not attracted by Zionism, he saw 'rigid and intolerant' Judaism as unfit for the modern world; it ought to 'remove from itself relics of barbarism alien from the spirit of today'.

Before long, Laski had become one of those who thought that their Jewish identity should be suppressed in the name of socialism. He became also a university teacher in north America and then at the London School of Economics (where his pupils in the early 1920s included Moshe Shertok), a well-known political theorist, a Marxist of sorts, a fantasist, a master of inextricably convoluted English, a member for years of the National Executive Committee of the Labour party, and for most of his life an assimilationist and anti-Zionist. He was nevertheless a friend of both Brandeis's and of Frankfurter's. After the 1929 violence, he advised Brandeis to remain calm, advice which was partly ignored: Brandeis lectured the British ambassador in Washington about the political strength of the American Jews.

But by then events were slowly modifying even Laski's anti-Zionism. When he complained to the Labour Prime Minister, Ramsay MacDonald, about the unfair treatment of the Jews in Palestine, and MacDonald expressed surprise at this protest coming from whom it did, Laski replied that 'My views on Zionism had not changed, but that as a Jew I resented a policy which surrendered Jewish interests in spite of a pledged word, to the authors of an unjustifiable massacre. No doubt when the Arabs killed the next lot of Jews, Webb would be allowed to expel all the Jews from Palestine.'

This exchange would have amused Jabotinsky, as would the idea that there was a community of interest between Jew and Arab. What did Webb expect, or Laski? And what for that matter did the liberal Zionists expect? The Jews could rely on no friends to help them and must defend themselves. Jabotinsky would have warmly echoed Bismarck's famous or notorious saying that the great questions of the day would not be decided through speeches and majority resolutions but through iron and blood. Did indeed echo it: the young men of Betar sang: 'In blood and fire did Judaea fall. | In blood and fire will Judaea rise again'; and Jabotinsky himself hymned the rebirth of the fighting Hebrews or Maccabees: 'With blood and sweat | Shall we beget | A newer tougher breed.'

In Palestine, these new Hebrews were vocal, and sometimes more than vocal. Norman Bentwich was an English Jew who had served in Egypt and then in the British Army when it conquered Palestine, where he became attorney general in 1922. Ten years later he was appointed professor of international relations at the Hebrew university. But his inaugural lecture, entitled with what in the circumstances was heroic optimism 'Jerusalem, City of Peace', was heckled and almost broken up by militant students who despised Bentwich's pacifism and hopes for a Jewish-Arab binational state. Arthur Ruppin was appalled by this demonstration – 'the whole world is mentally sick, much more so, we Jews' – and, despite his spiritual attachment to the idea of Zion, he became more disenchanted still with the prospect of a Jewish state. Even if it attracted a population of a few million, it 'will be nothing but a new Montenegro or Lithuania. There are enough states in the world.'

The next year worse followed. Chaim Arlozorov was one of Ben-Gurion's closest lieutenants in the Labour Zionist movement. Like his chief, he was publicly open to compromise with the Arabs, but, as the shadows lengthened in Europe, he privately wrote to Weizmann saying that an uprising in Palestine might be necessary to take control over immigration out of British hands. In 1933, he took another pragmatic course by visiting Germany to discuss the emigration of German Jews with the new National Socialist government, a form of collaboration which was anathema to the Revisionists. On his return, Arlozorov was walking on the beach by Tel Aviv with his wife, when he was killed by a gunman. This was the first but not the last fratricidal breach within Zionism, and sent out a tremor of shock. A Revisionist radical, Abraham Stavsky, was tried for the murder; although he was acquitted, most Labour men were sure the Revisionists were responsible, and at the subsequent Zionist conference Jabotinsky and his colleagues were ostracised.

And yet, if some Jews found Jabotinsky absurd or repellent, others found him compelling. Arthur Koestler was born in Budapest in 1905, forty-five years after Herzl, and like him moved to Vienna in adolescence. Between the wars he was caught up in two movements, Communism and then Zionism, and for psychologically similar reasons. In his own words, 'I became a Communist because I hated the poor and a Zionist because I hated the Yid.' In the first case, he was slowly detached by the events of the 1930s: he was one of those for whom Communism was 'the God that failed', and he wrote the classic *Darkness at Noon*, explaining the moral collapse of Soviet Communism and the apparent puzzle of the Old Bolsheviks' confessing to crimes they had not committed at the Moscow Trials. He also fell under the spell of Jabotinsky and helped to organise the Revisionists in Austria. He later wrote *Promise and Fulfilment*, an historical narrative about Palestine in the three decades after the Balfour Declaration, and a didactic novel, *Thieves in the Night*, dedicated to Jabotinsky's memory.

It is a quaint work. Its Anglo-Jewish hero Joseph is converted to Zionism in a wonderfully implausible manner. While he is at Oxford he is seduced by a 'blonde, slim, pretty' English girl who turns out to be an ardent supporter of Mosley's Blackshirts, the British Fascist movement. After their passion has been consummated, she turns on the light to see 'the sign of the Covenant on his body, the stigma of his race incised in his flesh'. Horror-struck, she sends him packing.[4]

Apart from other implausibilities, Koestler never quite understood English society or even English antisemitism. Later on, another immigrant from the Habsburg succession, George Weidenfeld, said correctly (and perhaps with feeling) that English antisemitism was largely an *ad hominem* thing, while one of Philip Roth's characters saw English antisemitism as closely linked to snobbery. And that was much what the formidable Circe, Lady Londonderry meant also. She was sitting out at a ball in London before the war with the writer Compton Mackenzie. He held forth about the 'impossible English women' of Georgian times, the hysterical Lady Caroline Lamb, or Lady Hester Stanhope running off to marry a sheikh of Araby, or Lady Ellenborough actually marrying another sheikh, and concluded that we no longer produced these extraordinary, impetuous women, capable of anything. 'I don't know,' Lady Londonderry replied. 'One of my daughters married a Jew.'

At any rate, Koestler's hero runs away to Palestine and becomes a 'thief in the night', an armed warrior serving the underground leader Bauman. Joseph is captivated, though also alarmed, by 'these Hebrew Tarzans' who know almost no European culture, but 'know all about fertiliser and irrigation and rotation of crops; they know the names of birds and plants and flowers; they know how to shoot, and fear neither Arab nor devil.

'In other words, they have ceased to be Jews and become Hebrew peasants.

'This of course is exactly what our philosophy and propaganda aims at. To return to the Land, and within the Land to the soil; to cure that nervous overstrungness of exile and dispersion; to liquidate the racial inferiority complex and breed a healthy, normal, earthbound race of peasants.'

This was the heart of Jabotinsky's career. He wanted to create a new Hebrew people. And in the process he laid down a challenge to mainstream Zionism. It was, during his lifetime, less of a political challenge than a moral one. Where they equivocated, he said what he meant. His posture and his advocacy of force led Ben-Gurion to call

---

[4] If Koestler had been as intimately familiar with male as he certainly was with female physiology in his adoptive country, he would have known that circumcision is quite common in England.

him 'Vladimir Hitler', but Jabotinsky was unabashed. His strength was his honesty. He wanted a Jewish state, as soon as possible, by whatever means necessary. And he could always reply, like other 'extremists' challenged by moderates who desired the same ends: 'Why should our endeavour be so loved, and the performance so loathed?'

11

Fulfilling the American dream

For my brethren and companions' sakes:
I will wish thee prosperity.

Ps.cxxii.8

While the centre of gravity of the Zionist movement had inevitably passed to London with the Balfour Declaration and the Mandate, the centre of gravity of the Jewish people had moved still further west, across the Atlantic. The same debates between Zionists and assimilationists took place among American Jews, but this was less significant than a practical development: the steady emergence of American Jewry as the most formidable Jewish community in the world, the most formidable indeed that the world had seen since Antiquity.

It did not come into being without suffering. The American Jews still knew much hardship and prejudice between the wars. The most drastic effect of this prejudice for the Jewish people as a whole was the closing of American doors to the millions who remained behind in Europe. They were closed by successive legislation, all of it undisguisedly designed to protect the Protestant, gentile, and north European character of the American people. Its basic principle was that immigrants were to be categorised by ethnic stock. Each group was graded by its supposed proportion of the population in 1910, and its annual immigration restricted to 3 per cent of that earlier stock. The 1924 Johnson-Reed Act reduced the figure to 2 per cent and pushed the 'stock' date back to 1890. In practice this meant that, for decades to come, there were far more places available for English (or German, or Swedish) immigrants than there were applicants, but that immigration from Italy, Poland and Greece was sharply restricted, and that there were very few places for European Jews. Since the decades in question saw catastrophe fall upon the European Jews, the effect of this legislation was to condemn untold numbers to death.

For the Jews already inside the United States, numbering more than four millions by the mid-1920s, life was nevertheless far better than anything their ancestors had ever known. This community was destined later to become strongly Zionist, in a sentimental rather than a practical sense. And yet it was to be this community more than any other which experimentally confuted the Zionist thesis that the Jew must always be an endangered outsider in a gentile society. The Jews were no more outsiders than many others in the heterogeneous American society; and they were not endangered, they were challenged. There were individual Jew-baiting demagogues like the radio orator Father Charles Coughlin, who tapped the far from latent Jew-hatred of Irish-Americans, but who never held any public office. The greatest entrepreneur of his age, Henry Ford, published the rantingly antisemitic *Dearborn Independent*, but the newspaper was denounced in 1921 in a proclamation signed by 123 prominent Americans, including every living President. And no open antisemitic movement arose in the United States, nothing to compare with the Action Française or Lueger's Christian Socials, let alone National Socialism.

In all of this, America followed the English rather than the Continental pattern, of social but not political antisemitism. On the one hand was a continuing undercurrent of hostility, which in many ways increased rather than diminished in the course of the first half of the twentieth century, at least as expressed in the exclusion of Jews from many social clubs and the very widespread use of covenants in housing sales forbidding the resale of property to 'Hebrews'. The Jewish response was communal solidarity: their own country clubs, their own holiday resorts, their own suburbs outside the great cities from whose centres they were emigrating. That, and a distinctive culture of their own: what now emerged was neither the old 'high' German-Jewish culture of uptown New York nor the old 'low' Yiddishkeit transplanted to the Lower East Side, but something new, unmistakably Jewish-American.

On the other hand, there were the huge, overwhelming advantages of living in a pluralistic immigrant society, and one in which different interest groups were a long if not always happy and honourable tradition. 'Hyphenated Americans' may have had a derogatory overtone, but it was a reality of American political life, as gently mocked by the Gershwin brothers in their 1931 satire on American politics, *Of Thee I Sing*. The campaign song 'Wintergreen for President' goes, 'He's the man the people choose, Loves the Irish, loves the Jews . . .'. This did not mean that there was, between the wars, a 'Jewish vote', as there unmistakably was later. Indeed, in 1923 Israel Zangwill had said that the absence of a Jewish vote was a disgrace, while Louis Marshall, president of the American-Jewish committee, had said 'it would be a misfortune if there were'. But American politicians not only eschewed public antisemitism, they began to pay attention to Jewish sentiment.

For most American Jews in this period, life was not about wielding political power but about social and economic advance. More important than party politics was the central plank of classical liberalism, the career open to the talents, specifically freedom of access to colleges and professions. Once they had been set free in a new-found land, the Jews' ability and energy began to produce explosive results, as long as they could compete on equal terms. In fact, access was far from open to begin with. Some civic colleges became well-nigh Jewish institutions – by 1920, enrolment at City College of New York was more than 80 per cent Jewish, at the Washington Square campus of New York University, more than 90 per cent – but the older Ivy League universities were less welcoming. Columbia moved to the remote Morningside Heights of Manhattan almost deliberately to distance itself from the immigrants, but by a nice irony William Parsons, a trustee of the university, helped to design and fund the subway up to the West Side which had the unintended consequence of making Columbia physically accessible to those poor Jews.

Harvard was likewise within reach of the 80,000-strong Jewish community of Boston, and in the first two decades of the century Jewish enrolment rose sharply, to 20 per cent. The college could scarcely remove itself physically from Cambridge. And so, Harvard began to introduce quotas. Abbott L. Lowell, president of the college, proposed, and the Board of Overseers accepted, 'methods for more efficiently sifting candidates for admission', which patently meant controlling the number of Jews. When a Jewish Harvard man protested, Lowell did not deny what he was doing, but said, 'If their numbers should become 40 per cent of the student body, the race feeling would become intense.' Meeting Victor Kramer, another alumnus, during a long delay on the Boston to New York train, Lowell was even more candid: 'Jews and Christians at Harvard just don't mix.' The Jews ought to become Christians: 'To be an American is to be nothing else.'

This sharp controversy was resolved, after a rather sordid fashion: although formal quotas were forsworn, the fact that Jewish numbers at Harvard in the 1930s had fallen back to 10 per cent suggested a discreet informal quota instead. But the affair sent out tremors. Not merely did it raise the spectres of privilege and prejudice, it caused rifts within Jewry, and raised other spectres of Jewish subservience and self-hatred. 'One of the saddest features of the whole matter', to Louis Marshall, lay 'in the fact that some of our Jewish snobs are openly favouring a limitation which would exclude a large percentage of the Russian Jews'. He was thinking of men like Julian Morgenstern, president of the Hebrew Union College which was the rabbinical school of Reform Judaism, who thought that the problem lay with the 'not yet American Jew' who was going to college a generation too early.

And he was thinking of Walter Lippmann. The reaction to quotas and other forms of discrimination might be protest, or defiance – or acquiescence. This was the path Lippmann chose. He had been born into the old *haute juiverie* of uptown New York, German Jews who worshipped at the Emanu-El Reform synagogue on Fifth Avenue and 43rd Street and sent their sons to the expensive Sachs School. He grew up in 'a gilded Jewish ghetto', passionately assimilationist and American, and quite cut off from the horde of poor Yiddish-speaking Jews flooding into New York. In 1906 Lippmann went to Harvard, at that time noisily snobbish and quietly antisemitic. He wrote back to his school magazine that 'at Harvard class distinction counts for nothing'. This was an early exercise in denying the truth, and Lippmann soon found that the grander clubs were closed to him as a Jew; but then denial was to become part of his make-up. In his last year at college, Lippmann led a revolt of the Harvard Yard plebeians against the patricians of Mount Auburn Street who controlled the Institute of 1770 and thus the social activities of the whole college. The revolt was successful, but an aberration on the part of Lippmann, who would never again 'seriously challenge a system of discrimination that excluded people on the grounds of race or religion'. Twenty-five years later he could tell the widow of a friend at a class reunion that her husband had been one of the first gentiles to show kindness to him; such private confessions apart, Lippmann's whole life consisted in suppressing and denying these memories.

His career was astonishingly precocious and successful. Lippmann soon became the most influential and fashionable pundit of his age, turning himself into what he remained: a grave public commentator, who wore the cloak of responsibility with heavy self-consciousness, who walked with the mighty and gave them his reflective and sage support. In his twenties he was one of the founding team of the liberal-progressive *New Republic*. He publicly supported Louis Brandeis when he was the first Jew nominated to the Supreme Court in 1916 and was bitterly attacked, not least from Harvard, where Lowell organised a petition of eminent Bostonians against the appointment of the Boston Jewish lawyer. After this flourish, Lippmann's course of political as well as social assimilation continued. He married a parson's daughter, he joined the best clubs, usually as the solitary Jew, he took no interest whatever in Judaism, Jewish social movements, or Zionism.

So much of an American was he, so good a Harvard man, that Lippmann took a highly equivocal line over the Harvard quota. There was a short answer, then and later in the age when quotas reappeared in the guise of 'affirmative action'. The composer Alexander Glazunov, a good musician and a decent man as well as a hopeless alcoholic, was director of the St Petersburg conservatoire. When a Tsarist official once asked him how many Jews there were at the conservatoire, Glazunov replied simply, 'I don't know. We don't count.' But that admirable answer eluded Lippmann, as it has eluded so many others before and since. He conceded that a quota would be an abandonment of principle, but (it was always 'but' with him) it would also be 'bad for the immigrant Jews as well as for Harvard if there were too great a concentration'. He suggested ways 'to persuade Jewish boys to scatter', he agreed with the Harvard authorities that 'a concentration of Jews in excess of 15 per cent will produce a segregation of cultures rather than a fusion'. And he said – not for the first time or the last – that 'I do not regard the Jews as innocent victims. They hand on unconsciously and uncritically from one generation to another many distressing personal and social habits, which were selected by a bitter history and intensified by a pharisaical theology.'

Lippmann made a great conscious as well as unconscious effort to distance himself emotionally from his origins. He could sometimes speak about the Jews in the tones of the Irish land-owner who replied to threats from the Fenians, 'Be assured that nothing you may do to my land agent will in any way intimidate me.' Lippmann never wavered from his belief that the Jews were the architects of at least some of their own misfortunes. Because the Jews were 'fairly distinct in their physical appearance and in the spelling of their names ... they are, therefore, conspicuous', and so 'sharp trading and blatant vulgarity are more conspicuous in the Jew'. And he repeated the well-worn charge that 'the rich vulgar and pretentious Jews of our big American cities are perhaps the greatest misfortune that has ever befallen the Jewish People. They are the real fountain of antisemitism.'

That was written in 1922, and even then 'ever befallen' showed a curious sense of Jewish history. Within a dozen years it was clear that there was something worse in the offing than hostile reaction provoked by the ostentatious display of Broadway on a Sunday. Lippmann believed that Germany had been treated oppressively at Versailles, and had justifiable grievances. Up to 1933, and even well after, this belief was common among enlightened liberal opinion in the West (and largely explains the policy of appeasement which is so much condemned with hindsight). But Lippmann's analysis did not stop there. In May 1933 he wrote with his chilly even-handedness that National Socialist aggression against other European countries might be held in check by several factors, not excluding the persecution of the Jews, which, 'by satisfying the lust of the Nazis who feel they must conquer somebody and the cupidity of those Nazis who want jobs, is a kind of lightning conductor which protects Europe'. A week later he wrote again about Hitler. Despite the brutalities already committed by his regime, through the 'hysteria and animal passions of a great revolution' could be heard 'the authentic voice of a genuinely civilised people'. Any people had its dark and light side, evil and good; those who wanted to judge the Germans by cruel stormtroopers should ask whether it was fair to judge the French by the Terror, Protestantism by the Ku Klux Klan, or 'the Jews by their parvenus'.

This was too much for Felix Frankfurter. The famous jurist, Harvard professor and later justice of the Supreme Court had been a friend of Lippmann's for many years; they had fought side by side on behalf of Brandeis's Supreme Court nomination. Now he wrote to Lippmann in bitter reproach, saying that 'something inside of me snapped' when he read those words. Certainly Frankfurter, like Brandeis, shared none of Lippmann's hang-ups. Brandeis had been the forerunner, not only demonstrating how far a Jew could rise in America but laying down the cardinal principles for the future: you could be a good American while being a Zionist, and you could be a good Zionist without intending to settle in the Land of Israel.

Frankfurter basked in the same self-confidence. He too was a Zionist, chosen to represent Zionist interests at the Paris Peace Conference in 1919. Well before those strange columns of 1933, he must have resented Lippmann's antipathy to Zionism, especially the way he expressed it: just as 'Jew-baiting produced the ghetto and is compelling Zionism, the bad economic habits of the Jew, his exploiting of simple people, has caused his victims to assert their own nationality'. Lippmann had been asked to review a Zionist book, Leon Simon's *Studies in Jewish Nationalism*, for the *Menorah Journal*. The review was never published: Lippmann delivered it, and then withdrew it. Perhaps he thought it was too revealing. He recognised that 'I am obviously one of the Jews whom Mr Simon deplores, regrets, shakes his head at, and regards as "The Problem", one of those assimilated creatures to whom the Jewish past has no very peculiar intimate appeal, who find their cultural roots where they can, have no sense of belonging to a Chosen People, and tremble at the suggestion that God has imprudently put all his best eggs in one tribal basket'.

Following the line of Brandeis, American Zionists had not rejected but embraced the charge of dual allegiance: they would be Jewish-Americans and Zionist Jews all at once. To Lippmann, this was 'other-worldliness of a peculiarly dangerous sort', resting as it did on a belief that while Jews settled in Palestine could integrate body and soul, 'the extra-Palestinian Jew is to keep his body in one place and to attach his mind somewhere else'. It seemed no tragedy to Lippmann, as it did to the Zionists, that western Jews were dissolved into their communities: 'It is a splendid thing to build Zion in Palestine, but it is no less splendid to fulfil the American dream.'

However much many American Jews might have recoiled from Lippmann's self-hating strictures, most also shared his lack of enthusiasm for Zionism in practice. The American movement was seriously weakened in 1921 when the Zionists split at the Cleveland convention. The group led by Brandeis and Frankfurter – assimilated and, in terms of Zionist politics, moderate – were defeated by a more radical and aggressive faction. Brandeis resigned, and the organisation slumped. By 1918, following the Balfour Declaration, the Zionist Organisation of America could claim 200,000 members; a decade later the figure was 22,000, or back where it had been a few years before Balfour. The international movement despaired of America. As one historian put it, 'convinced that American Jews lacked Jewish spirit, many eastern European Zionists viewed them simply as a source of funds'; or, in a contemporary joke, a Zionist was a person who solicited money from another person to send a third person to Palestine – a portent of relations to come between Israel and American Jewry.

There were contrary signs of a new political consciousness in Jewish America, especially in New York. A rally was held at Madison Square Garden in November 1930 to protest against the Passfield White Paper. Mayor Jimmy Walker said that 'there are more Jews in New York than in any other city in the world, and the message that the mayor of that city sends to Downing Street is that I wish we had twice as many', rhetoric which might have sounded rather more convincing if the American gates had not recently been so firmly shut. And a few years later Harold Laski saw the American Jews as deserving 'a study all to themselves' (an omission, if it was one, which would certainly be rectified before long), but worried that Zionism might have 'done them harm rather than good by making them less integrally a part of America'. This was scarcely true in the 1930s, though it might have been written with foresight.

At the time it was rather a case of most American Jews' practical indifference to Zionism, and dedication to integration in their own country. And there they had two advantages. There was the sheer newness and kaleidoscopic diversity of American culture which meant that Jewish alienation and otherness could never be the problem they had been in Europe, and that there was never in America a 'Jewish Question' on the European pattern. Despite a very real climate of hostility from cultural nativists, who thought that Jewish immigrants had polluted or at least diluted American civilisation, Wagner's argument that the Jews could never be truly rooted in a national culture simply did not apply in this new-found land. If 'the real American folksong is a rag', then blacks or Jews were at least as much part of that folk as any Yankee. And there was the astonishing Jewish-American success story, the like of which Jewish history had never seen. The two themes came together in one place: Hollywood.

In 1908, the Yiddish newspaper *Forward* had lamented the decline of Yiddish music halls in New York. Instead, 'there are now about a hundred movie houses in New York, many of them in the Jewish quarter . . . people must have entertainment, and five cents is little to pay'. Soon the new entertainment had swept the country, and then the world. The period from the Great War to the 1950s was dominated by two mass mediums, radio and cinema (their dominance only ended when another medium came along which combined, though in a lower form, the immediacy of the one and the hypnotic visual imagery of the other). In America, radio was largely run by Jews, but then radio was by definition a national medium limited to a local culture and language.

The movies were universal. Nothing else in the twentieth century had quite the impact on the consciousness of the human race. Stalin recognised this when he said once that if he could control Hollywood he could control the world. This extraordinary business was soon taken over by a small group of Jewish entrepreneurs: Adolph Zukor, born in a Hungarian village, Louis B. Mayer, born in a Russian shtetl, the Warner Brothers, born in Poland, Carl Laemmle, born in Germany; all brought to America when young, to join others like William Fox and Harry Cohn, the sons of recent immigrants. Their infant industry had taken itself off to southern California, in search of regular sunlight (which, as it happened, studios and artificial lighting quickly made unnecessary). Here they brought to perfection their new popular art, or at least entertainment, and here they created a discrete society. It was to an astonishing extent a Jewish society. The moguls who commanded the industry were served by a corps of producers; in 1936, an observer reckoned, fifty-three out of eighty-five men engaged in production were Jewish. So were many of a larger, ill-regarded brigade of screen writers, so were large numbers of directors, technicians, actors, musicians who worked in the movies. Non-Jews knew whom they were working for, whether they cheerfully took this as a test of their own worth, like Sir Ambrose Abercrombie in *The Loved One* – 'Your five-to-two is a judge of quality' – or saw Hollywood, in F. Scott Fitzgerald's sour phrase, as 'a Jewish holiday, a gentile tragedy'.

It was not always a happy holiday. Those who had created Hollywood were rarely at ease with themselves as Jews. Considering who made them, Hollywood films were quite strikingly empty of Jewish themes or even Jewish echoes. The very first talking film was *The Jazz Singer* in 1927, in which Al Jolson plays the son of a cantor to a New York synagogue. The son becomes a nightclub singer; his father's heart is broken, and he cannot sing the 'Kol Nidre', the prayer for forgiveness on the Day of Atonement; the congregation wants the son to take over, but on that holiest of days he is opening on Broadway; and so to the sentimental climax. Warners made a few other Jewish films, *Sailor Izzy Murphy* and *Ginsberg the Great*; then nothing. For decades Hollywood portrayed almost every aspect of American life, or at least its own version of American life. One movie after another had pious preachers, or kindly priests (always played by Pat O'Brien). But no rabbis, no more cantors, scarcely any allusion to Jewry. Twenty years after *The Jazz Singer*, in a brief period of social-conscience films, Zanuck made *Gentleman's Agreement*. But, although this somewhat prim and self-congratulatory denunciation of antisemitism received an Oscar, it was the rule-proving exception. Few of the Jews who made Hollywood publicly denied their heritage. They were famously nepotistic, as commemorated in several classic Hollywood jokes: 'Uncle Carl Laemmle | Has a very large faemmle', 'The son-in-law also rises', and what M-G-M supposedly stood for in Yiddish: '*Mayers ganze mishpoche*' ('Mayer's whole family'). But they made little parade of their Jewishness.

After visiting the Holy Land, Kipling wrote a strange poem, 'The Burden of Jerusalem', about the atavistic quarrel 'Twixt Sarah's son and Hagar's child | That centred round Jerusalem'. The poem remained unpublished in Kipling's lifetime and for decades after, although Churchill sent Roosevelt a copy during the war. It expressed Kipling's own complicated feelings towards 'The Unloved Race', who 'amass their dividends' while 'at the last | They stood beside each tyrant's grave, | And whispered of Jerusalem'. And yet when he further illustrated this age-old visceral yearning in the words 'For 'neath the Rabbi's curls and furs | (Or scents and rings of movie-kings) | The aloof, unleavened bread of Ur, | Broods steadfastly on Jerusalem', he was wide of the mark as far as the movie-kings went. Few of them even identified with Jewish causes. One studio mogul is supposed to have told a Jewish fund-raiser that the Irish and the Jews were responsible for most of the world's troubles, and Harry Cohn, asked to contribute to a Jewish relief fund, said, 'Relief *for* the Jews! How about relief *from* the Jews?'

Before long there was a cause which captured the imagination of the Jewish salariat of the Hollywood studios, but it was not Judaism, Jewish humanism or Zionism, it was Communism. In the late 1930s, after a successful recruiting drive by the party's cultural commissar, V. J. Jerome, well over half the Hollywood Communist party was Jewish, with unhappy consequences for the image of Jewish America when the anti-Communist purges began in the following decade. Apart from the usual motives which drove clever men and women, not least Jews, into Communism, there was the added feeling of guilt among script-writers who felt that they were prostituting themselves by turning out commercial tripe for very large salaries and could atone for this in turn by joining the Party. Their feelings about themselves were famously expressed by Budd Schulberg in his short story, 'What Makes Sammy Run?', about an ambitious and unprincipled first-generation Jew fighting his way up the Hollywood ladder. When Schulberg raised his hero from the decent obscurity of a short story in a magazine to a novel, it caused storms in the two communities to which the writer belonged, Jewish Hollywood and the Communist party. That was not surprising: the book was a powerful if not very subtle study of Jewish alienation, of the ostensibly emancipated and successful Jew in rebellion against the gods of his fathers, not to say his father and God. Sammy turns on his devout father: 'While you was being such a goddam good Jew, who was hustlin' up the dough to pay the rent?'

By the time Schulberg's novel was published in 1941, this sort of Jewish angst and self-laceration was horribly overshadowed by events. Hollywood had been that much more complacent, or at least ignorant, than the rest of Jewish America about the coming of National Socialism. 'Who *is* Hitler?' Carl Laemmle asked a newly arrived German Jew at a cocktail party, his question prompted not by other outrages so much as by the news that in his own home town of Laupheim, a street which had been proudly named after him had just been renamed after the new German dictator. Irving Thalberg went to Germany in 1934, and returned confident that 'Hitler and Hitlerism will pass; the Jews will still be there'. Louis B. Mayer did not go to Germany himself but asked his friend William Randolph Hearst to talk to Hitler, and was reassured when Hearst told him that Hitler's motives were decent.

This grotesque exchange was an example, albeit an extreme one, of the mood of deliberate oblivion which gripped many American Jews in the 1930s, from Lippmann with his nervosity about condemning National Socialists – or condemning them more strongly than Jewish parvenus – to the febrile hedonism of Hollywood. And yet even there it was possible for Jewish nationalism to strike a chord, and find an ally. One such ally was a surprising figure. Ben Hecht was no poor Jew from the Lower East Side but an assimilated son of a prosperous mid-western family who became a cynical, hardbitten journalist. His play *The Front Page* was a classic of cynical, hardbitten journalism and, literally, of gallows humour. Hecht also wrote his novel *A Jew in Love* in the same spirit of smart, tough mockery, to the point where some took it as an example of self-hating caricature.

Then Hecht found himself. 'Although I had never lived "as a Jew" or even among Jews,' he wrote, in words reminiscent of Moses Hess, 'my family remained like a homeland in my heart.' Before long Hecht was a Revisionist Zionist activist. This was a reaction to what he saw around him. Working in Hollywood in the 1930s, he became more and more conscious of the way that the leading American Jews, 'social, political and literary', were reluctant to speak out as Jews under attack and preferred to conduct themselves as 'neutral Americans'. It was quite true that most Jews there in the 1930s were trying to become, and remain, Americans. Many were politically active, but (as has been suggested of Marx himself) they transferred their Jewish concerns into the class politics of the Left rather than diverted it to Jewish nationalism. Not only in Hollywood but on the east coast, Jews played a disproportionate part in far-left politics, although not all were Stalinists. In New York, much more than in London or Paris, there was a lively and influential, albeit numerically small, Trotskyist movement. Indeed it was said that New York in the 1930s and 1940s was the most interesting part of the Soviet Union, since it was there alone that the conflict between Stalinist and Trotskyist Bolshevism was conducted noisily in public. And those who conducted it were mostly Jewish.

So had been many of the Bolsheviks in Russia itself, too many for their own good. The October Revolution had given a new stimulus to antisemitism in the West, which was shaken by revolution, expropriation and terror. A high proportion of the Bolsheviks were Jews, most notably Leon Trotsky whose *nom de guerre* concealed his original name of Bronstein but scarcely disguised his origins. This did not escape notice; it kindled much hatred in return, and even saw a reprise of a classic antisemitic fantasy. 'The Protocols of the Elders of Zion' was a fabrication which purported to set forth a great world-wide Jewish conspiracy. It had circulated in Russia before the war and made its way west after. It was a comment on the climate of the time that the 'Protocols' were taken seriously by *The Times* in May 1920, and that the editor of another London paper, H. A. Gwynne of the *Morning Post*, wrote a respectful introduction to them. Even Winston Churchill – in whose extraordinary and chequered career philosemitism was generally a fixed point – could denounce 'the international Jews'. Their 'world-wide conspiracy' was dedicated to 'the overthrow of civilisation', he wrote in 1920, and warned of 'the international Soviet of the Russian and the Polish Jew', as well as of a 'very powerful' lobby of English Jews. This was a man who had and was to have many Jewish friends and associates, Weizmann among them. The aberration can only be understood in terms of the violent anti-Bolshevik mood in which Churchill was caught up.

Those who visited Russia and were disillusioned by the reality of Communism were sometimes infected by antisemitism in the process. Malcolm Muggeridge went to Russia in 1931. He was disgusted by the famine, the terror, the lying; and by the sort of people who had risen to the top, 'petty Jewish Foreign Office officials', and other Jews who participated so heartlessly or even enthusiastically in the terror. The phrase comes from Muggeridge's barely fictionalised account of his visit, *Winter in Moscow*. Towards the end of the book, Wraithby, the author's point-of-view character or alter ego, finds himself arguing with a Russian-Jewish woman.

' "Supposing two or three million peasants do die this winter," the Jewess said mechanically, getting up. "What of it?"

'She was off to a lecture on The Film and the Class Struggle. As she revolved with the revolving hotel doors, red lips flashing like a lighthouse lamp, Wraithby understood pogroms.'[1]

All of this was to prove bitterly ironic. Marxism, certainly in its Communist or Bolshevik-Leninist variety, proved the cruellest of all false dawns. At first the Soviet regime preached an end to the Jewish Question by a complete equality of the peoples. The Bund, the Jewish movement which had combined socialism with Yiddishkeit, was suppressed by the Communists along with every other political party or movement apart from Communism itself. And the Communists early on adopted a policy of unremitting hostility towards Zionism. It was spelled out by a senior apparatchik, Michael Kalinin, president of the Great Russian Republic, in 1926: 'I consider that it would be absolutely inadmissible from the point of view of the Soviet regime that the Jewish toiling masses should desert us in search of happiness elsewhere [loud applause]. Comrades, I hold that the Soviet Union should be the fatherland, ten times a more real fatherland for the Jewish masses, than any bourgeois Palestine [loud applause].' This, applause and all, remained Soviet policy even when a Communist party was organised in Palestine.

But cultural autonomy was encouraged among Yiddish-speaking

---

[1] When it was proposed to reissue the book forty years later, the distinguished historian Leonard Schapiro told Muggeridge that he could not write a new introduction because of this antisemitism, much as he otherwise admired the book.

citizens of the Soviet Union. Jews were settled on the land, and the antisemitic propaganda among the peasantry which this rekindled was vigorously suppressed. And, in a strange, doomed experiment, a Jewish autonomous republic was created in the far east of Siberia, in Birobidzhan. It was hoped that this project would attract financial and moral support among western, principally American, Jews, and it was intended also, in the words of Alexander Chemirsky, one of its apostles, that 'the autonomous Jewish territory will be the heaviest blow to the Zionists and religious ideology'. Building a Zion without Zionism was a tricky feat. Enthusiasts for the scheme continually lapsed into language which echoed Zionism: '*Zu a Yiddish Land*' ('Towards a Jewish State') or, paraphrasing Herzl, 'If you want it – then you will achieve it.'

Before long the autonomists were forced in the best Soviet style to recant their crypto-Zionism. That was only a taste of what was to come. By the 1930s, Stalin's personal dictatorship was complete. He turned savagely on his comrades, especially on the Old Bolsheviks who had made the revolution. A disproportionately high number of these were Jewish, a disproportionately high number of Stalin's victims were thus also Jewish. This scarcely worried Stalin himself, a man who, for all that from well before the revolution he had been the Bolsheviks' chief expert on the national question, was in his heart a deep-dyed Jew-hater. And so, along with Zinoviev and Kamenev (and Trotsky assassinated in exile), along with Chemirsky and other leaders of Soviet Jewry scores of thousands of Jews were 'purged', that euphemism for extermination which Soviet Socialism added to the language. The Birobidzhan project struggled on. Religion revived surreptitiously, and a synagogue was even built in 1947, to be burned down in 1956. Two years later, Stalin's successor Khrushchev declared the project a failure, and attributed this to Jewish individualism and incapacity for agriculture.

Many western Jews nevertheless remained in thrall to the 'socialist idea', which had struck roots in Palestine also. A few like Koestler oscillated between Communism and Zionism or even tried to combine the two. Most practical Zionists were not Communists, but called themselves socialists and combined their Jewish patriotism with collectivism, in the kibbutz movement or the larger Labour movement in Palestine. Labour Zionism rejected Jabotinsky's militant rhetoric. Instead of winning the land by blood and fire, they wanted to win it 'dunam by dunam, goat by goat', gradually acquiring land from the

Arabs who were often keen enough to sell it. Their slogans were Hebrew Land, Hebrew Labour and Hebrew Defence, though the implications of those principles were not fully understood outside Palestine at the time.

'Hebrew Labour' in particular had a noble ring to it, until examined more closely. It seemed admirable that Jewish immigrants should do their own manual work rather than employing cheaper Arab workers. At the same time, the Labour movement as it had developed was everywhere tinged with racism in practice if not in theory. By definition, unions are combinations designed to preserve or promote the interests of comparatively privileged workers when there is always someone available to do the same work for less money. Early in the twentieth century, the labour unions in California had prevented the immigration of Chinese workers. The 'White Australia' policy which governed immigration to that country from the 1890s to the 1970s was purely a creation of the labour movement, concerned about cheap Asiatic workers undercutting Europeans. Where appropriate, the British Labour movement ensured that its members were protected from non-white competition, British seamen from Lascars, or Indian seamen, for example. And, most dramatic of all, the Labour movement on the South African gold mines fiercely fought both capitalist and black workers, a struggle culminating in the great Rand Revolt of 1922 when a miners' strike turned into armed rebellion under the slogan 'Workers of the World Unite and Fight for a White South Africa'.

None of these comparisons can have occurred to the exponents of Hebrew Labour in the early days. For that matter, very little was known of life in the Yishuv by western Jews at the time, for most of whom it was an attractive but very remote idea. The membership of the Zionist Organisation of America, which had slumped in the 1920s, rose sharply in the 1930s, but this was in response to events not in the Levant, but in Europe. The man responsible for transforming the story was not Herzl, Weizmann or Jabotinsky, but Adolf Hitler.

12

To the gates of Hell

If thou, Lord, wilt be extreme to mark what
is done amiss: O Lord, who may abide it?

Ps.cxxx.3

Just at the moment when political Zionism had enjoyed its first triumph with the Balfour Declaration, the old order had come to an end. The European empires were broken up and replaced by new, ostensibly rational, modern states. In Germany, one of the defenders of the Jews against Treitschke's polemical abuse had been the great ancient historian Theodor Mommsen. It was Mommsen who had once expressed the noble but defeated resignation of good German liberals when he said, 'My greatest wish was to live in a free German republic, but failing that I wrote the History of Rome.' In 1919, Mommsen's wish came true; and the free German republic proved yet another false dawn, for the Jews above all.

A large part of Germany never accepted the moral validity of the republic whose constitution was drafted at Weimar. Many Germans believed that it had been born in dishonour, out of a treacherous surrender in 1918, the army 'stabbed in the back'. Unreconciled reactionaries sneered at the republic, and at its red-black-yellow flag whose colours were said to represent the 'Reds', the Roman Catholics, and the Jews. In a sense this was true: the democratic parties which supported the republic were the Social Democrats, the Centre or Catholic party, and the Progressive party which was largely Jewish in leadership. The republic was attacked from Left and Right, by the Communists and by the nationalist and radical parties of the right.

One of these swept the others aside, the National Socialist German Workers' Party. Although German by name, its leader Adolf Hitler was Austrian, and had learned all his politics in Vienna – his nationalism from Schönerer, his antisemitism and appeal to the 'little man' from Lueger. He went further than either. However brutal and revolting the antisemitism of turn-of-century politics had been, it had often also been more calculated than heartfelt. That was true of Lueger with his 'I decide who's a Jew', echoed by his successor as leader of the Austrian Christian Socialists, Monsignor Seipel, who dismissed his party's antisemitic policy with the words '*Das ist für die Gasse*' – 'that's for the streets'. Hitler *was* '*die Gasse*', the streets incarnate. And his Jew-hatred was passionately sincere. After his abortive putsch in 1923 he was imprisoned and wrote his testament, *Mein Kampf (My Struggle)*. His greatest struggle was against the Jews, the theme which obsessively dominated the book.

To most German Jews in the early 1920s, Hitler was an obscure madman whom they could ignore. Indeed throughout the Weimar years, the German Jews seemed to enjoy another golden age. Antisemites who claimed that Weimar culture was 'Jewish culture' were not far wrong. Jewish writers, musicians, theatre directors flourished as rarely before. In the new and diminished Austrian republic, a chill wind had begun to blow. The great Viennese composer Arnold Schoenberg found this on holiday at a mountain resort where the hotel he wanted to stay at asked him for a certificate of baptism. But he happily settled in Berlin in 1926 to teach and compose, Jewish writers were prominent as ever there, many or even most large newspapers and department stores were Jewish-owned. Despite the assassination of the revolutionary leader Rosa Luxemburg and of Rathenau, the Jews believed that their position was secure. So much so that few of them saw the way that this identification of Weimar with Jewry threatened themselves.

The German Jews had tried so hard to identify with the nation, the people and its culture. They had fought, bled and died for the Fatherland in numbers at least commensurate with the Jewish proportion of the German population, as Jewish spokesmen continually pointed out. It did them no good. The most ardent manifestations of patriotism backfired. One case was Rathenau, with his impossibly complex attitude to his own Jewishness and his frank admiration for the tough German nationalism which was in the end to murder him. Almost more poignant a case was Maximilian Harden. His review, the

Zukunft, had once been a savage and irreverent critic of the Kaiser's government. He and it had moved steadily towards the jingo right, until the day came when he could hymn the German invasion of Belgium in 1914. This inspired the contempt of Karl Kraus,[1] who had once been an admiring friend of Harden's. But that did not prevent Harden from being beaten almost to death by antisemitic louts in 1921, nor the court's subsequently deciding that Harden's unpatriotic writings extenuated the beatings.

Despite this, despite the crescendo of hatred throughout the 1920s, the German Jews continued to delude themselves. Why they did so may be explained by a bitter phrase of A. J. P. Taylor's. Antisemitism was the great animating passion of Hitler's life, 'the one thing in which he persistently and genuinely believed from his beginning in Munich until his last days in the bunker. His advocacy of it would have deprived him of support, let alone power, in a civilised country.' Many German Jews' deepest instinctive conviction was that Germany was a civilised country; *ergo*, an antisemitic movement could not come to power there.

In February 1933 they were proved wrong. Hitler's New Order was something undreamt of by anti-Dreyfusards or Lueger; or for that matter by Zionists as much as by confident assimilated Jews. His triumph in the most 'advanced' of European nations, as so many had thought it, left European Jewry emotionally shattered as well as physically threatened. The clouds darkened for the European Jews throughout the 1930s. In some countries like Poland and Hungary it was the traditional, nationalist brand of antisemitism, often encouraged by the Catholic church. In 1936, the Catholic Primate of Poland wrote in a pastoral letter, 'There will be the Jewish problem as long as the Jews remain ... It is a fact that the Jews are fighting against the Catholic church, persisting in free thinking, and are the vanguard of godlessness, Bolshevism, and subversion.'

By these standards – by any standards – Hitler was different. Any number of traditions of Jew-hatred found their culmination in him, magnified with demonic force. Religious contempt had been bred into Europe for centuries, and Hitler could draw on that tradition even though he was profoundly pagan, almost as contemptuous of Christianity as of Judaism. He was indeed that 'Satan or sinful

---

[1] As much as did Harden's abstruse and pompous prose style, which Kraus mocked in the *Fackel* by quoting it, with translation into intelligible German, under the heading 'Desperanto'.

pantheism' whose conquest, Heine had predicted, would bring a tempest of persecution the Jews had never known. Hitler summed up every brand of social, political and economic antisemitism; the word was made flesh. And Hitler seemed the final answer to the assimilationists. For decades they had scorned Zionists who said that the Jewish Question was insoluble without a Jewish state. Assimilationists had preached that the progress of mankind would end these absurd, mediaeval passions. The preachers were now baffled. Karl Kraus had spoken for assimilationists, and for the culture of the German language, which he loved as dearly as he despised political nationalism. He had condemned Zionism as 'the unpleasant spectacle of clumsy hands scratching at the 2000-year-old grave of an extinct people'. He now faced the same threat as those people about his kinship with whom he had always been so equivocal.

The Jews did not seem extinct to Hitler who, on the contrary, wished to extinguish them. And so like others – other assimilationists, others who were called 'self-hating', others who had tried to evade the issue – Kraus was forced to take sides. He did not retreat into further evasion. In April 1933, a German radio station, now under the jurisdiction of the New Order, wrote asking permission to broadcast Kraus's celebrated translations of Shakespeare. He replied that he would want to spare the station any embarrassment in view of current regulations governing cultural criticism in Germany: 'We thus wish to call your attention to the fact that this translation of Shakespeare's sonnets was made from the Hebrew.'

This was droll enough; but what use was Kraus's Viennese irony now to that 'extinct people' threatened with real as opposed to metaphorical extinction? He answered himself, in a much-quoted sentence. '*Mir fällt zu Hitler nichts ein*': 'I can't think of anything to say about Hitler', or, 'Hitler leaves me speechless'. Here was all the old sardonic weariness – and in one way it was not hard to see what Kraus meant. There is a sense in which the phenomenon of Hitler left and still leaves everyone speechless. And yet Kraus's mordant phrase was also a groan of cosmic despair. Thirty-five years earlier Kraus had poured his scorn on Herzl in *Eine Krone für Zion*. Now another product of late-Habsburg Vienna had taken power in Berlin, determined to implement the pan-German scheme he had learned from Schönerer by absorbing Austria in the Reich (which he accomplished not long after Kraus's death), and to take the antisemitic programme he had learned from the Christian Socialists further than Lueger had even dreamed of. What now could Kraus say to Herzl's shade? The least he could do was to ensure that *A Crown for Zion* was not published again in his lifetime.

Not only Kraus was silenced. Hitler appeared to answer every other of the liberal and assimilationist critics of Zionism. He answered the German, Ernst Lissauer, who had deplored the radicalism of too many German Jews but insisted that Jewish alienation would end when the last barriers of prejudice had inevitably come down, and Rabbi Vogelstein, who had conceded that a Jewish state had been needed in Biblical times to foster the birth of monotheistic religion, but was now quite unnecessary. He answered Englishmen like Claude Montefiore, insisting that liberal Jews did not wish to pray for the restoration of the Jews to Palestine, and Americans like Rabbi Isaac Wise, with his 'modern Jew' who looks upon his own country as Palestine.

Above all, Hitler seemed to answer those like Kraus who had called Zionism a new form of antisemitism; or like Joseph Reinach, who said that Zionism was a trap set by antisemites for innocent or thoughtless Jews; or like Laurie Magnus, who said that Zionists stimulated the antisemitism they claimed to oppose. Whatever else he was, Hitler was not a product of Zionism, nor National Socialism a reaction against the writings of Herzl and Nordau, or the activities of Weizmann. Year by year after he came to power Hitler advanced his great obsession, from the first harassment of Jews to their exclusion from public life, to the 'Aryanisation' of business to the Nuremberg Laws of 1935 – racist decrees of a kind western Europe had not known for centuries – to the great *Kristallnacht* pogrom of 1938, which in kind and degree western Europe had not seen the like of since the Middle Ages. It would have been grotesque to claim that all this was a response to *The Jewish State*, or what was then a small and embattled Jewish settlement in Palestine. It seemed far truer to say, not that Hitler was a reaction against Zionism, but that he was its final justification, the conclusive proof that the Jews would never live at peace and at ease in exile, that the Jewish Question was unanswerable except by the creation of a Jewish state, and the Jews must find their own destiny. Hitler did not, in the years up to 1939, convert all Jews everywhere to Zionism. But he gave the project an entirely new impetus.

He also seemed to take sides in the debate within Zionism. General and Labour Zionists implied that a Jewish homeland could be established without force. As late as 1938 Albert Einstein hoped for 'reasonable agreement with the Arabs on the basis of living together in peace' rather than a Jewish state. 'My awareness of the essential nature of Judaism resists the idea of a Jewish state with borders, an army and a measure of temporal power, no matter how modest. I am afraid of the inner damage Judaism may suffer – especially from the development of a narrow nationalism within our own ranks.' This was an echo of the fears expressed ever since Tolstoy. It was what Gandhi now said when he reprobated the use of force on behalf of Zionism. It was what many Zionists themselves said, hoping against hope that force could be avoided. They included the Jews of the settlement in Palestine, most of whom were horrified by the violence between Zionists and Arabs, many of whom still thought of a Jewish homeland rather than a Jewish state and did not advocate a Jewish majority inside that homeland, and some of whom continued until the 1940s to abjure the use of force except in the most narrowly defined terms of self-defence, if even then. The Haganah stuck to its policy of havlagah, or 'restraint', in the face of armed attack.

In contrast, Jabotinsky's position remained resolute. He had always taunted those who believed Zion could be won with sweet talk and goodwill. To him, the idea of restraint was absurd. As he said, 'It is impossible to dream of a voluntary agreement between us and the Arabs . . . Not now, and not in the foreseeable future . . . Every nation civilised or primitive, sees its land as its national home, where it wants to stay as the sole landlord forever. Such a nation will never willingly consent to new landlords or even to partnership.' His words were a challenge to the Arabs, but even more of a challenge to the illusions of moderate Zionists. His logic remained remorseless. Either Zionism was in principle moral or it was not. If morally sound, then others' opposition did not affect that principle. Jabotinsky went straight to the points which other Zionists evaded: a Jewish majority must be established in Palestine as soon as possible, with the object of creating a Jewish state. And force should be used if and when required. Spiritual Zionism was a pretty idea, but what could it do for the Jews in their suffering, here and now? Jabotinsky might have echoed Stalin's famous question about the Pope: How many divisions had Ahad Ha-am or Judah Magnes?

As Hitler's persecution intensified, as the pressure mounted of Jews wanting to escape from it, to Palestine or to anywhere, Jabotinsky's own position hardened. He saw clearly that the Jews of Europe were facing 'a disaster of historic magnitude', as he told the Royal Commission on Palestine in 1937. And he attributed this not to 'the antisemitism of men' but to 'the antisemitism of things, the inherent xenophobia of the body social or the body economic'. In his submission to the Commission he not only made his haunting comparison between the claims of Arabs and Jews to the Holy Land as the difference between demands of appetite and the demand of hunger, he also embarrassed other Zionists by insisting that the Jews must have the whole of the Land of Israel rather than part: 'A corner of Palestine, a "canton", how can we promise to be satisfied with it? We cannot. We never can. Should we swear to you that we would be satisfied, it would be a lie.'

All this may have been said with intellectual honesty. But Jabotinsky suffered from his own delusions, at least if he meant what he said: 'Tell the Arabs the truth, and then you will see that the Arab is reasonable, the Arab is clever, the Arab is just; the Arab *can* realise that since there are three or four or five wholly Arab States, then it is a thing of justice which Great Britain is doing if Palestine is transformed into a Jewish State.' This justice was not evident to the Palestinian Arabs. They did not see why they should atone for the antisemitism either of men or of things in Europe. Even after Hitler came to power, it would have been a Palestinian of remarkably altruistic disposition who wanted to hand over the country to the Jews as a refuge. And, as Jabotinsky with all his apparent ruthlessness and intellectual clarity failed to see, part of the tragedy of the Zionist project was that it coincided with another national consciousness coming to life. From the beginning of the British Mandate there had been intermittent Arab resistance and violence, but it took fifteen years for full-scale rebellion to break out. Jabotinsky spoke in London in February 1937: the previous April the greatest of rebellions in the Holy Land, known as the Arab Revolt, had broken out; and a year later the most gifted of Arab leaders, George Antonius, published *The Arab Awakening*, which put an intellectual and historical gloss on revolt. For the moment, the Zionists could shrug this off, though they either publicly insisted like Jabotinsky that the Arabs would have to be met with an 'iron wall' of Jewish bayonets, or privately admitted, like Ben-Gurion, that agreement with the Arabs was highly unlikely.

Serious as the Arab Revolt was for the Jewish settlement in Palestine, it was trivial compared with what was happening to the Jews of Europe. Very few Jews read Antonius's book; every Jew was aware of the rising pitch of National Socialist persecution, as it reached a frenzy. Nothing mattered now except to rescue as many Jews as possible. But where to? In 1938 a conference was held at Evian in France, to discuss what, if anything, was to be done with Jewish refugees from Hitler. The British insisted that immigration to Palestine was not the answer, and practised what they preached. Immigrants to Palestine had been 61,800 in 1935. The Peel Commission recommended in 1937 that it should be held to 12,000 a year, and in that year it actually fell to 10,500. It increased slightly to 16,400 in 1939, when the British government recognised that Peel's proposed partition between Jews and Arabs was hopeless, and that the whole Mandate was falling apart, as it did over the next nine years. The White Paper of 1939 recommended that 75,000 Jews should be admitted over the next five years, after which immigration would cease altogether. This was seen by Zionists as a final betrayal. Then and since, the British received no sympathy, and they deserved none. Their plight was of their own making. All the same it was a plight (as Zionists did not always choose to recognise) which went back to the Balfour Declaration and to the incompatible promises to Jew and Arab.

With Palestine ruled out, the Evian conference became an embarrassing and humiliating business. No one wanted to take in the persecuted Jews. Few were as blunt as the representative of Australia – a country scarcely short of space – who said that Australia had no Jewish problem, and was not about to import one. Few were as evasive as the Americans. The Roosevelt administration encouraged the convening of the Evian conference, and then announced as its own contribution that the United States would accept rather fewer than 28,000 refugees. Such prizes as there were for generosity went – little known but worth recording – to Latin America. The Dominican Republic's offer to take in as many Jewish refugees as it could may have been more publicity value than reality, but Brazil and the Argentine did in fact take in, proportionate to their own populations, more refugees from Hitler than any English-speaking country. These embarrassments added to Hitler's glee. He taunted 'the other world' which had 'such deep sympathy for these criminals', the Jews. If they were only ready to translate sympathy into action, he would be happy to put the Jews at other countries' disposal, even providing luxury ships. This was only one side of his sadistic baiting. In 1939 he was threatening, without any obvious irony, that if war came it would lead to the extinction of the Jews.

What Hitler had in mind at that moment is unknowable. Jew-hatred had been the consuming passion of his life, but he made up policy –

economic, military, racial – as he went along. War did come in September 1939. Within weeks of its outbreak Hitler had conquered Poland; within a year, western Europe from the North Cape to the Pyrenees; within two years, Lithuania, White Russia, Ukraine and western Russia from the Gulf of Finland to the Black Sea. Until the war fewer than a million Jews were within Hitler's grasp; now eight or nine millions were, most of the Jews on earth.

If we cannot know what Hitler had always intended, we know what happened. In the first years of the occupation of Poland and the invasion of Russia there were random massacres of Jews, who were otherwise rounded up and herded into ghettos. By early in 1942, Hitler and his National Socialist élite had decided upon something else. Earlier in the century, Zionists and non-Zionist Jews alike had spoken of a 'final solution of the Jewish Question', either through a Jewish state, or through complete assimilation. Now Hitler adopted that phrase. His Final Solution was extermination. In less than three years, the greater part of the Jewish population of Europe was put to death, either where they were found or in specially designed killing centres. Most of the victims, including all the Jews of Poland, were killed in one great spasm of murder between the spring of 1942 and late 1943. In all, nearly six million Jews were killed.

A million of them were children. There were other great massacres in the twentieth century. Quantitatively, Stalin and Mao each killed more people than Hitler. The Final Solution was qualitatively different. It meant the methodical, careful selection and killing of men and women and children because of their birth.

Although this is obviously the central event of modern Jewish history, there is another sense in which it is not part of the 'Jewish problem' but rather of the 'gentile problem'. The fact that it could take place in the heart of Europe, in the middle of the twentieth century, carried out in the name of what had seemed to be and in many ways indeed was the most developed of nations, called into question every notion of Christendom, of European civilisation, of enlightenment, of progress. Writing shortly after the event, Dwight Macdonald saw this. Liberalism, socialism, Marxism, 'progressivism': all these had rested on the belief, rooted well before the French Revolution, that human happiness and betterment would come through the material advance brought about by man's control over his environment. This belief had now been experimentally tested, and falsified in the most dramatic way possible: 'The environment was controlled at Maidanek. It was the human beings who ran amok.'

It also posed terrible questions of responsibility. Hitler did the deed, and National Socialism, and the Germans. Not all of them, of course; but most of them knew that something frightful was happening to the Jews, many knew just what it was, and a fair number were active participants. So were many in other European countries, from French policemen to Croat politicians to Lithuanian peasants, who joined with various degrees of enthusiasm in the greatest massacre Europe had ever seen. There were exceptions, who should not be forgotten. Lone German sergeants here, poor Poles there, gave their lives trying to protect Jews. Many Italian soldiers and civilians helped Jews to escape. It was not even true that the European Right as a whole approved the murder: both Mussolini in Italy and Admiral Horthy in Hungary were shocked by what Hitler was doing, and even made halting attempts to keep their Jews from deportation and death. And in a nobler case, the Danes made heroic efforts to guard and spirit away their Jews, while King Christian X told the Germans, 'We have no Jews, only Danes.'

The Allies who were fighting Hitler could perhaps have done little to prevent the Final Solution; at any rate they did nothing, except to threaten punishment for the murderers. Larger gestures could have been made, bombing the railway lines to Auschwitz, or simply helping more Jews to escape by offering them shelter. This was not done. Great Britain continued throughout the war to keep Jews out of Palestine, and the attitude of many of its rulers was summed up in a Foreign Office memo in 1944 which complained that too much time was being spent on 'these wailing Jews'.[2] The Americans were worse. They harassed the British over Palestine, they struck attitudes, and they resolutely refused to take in more than the smallest numbers of victims. It is a bitter irony that the American Jews remained devoted to Roosevelt when, in the words of one historian, the conduct of the American administration was despicable throughout.

With nothing and no one to rescue them, the Jews of Europe awaited their fate. Whoever bore the ultimate responsibility for the Final Solution, there were those who wondered whether it could have been carried out without, if not the co-operation, then an unusual degree of passivity on the part of the victims. In the territories they

[2] The official who wrote this was shortly afterwards killed in an air crash, else who knows to what diplomatic heights he might have risen.

controlled, the Germans organised Jewish Councils under Jewish leadership which were used to effect the orderly collection and departure of the victims to the killing centres. It was later suggested that these Councils had been a form of collaboration; and that the victims had gone like sheep to the slaughter. The accusation was monstrously unfair: the victims had nothing and no one to help them, and no recourse. There was physical resistance, in the heroic rebellion of the Warsaw ghetto and in smaller risings even in heavily guarded death camps. But ultimately there was nothing the doomed could do. The Councils belonged to a long tradition of Jewish co-operation with authority, and to a belief that, if the persecutors were not provoked too much, the storm would pass.

To accuse the victims of passivity is deplorable, and to accuse the Council leaders of collaboration is to use hindsight. Maitland's warning that 'It is hard to think away out of our minds a history which had long lain in a remote past but which once lay in the future' applies with peculiar force to a history which lies in no remote past. Despite Hitler's bloodcurdling warnings before the war and as it began, it was hard to believe that what would happen was to happen. It was hard to believe as it happened. It still defies belief. If Hitler, his Third Reich and the Final Solution had not been outside history, unique and unfathomable; if the persecution had merely been a severer version of what the Jews had endured, and survived, before; if the war had taken a different course and Germany had been defeated earlier; then much larger Jewish communities might have survived, and those who had organised them might have been acclaimed as heroes rather than reviled as traitors.

Jewish responses to the catastrophe took different forms, from resistance, to defeat, to despair, to the ultimate logic of suicide. Before the war Gandhi had condemned Zionism when it resorted to the use of force, and not even shown much sympathy for it as a national movement. More startlingly, asked in 1938 how he thought the German Jews should respond to their persecution, the sainted apostle of passive resistance replied that they should collectively commit suicide, which 'would have aroused the world and the people of Germany to Hitler's violence'. The politest thing to say of this suggestion would be that it was logical and insane at once. And yet Gandhi's advice was all too often followed. In Germany after 1933, in Austria after 1938, there were many suicides, as there were also recorded in the Jewish cemetery in Berlin in 1942–3; and there was another rash of suicides among the refugees of cities like London after the war, when the full extent of the Final Solution became known.

Suicide was less common among the millions of ghetto Jews, for whom it contravened their Orthodox faith and even their traditional acceptance of fate, of God's will. One emancipated Viennese Jew, the musician and writer Hans Keller, had been arrested in 1938 and held by the Gestapo with numerous others, mostly poor Jews from the Leopoldstadt. What struck him most was 'the composure and behaviour of the Orthodox Jews'. When they were forced through a gauntlet of SS men beating them with rifles, along which others ran as fast as they could, 'they slowly walked through those corridors, in an upright position, with the result that you couldn't identify them when they came out at the other end – but at the same time, without showing the slightest sign in their behaviour of having been touched'. One of them was a sixteen-year-old newspaper boy. After the gauntlet he was literally unrecognisable. Asked how he could be so calm, 'he laughed and answered, "Well, we have had a few thousand years' training, haven't we?"' And then he told 'a Jewish joke which was appropriate to the occasion'. This acceptance was sublime in its way; as a Zionist might have warned, it was also fatal.

For emancipated Jews, acceptance was harder, despair easier. A symbolic succession of self-deaths took place. Otto Weininger had analysed his own Jewish problem with deranged clarity, and dealt with it logically by his own lights when he killed himself in 1903, aged twenty-three. His example was followed, as if in refutation of their father, by two of Herzl's children, though a third survived only to perish at the hands of the Germans. In the succeeding generation, suicide became an epidemic: Kurt Tucholsky in 1935, Joseph Roth in 1939, Walter Benjamin in 1940, Stefan Zweig in 1942. All of these were writers of distinction. Tucholsky had been the cleverest, and the most savage, of the satirists in Weimar Germany, pouring scornful invective on every established institution from the army and the churches to the unions and the Social Democrats. On one view he may have undermined the morale of the Republic, increased the unpopularity of the Jews, and hastened Hitler's arrival. At any rate, his suicide was an admission of defeat.

So was Roth's suicide in Paris at the age of forty-four. He had looked longingly back at the Habsburg monarchy in his novels *Radetzkymarsch* (1932) and *Die Kapuzinergraft* (1939). In *The Radetzky March*, a Polish aristocrat gloomily gazes around him in the last years of

Austria-Hungary – 'Even the parsons are going red, they've started preaching in Czech in the churches. At the Burgtheater all the performances are filthy Jewish plays. And every week another Hungarian water-closet manufacturer is made a baron' – before envisaging that 'each nation will set up its own dirty little government, even the Jews will have a King in Palestine'. This vision did not inspire Roth himself. In fact he had come to detest the Zionist idea, as he retreated into a shell of conservatism, Catholicism, and alcoholism. He told his friend Zweig that there was 'no road other than that which leads to Calvary, to Christ – no greater Jew. Indeed, perhaps I shall go even further and find the fortitude to enter an Order. Call it a kind of suicide . . .' Four years later, and in defiance of the teaching of his adoptive church, he admitted final defeat and committed the more literal kind.

For Walter Benjamin there was a more practical impulse. His own brilliant pyrotechnic contribution to German thought and Marxist theory were no help to him when persecution drove him to exile in France, then to the Spanish border in the hope of escape, then to end his own life in despair. He disappeared. His friend Hannah Arendt later came to look for his grave, but it was unmarked. Two years later he was followed by Stefan Zweig. Born in Vienna in 1881, he grew up in what, with hindsight, he had looked back on as the last golden age of Habsburg Austria. His deep nostalgic love for those last decades was partly self-deception, but was based also on the memory that 'nine-tenths of what the world celebrated as Viennese culture in the nineteenth century was promoted, nourished or even created by Viennese Jewry'. The domination of Austrian culture had been the Jews' form of citizenship and assimilation in a country which did not accept them socially or politically despite Zweig's claim that at school, university and in his literary career he had never 'experienced the slightest suppression or indignity as a Jew'.

That must have been very hard for his contemporaries and compatriots to believe, and in fact Zweig was not only a conscious Jew but one who for a time was attracted to Zionism and its founder (Herzl had published Zweig's first newspaper piece, which may have helped). He told his friend Martin Buber that, although he was wary of Jewishness 'as an emotional prison', it 'does not torment me and it does not sunder me; I feel it in the same way as I feel my heart beat when I think about it and I don't feel it when I don't think about it'. And yet he came to reject 'the dangerous dream of a Jewish state with cannon, flags, and decorations'. The more that dream threatened to become real 'the more determined I am to love the painful idea of the Diaspora, to love Jewish destiny more than prosperity'.

And yet it was not that dangerous dream's nearing realisation that crushed Zweig in the end, but the collapse of his own world, of Austro-Jewish *Kultur* and German-Jewish hope. 'What could the ideals of culture and *Bildung*, of Europe and Enlightenment mean in the face of Hitler?' The Wannsee conference in Berlin decided upon the Final Solution in late January 1942. Zweig did not know that, or the precise fate awaiting the Jews, but when, just over a month later, he and his wife took their lives together, it was another admission of defeat. Exile had driven them to Brazil, whose hospitality he warmly acknowledged in his suicide note; he might even have tried to begin a new life, 'the world of my own language having disappeared and my spiritual home of Europe having destroyed itself', but he was too old and too tired. He went on before, he said, impatient, but hoped that others would yet see the dawn after the long night.

These suicides spoke eloquently of what all Jews felt then, and after, an overwhelming sense of abandonment. The whole world had turned against them. Even when they did not actively take part in the murder, most of Europe turned its back, or even, like some Polish peasants, gloated at the Jews' torment. The few exceptions themselves had paradoxical implications for Zionism. King Christian's 'We have no Jews, only Danes', was a noble expression of the assimilationist tradition. Which, if it had been echoed throughout Europe – as of course it was not – would have made persecution unknown and Zionism unnecessary.

The Italian story was more revealing. Jabotinsky did not live to see the catastrophe he had accurately predicted, dying in American exile in 1940, oppressed by the 'elemental calamity' awaiting his people. He had always been fascinated by Italy, had used an Italian pen-name, and took Italian nationalism, before and after Mussolini, as his model. Just as Hess had been at the time of the Risorgimento, Jabotinsky had been deluded by Italian nationalism, taking the later patriotic rhetoric of Mussolini at face value just as Hess had the rhetoric of Garibaldi. 'The New Italian is organised and orderly,' Jabotinsky said, 'a builder and a conqueror, obstinate and cruel.' In truth, there was no new Italian. The Italians never came up to Mussolini's expectations,[3] they

---

[3] As he recognised: he kept a file of press cuttings illustrating the fecklessness and unreliability of his people.

remained largely untouched by his doctrine of state-worship, they kept their roots in their old traditions of family life and solidarity. They did not become builders and conquerors for long, and they did not play a distinguished military role in the World War. Instead, the Italian army had another battle honour: the part played by many Italian officers in the Balkans, at great personal risk, in protecting Jews from their persecutors. And when the Germans tried to implement the Final Solution in Italy, they received almost no co-operation from the Italians, with the result that a large proportion of Italian Jewry survived. Adolf Eichmann complained bitterly that by refusing to help in his great task the Italians had shown a lack of civic duty; no greater compliment has been paid to a people. But if Eichmann was disconcerted, so, as it were, was Jabotinsky: if the new Italian had indeed been as obstinate and cruel as he believed, fewer Jews would have been spared.

In Palestine his own spirit lived on. While part of the Yishuv joined the British in the war against Hitler, young Revisionists like Menachem Begin, Abraham Stern and Yitzhak Shamir, fought a campaign of their own throughout the World War. Where once Jabotinsky had raised a Jewish Legion to fight in the British Army, these followers rejected British rule, morally and physically. They might have chosen the Irish republican name 'Sinn Fein', 'ourselves alone'; they certainly followed the Irish nationalist precept, 'England's danger is our opportunity'. In his struggle for a Greater Israel stretching as far as the Euphrates, Stern led a violent group called Lehi in terrorist acts against the British; he met a representative of Mussolini; going further than Jabotinsky, he sent an agent called Naftalli Lubentschik to Beirut – at the time part of French Syria and controlled by the Vichy regime – to talk to a representative of the Third Reich, Otto von Hentig of the Berlin Foreign Office. Stern's emissary expressed his sympathy with the National Socialists, whose goal of removing the Jews from Europe he understood, spoke of 'the goodwill of the German Reich government and its authorities towards Zionist activity inside Germany and towards Zionist emigration plans', and proposed the 'establishment of the historical Jewish state on a national and totalitarian basis, and bound by a treaty with the German Reich', concluding with a formal offer to take part in the war on the German side.

Early in 1942 Stern himself was cornered by British police and shot dead while trying to escape (the phrase might be literal or conventional); but his gang continued under the leadership of one of his closest lieutenants, Yitzhak Yezernitsky, later known as Yitzhak Shamir. Contact with Berlin lapsed, but the Stern gang increased its activities. These were politically as much as militarily successful inside Palestine. In such situations, the groups who are seen to be 'doing something' – even if what they are doing is misguided or brutal – will always win converts from rivals who try to use peaceful methods. And although the majority of Palestinian Jews rejected Irgun and Stern – the *Palestine Post* saying that 'the authorities may rest assured that the Yishuv as a whole has its own accounts to settle with the terrorists' – the British found as they had earlier in Ireland that, whatever any terrorist might have done, any threat to execute him will produce a great revulsion among the peaceable community. That was understandable, as was the reprieve of some Jewish terrorists by the British under political pressure. Also understandable were the feelings of those who were still the majority in Palestine, and who remembered that during the Revolt more than a hundred young Arabs had been hanged by the British, with no eloquent voices to intercede on their behalf.

Lehi's most striking deed came in November 1944 when Lord Moyne was assassinated in Cairo. Moyne was British representative in Egypt and had earned the hatred of the Zionists by his opposition to immigration to Palestine and what was seen as his hostile attitude (though when he became Colonial Secretary in 1941 he had released forty-three Haganah men from imprisonment). His killing was meant as a further demonstration of ruthlessness, by men who would now stop at nothing. Its immediate effects were disastrous. Moyne was an old friend of Winston Churchill's, himself for long a Zionist sympathiser who had kept up his support for a Jewish state against the protests of colleagues in his government,[4] and who, in contrast to so many western leaders, was conscious that what Hitler was doing to the Jews was 'probably the greatest and most horrible crime ever committed in the history of the world'. The killing of Moyne also killed Churchill's Zionist enthusiasm for ever. He told the House of Commons that 'If our dream for Zionism should be dissolved in the smoke of the revolvers of assassins and if our efforts for its future should provoke a new wave of banditry worthy of the Nazi Germans, many persons like myself will have to consider the position that we have maintained so firmly for such a long time.'

[4] Though one colleague, Lord Cranborne, hoped for a Jewish settlement in Africa: 'only thus will we be able to get some of the Jews out of this country, in which there are now far too many.'

For his part, Weizmann was appalled by the assassination, and Ben-Gurion bitterly denounced the terrorists, who 'constitute a far greater danger to us than they do to the authorities and the police'. But there were others who greeted the news with approval, even if in private. Irgun had not known about the planned assassination and were annoyed at not having been warned, but came before long to the view that Moyne's killing was a brave and just deed. This view took a generation to come to term. For the moment, Sternists and Irgun were outcasts and outlaws, as the respectable Yishuv joined the British in hunting them down. Menachem Begin, head of Irgun since December 1943, told Haganah, 'We shall repay you, Cain.'

In America, little attention was given to those struggles in Palestine, much to the catastrophe of European Jewry. The Jews of America were stunned, numbed by the horror of what was happening to those who were not merely their co-religionists but quite literally their cousins. There were few Jewish families in New York, Boston or Chicago without kin in east Europe, whose fate slowly but appallingly emerged from the summer of 1942 onward. For American Jews, and British, and those in Palestine, the next three years were an agony, not of physical pain and death but of mental torment: horror, shame, rage, mitigated at first by hope that some somehow might survive. Then in the years after the war came the realisation that there was no hope at all; that in those very lands where most western Jews had come from, Poland, Lithuania, White Russia, Ukraine, the Jewish population had been almost entirely and hideously wiped out.

Jewish America stood appalled by the fate of Jewish Europe, but also paralysed by it. The Jews were the most loyal of Roosevelt's supporters. Any opposition to, or protest against, his administration's refusal to thwart or alleviate the fate of the Jews under Hitler, was inhibited by this. In one Jewish historian's harsh words, prominent American-Jewish leadership 'acted like court Jews who disdained above all to upset the king and instead waited patiently for a better day. It was a time-honoured policy of Jewish leadership, now exercised with incredibly lethal consequences.'

What did happen as a consequence of the horror in Europe was a sea-change among American Jewry in its attitude to Zionism. In May 1942, the main American Zionist organisations held a conference at the Biltmore hotel in New York. In the quarter-century since the Balfour Declaration, the debates had been unresolved: between assimilationists and Zionists, between cultural and political Zionists, between Labour and Revisionists, and between proponents of a Jewish homeland and a Jewish state. Individual men and women had shifted – and so had the centre of gravity of the Zionist movement – towards statehood. By 1937, Weizmann had been converted to a Jewish state though also to partition, as recommended that year by the Peel Commission. If Cis-Jordanian Palestine (i.e. the territory governed by Israel after 1967) were divided, the Jewish part could become solidly Jewish in population, as it would be free to control its own immigration. This seemed more logical still in 1941, when Weizmann foresaw with tragically misplaced optimism 'a problem of at least three million people' who would want to leave Europe after the war and be resettled, when 'a Jewish state is essential to carry out a policy of such magnitude'. By the following year he was persuaded, and hoped to persuade others, that a Jewish state had become both a practical necessity and 'a moral need and postulate, a decisive step towards normality and true emancipation', the old Zionist dreams of happiness. And he added that the Arabs would have to be told that they could not hinder further Jewish immigration. At the same time, he spoke still of this Jewish commonwealth's having close links with a neighbouring Arab Federation.

This was the language also of Ben-Gurion, who had been engaged in an elaborate, if sometimes unacknowledged, political duel with Weizmann and was emerging more as his rival for the leadership of Zionism and of the potential state. Ben-Gurion had certain advantages. He had a formidable power base in the Yishuv and its mighty union-welfare-kibbutz complex. He also was making his political pitch towards the Americans rather than the British, on whom Weizmann still pinned his hopes. After Pearl Harbor, Ben-Gurion percipiently foresaw that the United States would soon be the dominant Power. It had a great Jewish community, and its government was free from any actual responsibilities in the Levant. He saw that the dispute in Palestine was not going to be resolved by diplomacy but by force, and that American support could be crucially enlisted. He saw above all that the moment had come when the Zionists could shed the coy evasions in which they had indulged ever since Herzl had refrained from asking the First Congress explicitly to endorse a Jewish state.

Now Ben-Gurion seized the moment. At the Biltmore he put forward a resolution designed to answer 'the problem of Jewish homelessness'. It urged 'that the gates of Palestine be opened: that the Jewish Agency be vested with control of immigration into Palestine and with the necessary authority for upbuilding the country, including the development of its unoccupied and uncultivated lands; and that Palestine be established as a Jewish commonwealth integrated in the structure of the new democratic world'.

The passage of this resolution was a *coup d'état*, and a brilliant *coup de théâtre* by Ben-Gurion, which Weizmann chose to regard as a *coup de Jarnac*. He was still concerned to maintain the friendship with the British, concerned also that a violent Arab reaction might damage the war effort. He criticised Ben-Gurion when he openly demanded the admission of two million Jews to Palestine, and Ben-Gurion in turn denounced Weizmann in bitter terms: 'He wants always to be reasonable . . . he hears more what he would like to hear than what he hears . . . it is not in the interest of the movement that Dr Weizmann act alone.' Its brutality was effective because Ben-Gurion had the winning cards in his hand. Even before the war the majority of American Zionists, if not of all American Jews, seem to have been converted to the idea of a Jewish state, which the three leading Yiddish papers now backed. In November 1942 the Zionist Action Committee endorsed the Biltmore programme, and this was amplified in Atlantic City in October 1944, when the American Zionists, the largest and most powerful section of the World Zionist Organisation, demanded a Jewish state comprising 'the whole of Palestine, undivided and undiminished'.

All of this did not go without protest. Far away in Jerusalem, Magnes said that the Biltmore demand for a Jewish state was 'a declaration of war by the Jews on the Arabs'. In 1943 the American Council for Judaism was founded on a policy of opposition to 'a national Jewish state in Palestine or anywhere else as a policy of defeatism . . . We dissent from all these related doctrines which stress the racialism, the national and the theoretical homelessness of the Jews. We oppose such doctrines as inimical to the welfare of the Jews in Palestine, in America, or wherever Jews may dwell.' But this was now an unpopular dissident voice. The British were naturally dismayed by Biltmore and the new maximalist policy which, as the British Embassy in Washington pointed out to the State Department, was effectively the Revisionist programme.

During these years, the interaction between events in Europe, America and Palestine was complex both politically and emotionally. Unable to do anything for their doomed cousins in Europe, many American Jews transferred such reserves of hope as they still possessed to the Holy Land, to the Yishuv, and to the quest for a Jewish state which until recently had left so many of them cold, or at best tepid. The European Jewish catastrophe may or may not have justified the creation of a Jewish state – rigorous Zionists would insist that their case was self-sufficient without the Final Solution – but it was patently the catastrophe which converted the bulk of the Dispersion to Zionism, and to what had not long before been seen as an extreme doctrine.

So Hannah Arendt pointed out. German-Jewish by birth, she had made her way to America and had slowly become known as a formidable if often unsettling and unloveable member of the New York intellectual community. She now turned her trained philosopher's lens on to the Zionist controversy. The Atlantic City resolution, she said, went further than Biltmore, in which the Arabs had at least been granted minority rights. The development inside American Zionism in 1942–4 meant 'that the Revisionist programme, so long bitterly repudiated, has finally proved victorious'. The Arabs were left thereby with nothing but 'the choice between emigration and second-class citizenship. It seemed to admit that only opportunist reasons had previously prevented the Zionist movement from stating its final aims.' And it was a deadly blow to those Jews in Palestine who had tried to preach understanding between Jew and Arab. This carried a large weight of truth, though when Arendt predicted that general Zionism and Revisionism were objectively now so close that they might merge, she fell into the error acute minds often make when they pass from analysis to prophecy.

Few Jews read Hannah Arendt in an obscure journal, and many would scarcely have followed her arguments. For most Jews at the time, the task was coming to terms with what had happened in Europe. Some could not do so, and in these years that the scale of the horror became clear there were many more suicides among Jews in the West, especially and not surprisingly among those who had escaped, leaving family behind. Even to those who were determined that life, and Jewish life, must go on, the horror seemed an almost intolerable blow to faith and hope. In November 1944, Judah Magnes gave an address at the Hebrew university in Jerusalem, in which he tried to make sense of events. He read a description of the gassing and burning of Jews by the hundreds of thousands at Birkenau, and said truthfully that 'in all human history there has never been anything like this either in extent or in the methods employed . . . The hunt for myriads of human beings created in the Image is organised scientifically, and they are transported to the gates of hell and destroyed scientifically.' And he asked the question which all asked and none could answer: 'Is it possible that this can happen under God's heaven?'

In so many ways, Hitler had altered the terms of every argument. He had killed more than millions of people, he had destroyed an entire community, not to say a culture and a language. In 1939, Yiddish had been spoken by more than ten million people, more than spoke Danish and Swedish combined. Yiddish effectively perished in the death camps. The old Yiddishkeit lingered on, from New York to Jerusalem, lovingly cherished indeed; but the language was mortally stricken. So was its little cousin, Ladino spoken by the Sephardic Jews of south-eastern Europe. Its chief centre had been Salonika in Greece, whose Jewish population was wiped out.

Another civilisation had died also. The German-Jewish culture which had produced Heine, Marx, Mendelssohn, Mahler, Freud, Kraus, Kafka and Einstein, that extraordinary blend of anxiety and hope, was extinguished for ever. Its surviving remnants were scattered across the globe, but now mostly found themselves speaking and writing English. There were surviving Jewish communities in Italy, where the Turin chemist Primo Levi was to write the enduring masterpiece of Auschwitz, and in France, as well as in England. But in a sense European Jewry was ended – and Hitler had created an entirely new balance. Years earlier Namier had seen the centre of gravity of the Zionist movement shifting from the German-speaking to the English-speaking world. Now the centre of gravity for all of Jewry had moved across the Atlantic. The one really large Jewish community, several million strong, was in America. As immigrants flooded to the Holy Land, there too a community was to grow, rivalling the American in size, though not in economic weight and influence. And the pattern of Jewish history over the next half-century was to be dominated by the relationship between these two communities.

One other crucial change had been wrought by Hitler. In its earliest years, the Zionist project had been ignored by most Jews and bitterly opposed by some, especially the richest and most successful Jews in the West. This indifference and opposition was effectively silenced by National Socialist persecution. For generations, Jews physically emancipated from the ghetto had asked themselves a series of questions. Am I a Jew? In what sense? Do I affirm my Jewish identity? Do I like being a Jew? Do I consider myself a Jew first or a German (or Englishman or Frenchman or American)? With a kind of superb resilience of spirit, debates about Jewish identity and Zionism went on even among the huddled victims of the camps. And yet all these painful, subtle questions had been kicked aside by a jackboot. Hitler had allowed no one the luxury of worrying about identity and affirmation. Like his mentor Dr Lueger, and in insanely more cruel fashion, he decided who was a Jew – and marked them all out for death, rich and poor, young and old, learned and ignorant, good and bad. No one of Jewish birth and descent, however assimilated, 'evolved' or rootless, could ever feel the same again about that descent. And it was very difficult indeed for any Jew to disown, as so many recently had, what was done in the name of the Jewish people.

Much was being done. In the three years which followed the defeat of Germany, the struggle in Palestine intensified, with Jabotinsky's successors moving to the fore. Both the Zionist factions had private armies; Labour's Haganah was the larger, but the Revisionists' Irgun Zvei Leumi was the fiercer. Both had been operating during the war. Haganah had originally been created from a legal Jewish police force raised by the British to combat the Arabs (itself a genesis with interesting implications). When Haganah men, like the young Moshe Dayan, were captured they claimed that they wanted to fight the Germans. The British commander General Barker said to Ben-Gurion in reply that their real aim was clear: 'They are preparing for rebellion against Great Britain.' But both were true. The senior Zionist leaders deplored this armed rebellion. The idea, Weizmann said, was 'fantastic. No doubt there were a few extremists who toyed with the idea, but it was repulsive to the Jewish community as a whole.' He was powerless to prevent it, and indeed when it took place was loath publicly to condemn it, even when it became increasingly savage. And for their part, the militant extremists were not only physically brutal towards the British extremists but emotionally brutal towards their moderate Zionist critics.

Quite apart from what had happened under Hitler, there was the continuing legacy in Europe. In 1946 camps were overflowing with survivors of the Final Solution. Their treatment by the victors was an improvement on their treatment by the defeated Germans, but it was all the same thick-skinned and heartless, and the record shows again how little comprehension there was of the enormity of what had happened. During the war, there had been evidence in the United States of increasing antisemitism, or at least resentment of the Jews in their time of torment. In England, a Labour government had come to power in the summer of 1945 after a landslide electoral victory. The new Foreign Secretary, Ernest Bevin, was hostile to the Zionists from the beginning, but then his Prime Minister, the middle-class socialist C. R. Attlee, was also touched in private by the usual prejudice of his age and class, and this sometimes showed in his political words and deeds. In September 1945, he told President Truman that there should be no special sympathy for the Jews: members of every people in Europe had been rounded up and sent to camps, and 'there appears to have been very little difference in the amount of torture and treatment they had to undergo'.

This astonishing phrase is not evidence of hatred of the Jews so much as of something else very familiar to students of English history: the irritation felt by the governing class (of which Attlee was certainly a member) at anyone who got in the way of smooth administration, whether the starving Irish at the time of the Famine, educated agitators in India, or troublesome Jewish refugees. For the London government, the whole question of Palestine, Zionism and the Jews had now become just a nuisance. To be fair to the British during this lamentable passage in their history, they were worn out by the effort of fighting the greatest and noblest of all their wars and by their continuing burdens. Their reign in Palestine had proved entirely thankless, winning them the enmity of Jews, Arabs, Americans, and the friendship of no one. As J. M. Keynes told his friend Weizmann, England after 1945 was simply too poor and exhausted to sustain the burden of its incompatible problem 'and consequently must abandon both parties to their own devices'. That was what happened.

As the political and physical struggle continued in Palestine, a moral struggle was unresolved. Most Jews of the Dispersion were reconciled to Zionism, even if in a passive sense without any intention of living in the Jewish state. Few really bothered to wonder and worry about the means being used to achieve the Zionist dream. Only months after his great sermon, Judah Magnes wrote to the *New York Times* proposing a fair settlement in the Holy Land, though he recognised that 'the very idea of compromise – the word itself – has been made abhorrent to too many of the inhabitants of Palestine'. He proposed a Regional Council in Jerusalem, and an administration in Palestine on a binational basis, 'between Jews and Arabs in government, so that neither would rule the other'.

Magnes was far from proposing Jewish withdrawal from the Holy Land. He advanced again the beguiling but misleading example of

Switzerland. He believed that most of the survivors in Europe would come to Palestine, and that it was perfectly reasonable to expect 'parity', or the immediate immigration of half a million Jews, on top of the half million in Palestine at the beginning of 1945, to reach the same level as the million Arabs. And he opposed partition, foreseeing that 'all it will do is to create two irredentas, irreconcilable and activist, on either side of the border', though also and significantly on the ground that partition would limit the territory for Jewish settlement.

As events moved apace, Magnes watched critically but impotently. He recognised that there was evidence of growing antisemitism in America, but regarded this as an ignoble argument for Zionism, and perceived something profoundly important: 'Woe betide Zionism if the world be such as to have an America one of whose ruling forces is antisemitism.' Magnes tried to keep open a dialogue with Arabs like Azzam Pasha, the English-educated Egyptian diplomatist who had been expelled from Palestine by the British in 1933.[5] With all of what he – understandably from a subjective viewpoint – regarded as his philo-Arabism and moderation in only asking for parity of population, Magnes was surprised to be told by Azzam that 'one could see how far the spirit of Jewish aggression had gone if the proposals for parity were regarded as too moderate'.

The last years of Magnes's life were the stuff of tragedy. His Ihud (Unity) association continued to campaign for a binational Palestine. But although its spokesmen appeared before Anglo-American Committees of Inquiry and United Nations Special Committees, its words were drowned, by the noise of militant Zionism, of Arab nationalism, of armed violence. He was deserted by the small band of Americans who had once supported him, like Arthur Hays Sulzberger, Maurice Wertheim and Herbert Lehman. He found new allies in the League of Justice and Peace for the Holy Land, but this only distanced him further from most Jewish colleagues: the League, organised by Virginia Gildersleeve, dean of Barnard College, was openly pro-Arab, and the only Jew on its executive committee was Rabbi Morris Lazaron, a leading light of the American Council of Judaism, itself one of the last outposts of Jewish opposition to political Zionism and the Jewish state.

The truth was that Jewish anti-Zionism was now a lost cause, overwhelmed by the force of history. In Palestine, Ihud were not

---

[5] For, of all things, denouncing what he correctly called the barbarous suppression by the Italians of the Senussi revolt in Libya.

merely beleaguered but reviled, attacked as traitors. The mood of the Yishuv was exultant, almost necessarily so, determined to press on to the finish, and the American Jews for the most part did not think they had any right to tell their cousins in the Holy Land what to do and what not to do. Hitler had destroyed European Jewry, had indeed provided a 'final solution' for Jabotinsky's 'objective Jewish question'; as Walter Laqueur said: 'The idea of the Jewish state seemed to have lost its historical *raison d'être*', just before, as it turned out, the state came into being. Herzl and Nordau had dreamt of a haven for the Jews of Europe, even the Biltmore programme of 1942 had supposed that millions would survive in Europe. 'The prophets of Zionism had anticipated persecution and expulsion but not the solution of the Jewish question by mass murder. As the war ended Zionism seemed to be at the end of its tether.'

At just this moment it found a new role. Dispersion Jewry was converted to Zionism almost as suddenly as Clovis's army had been to Christianity. Where not many years earlier there had once been equivocation or indifference towards Zionism on their part, an opinion poll in November 1945 found 80.5 per cent of American Jews favoured a Jewish State, with only 10.5 per cent against. In England the conversion was epitomised by one man. Until the war, Harold Laski had remained detached from Zionism, if not as hostile as his father. In 1937, Nathan Laski had met the grandees of Anglo-Jewry, Rothschilds, Montagus, Montefiores and Cohens, and expressed concern about the possible establishment of a Jewish state and its effect on the political position of Jews in the countries of their birth. Zionism remained for him 'a surrender by the Jews to their enemies and an admission that emancipation had failed'.

By 1945, Harold was chairman of the Labour party (to the considerable embarrassment of its leadership); the story had changed dramatically; and on May Day of that year he proclaimed the immediate necessity of a Jewish state. He was still something less than a fully fledged zealot, insisting that the Arabs had as much right to be in Palestine as the Jews, and that the Jews' great contribution could be made without dominating their neighbours, 'any more than [in a curious analogy] the Scottish people have dominated the English since the Act of Union'.

Within his own party, he was by then preaching to the converted. This was a dramatic illustration of how liberal and 'progressive' opinions had been persuaded by the tragedy of the European Jews to

To the gates of Hell 227

take up the Zionist cause, once so esoteric or unpopular. Some months before Laski spoke, the Labour party had issued a policy statement, 'The International Post-War Settlement', principally written by Hugh Dalton.[6] A paragraph on Palestine recommended not only the creation of a Jewish National Home, not only unrestricted immigration, but 'Transfer' of population: 'Let the Arabs be encouraged to move out as the Jews move in ... The Arabs have many wide territories of their own; they must not claim to exclude the Jews from this small area of Palestine.' Shortly after this remarkable statement, George Orwell observed that the Left generally was 'strongly committed to support the Jews against the Arabs'. And yet, he added, 'the Palestine issue is partly a colour issue', in which 'an Indian nationalist, for instance, would probably side with the Arabs'. The prescience of this would echo louder and louder over the following decades.

The conversion of Jewish America meant a shift in American politics. In private, many American politicians were far from philosemitic. President Roosevelt, supported and revered by so many Jews, once told a colleague that 'this is a Protestant country, and the Catholics and Jews are all here on suffrance', while his successor, President Truman, was not only personally unsympathetic to a Jewish state but once mused whether an antisemitic movement might not sweep the country. But these were private thoughts, not the language of the campaign trail. Within months of succeeding to the White House in April 1945, Truman was advocating free Jewish immigration to Palestine. A cynic might have said he was in favour of free Jewish immigration to any country except the United States – and this was just what Ernest Bevin did say to the Labour party conference the following year: Truman was keen on migration to Palestine because 'they did not want too many Jews in New York'.

Though said with the customary brutality which so many of his colleagues as well as enemies had experienced, this had a grain of truth, whatever Mayor Walker had said sixteen years earlier. Both Roosevelt and then Truman paid court to the Jewish vote. The New York mayoral election in October 1945, which the Democrats particularly wanted to win, was maybe the first American election in which the new 'Jewish Question' played a part. The Jewish electorate –

---

[6] Who privately sneered at the 'Yideology' of the 'undersized semite' Laski; an illustration once more that a sympathy for Zionism was not the same as philosemitism.

a third of the population of the city – was crucial, and a Jewish topic, the future of Palestine, was of central importance to that electorate. Bevin said irritably that for the Americans 'to play on racial feelings for the purpose of winning an election is to make a farce of their insistence on free elections in other countries', although he seemed unaware that ethnicity was a fact of life in American politics. What was true enough was that Truman, like his predecessor and successor, was a great deal happier for Jews to enter Palestine, whatever difficulties that made for either the British or the Arabs, than for renewed Jewish immigration to America on the scale known before 1914. The tragically depleted numbers of European Jews were tired, poor, huddled masses yearning to breathe free; but the American republic was no longer so keen to give them breathing space. This was obvious enough, not least to the American Jews. But they now acquired a habit of selectively choosing which facts to make much of and which to ignore. The British policy of keeping Jews out of Palestine was denounced as a crime; the American policy of keeping Jews out of America was overlooked.

If most American Jews were now sentimental Zionists, in the sense of giving at least part of their hearts to the Zionist cause, many were Zionists in a more committed sense, like the young men and women of the socialist Habonim group. Their mood of exultation was caught in a resolution of 1947, whose tone was extraordinary enough at that moment in Jewish history. The Jews had dreamed and remembered Zion. 'In song, in prose, in their hearts and thoughts, Jews kept alive the dream of the Return to Zion . . . It has happened and is happening in our time . . . How fortunate we all are! How happy we all are!'

Few were publicly committed followers of Jabotinsky and his heirs. And yet those heirs were their nagging voice of conscience. In late 1946, scores of thousands of New Yorkers went to see a play by Ben Hecht, now an ardent supporter of the Irgun. *A Flag is Born* was one of the first in what was to be a long line in triumphalist agitprop. 'The English have put a fence round the Holy Land,' one character says. 'But there are three things they cannot keep out – the wind, the rain and a Jew.' Hecht threw himself into the task of polemising, on behalf of the illegal immigrants who were trying to enter Palestine, and the militant armed men already there.

As the twentieth century progressed, if progress is the word, the distinction between a 'terrorist', a 'guerrilla' and a 'freedom fighter' in one country or another was to become a nice semantic problem for journalists and politicians. Hecht did not shirk it. The following May he published an open 'Letter to the Terrorists of Palestine' as a full-page ad in several New York newspapers. 'My dear friends,' he addressed the Irgun men, 'on my word as an old reporter, what I write is true. The Jews of America are for you. You are their champions. You are the grin they wear. You are the feather in their hats.' In a further rhetorical flourish, remembered for years after in England, Hecht wrote, 'Every time you blow up a British arsenal, or wreck a British jail, or send a British railroad train sky high, or rob a British bank, or let go with your guns and bombs at British betrayers and invaders of your homeland, the Jews of America make a little holiday in their hearts.' Anglo-American relations worsened, as Bevin protested vigorously at this, and many Jews protested also. Eleven weeks later two captured British sergeants were hanged by Irgun in reprisal for the execution of two Irgun men; reporters telephoned Hecht to ask him whether he had a little holiday in his heart. Hecht was untroubled, just as he was enraged when illegal immigrants on the *Exodus 1947* (as the old Chesapeake Bay steamer *President Garfield* was renamed) were turned back to Europe.

In blood and fire did Judaea fall, in blood and fire did Judaea rise again. Jabotinsky's heirs, Stern earlier, then the assassins of Moyne, now young Irgun men like Menachem Begin and Yitzhak Shamir, were as good as the song they sang. They blew up not only arsenals and trains but civilian centres, most famously the King David hotel in Jerusalem, with heavy loss of life, British, Arab and Jewish. They put to death British prisoners. They were ready, as it proved, to massacre whole Arab villages. And they apologised to no one, not to the more moderate Jews of the Yishuv, not to Jews of the Dispersion (including British Jews, who had been horrified by the hanging of the sergeants and alarmed by the anti-Jewish demonstrations which followed), not to the goyim anywhere.

Nor was the real explanation for this ferocity far to seek. '*Si vendicano gli uomini delle leggiere offese; delli gravi non possono.*' As Machiavelli said, men seek revenge for smaller wrongs, unable to avenge the greater. When the Irgun killed Englishmen and Arabs, they were, in a tiny way, avenging something incomparably worse than British misrule or Arab resistance. And they were making a point. However unfair the accusations that Hitler's victims had accepted their fate passively, however exaggerated the charge that Churchill and Roosevelt had colluded in the catastrophe through their inaction, the event had seared itself into the Zionists' soul. Never again: never again would there be Jewish Councils and Jewish collaboration with the Jews' enemies; never again would the Jews look for help in a friendless world; never again would they even care what the world thought of them; and never again would they rely on gentleness or patience. The Irgun's slogan and symbol were the words 'Only thus' under a gun held across the Jordan. Only thus, in blood and fire, would the new Hebrews build and guard their new state.

As the drama in Palestine approached its climax, the debates continued elsewhere. One was the political debate, in the House of Commons and Foreign Office, Congress and State Department, and at the temporary headquarters at Lake Success of the newly founded United Nations. In August 1947, the United Nations Special Committee on Palestine pronounced the failure of binationalism and recommended partition into Jewish and Arab states. The proposed boundaries of the Jewish state were much more generous than those suggested in either the Peel Commission Report of 1937 or by the Foreign Office in 1944. It would include most of the citrus orchards, which were then the most important part of the Palestinian economy, and half of which were Arab-owned. It would also include, on the existing balance of population, almost as many Arabs as Jews, 450,000 against 500,000. Bevin objected strongly to this, saying he could think of no way of justifying the placing of so many Arabs under Jewish rule. He was advised that an extra division of British infantry would be needed to enforce the plan, which would be seen as a breach of faith by all Arabs.

Then and later Bevin was reviled as an enemy of the Jews; it was said, not without any evidence, that the Foreign Office was a hotbed of Jew-hating Arabists, the sort of people who had complained about 'wailing Jews' while the death camps were at full pitch. But Bevin and his officials had a case to answer. The failure to rescue the European Jews from their torment was an appalling stain on the record of the whole West; this did not in itself mean that the West was right to expiate the offence at someone else's expense. However bitterly Zionists complained about the motives of the British, and with however much justice at times, the fact was that the British had no permanent interest in Palestine and would leave before long. Who lived and ruled there was in a sense a matter of no consequence to them.

By late 1947, the British rulers of Palestine were despairing of their task. In August, the British Raj had become independent, divided between India and Pakistan after another hopeless attempt to find an alternative to partition, and the British were, not surprisingly, unenthusiastic about imposing another such solution – or presiding over a repeat of the frightful communal massacres which the partition had led to. They were still baffled by illegal immigration to Palestine. The American journalist I. F. Stone recorded his journey *Underground to Palestine*, accompanying the illicit migrants from their 'displaced persons' camps in central Europe to the promised land. Thanking him for a copy of the book, Magnes said that he had not quite given up hope of the binational scheme though he realised how slim its chances were, not least, as he had been told, because of 'the Jewish vote in New York, Chicago and one or two other places'. Partition had been rejected by the Arabs. They were still a large majority in Palestine and, as the British discovered over the course of the century, it was always the minority – Ulster Protestants, Indian Muslims, Turkish Cypriots – who wanted, or were prepared to settle for, partition, and the majority – Irish Catholics, Indian Hindus, Greek Cypriots – who were not. But, even as he recognised that partition of some sort was likely to come, Magnes prophesied that it would mean 'setting up two tiny principalities with chauvinist education for the youth, their irredentisms, their hatreds, and their almost inevitable clash'. He foresaw, he told another correspondent, that 'the rift between the two people will grow deeper, destroying all chance for some kind of peaceful life here'.

Both sides in this argument were right. In November 1947 the General Assembly of the United Nations voted in favour of the partition plan, thanks to the Americans (all eleven Muslim states represented voted against; there were other votes against, including Great Britain, but at the time, and for some time after, the State Department controlled a tame, mostly Latin-American, majority in the General Assembly). The British declared that their mandate would end on 15 May 1948, and by sporadic violence between Jew and Arab partition was now enforced. On 9 April, an Irgun attack led by Begin on the Arab village of Deir Yassin near Jerusalem resulted in a massacre of 250 civilians. It had a further result. In Begin's words, 'out of evil good came. This Arab propaganda spread a legend of terror amongst the Arabs and Arab troops who were seized with panic at the mention of Irgun soldiers. The legend was worth half a dozen battalions to the force of Israel.' He meant that a precipitate flight took place of Arabs from areas under Jewish control, a torrent of refugees which soon numbered many hundreds of thousands. There were Arab attacks on Jews in return, as the British pulled out. The day before the

Mandate expired, the leaders of Jewish Palestine declared independence. For all their hope and exaltation, they knew that the fate of the whole Zionist dream lay in the balance.

IV

From a
Jewish State
to a Jewish Solution?

13

Victors, not victims

Our soul is escaped even as a bird
out of the snare of the fowler:
the snare is broken, and we are delivered.

Ps.cxxiv.6

On 14 May 1948, a new state was born. The Zionist General Council proclaimed ('with unconscious irony', as a Gibbonian English historian put it shortly afterwards) that 'foreign rule' would no longer be tolerated in the country. In Washington, the Truman administration immediately extended *de facto* recognition to the new state of Israel, and three days later Soviet Russia capped this with *de jure* recognition. The latter decision requires complicated explanation, and perhaps cannot be fully understood until the day comes, if ever, when the inner workings of Stalin's regime can be studied from original sources. But in loose terms it can be said that, as the Cold War grew chillier, Russia did everything it could, and used every opportunity available, not necessarily to extend Communist revolution – Stalin often took actions which objectively frustrated that end – but to baffle and outwit the western powers. Whatever else, Soviet motives did not include any deep regard for the Zionist idea; still less, as became all too clear before long, any sentimental philosemitism.

The immediate problem for Israel was not diplomatic but military. Her neighbouring Arab countries, Egypt, Irak and Transjordan, determined to strangle the new state at birth and their armies moved in. King Farouk of Egypt, whose many pleasures and pastimes including philately, issued a set of stamps to mark his conquest of Palestine. But these Arab armies were thrown back by the Israelis, though with heavy losses. An Israeli position on the western edge of Jerusalem was held, with a narrow corridor attaching it to the main Israeli territory. A ceasefire was arranged, partly with the help of the United Nations, and came into effect on 13 June.

This did not end armed conflict in the new state. Its Prime Minister was David Ben-Gurion, and he wanted to enjoy undivided and unchallenged authority. By his order, the Israel Defence Forces were embodied, with the Haganah as their core, but the Irgun still existed. It had commissioned a ship, renamed the *Altelena* after one of Jabotinsky's old pseudonyms,[1] to bring in arms. Ben-Gurion determined to stop this challenge to his authority. On 21 June, Haganah-cum-IDF fired on the *Altelena* by the beach at Tel Aviv where she lay. Several men were killed (among them Stavsky, the man once tried for the murder of Arlozorov) and the ship was set ablaze. Begin was on board, and proclaimed a ceasefire, rather than a permanent peace, of his own. His movement would continue 'our political activities' within the jurisdiction of the new state, and confine physical force to 'the enemy outside'. Ben Hecht watched this from across the Atlantic with disgust and heart-break, his faith in the Jewish state betrayed as soon as she was born, and resolved to have nothing further to do with Zionism. Begin and his colleagues retired to lick their wounds, but they were not beaten.

To the extent that they were known of in Jewish circles in the West, the right-wing Zionist militants were still widely regarded with aversion, heightened by the assassination of the United Nations mediator Count Folke Bernadotte by Lehi or Sternist terrorists four months after the birth of Israel. In late 1948, Begin visited the United States to rally support and raise funds for Tnuat Haherut (Freedom Party) which he had formed out of the old Irgun. His visit was vehemently denounced in a letter to the *New York Times* signed by twenty-eight Jewish liberals, the best-known being Sidney Hook, Hannah Arendt and Albert Einstein. Begin was a 'terrorist, right-wing, chauvinist' leader, they wrote, whose movement was 'closely akin in its organisation, methods, political philosophy and social appeal to the Nazi and Fascist parties'. It was essential that Begin should not be able to claim that a large segment in America supported fascist elements in Israel, led by the man who had inspired the Deir Yassin massacre,

[1] Oddly enough, the penname was a mistake. Jabotinsky wanted to call himself 'Crane', like the bird, in Italian, but mistranslated it and lighted on the word for a swing or see-saw.

which 'exemplifies the character and actions of the Freedom Party'. And the signatories deplored the refusal of the American Zionist leadership to take the lead in denouncing 'the dangers to Israel from support to Begin' and 'this latest manifestation of fascism'. It would have been truer to say, not that large elements of the American Zionist movement, or of Jewish America as a whole, sympathised with Begin, but that they did not want to know; and American Jewry remained in blissful ignorance of many of the political realities of Israel for decades to come.

As independence dawned, Ben-Gurion echoed an old Zionist slogan: 'Like other nations, it is the right of the Jewish people to determine its history under its own sovereignty.' This seemed to be the central moral accomplishment, but the rhetoric obscured the reality. On the face of it the Jews had at last, for the first time in nearly two thousand years, taken their destiny in their own hands and were shaping their own history. The creation of Israel, with its subsequent history, was indeed a breath-taking achievement, a triumph of will and human spirit, won, as that one-time Zionist enthusiast Winston Churchill could have said, by blood, toil, tears, and sweat, by heroic battles against the odds.

But it was not that alone. Although the new Israeli people wanted to make their own story, it was in truth still to a large degree being made for them from outside. For all the heroism and sacrifice of the pioneers, for all Weizmann's long and patient diplomacy, for all the military discipline of the Haganah and for all the frank terror of the Sternists and Irgun, the new state would not have been born without factors which the Zionists did not control. One great war had led to the establishment of a Jewish homeland, another to a new conjunction in international affairs. Israel was born when the British were too worn out by war to continue their own imperial burden, when the American administration had decided to back the new state, despite many misgivings in the State Department and even in the White House, when Soviet Russia, for even more irrelevant and cynical reasons, decided that it too would act as a sponsor.

Above all, it was born after the greatest catastrophe in Jewish history. More than thirty years later, George Steiner wrote a strange fantasy, in which Hitler is found in Latin America where, not having died at all, he had fled like Eichmann. At one moment 'AH' muses about the fate of Germany and the Jews: 'And the Reich begat Israel.' To some Israelis this literary conceit seemed distasteful, and to some rigorous Zionists it was a point of principle that the Zionist vision was in no way affected or further justified by the fate of the European Jews. This flew in the face of common sense. Hitler was the most unsuccessful politician of all time, for all his vast and insane deeds: he left Germany divided for nearly half a century, left Europe as far west as the Elbe in the hands of his mortal enemies the Bolsheviks, and left his even more hated enemies, the Jews, with a voice in world affairs for the first time. But for him, Israel could not have been born when and as it was.

As for Ben-Gurion's other phrase, the old Zionist aspiration, that too was implausible. 'Like other nations' was quite obviously just what Israel was not. It was like no other country on earth, and in many ways did not pretend to be. This was no England or France, no United States or Soviet Russia, not even another Romania or Serbia, the pattern against which Tolstoy had warned the early Zionists. It was wholly original, an 'idea in history' made flesh. And, if its relationship with the outside world was different, its relationship with the Jewish Dispersion was also different from that of other new-born countries with their own Diasporas, a difference of kind rather than degree.

One uniquely distinctive feature which made the new state unlike other nations was its Magna Carta or Bill of Rights, the Law of Return which gave any Jew anywhere on earth (begging the question of who was a Jew) the right to settle in Israel. It was no abstract notion. In the first years from 1948 to 1951 there was a huge immigration, more than 650,000. They came as survivors from Europe, notably from Romania where a larger proportion of the Jewish population than in most east European countries had survived the Germans. They came in increasing numbers from the Arab countries, from Morocco far to the west of Israel, from Irak to the east, from Yemen to the south. This was something few had foreseen, certainly not Hess and Herzl. The creation of the Jewish state sent convulsions through the Arab world. In 1949, Israel signed armistices with the neighbouring countries which still did not officially recognise her, Egypt, Jordan, Syria, Lebanon. Humiliating defeat led in turn to a surge of populist nationalism in those countries, which threatened the old regime: the king of Jordan was assassinated in 1951, the stamp-collecting King Farouk of Egypt was deposed the next year. Under old or new leaders, these countries talked about crushing the Zionist interloper, but only talked. The fledgeling state profited from its neighbours: from their verbal violence, from their appearance of strength if only numerically, and from their actual military incompetence. It was not only that the Israelis could say, as the anti-imperialist (and antisemitic) Belloc had said, 'Whatever happens, we have got The Maxim gun and they have not.' Along with their great advantage in technology and weaponry, the Israelis had the crucial advantage of morale, of believing that they were fighting for something very precious, not to say for their very existence.

The 'oriental' Jews who began to arrive brought with them no fondness at all for those neighbours. On balance, the Jews may have been treated less badly over the centuries under Islam than under Christendom, but it was absurd to say, as a comforting myth did say, that they had been treated well. In one or two places like Alexandria and Cairo they had lived as part of a larger cosmopolitan community, along with Greeks, Armenians and Egyptians. This community was itself mortally threatened by the symbiotic growth of Zionism and Arab nationalism. For the rest, they avoided active persecution if they accepted their lot as an inferior minority; many of them, from Morocco to the Yemen, had lived in abject poverty even compared with the Jews of the Russian shtetl; and after the creation of the Jewish state they were harried and expelled. On top of Ashkenasi condescension towards the Arabs these new Israelis brought a distaste bred of intimacy; and they began to add something quite unforeseen, and slowly to change the character of the society.

Immigrants apart, there were many fascinated visitors to the new country, as pilgrims or curious reporters. Richard Crossman and Woodrow Wyatt were both British Labour politicians elected to Parliament in the landslide of 1945. Both were on the socialist Left of the party, as were other enthusiasts for Israel like Michael Foot: hard as it might later be to believe, most of the British and European, as well as American, Left was then deeply sympathetic to the Zionist experiment. Crossman visited what was still Palestine in 1946 as part of an Anglo-American committee of inquiry. Up until then he had been 'totally ignorant' about the subject, but he soon became an authority, in his own eyes at least. And he became a Zionist. It was often observed that Englishmen of the officer or official class in Mandatory Palestine had instinctively sided with the Arabs, and that this was in unconscious recollection of their own public-school days. The Arabs were the athletes, handsome, unintellectual outdoors men, while the Jews were the scholarship boys, clever, argumentative and to some tastes objectionable; true to public-school form, the 'masters' – the army and civilian officers – liked the former more than the latter. But this cut two ways.

A man like Crossman (for all that he was an Englishman of the official class, not to say a Wykehamist) instinctively sided with the Jews, just because they were clever and unruly, and above all because they stood for Progress. He predicted rightly that 'only a small minority of the Jews of the Dispersion will become members of the Jewish Commonwealth', and wrongly, though with characteristic assurance, that this commonwealth would become part of a much larger and predominantly Arab federation. 'Because it is a socialist community this small nation will have an influence on its backward neighbours disproportionate to its size, bringing to them the ideas and techniques of western civilisation.' Above all, Crossman admired (and doubtless identified with) 'the superb self-confidence of Palestine Jewry. They are troubled by no doubts or self-questioning. They cannot doubt the issue, because failure means extinction; and a nation which is never really a nation never believes that this is possible.'

This exalted tone was echoed by Wyatt, who visited Israel in 1950 to write a pamphlet about his visit with the evocative title, *The Jews at Home* (and with evocative drawings by John Minton, poetic artist of the English Neo-Romanticism). He was exhilarated by this extraordinary social experiment, though he also saw the dangers lurking. There was not only the potential conflict between the 'aristocracy' of Russian and Polish Jews and the scores of thousands of barely literate immigrants from Yemen, Irak and India (and even the Romanians were 'not as energetic or as purposeful as other Europeans'). There was another potential conflict between the secular Zionist state and 'the greatest danger of all ... a kind of clericalism similar to that in Roman Catholic countries'. And there was the hair-raising economy, with exports of £10.5 million in 1949 and imports of £87 million, a huge trade gap which could only be filled by outside subvention.

Another English visitor was shocked both by the economic folly and by the way nationalism was triumphing over humanity, even over common sense. Evelyn Waugh was no socialist, no Zionist, and no philosemite, but he was an astute witness. What he saw shocked him. As he wrote to his wife from the Jordanian side of the divided holy city in 1951, 'Both Jerusalems are full of huge cars flying UNO flags while both countries starve. Here there are half a million absolutely destitute and hopeless Arab refugees from Israel. Israel, starving and houseless, is importing 25,000 Jews a month from Mesopotamia, Abyssinia, the Yemen, everywhere. Neither side has any housing and both carefully demolish whole villages where enemies have lived.' Not only were villages demolished, the land on which they had sat was legally appropriated. For avoidance of doubt, as lawyers say, Israel passed a law which formally removed from Arabs who had fled (for whatever reason) any title to the land they had once owned. Thenceforth, many Israelis could have borrowed, if they had wished, the classic statement of brutal realism with which John Fitzgibbon, Lord Clare, tried to quieten the liberal posturing of his fellow Anglo-Irish landowners in 1789: 'The Act by which most of us hold our estates was an Act of violence – an Act subverting the first principles of the Common Law.'

There was more to the new state's curious social and economic condition. The definitive and characteristic social and economic institution was the kibbutz or collective, 'the purest form of socialism in existence'. Six years after the creation of the state, one more Englishman followed. The historian Hugh Trevor-Roper was likewise astonished by what he saw: 'What an extraordinary phenomenon of our time is Zionism! It was not only one of the great human movements of the age, it was the invasion of a new culture in an old world', with its bewildering paradoxes; 'a society cosmopolitan in its origins yet nationalist, even racialist, in its unifying tradition; a society modern in its technique yet of heroic archaism in its language and religion; a society which, at times, seems a little like Chicago in the Levant and, in places, like a monastic settlement in the mediaeval waste; a society with a western face, East European institutions, and an increasingly Levantine population.' He grasped that Zionism was, like socialism or fascism, a new secular religion – and that, unlike Judaism, it was active rather than passive, drastic not pathetic, 'a faith that can move mountains'.

He also saw, with greater penetration than most observers, the social objective of Zionism – 'the Jews are at last a society, not merely a class' – and yet, at the same time, how deceptive in appearance this was. It was a colonial enterprise, and ostensibly a parliamentary democracy with a mixed economy. And yet it had originally been created by east Europeans who brought with them not the ideas of western liberal, bourgeois democracy but the collective socialism of the old Russian intelligentsia. They had left as their legacy 'a society more collectivist than anything outside modern Communism'. Israel was not likely to become a Communist state on the Russian model. There was an Israeli Communist party, but it was tiny and its voters were mostly Christian Arabs of the Nazareth area. There was the larger Mapam party, Left-socialist, but it was dwarfed in turn by the great Mapai or

Labour party from which Mapam had seceded, which itself was profoundly collectivist but also profoundly hostile to Communism.

The antipathy was mutual, and a strange drama was now working towards its climax. This Jewish state was the most collectivised outside the Communist world; and yet it was sustained by charity from the greatest of capitalist countries. The American Jews had, at least by inheritance, a strong socialist tradition, and remained in general well to the left of the American average; and yet they were more and more of them riding high in that great capitalist economy. Some American Jews remained wedded not only to socialism but to its Soviet Communist form, and this might have seemed to endanger the reputation and position of Jewish America in the post-war decade, the first decade of the Cold War, the time of militant anti-Communism, of purges, of Senator Joseph McCarthy's brief but vivid career as a demagogue.

It might have seemed likely, or even inevitable, that all this would bring antisemitism in its wake. There were, from a demagogic point of view, reasons for identifying Jews with Communism. A much higher proportion of Jewish-Americans, from impoverished New York proletarians to overpaid Hollywood screenwriters, had at least flirted with Communism than of, say, Bible-belt Protestants or ethnic Catholics in big cities. At the height of the anti-Communist era, two Jewish Communists were convicted of espionage and executed. And yet, 'much to the surprise of American Jews', as one historian put it, 'antisemitism actually declined during this period'.

For one thing, McCarthy himself cast as his chief villains not Jews but WASPs, the Ivy League élite. Two of his sidekicks were called Cohn and Schine, one of his warmest supporters was Rabbi Benjamin Schultz of Mississippi. There were still Jew-baiters at large like Gerald L. K. Smith (who reproached McCarthy for not addressing the Jewish menace), there were still cranks putting out pamphlets called 'Jew Stars Over Hollywood', there was still much casual social and professional prejudice. But the fact was that militant anti-Communism was never transmuted into antisemitism.

The Rosenberg case was an intimately Jewish affair. All five defendants were Jews, but then so was the judge who sentenced Julius and Ethel Rosenberg to death for trying to pass secrets to the Russians. Although the Communist party and its stage army of hangers-on claimed that they were innocent victims of a frame-up, most Jewish Americans did not. Both Yiddish daily papers, the *Forward* and the *Day*, argued rightly that the Rosenbergs were guilty as charged and, also rightly, that the death sentence on them was barbarously harsh, especially when compared with the prison sentences on 'atomic spies' in England at the same time. Other Jews did not even complain about the sentence. The American Jewish Committee publicly supported the executions. So did Rabbi S. Andhill Fineberg. So did Lucy Dawidowicz, a future historian of the Final Solution, writing in *Commentary*, which was the most influential Jewish intellectual magazine in the country and at the time a bastion of anti-Communist liberalism.

There may have been in this an element of protesting too much, of falling over backwards to dissociate the community from guilt by association, but Jewish anti-Communism was terribly right, in a way not fully known at the time. The Rosenbergs were arrested in July 1950 and electrocuted in June 1953. This period coincided with the most savage phase of Soviet antisemitism. After a momentary lapse at the time Israel was born, when Moscow had been the first Power to recognise the new state *de jure*, Soviet Russia had reverted to its traditional anti-Zionism, indeed now added 'Zionist' to its vocabulary of demonising phrases. Numerous Jews had already been purged under the unmistakable euphemism of 'rootless cosmopolitans'. Now, in Stalin's last brutal years, the Slansky show trial in Prague and the 'Doctors' Plot' in Moscow were patently antisemitic exercises. And the Rosenbergs were in prison, exchanging their stilted party slogans from one cell to another, on 12 August 1952, the day when Dovid Hofstein, Dovid Bergelson, Perez Markish and other notable Yiddish-language writers and intellectuals were executed by Stalin. In this way the complicated, tormented relationship between the Jews and the Communist dream of hope came to a wretched end. Even when the full truth was not yet known, it was clear to all but the most pitifully deluded that Jews in search of a secular religion must look elsewhere.

Although a large shift from liberalism or social democracy (the terms varying from one country to another) was still a generation away among Dispersion Jewry during the first decade of Israel's existence, Jewish radicalism was inevitably eroded by Jewish social and economic success. Social antisemitism was far from dead even in those countries, England and America, which had just defeated National Socialism. In the United States genteel antisemitism fought a rearguard action, to the point where a sociologist could write that, in the years after 1945, the exclusion of Jews from clubs, hotels, resorts and residential districts was more widespread than in Germany in the year before 1933. These relics were a long time a-dying. In England the pattern was similar, though there the middle-class character of genteel antisemitism was more pronounced: for decades to come there were suburban golf clubs outside London which openly excluded Jews, but no West End gentlemen's club did so. Casual dislike of Jews was very prevalent in middle-class society, but there was less institutional exclusion in England than in America, just as there was less institutional colour-bar racism, and no doubt for the same reason, the fact that there were far fewer Jews, or black people, both in absolute and proportionate terms, than in America.

Even there, the lingering animosity mattered less than the explosive success of Jewish America in its third generation. Most academic barriers were now down, many Jews entered universities and professions. A particular group chose the new subject (not universally recognised as a true scholarly discipline) of English studies: it was a significant way of demonstrating identity with the mainstream culture; even more significant when critics like Lionel Trilling wrote about 'Eng. Lit.' in such a mandarin or even artificial style, as if trying too hard to prove a point. More important by far than critics like Trilling, Alfred Kazin or Richard Ellmann, or than the 'New York intellectuals' with their interminable intestine feuds, personal and political, were Jewish careers like those of film stars – Edward G. Robinson, Kirk Douglas or the enchanting Judy Holliday – and of Bess Myerson and Hank Greenberg, a beauty queen and a baseball player, both from the Bronx. The daughter of poor, radical, Yiddish-speaking immigrants, Myerson became Miss America in September 1945. At the end of the same month, Greenberg hit the ninth-inning home run which won the American League pennant for the Detroit Tigers. He had been playing for the Tigers since 1933, in what could claim to be the antisemitic capital of America, home of Henry Ford and Father Coughlin. He had twice been voted the League's Most Valuable Player, and once, in 1934, refused to play in a game which fell on Yom Kippur. Antisemitism seemed to have risen during the war, at the time of the Jews' great disaster, but declined by every perceptible measure after it, not least because, in Andrew Kopkind's words, recalling his childhood, 'Hank and Bess were winners, like Di Maggio and Grable – only smarter. They were as American as apple pie and the Fourth of July – and as Jewish as *knishes* and Yom Kippur. They belonged to a race of victors, not victims . . .'

So, of course, did the Israelis. The creation of the new state and its embattled survival were the cause of intense pride to Jews everywhere, even when the pride was tinged with incurable sardonic humour. The New York writer Delmore Schwartz was known for his brilliant story 'In Dreams Begin Responsibilities', for his inability to match it for the rest of his career, and for his inspiring the hero of Saul Bellow's novel *Humboldt's Gift*. In the summer of 1948, Schwartz gave his own verdict on the great adventure when he said that within a few months Israel would have changed its name to Irving. But this was just the self-mocking cynicism which humourless Zionism had put behind it.

Most Jews were happy that Israel had happened, and happy to leave it at that. They did not have the time or inclination to examine what the creation of a Jewish state had done to the Jewish Question. Some did, gentile as well as Jew. Shortly before Israel was born, Jean-Paul Sartre wrote a short book of *Réflexions sur la Question Juive*, published in English under the curiously different title *Portrait of the Antisemite*. It might have been an exaggeration to say of it, as George Orwell did, 'I doubt whether it would be possible to pack more nonsense into so short a space'; but not much of an exaggeration. Sartre insisted that antisemitism was artificial as well as irrational; that it was confined to the bourgeoisie, especially the petty variety, and unknown among the proletariat; and that it would disappear in a classless society ('the socialist revolution is necessary and sufficient to suppress the antisemite; we are staging that revolution for the Jews' sake *as well*', a claim which even Sartre might not have made so breezily if he had actually known anything about Soviet Russia rather than power-worshipped it from afar). He quoted the black American writer Richard Wright who had said that 'there is no black problem in the United States, only a white problem', and applied this without much originality to the Jewish Question; and, while asserting that assimilation was a dream as long as the antisemitism existed, Sartre praised the 'authentic Jew' who did not want to change his colours and disappear into gentile society. Orwell called this position dangerously close to antisemitism. It might alternatively have led logically to Zionism, though Sartre did not follow that logic.

Much more penetrating were two Jewish-American writers (both European by birth). Writing shortly before Israel was born, Hannah Arendt took as her subject 'Zionism Reconsidered', and, writing shortly after, Arthur Hertzberg saw 'American Zionism at an Impasse'. Arendt reflected at length on the history and philosophy of Zionism. She agreed with Sartre only to the degree that he had seen the Jew defined through the eyes of the antisemite, while she, though dismissing as absurd Herzl's definition of a nation as 'a group of people . . . held together by a common enemy' conceded that many Zionists had indeed been convinced that they were Jews by Jew-haters. She condemned the assimilation of the whole Zionist project to Revisionism, but she had something more to add.

Political theorists or historians are almost always unwise when they take on the role of prophet, as Marx had once shown, and as Arendt herself later demonstrated in *The Origins of Totalitarianism*. Here, however, she prophesied with great prescience. Moral consideration aside, she saw that a Jewish majority in Palestine – or 'even a transfer of all Palestine Arabs, which is openly demanded by Revisionists' – would leave Jewish Palestine dependent on the protection of an outside power. She saw that the old problem of dual loyalty had not gone away, least of all when Weizmann's British citizenship had forced him into a theory of predestined harmony of Zionist and British interests, 'which may or may not exist'. She saw at the same time the dual-loyalty problem might be solved by the differentiation between a 'Hebrew nation' in the Holy Land and a 'Jewish people' in America. At the same time, she was not optimistic about the hopes for compromise with the Arabs. Magnes and the socialists of Hashomer Hazair (Young Guard) in Palestine had advocated a binational state; but, Arendt said, this 'is no solution since it could be realised only as a result of a solution': a point which was to look unusually apt fifty years later.

Unlike Arendt, Hertzberg had been an active Zionist since adolescence. To begin with this had been an act of rebellion against his father, joining the Gordonia Labour youth group. This son of a rabbi became a rabbi himself and was serving at a synagogue in Nashville when he returned from a visit to the new-born state. This was after an episode which was dramatic in itself: the triumph of Zionism in the Dispersion in the aftermath of Hitlerism which had created 'a startling unanimity of Jewish opinion' in which Zionism became a 'moral crusade in which all world Jewry participated' with Bevin as the sworn enemy and the needs of the refugees paramount.

'We had all felt helpless, frustrated, and, in our inmost hearts immoral during the war as European Jews were being slaughtered. The fight for Israel united us so completely, I suspect, because it was at least a chance to make the world of murderers bend to our will, and also, perhaps, to relieve our guilt.' This was acute personal and collective self-analysis; but where did it leave Hertzberg and other American Zionists, who 'face an impasse'? At this remarkably early juncture, when 'Israelis' had existed for only a matter of months, Hertzberg recognised that by upbringing, American allegiance 'and by any desire to be part of the cultural traditions of the western world' he was not one of them, and was not going to become one. So, 'what shall I do with my Zionism?'

Despite the elation he shared with others, Hertzberg saw how the creation of Israel had created also a whole complex of new problems in the relations between Israelis and the Dispersion. 'Old-time Zionism' was almost at an end in an Israel which was its own justification. 'What the state wants is money, with no strings attached', and it would prefer to get it through Jewish leaders who would demand no influence or accountability. The Israeli leadership had made its position almost brutally clear: it expected financial support because of its open doors to refugees, it recognised an obligation to do nothing to injure the position of Jews in other countries, it acknowledged also the very real fear that the accusation of dual loyalty represented.

And yet, the conclusion drawn then from that acknowledgement was a curious one. In 1949, Moshe Sharett, now foreign minister of Israel, visited the United States and said (with more unconscious irony) that the Israeli government 'should allow no interference by Jews outside its borders'. He in turn met with repeated assurances from the American Zionist leadership that it would not meddle in the internal affairs of Israel. This was how the question of one relationship between Israel and Dispersion was seen in 1949; as events were to show, that was not the real nature of the problem.

Israel was now a sovereign state, with interests of her own, which she perceived through her own eyes, and which she defended as she saw fit. Having fought off the Arab armies in 1948, it faced years of gruelling guerrilla attacks across its borders from irreconcilable Palestinian exiles. These were met with more force; and at the same time the Israelis showed what they meant about not tolerating outside interference. In 1953, Israel proceeded with an irrigation plan to take water from the upper Jordan to the Negev desert, despite threats of war from Syria and despite remonstrations from the new Eisenhower Administration in Washington. Eisenhower's Secretary of State, John Foster Dulles, quietly held up a $26 million loan and, more seriously, threatened to cancel the tax exemption on charitable donations by the

United Jewish Appeal and this organisation raising money in the United States, but the Israeli government ignored these threats.

Later in the same year, a bomb was thrown into a house in an Israeli settlement close to the Jordanian border, killing a mother and two young children. According to the official story, enraged villagers spontaneously stormed across the border into the Jordanian village of Kibya and killed fifty of its inhabitants. The State Department again remonstrated, while Representative Jacob Javits of New York complained that the Administration was showing bias in condemning the response rather than the original atrocity: this was one of the earliest uses of the charge of 'double standards' which was to become so familiar. In reality, Kibya had not been spontaneous at all. It was a planned reprisal by Israeli troops under their chief of staff, Moshe Dayan, in which 250 soldiers led by a young officer, Ariel Sharon, had attacked the village with mortars and heavy machine-guns, blowing up forty houses and killing fifty-three civilians. Not long after this, at a meeting of the Israeli Cabinet, Dayan suggested that a war with Egypt could be provoked so as to open the straits of Eilat which were blockaded. This did not happen in 1954, but reprisal raids continued, the heaviest being against Gaza in early 1955.

All Israelis agreed that their country was besieged and embattled; not all agreed with armed ferocity. The most telling source for this disagreement is, indeed, a strange one. In December 1953, Ben-Gurion announced his retirement. This is still an obscure episode: he may have been suffering from some form of breakdown, or it may have been an elaborate ruse. At all events, he left behind a deliberately unworkable government in which Sharett became prime minister, but where the real power was held by Pinchas Lavon and Dayan, defence minister and chief of staff, who kept their prime minister in the dark. Sharett was a pioneer, brought to Palestine from the Ukraine in 1906 when he was twelve. He had grown up near Nablus in what was still an Arab village, and learned to speak Arabic as well as Hebrew. He was a founding member of Mapai and edited *Davar*, the Labour Zionist newspaper. Sharett was always overawed by Ben-Gurion, the more formidable personality though not his intellectual equal, and was willingly used by him. All Sharett's reservations were confined to his diary, which was not published until 1978, after his death, against the wishes of the Begin government, and then only in Hebrew.

He might be seen as a figure of fun, a head of government who wrote privately about the need for an understanding with Egypt while those who were meant to be led by him were organising military raids or spy rings in Egypt (with disastrous results) unknown to him. But from his weird position as ostensible leader, but sceptical critic, of his country, he played another part, as surreptitious truth-teller. He told the Cabinet that Kibya had 'exposed us in front of the whole world as a gang of blood-suckers, capable of mass massacres, regardless, it seems, of whether their actions may lead to war'. And when several army reserve soldiers confessed that, to avenge the murder of an Israeli couple, they had rounded up five Bedouin boys, interrogated them, and then killed them, Sharett pondered on the character of these new Hebrews whom he had helped to produce, with their ability and even spiritual grace combined with a capacity 'for calculated cold-blooded murder, by knifing the bodies of young defenceless Bedouin'; and he wondered 'which of those two biblical souls will win over the other in this People?'

Had Ben-Gurion known of these private musings he would have been even more contemptuous of Sharett than he was at the time, but he himself was not quite the man of uncompromising, bluff honesty he liked to appear. He scorned Sharett for worrying about 'what the Gentile will say', but Ben-Gurion did not neglect this consideration himself. In its early years, Israel was patently obliged to defend herself by force; her record was no worse, and in many ways much better, than other comparably embattled countries. Her neighbours were set on her extinction, and casualties from the hit-and-run cross-border raids were serious and rising (from 137 in 1951 to 238 in 1955). All of this might have been justification for self-defence. Certainly, Jabotinsky would not have hesitated to justify it. But Ben-Gurion's hostility to 'Vladimir Hitler' and his political heirs was both a strength and a weakness. It was highly convenient to him to have a, for the time being, discredited and marginalised right-wing opposition led by Begin, about which very few American Jews knew much and with which even fewer in the 1950s would have chosen to identify. At the same time, the claim that there was an absolute difference between, on the one hand, mainstream Zionism and Labour who were in charge of the new state, and the Revisionist tradition on the other, when, as Hannah Arendt had said, the very creation of Israel was in essence a Revisionist achievement, invoked a pretence and created a false position which stored up trouble for the future.

Gentile critics of Israel were met with an accusation of antisemitism, but this would not do against Dispersion Jewry. Something else was needed, and an elaborate game had begun. Not long before Israel was born, Weizmann had called on the American Jews to make aliyah. He was seconded more loudly after 1948. On his first visit to Israel, everybody asked Hertzberg, 'When are you Americans coming to settle here?' Ben-Gurion repeatedly said that, whatever else Israel needed, what it needed above all was Jews. He told a visiting delegation of American Zionists that the great project had only begun: 'the greater part of the Jewish people is still abroad. Our next step will not be easier than the creation of Israel. It consists in bringing all the Jews to Israel . . . We appeal chiefly to the youth of the United States and other countries to help us achieve this big mission. We appeal to the parents to help us bring their children here. Even if they decline to help, we will bring the youth to Israel.'

These strangely minatory words must have embarrassed their hearers. Perhaps they were meant to. But Jewish America was annoyed as well as embarrassed, and the American Jewish Committee threatened to turn off support for Israel if this demand was repeated. It was Ben-Gurion who backed down. In August 1950, he met Jacob Blaustein, president of the committee, and conceded that 'the Jews of the United States have only one political attachment and that is to the United States of America. They owe no political allegiance to Israel . . .

'The government and the people of Israel fully respect the right and integrity of the Jewish communities in other countries to develop their own mode of life and their indigenous social, economic and cultural institutions in accordance with their own needs and aspirations.' For his part, Blaustein added that 'to American Jews, America is home. Here, exist their thriving roots; there, is the country which they have helped to build; and there, they share its fruits and destiny. They believe in the future of a democratic society in the United States in which all citizens . . . can live on terms of equality.' Here was the making of an ingenious compromise. Israel publicly recognised what everyone had always known, that few Jews from the West would come to settle. To be sure, dramatically few did. Between 1948 and 1967, 1.3 million Jews came to Israel, an average of 45,000 a year. And yet, fewer than 3,000 a year came from England, and, in the first ten years of Israel's existence, north America with its Jewish population of more than five millions, the largest Jewish community on earth, provided an annual average of fewer than 5,000 immigrants to the new Jewish state. Brandeis had told American Jews that they did not need to leave

America to be good Zionists, and this was now something like a formal doctrine.

Lewis Namier's own relationship with Zionism had ended unhappily, as had so much else in his life. It had long been plain, as Isaiah Berlin put it, 'that his unwavering and withering contempt for most of his Zionist colleagues had made it certain that if an independent Jewish establishment ever emerged he would not be among its leaders'. He found some alleviation for his personal loneliness and bitterness in marriage to a gentile, but when this was accompanied with conversion to the Church of England it cost him the friendship of Weizmann, who reacted instinctively to 'an act of apostasy for which no decent motive could exist'. Namier visited Israel after Weizmann's death and was deeply moved, though he remained fervently anticlerical and early foresaw the growing power of the rabbis and religious factions.

But it was in another context that Namier unconsciously described what was happening to the Dispersion in its relations with Israel. He had suffered from grave disappointment in his own career. He longed to be a professor at Oxford, but whenever an apparently suitable Chair came up it went to someone else, usually someone inferior, in his view. He once bitterly told a friend how such appointments were decided. 'In the eighteenth century there was a club called the Koran Club. The qualification for membership was to have travelled in the East. Then it was found that there were various persons whom it was thought desirable to make members of the club and who had not travelled in the East. So the rules were changed from "travelling in the East" to "expressing a wish to travel in the East". That is how they make professors in Oxford.' However that may have been at Oxford, Namier was unwittingly but exactly describing the Zionism of western Jews. They could join the club merely by expressing a wish which all knew would never be carried out.

There was a price to be paid for club membership. The old anxieties, and accusations, about dual loyalty had been almost silenced, though not entirely. Shortly after Israel was born, Harold Laski had criticised the British government's failure immediately to recognise the new state. In reply, the *Spectator*, organ of civilised Conservatism, asked whether he spoke as 'a Jew or an Englishman?'. It would appear that 'Mr Laski is a Jew first and an Englishman second'. He was perfectly entitled to order his loyalties thus, the *Spectator* said, 'But if that is his choice, his right place would seem to be Palestine, not England.'

Across the Atlantic, not only was such a question no longer raised in public, but very few Jews expressed any public criticism of Israel, however little committed they might have felt to Zionism in a practical sense. This was true from the earliest moment after the foundation of the state. In 1949 the *Reader's Digest* published two articles under self-explanatory titles, 'The Case for Israel' by Rabbi Abba Hillel Silver, and 'Israel's Flag is not Mine' by Alfred M. Lilienthal, arguing for and against a close identification of Jewish America with the Jewish state. This marked the moment when reasoned and temperate opposition to Zionism became practically impossible for any American Jew outside esoteric intellectual circles, the extreme Left, or the most narrow Orthodoxy. Lilienthal was denounced from at least fourteen rabbinical pulpits; the *Intermountain Jewish News* of Colorado called on the Anti-Defamation League to recognise that 'Jews can be antisemitic and crack down on those who carp about dual loyalty in the public press'; a dozen other Jewish papers violently attacked the article; when Lilienthal sent a copy of it to Herman Wouk, a school-friend of his before he became the best-selling author of *The Caine Mutiny*, Wouk lamented 'a terrible personal blunder, probably the worst of your life ... at the cost of your co-religionists'. He added, in peculiarly significant words, '*The better your case, the worse your error would have been.* Your proper course, if you feel so strongly about this, was to dedicate your days to spreading your view in Jewish circles, as the Zionists do.' In other words, don't rock the boat, don't make waves, don't break ranks, don't let the team down by voicing any criticism which could be of value to Israel's foes. Wouk can hardly have guessed how he was setting the pattern.

A deal had been silently struck. The Jewish state had been created. Jewish opposition to Zionism, which had had such a long history, and often a morally and intellectually honourable one, was almost extinguished. It became morally intolerable for any Jew to oppose Israel, or even publicly to criticise her. At the same time, only a small minority of Jews actively wished to live in this Jewish state. Most of the Israeli population was composed of people, or the descendants of people, who had gone there because they had no choice: of refugees fleeing Polish antisemitism and Hitler's mad persecution between the wars, of the remnant of mass murder after 1945 who were offered refuge nowhere else, of the Jews of Araby who were now driven out of their native lands and likewise had nowhere else to go.

The increasingly assimilated and increasingly prosperous Jews of the West, above all of the United States, became sentimental Zionists in the sense that they admired Israel from afar, but did not intend to become practical Zionists in the sense of making aliyah. They thus felt that they not only should support Israel, but support it uncritically; that they had no right to tell Israel how to order its affairs; that they would obey Sharett's instruction that the Dispersion should not interfere in Israel's politics. And yet the bargain was not reciprocal. Israeli politicians believed, it soon became clear, that western Jewry owed them everything, but that Israel owed western Jewry nothing but its very existence.

14

They and we

I will magnify thee, O Lord, for thou hast set me up:
and not made my foes to triumph over me.

Ps.xxx.1

Before Israel reached her tenth birthday, her determination to look after herself at all costs was put to the test, and so was the question of loyalties for Dispersion Jewry. Israel's second war was one in which she played an almost consciously ignoble part, a role resented by her leaders even as the action was taking place. In 1954, two years after the preposterous King Farouk had been overthrown, power was taken in Egypt by Colonel Gamal Abdul Nasser, preposterous also though in a different way. The Levant and Araby had now become crucial battlefields in the Cold War and different countries were forced into surrogate positions not wholly of their own choosing. The Anglo-American Baghdad Pact forced Nasser into a Soviet alliance. In 1955, he made a large arms deal with Russia, and a military alliance with Syria. At the end of the year Ben-Gurion returned to office, almost as a precursor to hostilities; but, much as he saw Nasser as the enemy, the conflict of the following year was not of his design.

For different reasons, Nasser had enraged the British and the French, and they determined to get rid of him. More ambitious still, they hoped, as Conor Cruise O'Brien drily puts it, to perform the dextrous feat of toppling the most popular of the Arab leaders without forfeiting Arab goodwill. Following his nationalisation of the Suez Canal in July, a plan of baroque complexity, secrecy and mendacity was hatched. Israel would attack Egypt on a pretext and then, with this attack itself as a pretext, Anglo-French forces would intervene allegedly to separate the combatants.

This conspiracy proved a disaster for all the conspirators. Anglo-French military capability did not match the speed of the Israeli advance. The American Administration was outraged and pulled the financial rug from under the British government, which had innocently assumed at least the tacit co-operation of Washington. This had the incidental effect of exposing the grand illusion of post-war British policy, that British and American interests were congruent, and of demonstrating that the 'special relationship' was special chiefly in the degree of self-deception it required. The military operation was halted before it achieved its supposed objectives: Nasser was still in power, the canal was not reacquired by the West, and Israel was left high and dry, the object of much international obloquy. Almost every consequence of Suez was unintended, or at least unforeseen. Apart from Nasser, a new mood of nationalist militancy swept the Arab world. A radical revolution overthrew the Hashemite monarchy in Irak, Fatah was founded to promote Palestinian defiance to Israel, leading to the creation of the Palestine Liberation Organisation under Nasser's auspices in 1964.

Israel's international position had changed. In the early years her foreign policy had been 'non-identification', with, that is, either side in the Cold War, East or West. This policy may have been well-intended, but it was doomed, and within a few years it was effectively abandoned. Suez found Israel in alliance with the old European imperial powers, to the distress of many of her friends. The Jewish-American leadership had no more inkling of the plot than did the White House, had indeed repeated the assurances given by Ben-Gurion that Israel would not begin a war. One important Jewish-American businessman and friend of Israel, Philip Klutznick, insisted that rumours about an Israeli attack were false while speaking at a dinner, though the attack was under way as he spoke.

Greatly as they resented it, Jewish-American leaders swallowed this humiliation. Abba Eban, the Israeli ambassador in Washington, reported 'a difficult hour' of discussion with one Jewish-American eminence, and that 'for the first time in our memory there was a reluctance to justify Israel's action without reserve'. Dulles tried to enlist leaders to put pressure on Israel to withdraw and achieved a momentary success. Rabbi Abba Hillel Silver, who had already expressed his disquiet to Eban, passed on a message reminding Ben-

Gurion 'that Israel's power and future are in fact bound up in the United States', which was true and was to become truer every year. But no criticism of Israel's action was expressed in public; the bullet was bitten.

Critics on the Left were later to condemn the American-Israeli relationship as a corrupt form of quasi-imperialism or shabby power politics. That quite missed the point. Had Israel and the United States been old-regime autocracies, the relations between them would have been based on calculations of interest, or brutal realpolitik, and might even have been the healthier for it. Both were in fact modern mass democracies, with all that implied. The Israeli lobby in Washington had already begun to exploit very skilfully the division of power there: for the next forty years, Congress was always to prove more susceptible to blandishment than the White House. Just as Dulles was threatening Israel with financial sanctions, the Democratic majority leader in the Senate, Lyndon Johnson of Texas, one of Israel's most reliable friends on Capitol Hill, was telling Eban that the White House was not 'going to get a goddam thing' from Congress until it treated Israel fairly.

Both Eisenhower and Johnson were chosen by popular election, and in Eisenhower's case by national election, but it may be that Johnson was the authentic populist in this question, and his party also. Bevin had brutally accused the Truman Administration of playing for the Jewish vote. This was not so much true as becoming true. In the Roosevelt years, the Democrats had taken the Jewish vote for granted: not surprisingly when, in 1944, 92 per cent of Jews had voted for Roosevelt. The 1948 presidential election was the first in which the Jewish vote was an important, conscious consideration. From then on, American politicians in general and Democrats in particular clearly did work for this vote, sometimes to an almost comical extent. All American politicians, it was facetiously said, believed that every Jew voted twice; but behind the joke lay a curious reality. For one thing, if members of one group (say Jewish-Americans) were more than twice as likely to vote as members of another group (say black Americans), then the former did indeed proportionately 'vote twice' in statistical terms. Added to that, the Jewish community was concentrated in fewer than a dozen electorally crucial states, 4 per cent or more of the population in New Jersey, Florida, Massachusetts, Maryland, and all of 12 per cent in New York. Add finally the closeness of several presidential elections – 1960 decided by 119,000 out of 68 million votes, 1968 by 510,000 out of

63 million, 1976 by 1.7 out of 80 million – and the obsession of so many American politicians with Jewish votes seems rational enough.

Not that the equation was always simple quid pro quo. Truman recognised Israel in 1948, but fewer Jews voted for him later that year than had for Roosevelt four years earlier, and he won the election despite losing New York. Equally, presidents could favour Israel with no thought of electoral advantage. During the 1973 war, President Nixon gave unstinting support to Israel, despite the fact that only a third of Jewish-Americans had voted for him the previous November and that he was ineligible to run for the White House a third time in 1976 (even had other events not intervened). Support for Israel, in other words, was to become an imperative for any American politician of whichever party.

Congress had tilted heavily towards Israel from its creation, reflecting both a healthy respect for the Jewish vote and a recognition that broader public opinion was itself pro-Israeli. This disposition was strengthened in 1954 with the formation of the American Zionist Council for Public Affairs, which was renamed the American Israeli Public Affairs Committee in 1959. AIPAC was destined to acquire an awe-inspiring reputation as the most formidable – and sometimes least scrupulous – lobby in Washington. In 1954 also, the Conference of Presidents of Major American Jewish Organisations was created with the undisguised purpose, not of representing the common interests of American Jewry but of helping Israel in the face of the apparent hostility of the Eisenhower Administration.

The Administration was not wholly cowed by lobbying. In 1957, Dulles replied to remonstrations from Senator William Knowland, the Republican minority leader: 'I am aware how almost impossible it is in this country to carry out a foreign policy not approved by the Jews. Marshall and Forrestal found that. I am going to try to have one.

'This does not mean that I am anti-Jewish, but I believe in what George Washington said in his Farewell Address that an emotional attachment should not interfere.' His point was that Israel was entitled to pursue its own interests, but that 'we cannot have our policies made in Jerusalem'. This was to be the secret, though often vain, hope of all successors, and it was seconded by a few, though only a few, Jewish-Americans, who believed that, in Lilienthal's words, 'American Jews should no longer be forced, by smears and fears, to have a foreign policy separate from that of Methodists or Episcopalians'. As events would show, this wish was to prove vain also.

Similar tensions existed in other western countries. In England, Suez had been a great political upheaval, and had polarised politically conscious opinions like the Dreyfus Affair in France sixty years earlier. Broadly speaking, the liberal Left deplored the whole operation, which had been mounted by Anthony Eden's Tory government and which was backed by jingoists and imperialists, though also by those, led by Eden himself, who were still haunted – and misled – by the memories of Munich and appeasement. But there were exceptions to the broad pattern. Tories of Arabist sympathies regretted the attack. And although most British Jews still stood on the Left in the 1950s, a majority of them voting for the Labour party which condemned Suez, their sympathy for Israel took them against the leftist grain. There were even cases of Jewish-owned businesses threatening to withdraw advertising from liberal newspapers which had denounced the operation. In England and France, as in America, sympathy for Israel was far from confined to Jews, and it was not only British Jewry which was perplexed by Suez. The liberal Left as a whole was still strongly disposed towards Israel, though what Edward Tivnan says of Americans was true of most British and French people also, of all political opinions: they 'knew virtually nothing about Zionism, and less about events in Israel'.

Within Jewry, the debates over Zionism were not ended, but they were confined to small circles and esoteric journals. Writing in the *Menorah Journal* two years after Suez, Hans Kohn reflected on 'Zion and the Jewish National Ideal'. He saw that Zionism had combined the traditional of hypothetical longing for Zion with something new, borrowed from the political nationalism of late-nineteenth-century Europe, which was not only nothing to do with Jewish traditions but was in many ways opposed to them. He saw that the Palestinian Arab of *Altneuland* who said 'the Jews have enriched us, why should we be angry with them? They live with us like brothers, why should we not love them?' was in every sense a figment of Herzl's fictive imagination, as had been painfully shown: there was now nowhere in the world where a Jewish community was regarded with such distrust and hostility as in the Land of Israel; 'Nowhere have Jews felt so exposed as in Palestine.' He realised that 'in an indirect way, foreseen by neither Herzl nor Hitler, Hitlerism did make the Jewish state possible. Herzl's political Zionism had not only been an outgrowth of German nationalism, the theory that 'people of common descent or speaking a common language should form one common state'. This theory itself ran counter to the prevailing idea of the West, above all of the United States, in which nations were not the product of 'immutable laws of race' but were composed of people of entirely different and sometimes unknown descent, but owing a willed and subjective common allegiance. Zionism had succeeded in one way: a state existed, but 'military victory created the new state; and, like Sparta or Prussia, on military virtue it remained based'.

Unlike Kohn, most Dispersion Jews were impressed and excited by just this display of military virtue, but they, especially the Americans, might have pondered his point about nationalism. The triumph of the American Jews sometimes seemed to be symbiotically linked to the triumph of the heroic or new Hebrews more than five thousand miles away. A 'beautiful national legend' was taking shape, in fact and in fiction.

In 1958, Leon Uris's novel *Exodus* was published, and became a runaway best-seller. There can have been few Jewish-American households without a copy of a book whose different editions sold twenty million copies. Millions more saw the 1960 movie, directed by Otto Preminger and starring Paul Newman, Hollywood making one of its few contributions to Jewish history.[1] Not, however, an even-handed one. The book, and movie, gave what the *New York Times* called 'a passionate summary of the inhuman treatment of the Jewish people in Europe, of the exodus of the nineteenth and twentieth centuries to Palestine and the triumphant founding of the new Israel'. Uris showed some sympathy for the Irgun; the Arabs, as the *New York Times* meiotically said, 'come off badly'. They were almost a cross between two earlier Hollywood stereotypes, the simple darkie of the antebellum South, and the savage Indian of Westerns. *Exodus* gave an immensely heartening picture of the birth of a nation; Dispersion Jews could identify with their people undergoing unspeakable suffering, and then their people shaking off the shackles of spiritual and physical servitude, standing proud and free and walking tall. It was a view of what was, without question, an epic story, but unclouded by a hint of moral doubt about the use of force to establish the state or the way the Arabs had been driven out.

Something else happened, which is hard to date exactly but is

---

[1] Although there had been a quaint case of rewritten history in the 1951 film of *Ivanhoe*. In Scott's novel, the brave Jewish girl Rebecca is banished; in the movie, Elizabeth Taylor's Rebecca is fondly sent away to a promised Palestinian homeland.

unmistakable and most important. Often when a man is gravely wounded, the shock numbs him to pain. Only when the numbness slowly wears off does the wound become excruciating. Something like that happened to the Jews after the last survivors left the death camps. Another extraordinary event, the creation of Israel, took minds off what had happened, but in any case minds were dulled by the very horror. There is a parallel with another twentieth-century tragedy. The Great War was the first war which the English people ever fought on a continental scale, with a huge army and huge casualties, three-quarters of a million British soldiers killed, almost twenty thousand of them on one day in July 1916. After the Armistice in 1918, England was numb to pain. Ten years followed of frivolity and forgetfulness, the 1920s of *Brideshead Revisited* and flappers and Bright Young People. Then the numbness wore off. A decade after the war, in the space of two or three years, all the books were published which shaped our consciousness of it:[2] all of them telling explicitly or implicitly the same story, the stupidity, brutality and horror of war. This was the outlook which shaped English feeling – and also British foreign policy – during the following decade.

Something of the same kind happened with the Final Solution. To a degree which it would later be hard to grasp, the extermination of the European Jews either did not register in the world's consciousness or was underplayed. There was a vague awareness of the horrors of 'concentration camps', but this phrase in itself elided an essential distinction. During the Boer War, the British had interned or concentrated civilians in what they called 'concentration camps' and, when Hitler came to power, he borrowed the name in wicked mockery for the camps where he imprisoned his opponents. There was a difference of kind between these camps, like Belsen and Dachau, which were on German soil, which were publicly acknowledged for the purpose of terror, and which were liberated by the Anglo-American allies in 1945, and the wholly unique death camps, like Treblinka and Maidanek, which were in the East, which were shrouded in secrecy, whose purpose was extermination, and which were liberated (though as empty shells) by the Russians with less publicity.

The full horror was in some manner blanked out. This sounds

---

[2] In 1928: *Undertones of War* by Edmund Blunden; *Journey's End* (a play) by R. C. Sherriff; 1929: *Death of a Hero* by Richard Aldington; *Goodbye to All That* by Robert Graves; 1930: *Memoirs of an Infantry Officer* by Siegfried Sassoon; *Her Privates We* by Frederic Manning.

unlikely, but it is so. Attlee's 'very little difference in the amount of torture' is one example. An even weirder one is G. D. H. Cole, a desiccated, puritanical English historian and socialist. In 1947, he published an immensely thorough, if brisk and jejune, *Intelligent Man's Guide to the Post-war World*. Discussing the political prospects for Austria, he remarked on the strong Catholic influence, 'though Social Democratic Vienna, with its large Jewish population, would not be similarly affected'. This was written two years after the Red Army had reached the chimneys of Auschwitz. It had simply not impinged on Cole that Jewish Vienna, that birthplace of so much genius, anxiety, hope and fear, had been extirpated without trace.

No one even knew quite what to call the extirpation. From 1942 the German government used the word, *Endlösung*, Final Solution, as one euphemism for their systematic extermination of the Jews (they also used the code name '*Nacht und Nebel*', night and fog, a line taken – all too appropriately, some Jews might have thought – from one of Wagner's operas). Jewry had no real name to describe the event; the Hebrew words *hurban* and *shoah* (catastrophe) never passed into western languages. Another word did. From the Greek, 'holocaust' means a whole consumed by fire; that is, a sacrificial burnt offering. It has been used in English since the thirteenth century, with the sense of a great destruction and continues to be used occasionally in the context of a 'nuclear holocaust', but it was a literary, mandarin expression, what Fleet Street sub-editors used to call a seven-and-sixpenny word, even with overtones of polysyllabic humour: when James Stewart spoke of 'holocausts' of love as he wooed Katharine Hepburn in the classic 1940 Hollywood comedy *The Philadelphia Story*, the effect was deliberately facetious.

While the catastrophe was in progress and news of it seeped out, the word 'holocaust' came naturally to some writers and speakers. It was used in a London newspaper in 1942. The following year a speaker in the House of Lords spoke of 'this holocaust', in 1945 a writer referred to 'the Nazi holocaust'. By the late 1950s, the term was taking root with its definite article: the *Yad Washem Bulletin*, dedicated to the subject, mentioned 'the Holocaust Period' in 1957 and 'the Holocaust' the following year. But it was not fully in common currency: a best-selling book issued by an American publisher in 1959 under the name *Holocaust* was about a fire at a Boston night-club in 1942. A few years later, that name could not have been used for that book: 'the Holocaust' was a name that had entered the language.

It was all the same a sorry coining.³ To the end of his life Primo Levi insisted in print and in conversation that it should not be used: 'I never like this expression Holocaust; it seems to me inappropriate, it seems to me rhetorical, above all mistaken.' The British historian J. P. Stern, himself of Czech-Jewish origin, asked angrily: 'Why the misprision – the monstrous catachresis – of "the holocaust"? In what conceivable way was this a "sacrifice or burnt offering"? Where, above all, was the freedom which is entailed in every meaningful notion of sacrifice?' Equally, the Israeli novelist Amos Oz refused to use 'shoah': 'The word *shoah* falsifies the true nature of what happened. A *shoah* is a natural event beyond human control.' These linguists and moral critics were right, but wrong. Right, because the Final Solution was in no sense a natural disaster or a 'sacrifice', even by the barbarous standards of Antiquity when animals and sometimes human beings were sacrificially killed. No purpose was intended by the slaughter of those millions, and none was achieved. But wrong, because a deep psychological need existed among the survivors – and in this sense all Jews were survivors – to invest the incomprehensible event with meaning. The concept of a holocaust, sacrifice as well as catastrophe, was helpful to this end. It was intolerable to face the truth: that their deaths had no meaning beyond the fact that they had been killed. In denying that, the 'Holocaust' concept helped Jews, maybe American Jews most of all, to cope with the pain they felt as they emerged from their numbness.

During the second decade of Israel's existence, several events heightened consciousness of the Final Solution. One drama began in May 1960 when Israeli agents discovered Adolf Eichmann in the suburbs in Buenos Aires where he was hiding. Eichmann was an Austrian, like so many of the senior executives of the Final Solution. He had been closely connected with the extermination of the European Jews from 1941, when he had drafted Goering's order for 'a total solution of the Jewish question in the German sphere of influence in Europe', to the massacre of the Hungarian Jews in 1944. There was no question as to his identity or as to what he had done. He admitted everything, and at first (though he later conducted an elaborate defence) histrionically offered to hang himself publicly, 'if it would give greater significance to the act of atonement'.

There was little doubt in the minds of most Israelis, or of many

³ And has been avoided as far as possible in this book for that reason.

others, as to the justice of his trial, though it raised painful juridical questions. Eichmann was tried under the Nazi and Nazi Collaborators (Punishment) Act of 1950 by which the Israeli state authorised the trial and capital punishment of persons for deeds committed not only by foreigners and on foreign jurisdiction but before that very state had come into existence. This took 'retroactive legislation' to an extreme never seen before in legal history, and to say that the wickedness which the Act addressed was also unparalleled was, in terms of the rule of law, beside the point. On top of that, Israeli lawyers declined as a body to defend Eichmann, and the law had to be changed to allow a foreigner to do so. There was no question but that the trial of Adolf Eichmann was fair as it was conducted, in point of evidence and correct procedure. But it was also in the strict sense of the phrase a show trial, mounted with a plainly didactic and even dramatic purpose, emphasised by the spectacle of the defendant in his glass box. He was convicted and condemned in December 1961 and, after appeals and calls for clemency were rejected, he was hanged on 31 May 1962, his body cremated and the ashes strewn at sea.

The trial had been an international 'media event', covered by 166 Israeli correspondents and 976 from abroad. More than one of these correspondents wrote a book, but one book caused a controversy entirely of its own. In 1963, Hannah Arendt published her account of the trial, *Eichmann in Jerusalem*. The storm had already broken following its serialisation in the *New Yorker*, one Jewish-American paper ran its story under the headline 'Self-hating Jewess writes pro-Eichmann series'. Her book itself was received with uniform hostility by Jewish critics. Lionel Abel in the *Partisan Review* summarised a complaint felt by many, that Eichmann 'comes off so much better in her book than do his victims'. This was echoed by Marie Syrkin in *Dissent*, one of two leading intellectual magazines of Jewish America: 'the only one who comes out better than when he came in is the defendant. The victim comes out worst.' And in *Commentary*, the other magazine (whose development was to tell a story all of its own about Jewish America), Norman Podhoretz wrote that 'In place of the monstrous Nazi [Arendt] gives us the "banal" Nazi; in place of the Jew as virtuous martyr, she gives us the Jew as accomplice in evil; and in place of the confrontation of guilt and innocence, she gives us the "collaboration" of criminal and victim'.

Arendt's book had hit two raw nerves. Her subtitle gave a phrase to the world: 'the Banality of Evil'. Whether this concept was itself brilliant or banal, it stuck. The idea was really nothing new. It had always been obvious that Hitler, like Stalin, was a man of complete personal mediocrity and intellectual banality, and the contrast between this and the evil that Hitler, like Stalin, had done was one of the paradoxes of the age. From Caesar to Cromwell to Napoleon to Bismarck, earlier 'great men' may have been bad men, as Acton said, but they were often men of parts, whose thoughts and writings – whose musical compositions, in the case of Henry VIII and Frederick the Great – were interesting in themselves. So for that matter were Herzl, Weizmann and Jabotinsky personally remarkable men.

With the twentieth century came a new type of great man, capable of vast deeds of destruction and possessing a kind of genius for political manipulation, but otherwise utterly empty and uninteresting, Hitler and Stalin being the epitomes. Eichmann himself was a vapid and pointless human being, a bureaucrat who had applied himself to the task of killing Jews as he might have done to improving a water supply or a banking system, all part of a day's work. This much of Arendt's book was true; and it was painful. Part of the building of a 'holocaust consciousness', by Israelis and the Dispersion, had been to invest a cosmic significance in the event. The 'Jewish Holocaust' was an experience and a purpose unique to the one people. The great killing had mattered in the sense that the dead had died for something. The 'Holocaust' was to be seen as a battlefield, as Lincoln had seen Gettysburg. Israel did, consciously sometimes as well as unconsciously, see Hitler's victims in those terms: those who gave their lives that this nation might live, those honoured dead who gave the last full measure of devotion; above all, Jews resolved 'that the dead shall not have died in vain'. There was something intolerable in being told that 'too much meaning is being heaped upon the victims', as Ian Buruma later put it; that the awful truth might be that they died 'for nothing. There was no higher meaning attached to their deaths. They were killed, because they were denied the right to live. And that was all.'

Hannah Arendt may have been the first to suggest this possibility. Her portrait of Eichmann did not deny that he *was* evil, but painted him in terms which Dostoyevsky would have understood. The devil when he comes to Ivan Karamazov is a shabby-genteel flunky, who seems 'stupid and vulgar' to Ivan; he only wants 'to be a gentleman and recognised as one'. He replies to Ivan's abuse, telling him, 'You are really angry with me for not having appeared to you in a red glow, with thunder and lightning, with scorched wings, and for showing myself in a modest guise. You are wounded in the first place in your aesthetic feelings, and secondly, in your pride.' This was what many felt when told that the National Socialists were mediocre and banal, with the implication that what they did also was.

But one passage of Arendt's book caused outrage and anger beyond all others, her discussion of the Jewish Councils. In many territories they conquered or controlled, the National Socialists to some extent co-opted the local people to carry out their administration. Under German tutelage, Jewish Councils were formed to run each Jewish community; to collect and concentrate widespread Jewish population in easily suppressed ghettos; and in the end to oversee the orderly evacuation of the Jews to the killing centres where they were murdered. Arendt wrote of these Councils in harsh language: 'If the Jewish people had really been unorganised and leaderless, there would have been chaos and plenty of misery, but the total number of victims would hardly have been between 4.5 and 6 million people.' Even this statement is not so obviously true as Arendt thought. In central and eastern Europe, the Germans followed the imperial practice of delegating the management of civil society to local leaders. In conquered Russia, there were no Jewish Councils, no civil society, only a savage Hobbesian state of nature; and that had not stopped the Germans from very effectively exterminating all the Jews they could find.

For writing as vehemently as she did, Arendt was denounced with even greater vehemence by Jewish critics. They plainly felt that she had let the side down, insulted her own people in her icy pursuit of some abstract truth. Gershon Sholem made the reproach as gently as he could: 'In the Jewish tradition, there is a concept . . . we know as *Ahabath Israel*: "Love of the Jewish people". In you, dear Hannah, as in so many intellectuals who came from the German Left, I find little trace of this.' But if her Jewish critics were severe, Arendt's gentile defenders like Mary McCarthy and Dwight Macdonald were too breezy. The League of B'nai B'rith went to one extreme in denouncing *Eichmann in Jerusalem* as 'an evil book'; Mary McCarthy went to the other, not only calling the book 'splendid' but, in a flight of pretentious whimsy, finding in it 'a paean of transcendence, heavenly music, like that in the final Chorus of *Figaro* or of the *Messiah*'.

It was one thing to deride the calls for more Jewish team spirit, or for less morbid self-criticism; Norman Podhoretz's plaintively asked, 'the Nazis destroyed a third of the Jewish people. In the name of all that is human, will the remnant never let up on itself?' A more telling criticism of Arendt applied whether she was herself Jewish or not, and whoever Hitler's victims might have been. Her analysis was altogether too chilly and detached, and partook too much of the notoriously easy judgement of those who have never had to endure conditions, and face choices, too terrible to understand in the abstract. An English critic was more compassionate and acute: 'It is one of the horrors of the present age', John Sparrow wrote, 'that it has thrust upon the ordinary citizen the necessity of making choices of a kind that used to be familiar to us only from the pages of the historian or the casuist.'

Not all Jews were susceptible to these calls for group loyalty, not all rode along with the attempt to enlist their unconditional support. The question of Jewish identity was as fascinating, and as vexed, as ever. What did being Jewish mean after Hitler, and after the creation of the Jewish state? The bulk of Jews continued to live outside Israel; they could ask themselves, 'Who is a Jew?', the title of an article by Isaac Deutscher (conflated from interviews in 1963 and 1966), or even, 'Am I a Jew?', the title of an article by Bernard Levin in 1965. Jewish identity was a more practical question still in Israel. The question of who was and who was not Jewish was the defining factor of citizenship in the new state; paradoxically, the state was secular, but the question of who was a Jew was decided on religious grounds. A good old answer to the question of who was a Jew was that 'everyone who thinks he is a Jew is one'. But that would not do for the rabbis who were allotted the task of defining Jewishness, sometimes with results as painful as the exercise of the Classification Act in apartheid South Africa (itself a painful comparison). The classic rabbinical definition relied on descent through the female line, with the curious consequences that someone who had seven Jewish great-grandparents out of eight was considered non-Jewish if the exception was a mother's mother's mother, but someone with a Jewish mother's mother's mother was Jewish despite seven other gentile great-grandparents.

These questions (which had been so important a generation earlier in Germany) were not what concerned Levin and Deutscher. For Levin, a British newspaper columnist, the question was rhetorical: 'I know perfectly well that I am a Jew; what I am inquiring into is what this means to me.' Levin spoke for others in the late-twentieth-century West as he enumerated his qualifications and disqualifications: Jewish appearance, a taste for Jewish food, liking for Jewish jokes on the one hand; on the other, positive rejection of Judaism and even active dislike of the dietary laws and 'the savage monotheism of Jehovah', as well as an insistence that the Final Solution should be condemned, but no more strongly than Stalin's slaughter of innocents. He also combined an admiration for the incredible achievement of Israel and hope that it would continue 'with the strongest condemnation of her crime against the original Arab population and the campaign of lies she has waged ever since on the subject'.

As Levin said, this did not distinguish him from a gentile of similar political outlook, but it did distinguish him from many Dispersion Jews (as was made clear by the envenomed attacks on Levin in the London Jewish press following his article). He conceded, as any honourable Jew must, and as even a Jewish Marxist like Deutscher did not need reminding, that there was another test: the test of definition by antisemites. After generations of assimilation, of baptism, of intermarriage, of name-changing, even of deceit and pretence, there were great grey areas in the western Dispersion, where defining someone as Jewish was well-nigh impossible. In England, cases ranged from the Rothschild family, universally seen as Jewish but some of whose members by the end of the twentieth century were so interbred or married-out as scarcely to count as Jewish by rabbinical law, to the Hambro family, undoubtedly of Jewish origin two centuries before but so entirely Anglicised and Anglicanised as to be just another English family (at least as much, one could say, as families of Huguenot origin like the Courtaulds or the Portals), to the Lawrence family, whose Jewish origins were so remote and so forgotten that, when a member of the family came to marry the Princess Royal, his kinsmen were astonished to be told about them. Arthur Miller spoke for others when he said that he would not think himself Jewish if it were not for antisemitism. But, even as antisemitism dwindled, a haunting question remained: Was someone a Jew if Hitler would have thought he was one?

For Deutscher the problem of continuing Jewish identity presented itself differently. The biographer of Trotsky was a Polish Jew by birth whose father had died in Auschwitz. He did not – he could scarcely – evade the Jewish catastrophe of his time, but he found a convenient way out through Marxian alchemy. Trotsky had dismissed Hitler as an aberration produced by the, presumably temporary, failure of proletarian revolution: 'Everything which society, if it had developed normally, would have rejected it as the excrement of culture, is now bursting out through its throat.' Even if this had been true, it took Deutscher no further. 'As an unrepentant Marxist, an atheist, an internationalist – in what sense am I then a Jew?' he asked, and he came up with no real answer. It was indeed hard to be a Jew by the 1960s if you were as alienated as he was from both the large surviving Jewish centres, the Hebrew national state in Palestine and the Jewish community in the world's greatest capitalist democracy.

If Deutscher had been right, then the Jew in what he called with sneering sarcasm the Great Democracy would have felt an ' "other" Negro'. But he was wrong. The 'black question' was the one which convulsed American society in the 1960s; the Jewish Question was forgotten. In what remained in many ways a highly race-conscious and sometimes openly racist society, antisemitism had burned away to a faint ember. An opinion poll in 1962 found that only 1 per cent thought the Jews a 'threat to America', a striking contrast to the pronounced popular antipathy to, and fear of, Jews which remained in many European countries, including some like Austria and Poland whose Jews had been destroyed. Meantime the material success story of the American Jews continued. In 1965, one quarter of all American families had incomes between $7,500 and $15,000; one half of Jewish families did. The percentage of Jews in white-collar jobs was three times the national average, the old Jewish working class faded away, and Jews took on a role in cultural and intellectual life quite out of proportion to their numbers, not just in the traditional bastions of Hollywood and New York liberal-left polemics, but in universities, newspapers, book publishing and television.

Jewish integration, Jewish social ascent, were accompanied by a proud new Jewish self-confidence. The old Yiddishkeit was fading fast and the life of east European Jewry had been destroyed, but it could live on as a sentimental memory. In 1964, *Fiddler on the Roof* opened in New York. There, and in many other cities, it enjoyed a success few musicals (including better ones) have known. But it was more than any other musical; it was an ethnic rite of celebration, an affirmation of Jewish identity and pride.

All of this was reflected politically. For decades, politicians had paid obeisance to hyphenated groups, but Jewish-Americans had come to occupy a special place of honour. Until the second half of the twentieth century, the prefix 'Judao', 'Judaeo' or 'Judeo', or the suffix 'Judaic', had usually conveyed a pejorative put-down: Belloc's 'modern Anglo-Judaic plutocracy', a London newspaper's description in 1906 of 'the Judaeo-Masonic and Protestant coalition' governing France. Now, significantly enough, 'Judeo' was prefaced to 'Christian', as politicians extolled the 'Judeo-Christian tradition' which underlay American society. The very suggestion that someone was unsound in this area was damaging; as Edward Tivnan put it, 'No politician wants to be called an "antisemite", particularly a politician who is a genuine antisemite.' The philosemitism of many politicians resembled the sincere conviction that it was better to be a baptised professor in Petersburg than a melamed in Lithuania: politicians were convinced that it was better to win elections with Jewish support than lose without it. And they were convinced also that the way to win Jewish support was to offer their own support for Israel.

From when John Kennedy won his Massachusetts Senate election in 1952, he had been supported by Zionists like Dewey Sims, but he appeared uncommitted on the question of Israel. At the time of Suez, he did not take the Israeli side, as Lyndon Johnson for example did. But Kennedy soon learned. One of the leading lights of the Presidents' Conference was Philip Klutznick, who set himself the task of putting Senator Kennedy right. In 1958, the two met and Kennedy expressed concern about the Palestinian Arab refugees; Klutznick told him that 'if you plan to run for the presidency and that is what you're going to say, count me out and count a lot of other people out, too'. Kennedy counted him in. Shortly afterwards the senator made a speech praising 'the values and hopes which the state of Israel enshrines – and the past injury it redeems . . . it twists reality to suggest that it is the democratic tendency of Israel which has injected discord and dissension into the Near East'. At the 1960 election, four American Jews in five voted for Kennedy.

And yet, strangely as it seemed, Klutznick could write only three years later that, at any given moment, 'I don't know whether I am a Zionist or not'. He was a characteristic figure among the American Jewish leadership: a rich Chicago property developer, who had become president of B'nai B'rith, the oldest of Jewish fraternal organisations, and had helped to found the Presidents' Conference. Klutznick was a strongly self-affirming Jew, and a highly intelligent one, who ruminated on his identity. He recognised the accusation made by Ben-Gurion, that true Jewish life was only possible in a country where roads were paved, streets policed, harbours built, 'even the crimes are committed by Jews!' The American Jews had turned their back on Zionism, however loudly they proclaimed it, by abandoning any pretence that all, or most, or even many American Jews would ever go to chase the Zionist Dream.

Although he acknowledged the force of this, Klutznick did not take it quite lying down. He saw the way in which something vaguely called 'Zionism' had, for many an American, 'become his sheltering umbrella' with which 'he could walk through the storm with his Jewishness intact'. And yet he, one of the most prominent American friends of Israel, queried Ben-Gurion's premiss: was it really essential to his Jewish future that his coffee at lunch should be served by a Jewish waiter? Klutznick called his meditation *No Easy Answers*, and indeed provided none, but he did suggest that Israeli-Dispersion relations should become more emotionally honest: Israelis should stop sneering at Jewish Americans as rootless and sybaritic, American Jews should stop automatically deferring to Israelis and investing them with an aura of heroic infallibility.

Within months of Kennedy's inauguration in 1961, the young president met the septuagenarian prime minister of Israel in New York, and said to Ben-Gurion, 'I know I was elected because of the votes of American Jews. I owe them my election. Tell me, is there something I can do for the Jewish people?' To which Ben-Gurion supposedly replied, 'You must do what is best for the free world.' American-Israeli relations were not quite so simple as that mildly implausible exchange suggested. At that very meeting, Kennedy raised the question of the refugees again, but Ben-Gurion evaded it. The Kennedy administration subsequently floated a plan to deal with the refugee problem, by allowing at least some of the dispossessed Palestinians to return home. Ben-Gurion described this plan as 'a more serious danger to her existence than all the threats of the Arab dictators and kings'; it was opposed by American-Jewish groups;[4] it was dropped.

This was not the first, but it was one of the most impressive, demonstrations of the power of the Israeli lobby, and of the unity between Israel and American Jewry. At the time it seemed a triumph, in those terms. Very few Jewish-Americans can have stopped to ponder on the implications of it for themselves. No one accused them of divided loyalties, not in public at least. The charge was a potent and a sensitive one in a nation of immigrants. It had often been raised of

---

[4] Though the plan was also opposed for narrow reasons of their own by those Arab dictators and kings.

different groups, sometimes with justice, sometimes not. Earlier in the century it had been used against German-Americans – some were even lynched after the United States entered the war in 1917 – and against Japanese-Americans who in 1942 had been rounded up and deported to internment camps. It might have been used in different circumstances against Irish-Americans and Czech-Americans. It was never used against Jewish-Americans during the first decades of the Jewish state, and this repression stored up trouble in political and psychological terms.

When Kennedy was assassinated in 1963, the Israelis 'lost a great friend', his successor told an Israeli diplomatist. But, Lyndon Johnson added, 'you have found a better one', and his presidency saw the heyday of American-Israeli friendship. Johnson was in his way a genuine philosemite. He had several Jewish friends, including James Novy who had looked after his finances when he first ran for the Senate and Abe Fortas whom he appointed to the Supreme Court. Abba Eban recalled how when he was Israeli ambassador Johnson 'had come to my Washington residence in 1952 in an effort to find out everything essential about Israel in the briefest possible time'. He was a good learner.

Even as Israel played its role on the world stage with increasing confidence western Jewry remained curiously remote from it. Most Jews instinctively supported Israel, though often in a detached way. Some openly disliked what the Jewish State had become. The radical journalist Nat Hentoff may have spoken for others when he told the Jewish journal *Midstream* before the state was fifteen years old that if Israel was the promised land, 'then the promised land turned out to be another atavistic nation-state'. And in a survey of intellectual Jewish-American opinion published in *Commentary* in 1961, the young publisher Jason Epstein may have spoken for more when he called Israel 'an admirable experiment' but one about which 'I know little'. He doubted whether it would work. 'It is too much a creature of will and not enough of long, slow organic history . . . its foundations are too visible for its future to seem secure.' Other reflective Jews also had mixed feelings. Jakob J. Petuchowski weighed up the undoubted successes of Zionism against the failures. Since the birth of Israel, Jewish nationalism seemed to have received its final validation by history. Its premises could scarcely even be questioned any more, he observed. And the Israelis did have an obvious, practical existential weight of argument against those who remained behind in the Galut, however successfully integrated these seemed to be: 'The Jewish policeman on Tel Aviv's Dizengoff Square is a more concrete symbol of reality than the rabbi who, together with Protestant and Catholic clergymen, participates in the inauguration ceremonies of the American President.'

And yet, with its radical rejection of Jewish history and Jewish tradition, along with Jewish passivity and Jewish defeat, could this 'Jewish state' really claim to have a Jewish culture? Equally, however much of a liberation the Jewish state might represent for those who had only known the ghetto, might not the emancipated Jew reasonably feel that it represented 'an undesirable limitation and confinement'? The psychological need which Israel had fulfilled for the Dispersion was obvious enough, after 'My brothers are being killed in Europe, and I lead a life of luxury in America'. But at the same time this cult of Israel-worship might become an unhealthy substitute, and was quietly disliked by some pious Jews who saw it go hand in hand with the rapid secularisation of American Jewry. As for that uneasy if not unhealthy relationship between Israel and Dispersion, it was founded on an obvious fallacy. Of course Israel had given all Jews a new sense of pride and self-respect, but the idea that it was their spiritual home and ultimate refuge was unsustainable. Without the support of the West, Israel herself would not survive; and if America should become so untrue to her own nature that Jewish existence on her soil became precarious, 'then it was likewise impossible to conceive that Israel will fare any better'.

Petuchowski's *Zion Reconsidered* was published to little notice in 1966. Within a year the story was transformed in a way he could not have imagined. In May 1967, Russia warned Nasser that Israel was planning to attack Syria. Nasser responded vaingloriously by moving troops into Sinai, expelling the United Nations, and closing the Gulf of Aqaba to Israeli shipping. Israel in turn called this an act of aggression, and prepared for war. Dayan became defence minister, and Begin joined a government of national unity. The war began on 5 June. What happened next amazed the world.

As the fighting began, Israel was seen more than ever as David against the Goliaths of three surrounding countries supported by the whole Arab world. Some military historians later argued that not only had Israel begun the war but that her geographical encirclement and demographic disadvantage were more than offset by her technical superiority. That was not how it seemed at the time. Jews believed that their people stood on the brink of a second catastrophe within a quarter-century. All doubts about Zionism and the Jewish state vanished among western Jewry. British Jews rallied to the cause, 99 per cent of American Jews supported Israel without reserve, some flew to fight for Israel, huge sums were raised in her name, $15 million at one fund-raising lunch, $100 million in a matter of weeks; in Arthur Hertzberg's words, 'the immediate reaction to the crisis was far more intense and widespread than anyone could have foreseen.'

All wars begin with anxiety and end, for the victors, with jubilation. In 1939–45 this emotional experience was spread over nearly six years. In 1967 it was compressed within the Six Days which the war lasted and by which it is known to history. Under the command of Moshe Dayan, Israeli aircraft destroyed the Egyptian air force on the ground in a matter of hours, Israeli armour and infantry drove Jordanian forces from the west bank of Jordan, took Jerusalem, captured the Golan Heights from Syria and, most breathtaking of all, drove the Egyptians out of the whole Sinai peninsula to the line of the Suez canal, decisively opening the straits at the mouth of the Gulf of Aqaba. It was one of the most extraordinary victories in military history, and the words of Miriam come true: 'Sing ye to the Lord, for he hath triumphed gloriously; the horse and his rider hath he thrown into the sea.'

The world stood astonished, but for Jews everywhere emotion went far beyond astonishment. It was unimaginably exhilarating to see Israel free with one bound, David felling Goliath. It was exhilarating to belong to a race of winners, to enjoy the world's vicarious admiration; as one American Jew was told, 'You Hebes really taught those guys a lesson.' Most of all, it was exhilarating to be united with those far-off embattled cousins who had not submitted to extinction like other cousins a generation before but had fought and won. Writing in the New York *Village Voice*, Nancy Weber spoke for millions of other Jews throughout the world that midsummer: 'Two weeks ago, Israel was they; now Israel is we.'

15

Hebrew and Jewish

Thou shalt bruise them with a rod of iron:
and break them in pieces like a potter's vessel

Ps.ii.9

Bliss was it in that dawn to be alive, but to be Jewish was very heaven. Any ambiguous feelings Jews throughout the world may have had about Israel were dissolved; what had been suppressed broke out. The peculiar circumstances of the Six-Day War might have been deliberately designed to produce this emotional catharsis: first the dread, horror and incipient shame as millions of Jews were once more seemingly threatened with extinction; then the exultation as the new race of Hebrews surged to their astonishing victory, more dramatic than either 1948 or 1956. Israel's triumph seemed a triumph for Jewry as a whole, everywhere enhancing their position. More then twenty years later Arthur Hertzberg looked back on the mood which followed: 'After the Six-Day War in 1967, Jews in America were freer, and more powerful, than Jews had ever been before in the Diaspora.'

When the first exhilaration died away, the picture was not one of unalloyed ease and happiness. There were problems. For Israel itself there was a huge practical problem, though one which it was difficult to face up to. The war had brought large new conquered territories, not only the whole of the Sinai peninsula, most of it desert and eventually returned to Egypt, not only the Golan Heights, whose importance was chiefly strategic, but the West Bank and Gaza, two prizes which proved poisoned chalices. These 'Territories' were to become both a burden and a challenge. Some Israelis regarded the

West Bank as a temporary impediment: some as 'Judaea and Samaria', part of the historic and sacred Land of Israel. What was not in dispute was that they were peopled then by hundreds of thousands of Arabs. The problem was later summarised by the American reporter Glenn Frankel. It was 'a three-sided dilemma: to give back the territories and risk another Arab invasion; to retain the territories and give Arab residents full rights, which would inevitably erode the Jewish character of the State; or to keep the land and the Arabs in a state of animated suspension pending future development'. In truth, there was a fourth choice, but it was scarcely discussed in public, and remained a secret thought: somehow to remove the Arabs.

For Dispersion Jewry, there were different problems, barely recognised at the time. Despite the intense identification of almost all Jews everywhere with Israel in 1967, the old question of dual loyalty was not raised in America or England. But in France it was. Shortly after the war, the French president, General Charles de Gaulle, spoke off the cuff at a press conference, and in language which sent a shudder through his Jewish compatriots. 'Some even feared', he gnomically put it, 'that the Jewish people, who had until then been dispersed, who had remained what they always had been, an élite people, sure of itself and overbearing,[1] would, once they had come together, change the moving desire they had expressed for nineteen centuries – next year in Jerusalem – into an ardent desire for conquest'. Israelis had their suspicions confirmed that no gentiles were free from antisemitism, even the head of the country which had been an Israeli ally not long ago. France was the land of the Dreyfus Affair, after all.

One man stopped to think what this meant. Raymond Aron most certainly belonged to *un peuple d'élite*: a French Jew, from the highest intellectual class in the country, who was a contemporary – sometime friend, sometime foe – of Sartre's, who had joined de Gaulle and his Free French in wartime exile in London, and who had become after the war the best-known unreconstructed liberal commentator in the French press, an anti-Communist when Stalinist chic was all the rage among the French intelligentsia, an advocate of European union, a critic of France's war in Algeria, a candid friend to de Gaulle after his return to power in 1958. He was in his own words 'A Jew like me, de-Judaised, an unbeliever, non-practising, of French culture', and as such he had taken issue with Sartre over his facile saying that Jewish identity

---

[1] '*un peuple d'élite, sûr de lui-même et dominateur*'

existed only in the eyes of others (perverse reversal of 'whoever thinks he is a Jew is one').

He had, for most of his life, identified himself as a Frenchman rather than as a Jew. At the Ecole Normale he had encountered almost no antisemitism. Hitler had revived his Jewish consciousness, and after 1933 he had asserted his Jewishness, 'as much as possible without ostentations', so as not to conceal it through cowardice: and he was shocked by the climate of the 1930s, when Léon Blum was baited by Jew-haters. Even after 1945 his French patriotism was undimmed (though he did not know about the full complicity of the Vichy regime in the Final Solution, and the ambiguous role played even by a future socialist president like François Mitterrand). In this respect, he resembled other and nobler French Jews than Dreyfus. The great historian Marc Bloch served in the wartime resistance, before he was captured and put to death by the Germans. For him, his identity had never been a problem: 'I have felt myself during my whole life above all and very simply – French,' he said in words which Aron might have echoed. 'I have been tied to my fatherland by a long family tradition; nourished by its spiritual heritage and its history, unable to conceive of any country where I could breathe at ease. I have loved it very much and served it with all my strength.' And even more emphatically, as 'a stranger to all confessional formalism and to all racial solidarity', he requested before his execution that no Hebrew prayers should be said at his grave.

The creation of Israel 'provoked no emotion in Aron', and he continued to believe that 'a Jew of French culture, from a family which have been French citizens for generations, is required by no human or divine law to consider himself a Jew'. All the same, the 1967 war had profoundly affected even this most assimilated of Frenchmen, and he addressed himself to de Gaulle's strictures. While ironically wondering for a moment whether or not *dominateur* and *sûr de lui-même* might not have been compliments coming from the general, he deplored the revival, maybe unconscious, of antisemitic stereotypes: '*dominateur*' had been the very word once used by French antisemites like Xavier Vallat, the Vichy High Commissioner for Jewish Affairs, by way of justifying his loathsome treatment of the Jews. But if Aron recognised the language of antisemitism when he saw it, and had instinctively thrilled at Israel's triumph, he remained both open-minded and equivocal about Zionism. After 1967 and de Gaulle's press conference, Aron continued to defend anyone who chose to reject any solidarity between

Israel and French Jews. 'On what ground can he be condemned?' Aron asked, and added, in an unconscious inverted echo of Drumont's *'pour trahir sa Patrie, il faut en avoir une'*, 'One cannot betray or desert a community unless one has belonged or wanted to belong to it.' He similarly defended the right of any French Jew to take a strongly anti-Israeli position in the conflict with the Arabs. And, although he made the telling point that 'in a democratic regime, national allegiance does not have a totalitarian quality, and it should not', he accepted that there was a problem of loyalty to be addressed: Jews could not evade the question of self-definition posed by the Jewish state of whether they were Israelis or citizens of their own countries: 'Jews *and* French, yes; Israelis *and* French, no.'

There could not have been a better illustration of the difference between the Old World and the New. No American president could possibly have spoken in public in the terms de Gaulle used. But then almost no eminent American Jew would have debated the question as dispassionately as Aron: not one of his general political outlook, any more than many American Jews by the end of the 1960s could or would say, with Bernard Levin, that their admiration for Israel, combined with strong condemnation of the crime against the Palestinians, did not distinguish them from gentiles of similar politics.

The exception was on the hard Left, as opposed to the soft-liberal Left where most American Jews still resided. And the attitude of the Left was to be one of the factors transforming the political position of Dispersion Jewry. The Old or Stalinist Left had been ambiguous about Zionism, sometimes condemning it but also organising a Communist party in Israel, playing on the fellow-travellers of Mapam, and trying not to alienate entirely those western Jews who wanted to combine a sympathy for the Soviet version of socialism with a sympathy for the Jewish state. What was more, the Old Left had always been imbued with a residual feeling that socialism was a European blessing, to be brought to non-Europeans.

Now there was a New Left, a mixture of defectors from Communism after the rupture over Hungary in 1956, of Trotskyists and other revolutionary socialists, of younger people radicalised by the civil rights movement in the United States and opposition to the Vietnam War. This New Left did not merely support the cause of 'the colonial peoples' as the Old Left had in an abstract way, but was emotionally attached to one side in a *Kulturkampf* between the industrial West and what had come to be called the Third World. And, just as Orwell had predicted more than twenty years earlier, Zionism and Israel were cast on the wrong side of this melodrama. Only weeks after the Six-Day War, *New Left Notes*, published by the radical Students for a Democratic Society, laid down the new law: 'It is important that the American Left understand that Arab reaction will be a reaction of blacks to whites when the violence culminates against colonial settlers in their country. The importation of pro-Western settlers into the underdeveloped world to build a strong colonial base is hardly a new factor of imperialists and it is no more justifiable in Israel than in Kenya or Mozambique.'

Namier's sardonic '*Wir Juden und die anderen Farbigen denken anders*' rang very hollow now. Anti-colonial movements and leaders were increasingly backed by the Left without reservation, or reflection, though in all of this there was an absurd contradiction. The proponents of anti-colonialism, of Third Worldliness, of what came to be known as multi-culturalism, were invariably 'of the Left'. And yet, while there was a good – maybe an overwhelming – moral case to be made against colonial settlements, imperialism, white supremacy, 'eurocentricity', 1492 and all that, it could only be a good reactionary case, not a good progressive one. In that respect, Jabotinsky with his recognition that Zionism was indeed a colonial irruption into a backward land – 'We belong, thank God, to Europe and for two thousand years have helped to create the culture of the West' – was not only more honest but, paradoxically for an alleged rightist, more progressive than his opponents.

But the implications of this were as disturbing for liberal Zionists as they were for those like Edward Said who tried to combine anti-Zionism with political Left-radicalism. At all events, liberal Jews were increasingly stranded. By 1971, a writer in the liberal-left *Ramparts* lamented the polarisation of the Jewish community 'between pro-Israel cold warriors and simple-minded, anti-Jewish revolutionaries', and four years later a critic in the *New York Times* lamented more bitterly still that 'the New Left today stands in direct and open opposition to the entity, safety and aspiration of the Jewish people'. Many Jews quietly agreed. It was partly for this reason that, as Norman Cantor puts it a little rhetorically, the American New Left 'was dead as a political movement by 1971. Once the Jewish radicals saw the blacks taking over, they went back to graduate school and law school.'

Here was an agonising conflict. An undercurrent of hostility between black and Jew in America had been an open secret for decades past.

Many liberal Jews had applauded the cause of racial equality, and not only in theory. Jews had helped in the civil rights movement of the early 1960s, some had even given their lives for it. It was all the more bitter when this was repaid by an increasingly blatant black antisemitism. 'In every major ghetto, Jews own the major businesses,'[2] Malcolm X told the rabble he was rousing (with a tincture of factual accuracy, just as it had been factually true when the National Socialists said that German newspapers and department stores were largely Jewish owned before 1933). 'Every night, the owners of these businesses go home with that black community's money, which helps the ghetto stay poor.' The black poet Leroi Jones called Judaism a 'dangerous, germ culture' nearly twenty years before Louis Farrakhan called it a 'gutter religion'. Stokely Carmichael went even better in scoring a double: Zionism should be wiped out 'wherever it exists, be it in the ghettos of United States or in the Middle East'.

It was impossible for Jews to ignore this. Some gritted their teeth and hoped that the mood of black militancy – or this expression of it – would pass. Others did not. There had always been some reciprocal hostility. In Israel, the Yiddish word 'shvarzers' (blacks) came to mean the black-coated ultra-Orthodox haredim; in New York for a long time before that it had a simpler meaning. Lower middle-class Jews living cheek by jowl with blacks in Brooklyn or Chicago – or, more to the point, seeing blacks move into their districts – reacted not much differently from other 'ethnics'.

By 1968, this simmering resentment boiled over. The *Jewish Press* was already an aggressive Jewish-chauvinist paper, publishing stories about black antisemitism in New York. Now it published an advertisement seeking Jews interested in 'Jewish Pride' and soon the Jewish Defence League was born, meeting for the first time at the West Side Jewish Center on West 34th Street in June. Its only begetter was Meir Kahane, a young rabbi connected with Menachem Begin and others of the Revisionist tradition in Israel, where he had just visited; he stood himself in a kind of apostolic succession: in 1940, shortly before his death, Jabotinsky himself had stayed in the Brooklyn house of Rabbi Charles Kahane, whose son Meir was then a little boy.

The great talking point when the League was founded was a fierce

---

[2] A curious example of how the original meaning of words is lost: a 'ghetto' was once a quarter where Jews were confined by authority, not a black slum.

battle, building up for some time and now about to erupt, over the New York schools system. Its flashpoint was Ocean Hill-Brownsville in Brooklyn, just such a Jewish neighbourhood which had become a black 'ghetto'. The Board of Education proposed a plan for decentralisation, to allow local communities more control over the schools. This proved acutely sensitive and controversial: such communities were many of them now black, but most teachers were Jewish and were appalled at the prospect of being ordered about by local politicians, and that the principle of centrally administered promotion on merit should be threatened. In September, the New York teachers' union, three-fifths Jewish, went on strike.

Before long inflammatory propaganda was being broadcast from both sides. A black teacher called James Campbell denounced the Jewish teachers, and read on the radio a poem about their union leader Albert Shanker: 'Hey, Jew boy, with that yarmulka on your head, | You pale-faced Jew boy, I wish you were dead | . . . You came to America, the land of the free, | And took over the school system to perpetuate white supremacy', and more of the same tenor and poetic quality. In turn, a gang of several dozen Jewish Defence League members armed with clubs attacked the radio station. A little later the League attacked the headquarters of the Black Panthers.

Full-scale race war between Jews and blacks did not break out; violent dust-ups were confined to small groups. The Jewish Defence League made more noise than impact, and in 1969 the liberal John Lindsay was re-elected mayor of New York. But Kahane had made an important gesture, and he embarrassed other Jews not merely with his antics but, like Jabotinsky before him, as a reproach. His slogan 'Every Jew a .22' took militarism one step further, and challenged his fellow-Jews twice over. They were ashamed at the violence of the language, but perhaps also a little ashamed that someone else was sticking up for Jewish rights. More and more the American Jews were *embourgeoisé*: they moved out of those inner-city districts as poorer people moved in; in their leafy suburbs they were physically but not emotionally remote from those conflicts. It was very much as western Jews felt about Israel, where Kahane was running a parallel career as an agitator. Dispersion Jews disliked the violence which Israel was obliged to use, or at any rate did use. But those sitting in Hendon or Long Island or the valleys of Los Angeles felt guilty about their own comfort and security compared with the lives of those who had chosen to live in the Land of

Israel, and most felt inhibited to the point of catatonia from criticising them.

Now Kahane shrewdly lighted on another campaign, for the Russian Jews. He may not have known much in detail about their condition, which became clearer later when large numbers of them began to emigrate for the first time since 1914. A half-century of intermittent unofficial antisemitism and official secularism had wrought a great change in this community. But there had been physical causes also. The Germans had slaughtered the Jews in the territories they had overrun in 1941–3, up to the gates of Leningrad and Moscow and the Caucasus. The survivors had not only been persecuted by Stalin, in some cases unto death, but had intermarried at an increasingly rapid rate. By the 1970s it was said that there were around two million Jews in the Soviet Union; but, even more than western countries, it was impossible to give an accurate figure, as the numbers of full-blooded Jews (whether religious or not) decreased, and the numbers of the partly Jewish increased, with every generation.

Still, the harassment of those who considered themselves Jewish by the Russian government was a fact. By now, everyone not entirely blinded by incurable political prejudice knew about the condition of this large Jewish community. Antique leather-jacketed party members could still be found on the streets of New York handing out pamphlets called 'Soviet Antisemitism – a Cold War Myth'; mythical it was not. Despite – perhaps because of – the official climate, Russian Jews too had been thrilled by the Six-Day War and, as the black night of oppression in Russia slowly brightened, a Jewish activist movement emerged: 'If tiny Israel could lick the combined Arab armies, perhaps the 2.1 million Jews of the Soviet Union could live with dignity and respect.' Kahane campaigned on their behalf and he became a hero to many of them. In June 1970 a group of Jews tried to hijack an airliner out of Leningrad, in an operation probably planned in Israel with Kahane's knowledge. Before two of the hijackers were sentenced to death a bomb was exploded at the Aeroflot and Intourist offices in New York, and in 1971 there was a series of bombings at Russian and Communist offices. Most Jews shied away from Kahane's fanaticism, his open racial hatred of Arabs, his espousal of terrorism. And yet all of them sympathised with the Russian Jews in their plight and could not wholly disown anyone active on their behalf.

In 1973 Israel and its supporters received two unpleasant shocks, one physical, one moral. The Egyptians attacked at Yom Kippur and the

Israelis were caught napping.[3] Although the Egyptians were beaten back, it was only after a stiff fight which both restored Arab self-respect and suggested alarming Israeli vulnerability. Two conclusions could be drawn. One was that Israel could not live under siege for ever; it had best try to find some settlement, and earlier at that, rather than later on what might be less favourable terms. The Arab states had a declared policy of 'no peace, no recognition, no negotiation' with Israel, and the Palestine Liberation Organisation was committed in a far-fetched way to the complete extirpation of the 'Zionist entity', but this was bluster bred by defeat. Soon, they might not be so weak.

An alternative conclusion, which many did draw, might have been taken from the traditional slogans of Orange Ulster: 'No surrender', and 'Not an inch'. Why try to make terms with an implacable and irreconcilable foe who would take any hint of compromise as weakness? This was the conclusion of Likud, the block of Right-wing parties led by Menachem Begin, the old Irgun terrorist and inheritor of the Revisionist tradition, whose group was making steady headway at elections. That mantle was claimed by Kahane also. With his open talk of 'transfer', or physical expulsion of the Palestinians, he acted, as it were, as pacemaker for the Likud who were gradually emerging from their decades of opposition: the once unimaginable approached.

The other nasty shock was a resolution introduced at the United Nations in 1973, which denounced Zionism as a form of racism. Within two years, in October 1975, the same resolution was passed by the Third Committee of the General Assembly, and a few weeks later the General Assembly itself endorsed the resolution by 67 votes to 55, with 15 abstentions. The date of the resolution was 10 November; the anniversary, as the Israeli delegate and future president Chaim Herzog pointed out, of *Kristallnacht* in 1938.

This Zionism-equals-racism resolution was as gravely malicious as it was deeply offensive, and intended to be. To tell the people who were by far the twentieth century's worst victims of racial persecution that they themselves were racists was 'Jew-baiting' in the true sense. It was an accurate reflection of the malice and malignancy of the Arab states,

---

[3] The choice of timing was deliberate, but miscalculated: Yom Kippur was the one religious festival every Israeli at least made an appearance of observing, and so the citizen-soldiers of the army reserve were all at home and easily alerted. An Israeli cynic pointed out that if the Egyptians had known the country better they would have attacked at Rosh Hashanah or Purim, when a large part of the population would have been on the beach or the golf course.

and still more of Soviet Russia and its satrapies, who were really behind the resolution. At the same time, it was little more than a statement of the obvious: a statement which could have been made (as it was not) about almost any national movement, almost all of which were in some sense 'racist'. The Czechs had not struggled for a Czech state on behalf of the Austrians, or the Irish on behalf of the English (nor, it might be said, on behalf of the Bohemian Germans in the one case or the Ulster Protestants in the other). Nationalism is by definition exclusive, and in practice if not in theory all too often narrow and bloodthirsty as well.

Besides, Zionism did have certain features which distinguished it even from the general run of nationalism. Its great idea had been promoted for a people without a land or even to begin with a common language, a people who thus, whatever the meaning of 'race' or 'ethnicity' might be, had to be in some degree defined by descent or racial origin. Herzl, Dreyfus, Brandeis and the Rothschilds were all Jews, along with the Yiddish-speaking tailor from the Lithuanian shtetl, the penniless artisan from the Moroccan ghetto, Indians and even Ethiopians. It was quite obvious that these were not in fact one 'race', but Zionism treated them platonically as one. Judaism had always been distinguished from other religions by its non-proselytising – which was to say exclusive – character. With rare and quaint exceptions from Lord George Gordon to Elizabeth Taylor, there were no Jewish converts. Exclusive Judaism was at a great disadvantage in comparison with inclusive religions like Roman Catholicism once emancipated Jews began to mix in larger society, and the 'mixed marriage' became a grave threat to Jewry. Every time a Catholic married a Jew there was one more Catholic family and one fewer Jewish.

Secular Zionism unconsciously borrowed from religious Judaism. In some countries, citizenship was a matter simply of residence and loyalty to the state. That was peculiarly true of the United States. The country which had most strongly, and most crucially, supported Israel was founded on principles in opposite reaction to the European nationalism on which Zionism had modelled itself. It had fostered the greatest and richest Jewish community since Antiquity because of the freedom it had long offered to incoming citizens, gentile or Jew. In Israel by contrast gentiles were precluded from settling and taking citizenship; a hypothetical preclusion in the case of most people though very practical for the several hundred thousand Palestinians who had lived inside what became Israel and now lived outside it. At the same time, one of the central principles of the Jewish state was the Law of Return, begging the question of how 'a Jew' was to be defined, which entitled any Jew to settle in Israel. The very principle of 'Hebrew land', so important to early Zionists, spoke for itself.

What the 'racism' resolution really demonstrated, apart from malice and base intrigue, was the way in which Israel, and Zionism, had fallen on the wrong side of the argument. Orwell had correctly predicted that the conflict in the Holy Land would become a 'colour question'; but even he had not foreseen how an obsession with anti-colonialism and racism would come to alter the terms of debate. When Israel was created, and for at least a decade after, the United States still had a safe majority in the General Assembly of the United Nations: the largest single bloc was the Latin-American republics, who then followed the State Department's lead. By the 1970s all had changed. Thanks to decolonisation there was now a clear anti-American, anti-imperialist, anti-western majority, comprising Arab and Asian states and the forty-odd (some of them very odd) African states which had become independent since Ghana led the way in 1957.

The world-view – the Third-World-view – of these states was Manichean: life was divided into the good, the tropical, post-colonial countries; and the evil, the West (or 'the North': neither was geographically precise). Not only Manichean, it was Antinomian. Those quaint sixteenth-century heretics had believed that 'to the pure all things are pure'. If you were of the elect, the saved, you could do no wrong; you could merrily eat, drink and fornicate (as they duly did) in the certainty of salvation. This convenient doctrine was borrowed by anti-colonialism. India had led the moral campaign against the unarguable cruelty and injustice of apartheid, perpetrated by white on non-white; being a non-white country with impeccable anti-colonial credentials, India herself was free from criticism of the sundry forms of institutional or informal racism which flourished on her soil. A matter of days before the Zionism-equals-racism resolution, the General Assembly in stately conclave had received the Ugandan ruler, Idi Amin, who had himself denounced the 'American-Israeli conspiracy' and called for the expulsion of Israel from the United Nations. He was not only an egregious buffoon but a murderous maniac, who had harried and butchered Asians unfortunate enough to live in Uganda, had not only denounced the 'American-Israeli conspiracy' and called for the expulsion of Israel from the United Nations but had applauded the Final Solution, and proposed to erect a statue to Hitler. By any honest or objective measure Amin was himself an appropriate figure for expulsion. But he was incontrovertibly a black African, and thus one of the elect, free from sin.

It was said more and more often that Israel was being judged by a 'double standard'. This double standard was said to ignore the fact that Israel was not only the West's, and especially America's, truest friend in a strategically vital region, but the only democracy there, surrounded by Arab states which were all of them autocracies or despotisms, which frequently oppressed their populations in various degrees, and which invariably suppressed the free speech and open society which flourished in Israel. All of which was quite true. Over the years, many brutal things were done in the name of Israel, usually to Palestinian Arabs. But, if some Arabs were falsely imprisoned, deprived of rights, tortured or killed by Jews, an enormously larger number of Arabs were tortured, imprisoned and murdered by Arabs.

And yet the 'double standards' argument was an awkward one for Israel's defenders. Apart from the fact that '*Tu quoque?*' is never a really good answer, Israel had positively asked to be judged by double standards: it did not want to be ranked with, and have the same excuses made for it as, Afro-Asian despotisms. *Tu quoque?* tends to become *ignoratio elenchi*: the term in formal logic for refuting the proposition which has not been advanced. Thus a man who comes home late and whose wife says 'You're drunk', replies, 'Your cooking stinks'. The latter statement may be true, but it is not addressed to the original proposition. Well-meaning defenders of South Africa in the 1970s and 1980s were addicted to *ignoratio elenchi*. Asked about conditions in black townships they would point out correctly that conditions in Addis or Kinshasa were far worse. But the proposition advanced had not been that conditions in Addis and Kinshasa were good, rather that conditions were bad in the Soweto. The cry of double standards came near to this logical error.[4]

It was difficult also for the reasons shown by the comparisons with Uganda and South Africa. During the more than forty years of institutional racial oligarchy called 'apartness', the South African regime oppressed the black masses with great cruelty. All the world knew of the disenfranchisement and lack of civil rights of the majority,

---

[4] In Soviet Russia, *ignoratio elenchi* was elevated into a classic joke, one of those associated with the legendary Radio Armenia station. A caller asked the radio commentator what was the average wage of an industrial worker in the United States. After a long pause the answer came: 'They kill Negroes.'

of the pass laws, of the massacres at Sharpeville, of the categorisation of population, of the laws against sexual relations, let alone marriage, across the colour line. At the same time, curiously enough, South Africa remained in its fashion and in certain limited aspects a free country. It was even, in a bizarre way, a democracy. For those brought up to admire the city states of ancient Greece, it was a disturbing thought that apartheid South Africa was the closest thing in the modern world to Periclean Athens: a minority enjoying full democracy, and a considerable degree of social equality among themselves, supported by a servile helotry without civil rights. South Africa kept free speech and a rule of law, as was demonstrated by the very outrages of the system. The police could beat to death a dissident like Steve Biko, but then the murder was exposed by the press and by judicial inquiry. Free speech and rule of law distinguished South Africa not only from mad tyrannies like Uganda, but from most of the other countries of independent Africa. And yet much good did that do when South Africa was weighed in the scales.

Less and less good did it do Israel that it, too, was a functioning democracy and a free country. It was on the wrong side of that great *Kulturkampf* of the age. As the criticism of Israel became more and more malevolent, critics sometimes compared the country to South Africa, or even to Hitler's Third Reich. A cartoon in a magazine subsidised both by the Labour-controlled Greater London Council and the National Union of Journalists[5] showed the Israeli prime minister in full SS uniform standing on top of a pile of corpses, above the slogan 'Final Solution'. This comparison was not only repulsive but grotesque. The comparison with South Africa, however, though far-fetched, was not entirely absurd. Abba Eban, the Israeli statesman who was foreign minister from 1966 to 1974, was asked once by a reporter if he foresaw the Territories becoming a 'bantustan', and affected not to understand. But Eban, himself born in Cape Town, must have been aware of the South African government's policy of 'grand apartheid' based on 'tribal homelands' or bantustans which would be ostensibly self-governing, and whose existence would theoretically solve the problem of maintaining white rule in a territory with a black majority. Just such a problem existed for Israel after 1967. All of which was hard to come to terms with for Israel's emotional supporters in the West, many of whom still thought themselves liberals, who abhorred apartheid, who

[5] And thus involuntarily paid for, in part, twice over, by the present author.

had identified with 'the colonial peoples' and who detested the idea of 'racism'. To some extent, the Zionism-is-racism resolution forged a bond between Israel and the Dispersion, united in resentment of the despicable accusation.

Another moment of bonding came with Entebbe in July 1976. A group of Israelis had been hijacked on a flight and held hostage by PLO men at an airport in Uganda. In a brilliantly planned and executed operation, Israeli special forces flew in to rescue them, the leader of the raid dying heroically in action. At this time, Labour was still in office in Israel after nearly three decades. Golda Meir had resigned as prime minister in 1974, taking Dayan – hero of 1967 but cast as the villain of national unpreparedness in 1973 – into the political wilderness with her. She was succeeded by Yitzhak Rabin, sometime soldier, sometime diplomatist; chief of staff in the Six-Day War and then ambassador to Washington; tough foe of Arabs and if anything tougher foe of his political rivals in Israel, above all his ostensible colleague Shimon Peres. Their bitter rivalry complicated Israeli politics for years, and the glory of Entebbe was slightly dimmed by the row as to which of them was entitled to it.

Labour was in any case in poor shape. The party had been born during the Mandate, and given further cohesion by the clandestine resistance to British rule. All underground movements operate of necessity by basic rules – unconditional loyalty to colleagues, and no questions asked – which become dangerous when carried on into constitutional societies. It is not a coincidence that parties which began underground, like the French Gaullists and Fianna Fáil in Ireland, have been so prone to corruption. Just how far this was also true of Labour became excruciatingly apparent in January 1977, when the housing minister, Avraham Ofer, committed suicide while under investigation for corruption, and the governor of the Bank of Israel, Asher Yadlin, was gaoled for taking bribes. Both men had been appointed by Rabin. And this was at a time when the country was racked by strikes, when inflation was approaching 40 per cent, and when the government, though Labour-led, was, as always, a coalition and a distinctly weak and fissile one at that.[6]

---

[6] It was a curiosity of Israeli politics that, under the system of proportional representation so much esteemed in countries which did not have it, not only were all governments coalitions, but the party bosses were strong and governments weak, while small fringe parties, notably the religious extremists, could exercise a political weight out of all relation with the popular vote they won.

Within months of those disgraces, an historic general election was held, and in June Labour's long reign ended. The new prime minister was Menachem Begin. It was more than a political change, it was a cultural revolution. Like other revolutions, it was long in the making. A large part of the political strength of Begin's Likud coalition lay with the oriental Jews who had steadily increased as a proportion of the Israeli population. And in another sense the revolution had been anticipated while Labour was still in office. One of the more contentious issues of the following years was to be the Jewish settlements in the Territories, but these had begun under Labour. Their existence only heightened the dilemma of occupation. Either the 'West Bank' was one day to be returned to Arab rule, in which case the settlers would have to be either unsettled or left to their own devices, or they were 'Judaea and Samaria', part of the historic and inalienable Land of Israel, with an unspoken message for their Arab inhabitants.

It was in 1975, still under Labour, that the Israeli government cocked another snook at its outside supporters when it was proposed to issue a new postage stamp, commemorating the men who had assassinated Lord Moyne in 1944. This sent a shock of horror through British Jewry in particular. By an appropriate congruity, the response fell to Lord Rothschild: third baron, and nephew of the 'Dear Lord Rothschild' to whom the Balfour Declaration had been addressed nearly sixty years earlier. In a letter to *The Times* – traditional medium for English indignation – he expressed 'the feelings of a vast number of British Jews and non-Jews who are well disposed towards Israel, in expressing a sense of outrage at the behaviour of the Israeli government . . .

'Reasonable people of all nationalities, religions and political persuasions reject the doctrine that "the end justifies the means", and this particularly applies to terrorism, a disease which greatly affects the civilised world at the present time and which all civilised people utterly condemn.

'Israel is by no means the only country which appears to condone terrorists. But standing, or purporting to stand, as it does, for adherence to the law, international and otherwise, and to the most famous Commandments ever propounded, their behaviour in this case is a source of indignation to all who believe in justice, peace and freedom.'

In Israel, Rothschild's protest was met with a shrug. Where were the Rothschilds when the state was forged in blood and fire? Where were the comfortable Jews of England in 1967 and 1973? The moral challenge remained. Israel would do as it liked, and Jews outside could choose which side they were on, with the clear implication that who is not with us is against us. None of Israel's so-called friends had any right to criticise her as long as they did not share her burden. This reproach was often passively accepted by western Jews, but, partly as a result, their attitude to Israel was becoming increasingly complex in the psychiatric sense, suggesting unresolved tension or trauma. Almost all Jews admired Israel and identified with it emotionally. They unconsciously constructed an image of it which was in many ways remote from reality, as Israelis themselves were well aware. Much of increasingly voluble and bitter criticism of Israel was called unfair by Israel's supporters, and so it was. But the supporters were engaged in their own form of self-deception. The whole purpose of Zionism had been to make Israel a nation among nations, but its partisans did not in reality regard it as one. They saw it as a sacred cause, as part of themselves, and took personally attacks on it, in a way in which nationals of other countries, or partisans of other national causes in foreign countries, did not.

In abstract terms this was illogical. W. H. Auden wrote once about G. K. Chesterton, whom he admired but whose antisemitism he deplored. Chesterton had tried to defend himself on the charge by saying that 'criticism of any other nation on the planet' was permitted, and that it should not be impermissible to criticise people 'merely because they happen to be members of a race persecuted for other reasons'. But, as Auden pointed out, this was disingenuous, with its 'quiet shift from the terms *nation* to the term *race*. It is always permissible to criticise a nation (including Israel), a religion (including Orthodox Judaism), or a culture, because these are the creations of human thought and will ... A man's ethnic heritage, on the other hand, is not in his power to alter.' That should have concluded the arguments. Zionism had turned a Jewish race or a people into an Israeli nation, which should have been treated on equal terms with any other and as open to criticism as any.

But it was not. Beyond the general tradition of Jewish solidarity, 'one for all and all for one', Israel and Zionism had become so emotionally charged that they could not be discussed in any calm way. It remained true that, as the Anglo-Jewish writer David Selbourne put it, 'few Jews, including anti-Zionists, can be convinced that anti-Zionism is not antisemitism in thin disguise'. This was a victory of sorts for Herzl over Kraus and all others who had claimed that Zionism was another side of the antisemitic coin, but it was an ambiguous victory. If anti-Zionism was disguised antisemitism, how could Jews criticise or distance themselves from the Zionist state? If any criticism of Israel was going to be met with a counter-charge of antisemitism, then in theory an Israeli government could do what it liked, knowing that the emotional supporters of Israel far away would be reluctant to voice any criticism, though they might increasingly resent the way they were being used, and the position this put them in with the countries where they lived; an ironical outcome to the Zionist psychological project of rescuing Dispersion Jewry from its false position.

The trauma this created was exaggerated by repression. Few American, British or French Jews wished to relieve the trauma by thrashing it out in public. Israelis had fewer inhibitions, and it was a curiosity of the story that, however envenomed debate in Israel could often be, it was often much franker and more open than debate among British, or American, or French Jews. Israel had always contained numbers of dissenters, on Left and Right. There was the apparently curious phenomenon of the ultra-Orthodox who lived on the soil of the Land of Israel but refused to recognise the State of Israel on the traditional grounds that it was an impious anticipation of messianic redemption. Some went so far as to form alliances with the Palestinian opposition to Israel. On the far Left were those who called themselves non-Zionist Israelis, or who made another surprising objective alliance, praising the Right, Jabotinsky's Revisionists and his heirs in Begin's and Shamir's Likud, for their intellectual honesty. Israel Shahak was one extreme radical, who despised the official Israeli liberal Left for its dishonesty. It was he, and others like him, who insisted that Labour had never enjoyed the reputation for moderation which it enjoyed among European social democrats and American liberals; that it was 'the trade unions and the kibbutzim which have always been the most sinuous and deceptive in pretending that a Zionist state need not conflict with the interests of the Arabs', a pretence in which the Right from Jabotinsky onwards had never indulged; and that the Israeli liberal Left had conducted a brilliant imposture in persuading American liberals to believe that Israel 'was effectively part of the United States and its professed value system'.

Shahak's paradoxical admiration for the Right went further. In the 1970s, he made two discoveries. 'The first was the dishonesty and spite of many liberals, and the second was the decency and fortitude of many conservatives.' After Shahak had met PLO supporters abroad,

Amnon Rubinstein, leader of the Shinui, or 'Change', party, said that there was a case for prosecuting Shahak for treason – 'he has a mental perversion worse than Lord Haw Haw and Tokyo Rose' – while the *Jerusalem Post* columnist Lea Ben Dor ended a denunciation of him with the words: 'What shall we do about the poor professor? The Hospital? Or a bit of the terrorism he approves? A booby-trap over the laboratory door?'

Another radical had made a similar discovery earlier. Uri Avnery was German by birth but had been brought to Israel as a child. In 1950 he had begun publishing a subversive magazine – subversive, that is, of the prevailing political and social ethos of the new-born state – called *Ha'olem Hazeh (This World)*. It was not suppressed, of course, since Israel remained a free country, but it was treated with contempt by the regime; it became informally known as 'a certain weekly', the only description which politicians and officials could bring themselves to use.

By 1968, the year after his country's greatest victory, Avnery was calling for an Israel without Zionists. He argued for a federation of Palestine which would belong both to Arab and Jew, a forlorn case in the circumstances, as he must have known. He conceded the extraordinary achievement of Zionism, incomparably more revolutionary than the nationalism from which it had grown and which itself was 'of course, a specific manifestation of the spirit of western culture'. Zionism had not only moved large numbers of people from one country to another, 'it transferred people from one social class to another, usually a much lower one. It changed their language, their environment, their culture. It completely cut them off from their former lives.' And at the same time, Avnery penetratingly analysed his own country and society, and saw the changes which had come over them, the way in which, under the long Labour hegemony, the programme and presuppositions of Revisionism had been imperceptibly absorbed. Moshe Dayan was Ben-Gurion's protégé and favourite soldier, the New Hebrew or reborn Maccabee incarnate, and he came to epitomise Israeli valour to the world, unmistakable in the piratical patch covering the eye he had lost fighting with the British in the World War. He had been brought up on the kibbutznik principles, Hebrew Labour, Hebrew Land, Hebrew Defence; on the slogan, 'dunam after dunam, goat after goat', implying patient and slow settlement. He was not raised, he said, on the contrary Betar slogan, 'in blood and fire will Judaea rise again'. And yet, now when his country stood at the apogee of power and success, he recognised that it was the later slogan which was true: 'The fact is that since 1936 all that we achieved was secured through force of arms.'

Although Avnery did not want to agree with this Hebrew militancy, he recognised another truth. The Israelis had become a nation, 'unmistakably and irrevocably, for better or worse'. It was a nation which compromised 'all of us'. But 'it does not include a Jew from Brooklyn, Paris and Bucharest, much as he may sympathise with our country and feel an affinity for it'. This existential rather than emotional gulf between Hebrew nation and Jewish people, Israel and Dispersion, was even illustrated in that most astonishing of all Zionist achievements, the creation of Hebrew as the everyday tongue of several million people. Speaking that language, all unconsciously but with great significance, Israelis actually made that distinction between 'Jewish' – the word for the Jews of the Galut – and 'Hebrew', the word for themselves. Best of all, Avnery pointed out, was an Israeli colloquialism: to 'talk Zionism' meant to talk blarney or highfalutin' nonsense.

What Avnery had to say about the relation between 'Hebrews' and 'Jews', was reflected – though as if in a distorting mirror, so different was the political outlook – by Hillel Halkin, an American Jew who had made aliyah. Ten years after the Six-Day War and in the year Begin became prime minister he published *Letters to a Jewish American Friend*, subtitled without exaggeration 'a Zionist polemic'. Ever since Brandeis, the largest of all Dispersion Jewries had been told that they could become better Americans by becoming Zionists, and that they could become Zionists without transplanting themselves to Zion. This was nonsense; Halkin said it was absurd for anyone to call himself a Zionist who did not intend to come to Israel. Zionism meant not a vague emotional support or financial contribution but the 'decision not to live in Los Angeles or New York'. The relationship between Israel and its supporters in the Dispersion was false: 'I am not sure what it means for a Diaspora Jew to respond to Israel in a free and open way, or for an Israeli to relate to him as though he could.' The Jewish-American long-distance goodwill was as absurd as the belief of German Jews earlier in the century that it had been God's will to scatter the Jews 'so that if anything happens to one part of it, the others will live' and that gathering all the Jews into the Land of Israel was a crazy scheme which would only mean that they 'can all be slaughtered there together some day or be swallowed up by some other catastrophe'.

To Halkin the real catastrophe was to be found in Dispersion, which, 'I am convinced, *is* doomed; Jewish life has a future, if at all, in Israel.' This was a familiar theme from other Zionist polemicists besides: the partly atrophied Jewish life of so many in the West – 'Bar Mitzvah, two or three years of Hebrew school, an annual family seder, Hanukkah gifts at Christmas time' – was ignoble. Although Zionism and Israel were themselves secular in origin, they at least offered a genuine Jewish identity, in contrast to those in the West who had been undone by assimilation as well as secularism: 'They are no more ashamed of their Jewish names than are other Americans of their Polish or Italian names, and no more conscious of them either.' Halkin had one other cruel shot: to be honest, the charge of dual loyalty was as painful as it was 'not because it is a malicious invention of rabble-rousers and antisemites . . . but because it reflects the real ambiguity of being simultaneously a Jew and a citizen of a country on which a Jewish state's future depends'.

This sounded honest, but was still ambiguous. It uncannily anticipated the Pollard case of a few years later. But Halkin was surely making what lawyers call a bad point. For a blissful moment after 1967, it seemed that Zionism really had solved the Jewish Question, by giving Jews everywhere an intense pride in Israel. Not only was it perverse, however, to try and destroy Jewish America by making it migrate *en masse*, which would destroy in the process Israel's essential support. More to the point, all the nagging of Zionists only served to remind Israel's supporters in the West that, in Mordecai Richler's words, 'Looked at closely, the interests of Diaspora and Israeli Jews are seriously at odds' – and that, far from having resolved their own social problems, the very practical achievement of Zionism had given Western Jews a quite new problem which would not exist if Israel herself did not.

16

Fractured friendships

Deliver Israel, O God: out of all his troubles.

Ps.xxv.21

In 1977, nearly thirty years after the state was born, and eighty years after the first Zionist World Congress in Basle, Menachem Begin became prime minister of Israel. Eight decades was a moral light-year. The transformation of the Jewish story had been strange, then appalling, then astonishing. But not least dramatic was the change in the last of those eight decades. In 1967 the Jews of the world were united, brought together by a threat and a victory, and bonded also in untempered admiration for Israel. Now, ten years after the Six-Day War, and almost thirty since the foundation of the state, something long unforeseen had happened. The Labour hegemony had ended and Israel was ruled not by men and women with whom American liberals and European social democrats could identify but by a man who had glorified in physical violence; by the heir to Jabotinsky whom Ben-Gurion had called 'Vladimir Hitler'; by someone who had himself been called a 'fascist' by Albert Einstein.

Whether or not Begin was a fascist (and if the word had any meaning in the context), he was plainly an embarrassment to those Jews who still believed that Israel was founded on liberal and consensual principles, or who wished away the problem of the Territories. Begin did not follow his master Jabotinsky in claiming the east bank of the Jordan as well, but he made no secret of regarding the West Bank, or Judaea and Samaria, as part of the Land of Israel. Settlements there and in Gaza were increased, which did not resolve the unanswerable mystery of what was to become of those territories and their Arab population. And yet Begin surprised friend and foe alike by breaking out of the impasse with Egypt which had lasted ten years since the 1967 war. Anwar Sadat, the Egyptian president, made overtures only months after Begin had taken office, a reprise of the approach which Sadat had made in 1971 and which had been rebuffed by Golda Meir's government. This time the overture was warmly encouraged by the State Department, which called for 'a comprehensive Arab-Israeli agreement', and then by the Americans and Russians together – those unlikely co-sponsors of Israel nearly thirty years earlier in unlikely unison once more – asking for new negotiations which would include representatives of 'the Palestinian people'. This represented a shift on the part of James Carter's Administration, which had taken office in Washington the year that Begin came to power in Israel: under Israeli and Jewish-American pressure, previous administrations had eschewed that phrase.

Now Sadat said that he would travel to Jerusalem. Begin responded with an invitation, and they met there in November 1977. It was an act of great courage on both sides. Sadat in particular thereby paved the way for the Israeli-Egyptian peace treaty of 1979, earned himself half of a Nobel Peace Prize, and signed his own death warrant. The negotiations were conducted against a background of violence. In 1978, a brutal Palestinian attack killed thirty-seven Israeli civilians; Israel launched a reprisal attack on Lebanon, a practice run as it turned out; the United Nations told Israel to withdraw. In September, nevertheless, the peace treaty was negotiated at Camp David. It was immediately and predictably denounced at an Arab summit in Baghdad, an anathema pronounced again the following year. There were other ominous portents in 1980. A revolution in Tehran overthrew the Shah. Iran, or Persia, was not part of Araby (the Persians like to imagine themselves Aryans and not semites), and its Shi'ite form of Islam differed from the Sunni mainstream. That may have added to the confusion, as at first this revolution was comprehensively misunderstood outside Persia. Only by stages did it become clear that it was a profoundly reactionary expression of religious zeal and rejection of the modern world, directed by the Ayatollah Khomeini and other mullahs; part of a new 'Revolt of Islam' which was to prove more dangerous for Israel than secular Arab nationalism. So little was this understood at the time that, in the late 1970s, the Israeli authorities surreptitiously encouraged what was then the little-known Hamas

Islamic movement in Gaza and the West Bank as a counter-balance to the secular PLO. The law of unintended consequences duly took its course.

These great diplomatic events caused a mixture of relief and unease among western Jewry. As soon as Carter took office, with Cyrus Vance as Secretary of State and Zbigniew Brzezinski as National Security Adviser, the new Administration began to move on the Middle East. American public opinion still inclined towards Israel; almost all American Jews had a deep attachment to Israel; most American Jews were also, however, still Democrats, and had voted for Carter. This produced a conflict political and psychological at once. The crucial question in this regard was not peace with Egypt but the question of the Palestinians and the intimately related question of Jewish settlements in the Territories.

The settlements had begun well before Begin, or for that matter Carter, came to power. The Labour government had sponsored settlements along the Jordan valley, with the clear if unstated intention of making the Jordan the permanent strategic frontier of Israel, but it officially deplored settlements throughout the whole West Bank, with its heavy Palestinian population. In 1973, an extreme group from the religious Right, Gush Emunim, or Block of the Faithful, began to form settlements in 'Samaria', the northern part of the West Bank. If this was contrary to government policy it was not contrary to Zionist history. This was after all, as Ehud Sprinzak puts it, 'the historical pattern of Pioneering Zionism: an illicit minority action followed by majority recognition and gratitude'. Some Labour ministers could not help privately thinking back to their own younger days as pioneers defying the British. The government disapproved of the settlements in theory, and in practice allowed them to stay.

Once Begin took office, the Israeli government no longer even bothered to condemn settlements in what it, as much as the settlers themselves, believed to be the Land of Israel. And yet Israel was 'the truest ally in the Middle East' of the United States, whose government, under whichever president, always opposed the settlements, the Carter Administration more outspokenly than its predecessors. This put Jewish America in a painful position. A survey of Jewish-American leaders in 1978 found that three out of four wanted Israel to follow more moderate policies, and one of those leaders gave an interview that year to the Israeli daily paper *Ha'aretz*. Laurence Tisch accused Begin of playing into Carter's hands by his obduracy, and he implicitly accused him of embarrassing Jewish America: 'The only thing that Israel can offer is its righteousness, and the Jews in America are on the right side of public opinion when they can prove that they are fighting for something which is right . . . but when Israel is in the wrong our strength is low. If Begin continues about the settlements, you will lose the war down to the last American . . .' He went on in telling words: 'for thirty years we have been building for Israel the image of a peace-loving country. Begin destroyed this image in three months.' As significant as the interview itself was the fact that Tisch refused to allow its republication in English translation in any American newspaper. His confusion spoke for many others. Israel had given so much to western Jews in emotional terms; now that great gift seemed threatened. In return western Jews had written a blank cheque to the Israel of Ben-Gurion and Golda Meir; now they found that Begin was trying to cash it.

Their pain was increased by a succession of events in sharp contrast to the Israeli-Egyptian peace treaty. Only months after Carter took office, Congress was circulated with a list of twenty-one Israeli grievances against the new administration; the White House was bombarded with letters complaining of its bias towards the Arabs; demands were made for the removal of some of Carter's Middle East advisers; and a board Member of the Zionist Organisation of America told *Time*, with more candour than caution, 'People thought they had seen a Jewish lobby operate before. They haven't seen anything yet.' The Israelis fought Carter bitterly over the sale of fighters to Saudi Arabia, but lost; this and other conflicts affected Jewish America to the extent that, in 1980, Jewish support peeled away from Carter, who won only 45 per cent of the Jewish vote in the New York primary, and then lost the presidential election. For Israel it was a Pyrrhic victory.

Although Ronald Reagan made all the conventional noises about the Judeo-Christian tradition and 'our truest ally' during and after his election campaign, he proved less pliant than the Israeli government had hoped. He was inaugurated in 1981, a dramatic year. There were armed confrontations between Israel and Syrian forces in Lebanon. The Israelis showed their usual determination to look after their interests as they saw them when their air force suddenly bombed and destroyed a nuclear reactor with military potential in Irak. Begin won another election and made Ariel Sharon his defence minister. Anwar Sadat was assassinated by Muslim zealots. But for Israeli-American relations the most important episode of the year was the AWACS affair: Reagan's authorisation of the sale of five surveillance aircraft to Saudi Arabia.

For the more than fifty years since its creation, that country had been an unflagging enemy of Zionism, an enmity often expressed in the most violent language. To call this 'antisemitism' was absurd, quite apart from the semantic quibble that the Arabs themselves were semites. King Ibn Saud and his successors had seen the Zionist settlers not as Drumont or Streicher saw the European Jews, a parasitic or sub-human species, but as Geronimo or Sitting Bull saw the wagon trains and the United States cavalry, an irruption by a more dynamic society. Saudi Arabia had survived the threat of secular Arab nationalism, partly thanks to the remoteness and backwardness of the country and partly, if contradictorily, thanks to the immeasurable wealth lying under its soil. A very small part of those oil riches had been used to promote the Palestinian cause, and to look after Palestinian refugees, whom the Saudis could have afforded to resettle in comfort if they had wanted. And the dynasty saw itself as a guardian of the Palestinians: that year of 1981, Prince Fahd advocated a Palestinian state with Jerusalem as its capital.

By almost every standard of liberal democracy, Saudi Arabia ranked near the bottom of the scale, with no pretence of representative government, freedom of speech, respect for human rights, or rule of law, except the harsh antique law which publicly beheaded thieves and stoned adulteresses to death. But, as Bismarck used to say, the rules governing the conduct of international relations are not those of a student duel. Like any other power, not to say like Israel, the United States was entitled or even obliged to think of its own interests, and those patently included remaining on good terms with Saudi Arabia, to which end the Reagan Administration wanted the AWACS sale.

Thus began a political battle which became an epic clash of wills, the most bitter to date. The American Administration wanted one thing, the Israeli government another. The arbiter was to be Congress, played on from one side by the White House, from the other by AIPAC, trying as usual to throw the weight of Jewish America into the tug-of-war. Accusations of outrageous Israeli interference were matched with accusations of antisemitism. Those accusations would have been sharper still if everything said in private had been known to the public. Ten years later, President George Bush's Secretary of State James Baker was reported as saying to a colleague in confidential discussion, 'Fuck the Jews, they don't vote for us anyway.' The words were blazoned as a headline in an Israeli newspaper which, not surprisingly, portrayed him as an antisemite. But Baker was unwittingly echoing others. During the AWACS debate Gerald Ford was enlisted by the Reagan White House. In a telephone conversation with one Republican senator who had been tracked down (at dinner with Jewish leaders, though Ford did not know this), the former president asked, 'Are we going to let the fucking Jews run American foreign policy?' And Ford in turn echoed President Carter, who had told some of his closest colleagues in the spring of 1980, 'If I get back in, I'm going to fuck the Jews.'

What explained this catalogue of profanity (all reliably documented at the time)? A simple answer, which many Zionists from Herzl's time on would have given, was that it merely displayed that ineradicable virus of antisemitism lurking in the breasts of all gentiles. Another explanation was even simpler. Ford, Carter and Baker were all politicians. Being American politicians in the second half of the twentieth century, they had all been obliged to respect the public pieties about Israel. But like all politicians they wanted to get their way, and found it intensely frustrating when they were blocked in what they tried to do – the rightness or wrongness of which was almost irrelevant – by such a formidable pressure group. The frustration was let off in private, in brutal and ugly language, but it was not so much the language of bigots as of thwarted men.

In October, the House of Representatives voted heavily against the sale, after intensive lobbying, though this was less one-sided than usual. The Saudis had hired as their Washington lobbyist Frederick G. Dutton, who had been an aide to Adlai Stevenson, then special assistant to President Kennedy, and was still a friend of Senator Robert Kennedy and of Benjamin Bradlee, editor of the *Washington Post*; not a negligible figure in Democratic politics. The other side redoubled its efforts: shortly before the next critical vote, every member of the Senate was sent a copy of the novel *Holocaust*, but even this did not work. The Administration had its own means of persuasion; as a White House official nicely described the approach made to one senator, 'We just beat his brains out. We stood him up in front of an open grave and told him he could jump in if he wanted to.' On the day, the Senate approved the sale by fifty-two votes to forty-eight.

The AWACS affair was a milestone not only for Israeli-American relations but for Jewish America. Despite all the abuse hurled at it, the Reagan Administration had only behaved as governments will. If the president had been in the habit of quoting nineteenth-century statesmen, he could have cited not only Bismarck, but Palmerston too: his country had no permanent friends and no permanent enemies, only permanent interests. Israel and her friends claimed, when it suited them, that an alliance with Israel, albeit informal, was such a permanent interest, but this needed to be demonstrated rather than merely assumed. After the dust had settled, the old questions remained. As Edward Tivnan put it: 'Were American interests in the Middle East the same as Israel's? Why did the American Jewish community differ so strongly with US policy? Were the current President of the United States and his three predecessors all really antisemites?'

Not only were these questions unanswered. Few chose to see that the relationship between Israel and the United States had become distorted and one-sided, and the relationship between Israel and the Dispersion still more so. Complaints about American 'bullying' of Israel were more and more heard, but this alleged bullying took the form of American failure to comply with Israeli diplomatic or military policy, or even any suggestion that the Americans might diminish the very large subsidies they paid to Israel. Any hint that this subsidy might be in some way conditional was resented by Israel and its lobbyists and friends in America. Thus another question was left unanswered. Although this particular flood of inter-governmental funds may not have quite fitted Peter Bauer's classic definition of 'aid' – the process by which poor people in rich countries give money to rich people in poor countries – it had an unmistakably deleterious influence on the Israeli economy; but any attempt even to discuss it was portrayed as unfair to Israel, even as an attack on her sovereignty. The psychology of this was almost droll. Parents of children growing up make an interesting discovery. In almost every way – socially, politically, not least sexually – these adolescents expect to be treated as adults. The exception is financially: in that regard, the kids want to be treated as kids until long after the age of majority. Israel's relationship with the United States was like that. Not only were its college fees to be paid, as it were, but all the costs of partying and cutting a dash as well, while no criticism of life-style was brooked. At the end of 1981, Begin turned angrily on the Americans: 'Are we a vassal state of yours? Are we a banana republic?' Given that, in the quarter century 1966–1991, Israel received more than $75 billion in American aid, this was a question he might have been better advised not to pose in those words. But then no good deed goes unpunished, and a consciousness of indebtedness notoriously causes sour resentment on the part of the indebted.

Israel indeed continued to go her own way whatever anyone else said. In the summer of 1982, in reply to terrorist attacks in general and in particular to the attempted assassination of the Israeli ambassador in London, Israel launched a full-scale military invasion of Lebanon. The PLO were driven out of their bases, large parts of the country were devastated, many thousands were killed, Beirut was heavily bombarded. It was a turning point not only in Israel's own history, but in the story of her image in the outside world. When the war began, Sharon had said that 'No one has a right to tell Israel what decision to take in defence of its own people', and Begin had told 'my dear friend' Alexander Haig, the American Secretary of State, that 'the man has not yet been born who will ever obtain from me consent to let Jews be killed by a bloodthirsty enemy'. Perhaps advice from a candid friend would have been worth listening to before Israel embarked on a fierce war into which Syria was inexorably drawn, so that much of Lebanon ended under Syrian control.

Much or maybe most of the Dispersion nevertheless accepted Sharon's and Begin's argument that summer and closed ranks. Prominent British Jews were taken on a thirty-six-hour guided tour of Lebanon, and were impressed by the Israeli achievement. Several signed a full-page advertisement in the *Jewish Chronicle* which gave their 'full support to Israel in Operation Peace for Galilee' (the Newspeak name for the invasion). The Labour MP Greville Janner reported that the Israelis had been welcomed as liberators: 'In East Beirut people were waving and cheering – I was absolutely astonished. Every Lebanese I met, most of them Christians, some Moslems, had only one criticism – that we should finish the job.' By 'we', Janner meant the Israelis, not the country of which he was a citizen and a legislator. Criticism of Israel by the British government was much resented by some British Jews. Comparisons were made with the Falklands War which England had just fought, or with the World War forty years earlier. Begin cited the British bombing of Germany,[7] while others insisted that the reports of casualties had been grossly and maliciously exaggerated. Sidney Brichto, director of the Union of Liberal and

---

[7] As did a very eminent British (though German-born) Jew to the author that late summer: the bombardment of Beirut was 'no worse than what we did to the Germans'. 'What we did' in 1942–5 was to destroy scores of cities and kill 600,000 civilians, 100,000 of them children; a revealing comparison.

Progressive Synagogues, spoke of the moral torment British Jews had suffered as a result, recalling Golda Meir's saying that she could forgive the Arabs for killing Jews 'but not for making killers of us'. This anguish had been inflamed by journalistic mendacity, Brichto claimed; 'I find it difficult to forgive the press'.

Not for the first time, this sensitivity and closing of ranks was more pronounced in the Dispersion than in Israel. In fact, Lebanon was the first of Israel's wars openly to divide rather than unite the country. At the time, Moshe Machover, a mathematician, was teaching in London and said that, as a supporter of the Israeli Peace Now movement, 'Paradoxically I feel more isolated here than in Israel itself', where debate was as vociferous as ever. He also disbelieved the motives of the Israeli government which really, he claimed, wanted to crush the PLO just as – and because – it was perceptibly shifting from pure violence to rational politics. And yet, 'Most Jews around the world think of themselves as potential victims, and when you have this state of mind you excuse the inexcusable.'

The grim climax came in September. West Beirut was controlled by the Phalangists, the Maronite Christian Militia which was acting as Israel's client. Two refugee camps there, Sabra and Chatilla, were packed with Palestinians. The Israelis had announced that their occupation was designed 'to prevent any possible incidents and to secure quiet', and Begin had himself told his chief of staff to protect the Muslims from the Phalangists. Days after he said this, Phalangists fell on those two refugee camps and massacred several hundred people. The world was horrified, but Begin was unmoved: 'Goyim kill goyim and then they come to hang the Jews.' Despite these dismissive words, the division within Israel, not to say the very fact that it was a free country, was shown when 400,000 people, or a tenth of the population, demonstrated in favour of an inquiry into the Beirut events. In a dramatic break with the tradition of unquestioning solidarity, Howard Squadron and Alexander Schindler, a lawyer and a rabbi, both past chairmen of the Conference of Presidents of Major American-Jewish Organisations, also called for an independent inquiry. And Arthur Hertzberg, another rabbi, wrote a fierce attack on Israeli policy under the headline 'Begin Must Go' for the *New York Times*, in which there were also paid advertisements protesting against the war, mawkish from Woody Allen, more serious from Jewish intellectuals. Hertzberg had long been a gadfly, from his early, quizzical essays wondering 'what shall I do with my Zionism?' after the creation of Israel. He had been a critical friend of Israel, and may have suffered from some of the same illusions as so many liberal Jews about the fundamental benevolence and peaceableness of Israeli leaders before Likud came to power. But he now became Begin's most vehement foe in the Dispersion, insisting that 'I am not in the dissenting minority; it is Begin who is in the minority, in Israel and the US'. He now argued that the invasion of Lebanon was designed partly to scare Palestinians out of the West Bank, and that the solution was to be found in a return to the original 1947 partition plan.

Although Begin was as indifferent to the reproaches of Dispersion liberals like Hertzberg as to what the goyim said, he was not emotionally invulnerable. In 1983, he sank into deep depression, brought on partly by the death of his wife but also by the continuing conflict in Lebanon which he had embarked on and which was taking a toll of Israeli life (though a heavier toll of Lebanese life). He resigned, to be succeeded by Yitzhak Shamir, an even more remarkable embodiment of the extreme Revisionist tradition. During the World War, Shamir had joined Stern, the man who had negotiated personally with Mussolini's representatives and, through colleagues, with Hitler's, even proposing an alliance with the Axis. Shamir was later closely involved in several violent acts, including the assassinations of Lord Moyne and Count Bernadotte. Yeshayahu Leibowitz, an Israeli dissenter, though also a self-proclaimed Zionist and sometime editor of the *Encyclopaedia Hebraica*, looked with disgust upon 'a prime minister who was a leader in an organisation which offered its services to Hitler'.

For all that, despite the shock of Sabra and Chatilla, despite all the protests, despite the plain embarrassment, an underlying sense of embattled victimhood still linked Israeli and Dispersion Jewry; which was to say, a common fear of lurking antisemitism. Rabbi Hugo Gryn, an Auschwitz survivor living in London, believed that the Lebanon war had 'made antisemitism respectable'. Respectable or not, there was some evidence that it could once again be publicly voiced. A line had always existed between anti-Zionism and antisemitism in theory, but it had become harder to draw in practice. Until Hitler and the creation of Israel, many Jews had themselves been strongly anti-Zionist, but in the following decades those voices were silenced. Perhaps it should have been possible to make Auden's intellectual distinction between criticising a people and a national state, but the emotional truth was David Selbourne's seeming paradox, that even anti-Zionist Jews suspected that anti-Zionism was antisemitism. Nor was this suspicion always just paranoid fantasy. The bitterness and violence of language which the Left had come to use about Israel – its tone as well as its content – was charged with significance.

When Harold Wilson abruptly resigned as British Prime Minister in 1976, the mystery of his departure was deepened by a resignation honours list which included some notably shady Jewish businessmen; one was subsequently imprisoned for fraud, one shot himself while under criminal investigation. Wilson devoted part of his retirement to the Zionist cause, publishing in 1981 *The Chariot of Israel*. It was a bizarre book, but no less telling were some of the reviews. The hard-Left journalist Paul Foot concluded that 'the whole wretched experiment of Zionism is in ruins', a proposition plausible on certain terms, though it could also (but by Foot would not) have been said more plausibly about the experiment of Irish nationalism, or indeed of socialism. His uncle Michael Foot had been a Labour MP on and off since 1945, had edited the left-wing *Tribune* and was a famous figure on the Left of the party until he accidentally and unhappily became party leader from 1980 to 1983. Back in the 1940s, along with other zealous socialists in his own party, Michael Foot had been a strong supporter of the infant Israel. The contrast between uncle and nephew was a vignette of what had happened between Zionism and the Left.

Others were more eloquent still. The English children's book author Roald Dahl wrote that 1982, the year of Lebanon, was 'when we all started hating the Jews', words which in themselves might have been designed to justify the equation of hostility to Israel with antisemitism. Among that political group for whom the only good Jew was a dead Jew (name of Leon Trotsky), the belief flourished that the Zionists had colluded with Hitler, a belief aired in the left-wing magazine, *Labour Herald*, co-edited by Ken Livingstone, then the leader of the Greater London Council and subsequently a Labour MP, who himself called the official Anglo-Jewish leadership 'neo-fascists'. In the United States little quite on that level appeared. But in every western country the rift between Jews and the Left widened, although the Jewish disengagement from radicalism and even liberalism was slow, and uneven. Carter's policy alienated many Jewish voters from the Democrats, but they swung back, and in the 1984 election more Jews voted for Mondale than had for Carter and the liberal third-party candidate Anderson combined four years earlier; Reagan scored 8 per cent better in 1986 than 1980 among the general population, but 7 per cent worse among Jews; and two-thirds of them voted for Mondale, more than any other identifiable groups except blacks or the unemployed.[8] The shift was taking place all the same, quite apart from the fissuring of the old Jewish Left. Raymond Aron had illustrated this in France: an old-fashioned liberal who ended as a supporter of the Vietnam War and a friend of Henry Kissinger's (who illustrated the Jewish rightward shift himself). In England, the shift was acted out on the stage of high politics. When Sir Keith Joseph was first elected to Parliament in 1955, there were numerous Jews on the Labour benches but he was one of only two Jewish Tory MPs. There were still only two in 1966, though thirty-eight out of 363 Labour MPs in that Parliament were Jewish, an astonishing proportion in a country where Jews were little more than one in two hundred of the population. A decade later, the Tories showed their cunning and instinct for survival when, a little more than a century after Disraeli had become their leader, Margaret Thatcher did. She showed an unusual affinity for Jews, encouraged by her sympathy for the Jewish accountants, dentists and businessmen of the parliamentary constituency of Finchley which she represented, who were almost as much 'the folk from whence she came' as her own Methodist forebears in Grantham. Her governments of the 1980s included in all six Jewish Cabinet Ministers, Joseph himself the first.[9] This was a remarkable achievement; it also contrasted with the diminishing number of Jewish Labour MPs.

Nearly a century and a half earlier, Disraeli had said that the persecution of the Jews had deprived the conservative element in society of an important ally and added to the destructive party. His assertion had now been addressed, and demonstrated empirically, in his own country and by his own party. It had always been true that wherever Jews had been treated reasonably well, from Austria-Hungary to the United States, they had become the most loyal citizens of those countries. All Jews had wanted was equality of respect and of opportunity. Now there were other forces at work driving western Jews to the Right, as the principle of strict equality of opportunity was abandoned by the Left. This was done in the name of 'affirmative

---

[8] This was despite President Reagan's parading on Long Island in a red-white-and-blue yarmulka and the telephoning of millions of Jewish voters by callers identifying themselves as 'Harry Goodman' or 'Betty Goodman', many of whom were in fact black.

[9] Also Leon Brittan, Nigel Lawson, David Young, Malcolm Rifkind and Michael Howard.

action' or reverse discrimination. Under whatever name, it cut to the quick, as Howard Jacobsen said, the Jews with their instinctive meritocracy. In order to enhance their position, supposedly ill-used minorities were given preferential treatment and, whatever disguises were adopted, this could only be done on a quota basis. Jews had long chafed under the *numerus clausus*, restricting their numbers in professions or institutions. Affirmative action looked like, and indeed was, a *numerus clausus* in reverse. It offended in general against the old liberal principle of the *carrière ouverte aux talents*, of appointment and promotion on merit. 'I don't know. We don't count,' Glazunov had nobly replied when asked how many Jews there were in his conservatoire. Affirmative action was counting with a vengeance, and offended Jews in particular.

In England, this rightward shift had little to do with the controversy of Zion; in America, much. The increasing political perplexity of Jewish America was related to *embourgeoisement* and suburbanisation, to tensions with blacks and fear of the underclass, to disenchantment with the welfare state; but above all to Israel. As the Left became more and more detached from, and then frankly hostile to, Israel, Jews almost inevitably became estranged from the Left. The process could be followed through the pages of one magazine. *Commentary* had begun as the property of the American-Jewish Committee; the voice of Jewish liberalism; and, under the editorship of Elliot Cohen, to publishing 'what Brandeis was to academia . . . a manifestation of the conviction that Jews had become part of the American mainstream'. As part of this process, the magazine had been both liberal and staunchly anti-Communist. More the latter than the former, its critics thought: radical Jews like Irving Howe saw the magazine as abjectly uncritical of McCarthy and his ism; as part of 'The Age of Conformity', in the essay of that name Howe published in 1954. Maybe Cohen felt these criticisms, as well as the tensions of the decade. Overwhelmed by events and by melancholy, he killed himself in 1959.

His successor was the young critic Norman Podhoretz, whose appointment was meant (however ironical it later seemed) to signal a move of the magazine to the Left. It did not immediately move the other way. Nor did Israel become its chief preoccupation then. When Podhoretz published an early autobiography in 1967 he called his memoirs *Making It* and its theme was his 'astonishing revelation' at the age of thirty-five: 'it is better to be a success than a failure'. But although the book was a detailed name-dropping chronicle of the ins

and outs and ups and downs of New York literary life, and inevitably
had a heavily Jewish flavour, it scarcely touched on Zionism, Israel and
American Jewry's relationship with them. By the time Podhoretz wrote
Breaking Ranks in 1979, life had changed, and so had he. The turning
point, in the view of Bernard Avishai, a critic who remained on the
Left, was the aftermath of the Six-Day War, when *Commentary* had not
only shared the near-universal, intense Jewish identification but had
become an organ of Jewish nationalism. Throughout the 1970s, the
magazine's denunication of Israel's critics became more bitter, and
Podhoretz wrote an unhappily timed attack on those critics under the
Dreyfusard title '*J'accuse*', which appeared in the September 1982
Commentary, printed before the Beirut massacres.[10] And he admitted
that he had come to judge every question by the simple test, 'Is it good
for the Jews?' This drew a deft rebuke from one critic. If that was
Podhoretz's only standard, Murray Rothbard said, what would happen
when those Americans who were not Jewish – after all, 97 per cent of
the population – asked of every proposition, 'Is it good for the gentiles?'

In the 1980s, the story moved down stranger paths. If western Jews –
or if Israelis – moved to the Right, they were bound to find themselves
some curious bedfellows. The distinction of Left and Right remained as
confusing and often as misleading as ever two hundred years after the
French Revolution, a metaphor which continued to do European and
American political thought and conduct more harm than good. But
everyone used it. The Left had been cured of its own antisemitism by
the Dreyfus Affair, and the whole world had at least affected to find
antisemitism intolerable after Hitler. Stalin had emerged in his true
Jew-hating colours, the Warsaw Communist government had used a
campaign against 'Zionists' to drive out the tragically tiny remnant of
Polish Jewry after the 1967 war, and on the insaner fringes of the Left
members of the Baader-Meinhof gang could justify Auschwitz in terms
of the need to purge corrupt Jewish capitalism. In the broadest terms,
however, the progressive, liberal 'Left' kept some credit through an
instructive identification with philosemitism, while the reactionary,
conservative 'Right' was still tainted with antisemitism, and not without
reason. American nativism, the nearest the country could come to
narrow European nationalism, had a long history of Jew-hatred. It was
succeeded by the militant anti-Communism of McCarthy and the John

[10] One of the most eloquent of gentile Zionists, Conor Cruise O'Brien, had even
worse luck: his defence of Israel in Lebanon appeared in the London *Observer* on
the Sunday morning that the news of the massacres broke.

Birch Society, which was itself slowly replaced as the dominant force of the Right of the Republican party by a new religious fundamentalism. This movement threw up some strange figures, whose attitude to the Jews was cranky at best and hostile at worst.

Even those Jews who had moved from radicalism through liberalism to neo-conservatism were disturbed by this; or some of them were. In 1984, Irving Kristol, once a stalwart of liberal anti-Communism, argued that Jews should not be squeamish about making alliances with America's own ayatollahs like Jerry Falwell, leader of the self-proclaimed Moral Majority. Nathan and Ruth Ann Perlmutter had already suggested in *The Real Anti-Semitism in America* that the said reality was now to be found among political radicals, black militants, Arab sympathisers in the mainstream Protestant churches, isolationists, businesses trading with Araby and, not least, the proponents of 'affirmative action'. They argued that while the Episcopalian and Presbyterian churches' members were likely to be less antisemitic, because better educated, than the membership of fundamentalist sects, the latter sects were far more inclined to support Israel than the former churches, and that the Moral Majority was where Jews should look for friends. Kristol agreed: 'This real world is rife with conflict and savagery. It is a world in which liberalism is very much on the defensive, in which public opinion runs in the grooves established by power, in which people back winners not losers.' Falwell and his kind may have been cranks and bigots, Kristol conceded, but that mattered not 'as against the mundane fact that this same preacher is vigorously pro-Israel', that fact itself a curious legacy of the link between Ashley's evangelicalism and his kinship with 'God's chosen people' in 1840.

To some liberals like Michael Kinsley his argument was poor on its own premises, as well as ignoble. American support for Israel could be justified in foreign policy terms, Kinsley said, 'but that case is complicated. What isn't complicated is the case for Israel as a unique exemplar of the American values of democracy and freedom in a region dominated by tyrannies of various sorts. Any Jew who's discussed the subject with gentiles knows that this is the real wellspring of American support for Israel.' In truth, the case went further than that. The cynical or *realpolitisch* argument, which neo-conservatives insisted was the only one which should be used, was logically flawed. If the most brutal self-interest or national egoism was to be the touchstone, then a plausible case could be made that the United States should abandon Israel to its own devices while making an Arab alliance. But equally, the easy assumption that Israel was a unique exemplar of democracy and freedom begged a few questions of its own. Perhaps most significant of all was the very existence of what Kinsley called 'the continuing war among Jewish intellectuals'. This war might have been waged in any case, about the position of Jews in a secular society. Instead it took the form of a renewed controversy of Zion; a debate focused on the Jewish response to the Jewish state; a dispute which could not have taken place at all if Herzl had not dreamt his dream.

Jewish disenchantment with the Democrats was increased by the rise in the party of the gifted demagogue Jesse Jackson, who was overheard referring to New York as 'Hymietown' and who flirted with a much more blatantly antisemitic mountebank like Louis Farrakhan. Thanks to the prevailing cravenness of American 'liberal' politics, this sort of bigotry on the part of an alleged victim group went largely unchallenged. Not that bigotry and demagoguery were confined to blacks, or gentiles. Rabbi Kahane transferred his operating base to Israel, where in 1984 he won a seat in the Knesset. There was never any chance that he would win real power, but his influence was alarming enough, so alarming that the Knesset subsequently voted to expel him even though he had been fairly elected. The heirs of Jabotinsky, the Likudniks, and their western supporters, liked to use the language of realism. Those who advocated compromise with the Palestinians, they argued throughout the 1980s, were deluded senti-mentalists. This was much what Jabotinsky had said sixty years earlier, when he challenged the delusions of Weizmann and the mainstream Zionists in terms likewise of realism and intellectual honesty, insisting that Zionism must mean a Jewish state with a Jewish majority and that it would have to be established by force against Arab resistance. The problem now for his heirs was that they in their turn were being challenged in terms of realism by Kahane, as well as other extremist parties, and the zealots settled in Judaea and Samaria.

Every Israeli knew about what George Steiner called 'the demo-graphic crises underlying the entire question of the future of Israel: the fact that more people are emigrating *from* Israel than *to* it and the great differential in birth-rate as between Arabs and Jews (to the Arabs' ineluctable gain) inside Israel itself'. So what was to be done if Israel remained within its post-1967 borders? For all their self-proclaimed realism, the Likudniks gave an evasive answer. There was nothing evasive about Kahane. His remedy was compellingly simple. The

Arabs should be removed from Judaea and Samaria as so many of them had been removed from pre-1967 Israel. One extreme party, Moledet (Homeland), was bluntly advocating forcible expulsion of the Arabs, asking 'who will go – us or them?', and posing an awkward proposition. 'We came to conquer the land and settle it. If transfer is unethical then everything we have done for a hundred years is wrong.' And Kahane said, 'I am telling you, what each one of you thinks deep in his heart: there is only one solution, no other, no partial solution: the Arabs out! . . . Do not ask me how . . . Let me become defence minister for two months and you will not have a single cockroach around here! I promise you a clean Erez Israel!' Here was a frighteningly brilliant slogan: 'I say what you think.' It was not, in fact, what many Israelis consciously thought, or wanted, but it implied that he was speaking a truth which at some deep unconscious level they all recognised.

For western Jews, Kahane was a problem also, even if they tried to ignore him. And Israel itself was a difficulty as well as an inspiration. The charge of dual loyalty had not gone away. Hillel Halkin had told his American-Jewish friend that it could not be brushed aside, and from an entirely different angle Gore Vidal repeated it with envenomed glee. There had long been two liberal American weeklies, the *Nation* and the *New Republic*. The *New Republic* was Walter Lippmann's old paper, a voice of earnest, sometimes anguished, reason. In the 1930s and 1940s it had lost its way, as had the *Nation*, when both became more or less embarrassed apologists for Stalin, or adopted a position Dwight Macdonald had called 'totalitarian liberalism'. From the 1970s, the *New Republic* acquired another King Charles's head, in the shape of Israel and the need for continued American support for its truest friend. On the twentieth anniversary of the 1967 war, the magazine published a cover stylistically cognate with socialist-realist art of the 1930s, showing a man with a child in his arms looking out over the land of Israel as the blue-and-white flag fluttered aloft. The *New Republic* did attack Shamir, whose extremism provided a useful means of striking an apparently even-handed stance; and, like those *New York Times* columnists who strongly supported Israel, A. M. Rosenthal and William Safire, it also attacked the economic decadence of Israel and recognised that this was caused by Israel's dependence on a financial life-support system provided by the American taxpayer.

By contrast, the *Nation* did not shift to the Right, and did not become an uncritical supporter of Israel, far from it. It was there, in 1986, that Vidal published an attack on Podhoretz, his wife Midge Decter, and other members of the 'Israeli Fifth Column'. He ascribed *Commentary*'s and the Podhoretzes' well-known move away from liberalism to their desire to get American money for Israel, and this was their first priority even if it meant making common cause with the lunatic Right. Vidal went further. He told an anecdote. When he had been working on a play about the Civil War – 'to the United States what the Trojan War was to the Greeks' – Podhoretz had told him that the Civil War was to him as remote and irrelevant as the Wars of the Roses. From his exchange, Vidal inferred that Podhoretz was not, and did not want to be, even an 'assimilated American' (let alone one of old American stock). Nor was his wife: 'Like most of our Israeli fifth columnists, Midge isn't much interested in what the *goyim* were up to before Ellis Island.' She had accused Vidal of not liking his country; 'now that we're really levelling with each other,' he replied, 'I've got to tell you that I don't much like your country, which is Israel.'

This age-old accusation of disloyalty was bitterly offensive to most American Jews, but it was not as damaging as their own intestine disputes and their own more reflective critics. Shortly before Vidal's pasquinade, Amnon Rubinstein published *The Zionist Dream Revisited*, and Bernard Avishai, *The Tragedy of Zionism*. Rubinstein correctly saw the Israelis not as 'a new branch grafted on to an old tradition [but] a new tree'. At the same time he voiced a doubt, which others surely felt even if they did not always voice it or even consciously recognise it in themselves, whether he entirely admired this new growth. Jewish soldiers were shedding the blood of Arab children, 'and real blood . . . this is no libel'. Avishai went further, in a literal as well as literary sense. He was a Canadian Jew who had made aliyah, lived in Israel for several years, but finally returned to America, not so much bitterly disappointed as quietly disillusioned. So he explained at length in the pages of the *New York Review of Books* as well as in his own book. Perhaps he retained as well as shed illusions of his own, ones which fitted in well with the presuppositions of academic Jewish America, of many New Yorkers, and of the *New York Review*. He believed, that is, that 'Labour Zionism is a good revolution that long ago ran its course, that it stopped short of its liberal-democratic goals'.

Israel had declined into militarism and reaction, he argued in the aftermath of the Lebanon war, but he took on trust the essentially worthy nature of the early settlement and the principle of 'Hebrew Labour': in the pioneering days of the Yishuv, 'the revolutionary institution of Labour Zionism understandably discriminated in favour of Jews and excluded the interest of Arabs', something which might not have seemed quite so understandable to those Arabs. He also ignored the possibility that Revisionism and its heirs had all along been more intellectually honest than the Labour movement, and that Ben-Gurion's successors were neither blameless, nor always constructive, about what Avishai called 'the West Bank tragedy'. What haunted Avishai was an underlying conflict: 'Democracy or Zionism?' but it was too convenient to suggest that this conflict had suddenly emerged with Begin's premiership. The position of Israeli and Dispersion liberals sometimes resembled that of South African white, English-speaking liberals, who had persuaded themselves that not only the name 'apartheid' but white supremacy itself had sprung up as if from nowhere with the Nationalists' victory in 1948; a view which required selective historical amnesia.

There were still moments when Israel could tug at the heartstrings. Another threatened Jewish community, though a mysterious one, was rescued when, in a stunning logistical feat, 'Operation Moses' brought out 14,000 people from Ethiopia in a single weekend in 1984. In all, 21,000 Ethiopian Jews were brought to Israel. These people claimed to be a long-lost branch of the Hebrew nation, although they appeared in many ways little different from other Africans in the upper Nile region. Whether most Israelis truly regarded them as their own kith and kin was a delicate question; certainly, the official Israeli rabbinate did not recognise their religious leaders. On a cynical view, it was convenient for a country accused of racism to find a group of poor blacks whom it could call its own and patronise. And the Dispersion was cheered by a new good cause to support. According to an Israeli reporter, one rich Jewish-American businessman was solicited for his support, asked how much the resettlement of each Ethiopian cost, and said, 'Okay, put me down for four *shvartzes*.' Later on, the story turned rather sour when most of these *shvartzes* were still living in bleak trailer parks, when their children were largely (and some said needlessly) being educated in schools for the backward, and when it transpired that the Israeli medical services were surreptitiously destroying blood donated by Ethiopians, ostensibly for fear of AIDS contamination.

For American Jewry there were, in the 1980s, more painful conflicts than the treatment of Ethiopians, or than the taunts of WASP litterateurs. In March 1987, Jonathan Pollard and his wife Anne were convicted of espionage on behalf of Israel. Pollard was an American who had been suborned by Israeli agents, playing on his sentiment as a

Jew. It would have been hard to think of a more brutal way of raising the spectre of 'dual loyalty'. The head of the Conference of Presidents publicly supported the life sentence on Pollard, and even the tireless lobbyists of AIPAC worried about the effect the case might have on American-Israeli relations. In reply, the Israeli historian Shlomo Avineri published an open letter to an imaginary 'American-Jewish friend' in which he accused Jewish-Americans of having displayed over the Pollard case 'nervousness, insecurity and even cringing' – *mauscheln* again – and perceived an anxiety 'deep in the soul' of Diaspora Jewry. The accusation was designed to wound the Dispersion, and to increase its anxieties; it did not help when Rabbi Avi Weiss of Riverdale, New York, organised a 'freedom seder' outside the prison where Pollard was held, to protest at the incarceration of this 'Jewish political prisoner'.

Some of Pollard's defenders compared him with Dreyfus. The comparison was bizarre. Dreyfus was a passionately patriotic and loyal Frenchman falsely accused of treason; Pollard's want of loyal American patriotism had been experimentally demonstrated.[11] But echoes of the *Affaire* were indeed ominous. When the veteran reactionary writer Charles Maurras had been convicted of collaboration after the liberation of France in 1945, he had left the dock shouting *'C'est la revanche de Dreyfus!'* The Pollard case was the revenge of Charlus. Proust's cynical ogre had thought that Dreyfus should not have been accused of treason, at worst of an offence against the laws of hospitality; that his only true loyalty was to Judaea. Those who suborned Pollard seemed to have agreed. Equally, those Americans who attempted to defend him seemed not to realise how damaging they were to themselves. Alan M. Dershowitz had become one of the best-known trial lawyers in America, famous for pleading and winning the most unlikely cases, and was also an acutely conscious (or self-conscious) Jew. In his book *Chutzpah* he put forward the notably unlikely case that in general American Jews were not assertive or 'pushy' enough, and that in particular Pollard was a victim.

Dershowitz claimed that he had been sharply aware of antisemitism from his childhood in Brooklyn, that the senior administration of Harvard 'was virtually *Judenrein*', that American Jews should 'shed our second-class status, drop our defensiveness, and rid ourselves of our

---

[11] Another defence was ill-chosen: that Israel was a friendly country, to spy on whose behalf was no real treason. It was unfortunate that an identical argument – that Great Britain and Soviet Russia had been wartime allies – had been used a few years earlier by those who wished to gloze the treason of Anthony Blunt.

pathological fear of offending our "hosts" ', characteristics of which, by
the 1980s, many Jewish as well as gentile Americans were unaware. He
saw Pollard as a 'Jewish zealot' who had put Israeli interests as he saw
them 'before the bureaucratic niceties of the classification system'. He
made some half-hearted criticism of Israel and some of its flagrant
official as well as informal discriminations against the non-Jewish
population, but found nothing objectionable in forcible transfer of
population. To all of which Leon Wieseltier replied crisply that the
idea of American Jews cringing before an antisemitic WASP hegemony
was a parachronistic fantasy; that 'Dershowitz's Jewishness, morbid,
bellicose, middlebrow, political, comes down to this: if you bleed us,
are we not pricks?'; and that, in view of the astonishingly constant and
generous American support for Israel, it was Pollard's crime which had
broken new ground in chutzpah.

With or without her own brand of chutzpah, Israel had shown she
could look after herself outside her borders. At the end of 1987, she was
challenged inside them in a way which was frightening both physically
and, still more, morally. The 'Intifada' or uprising rocked Israel.
Dealing with riotous youths, Israeli soldiers found themselves using
methods and doing things unknown before. There had been no
television coverage of the Deir Yassin massacre or the Kibya raid. Now
the lens and the microphone were everywhere, to pick up every detail
and magnify them through the prism of publicity. Israel learnt, and the
world learnt, about the ninety Palestinians aged under seventeen –
twenty of them under thirteen – who were killed in the space of
eighteen months. They learnt that Yitzhak Rabin had urged his
soldiers to use 'force, power and blows' to crush the rising, and that this
had been done to a fault. They learnt that prisoners had their bones
broken and that on one notorious occasion a prisoner was buried alive.
It was not only that, as one reporter put it, repressing the Intifada ate
away at the moral core of the Israeli army; it did further huge damage
to the reputation of Israel, to its relationship with its traditional
supporters, and even to their self-esteem. George Steiner expressed the
anguish of many others when he wrote that he had always believed a
Jew was someone who was incapable of burying another person alive.

His words demonstrated not only genuine shock, but embarrassment. The Intifada made criticism of Israel by its enemies, or the
media, or foreign politicians so much easier, and it was that much
more painful for Israel's friends. Criticism was as bitterly resented as
ever by Israelis, and sometimes understandably so, as when David

Mellor, then a junior minister in the British Foreign Office, turned up
in Gaza and harangued an Israeli subaltern in front of the cameras.
Even the most pacific or least chauvinistic Israeli felt entitled to ask
how the English would have liked it if some self-publicising shmendrik
of an Israeli politician had likewise publicly dressed down a British
army officer in Belfast for his alleged misdeeds. But, as so often, logic
and objective right had little to do with subjective feelings of
embarrassment or disenchantment. The Israeli journalist Matti Golan
sourly reproved western Jews on just this point: 'It's not our being
crooks that bothers you, it's our getting caught.' But indeed it was,
from the point of the Dispersion: they wanted an Israel they could be
proud of, not one they had to apologise for.

The relationship between Israel and its friends became tenser in
1988 with the 'Who is a Jew?' controversy. The Law of Return entitled
every Jew to settle in Israel but left undefined the question of whom
this described. Earlier visitors to Israel had asked how to define a Jew.
'Immigrants from every clime from China to Peru were jostling round
us. There were atheist Slavs, orthodox Semites from the ghettos of
Morocco and Negroes from the Upper Nile who are reputed to eat
snakes. It seemed a pertinent question. He answered: "Everyone who
thinks he is a Jew is one." ' This workable definition had satisfied the
state, but had never satisfied the Orthodox. In the November 1988
Israeli election, Shamir's Likud won by a small plurality over Peres's
Labour but as usual no one had an absolute majority. This led to the
most acute demonstration so far of how, so far from representing the
will of the majority, 'proportional' representation had placed utterly
disproportionate power in the hands of small, fringe parties. The
religious extremists had already imposed sabbatarian observance laws
on a mostly secular, or at any rate far from devout, Israeli population.
Now they flexed their muscles again.

For some time, the question of who was and was not Jewish had
been contentious, and at the same time a powerful lever in the hands of
religious reactionaries. In 1970, Benjamin Shalit, an Israeli, and his
wife Ann, Scotch by birth, had petitioned to have their children
classified as Jews. Like many Israelis, both parents were open atheists,
'but Jewish status was an important legal designation, especially in view
of the social and economic benefits accruing to Jews' in Israel (as
Avishai puts it without further comment as to the justice of such
accrual). The courts decided in the Shalits' favour, whereupon the
Labour government immediately bowed to the demands of the

National Religious Party which supported it in coalition and passed a law amending the Law of Registration of Inhabitants to overturn that decision. Now, eighteen years later, as he bargained to stay in office, Peres offered three tiny ultra-Orthodox parties a sweetener to join his government: the Orthodox rabbinate would have the sole power to define which immigrants qualified as Jews. And the rabbis' definition told large numbers of American Jews – not to mention many who had been killed by Hitler – that they were not really Jewish. The news caused intense anger in Jewish America; as one Miami businessman said to a colleague of Shamir's (who had made the same offer to the Orthodox), 'Don't you people have enough problems without angering your only real allies in the world?'

But then in more ways than one the episode showed the gulf between Israel and those allies. Quaintly enough, the Israeli politicians – Likud as well as Labour – who played up to the religious extremists were themselves mostly secular and agnostic, and yet for that very reason had not given any special thought to the 'Who is a Jew?' problem. If not practising, or even believing, most of them were, on the other hand, 'full-blooded' Jews with few temptations or opportunities to marry gentiles. Intermarriage was now a fact of life for western Jewry. On every measure, not only religious observance but marriages between Jew and Jew to produce Jewish children, British Jewry was declining rapidly in numbers. By the 1980s, an estimated third of British Jews were 'marrying out' and a future Chief Rabbi of Great Britain, Dr Jonathan Sacks, could write a pamphlet gloomily asking 'Shall We Have Jewish Grandchildren?'. In some parts of the United States, intermarriage had reached and then passed the levels of the German middle class in the 1920s.

The rift between the two communities might have widened further, but there were always events to close it. From the euphoria of 1967, or even the solidarity of 1982, relations between the Shamir government and British Jewry had cooled by 1989 to a degree unknown before, to the point where a number of Anglo-Jewish leaders refused to attend a 'solidarity with Israel' conference in Jerusalem and meet Shamir. Sir Isaiah Berlin told the *Jewish Chronicle* that Shamir's policies were mistaken and counter-productive, and that talking to him was like talking to a brick wall. But the following year, Saddam Hussein of Irak invaded Kuwait, and the United States formed an alliance to remove him. Since the alliance contained Arab states it could not include Israel, and it was essential that Israel took no action. With unwonted forbearance, she did not, even when Iraki rockets fell on her soil. But some Americans still chose to see it as a war on Israel's behalf.

One conservative Catholic journalist, William Buckley, had a few years earlier used a lurid phrase when he said that Cardinal O'Connor of New York had 'declined to be circumcised into Israeli dogma'. Now, another, Patrick Buchanan, before long to be a presidential aspirant, joined in. He opposed the Gulf War on old-fashioned isolationist grounds, but added that the war was being fought for an Israel desperate to destroy the Irak war machine, and that there were 'only two groups that are beating the drums for war in the Middle East, the Israeli Defence Ministry and its amen corner in the United States'. This was an echo of the nationalist and sometimes frankly antisemitic rhetoric of 1930s isolationists who had opposed American entry into a Jewish war against Hitler. To make the point clearer still, Buchanan compared 'kids with names like McAllister, Murphy, Gonzales and Leroy Brown', who would soon be fighting on behalf of polemicists and pen-pushers called 'Kissinger, Krauthammer, Rosenthal', almost a reprise of Irving Berlin's song seventy years earlier, 'No, you better mind the store Let McCarthy go to war'. In the eyes of A. M. Rosenthal, one of his targets, Buchanan was now an unmistakable antisemite whose new 'blood libel' held that 'Jews are not like us but are others, with alien loyalties', and that they want 'to spill American blood for Israeli interests'. Accusations and counter-accusations raged on. Rosenthal could plausibly detect the obsessive language of antisemitism, and it could be just as plausibly said that he and other commentators were displaying an obsession of their own in promoting Israeli interests above all other considerations (not least the simple humanitarian plight of the Palestinians, in which the *New York Times* had long shown little interest).

The amen corner, if such it was, was heard again in 1991 during the next fierce Israeli-American controversy, the loan guarantee. In outline, Israel asked for another subvention, a loan guarantee of $10 billion. The loan was on top of, and for the same purpose as, a loan of $400 million already approved by Congress in 1990, to facilitate the resettlement of Soviet immigrants. This immigration was the largest in Israeli history since the early years of the state; and it was a very curious affair. Many Jews had long wanted to leave Soviet Russia (so, of course, had many others). Many of them were in any case even more remote from their Jewish heritage than the most emancipated western Jews, possibly more of them of mixed than of pure Jewish descent, with no tincture of traditional Jewish culture, and so completely secularised that many 'Jewish' men arriving from Russia were uncircumcised and had to undergo what is for adults a painful operation.

As the row over the American loan guarantees warmed up, more than one pro-Israeli commentator used the same figure of speech: America should not take hostages. This intended that it was indecent to use the resettlement of those Russian migrants as a bargaining chip. But the phrase was a kind of Freudian slip. The Zionist idea had been for a place where the Jews could be gathered, whither they could 'ascend' through aliyah, which word had suggested an act of will. And yet, if the Soviet emigrants wanted to leave Russia, most of them would have gone somewhere other than Israel, notably America, if they had had a free choice. Israel put pressure on the Americans to encourage emigration from Russia but to discourage immigration to America, something unique in the whole history of migration. Israel wanted the Russians to come to Israel whether they wanted it themselves or no. Who was holding whom hostage?

It was the clear Israeli intention not merely to receive these immigrants but to settle many of them in the Occupied Territories. In early 1990, David Levy said that he would build apartments for settlers in East Jerusalem, despite American disapproval. In October, he promised the Americans that there would be no Russians settled beyond the 'green line' of demarcation. Into early 1991 and then the summer, the Shamir government repeatedly told the Bush Administration that no large-scale settlement programme was under way. And all the while the Americans' own intelligence, notably satellite data, told them it was. Bush resolved to hold up the loan, but Congress could override his veto. The most telling moment of the story came in March 1991 when Shamir told his finance minister that he could incorporate the first $2 billion of the guarantee into next year's budget. The implications of this were startling. Here was a conflict of wills between the Israeli government and the American President over a matter which both deemed important; as in the AWACS affair, the rights or wrongs might have been neither here nor there for the sake of argument; it was to be settled in the United States Congress; and the prime minister of Israel assumed as a matter of course that he would win. The showdown came in September. Bush reminded a press conference that only months earlier 'American men and women in uniform risked their lives to defend Israelis'. He was now trying to bring Israel into direct talks with its Arab neighbours for the first time but this was frustrated by Israel's intransigence – and he was barely able to carry out his own policy in his own capital. He was 'up against some powerful political . . . we're up against very strong and effective, sometimes, groups that go up on the Hill. I heard today there was something like a thousand lobbyists on the Hill working on the other side of the question. We've got one lonely little guy down here doing it.'

For all the risible bathos of the last words when used in self-description by the most powerful man on earth, Bush had spoken for every post-war American president. It was a 'gaffe', but in Michael Kinsley's definition of political gaffe, as when a politician tells the truth; not necessarily the objective truth (whatever that might be) but the truth as he sees it at that moment. Almost inevitably, Bush was called an antisemite by two Israeli cabinet ministers, though Shamir tried to quieten them. More surprisingly, the president's outburst worked. Jewish-American support for the loan guarantee crumbled. Some Jewish leaders were shocked by what they too thought were Bush's antisemitic overtones – any suggestion that Jews were conspiratorial or over-mighty was bitterly resented – but they were also winded and taken aback. The accusation that they were agents of a foreign power had always been potentially damaging to Jewish-Americans, but the damage had remained only potential because no American president had ever dared make it, or even refer publicly to the lobby. Now one had, and the effect was dramatic. Support for the loan guarantee collapsed. As one Jewish leader put it, Bush 'clobbered the Jewish community, left us in a state of shock. People were deeply hurt and offended, and it also scared the shit out of us.' The guarantee was held up, then frozen. Shamir fumed that 'the American people will come to their senses', his aide Yossi Ben-Aharon sneered at 'the *galut* mentality' of American Jews. But they had lost: 'For the first time in the history of their relationship, the United States had demanded that Israel change one of its key policies as the price for economic aid and had inflicted the penalty when Israel refused.' As much to the point, for the first time American Jews had been effectively challenged to say where their loyalty lay. For all the taunts of Israelis – and the different taunts of antisemites – they had no difficulty answering.

Another, tragi-farcical shaft of light was cast on relations between Israel and Dispersion in the same year with the death of Robert Maxwell. Born wretchedly poor in a Carpathian *shtetl*, he had escaped the German terror, though his family had perished. After serving bravely in the British army he had settled in England where he enjoyed a very chequered business career, several times barely avoiding disaster, and even briefly and improbably became a Labour MP. Having tried to shed his identity when he came to England, Maxwell publicly reassumed it in later years, telling the *Jewish Chronicle* that he was born Jewish and would die Jewish, and forming close links with Israel, including its intelligence services as some believed.

In November 1991 he drowned near his yacht, perhaps accidentally, perhaps suicidally, perhaps, as some conspiracy theorists believed, at the hands of the same intelligence services. In what proved to be a misplaced gesture of solidarity, he was buried on the Mount of Olives in an Israeli state funeral at which President Chaim Herzog called him 'a figure of almost mythological status'. These words seemed all too apt when, within months, it transpired that Maxwell had been a fraudsman on an even greater scale than his foes or critics could have believed, reduced in his last years to looting the pension funds of his own companies. This embarrassing episode was a caution against the way the age-old Jewish tradition of solidarity against a hostile world could become uncritical and indiscriminate loyalty with no questions asked, a lesson with wider application than the case of one crooked entrepreneur.

In 1992, President Bush lost the presidential election. This had little to do with Israel and the Levant, or any other foreign question, although Jewish support for Bush did fall, despite his forlornly inviting Rabin to visit him at his Maine summer home. It fell to the newly elected President William Clinton finally to broke a settlement between Israel and the PLO which had been so long in the broking. As hands were shaken on the White House lawn in September 1993, the world applauded, but Israel was apprehensive and divided. So was Dispersion Jewry. Some American Jews who had not long before ranked Arafat with Haman and Hitler now competed for 'face time' with him. Others shared the apprehension of Israelis who saw the looming and dread form of a Palestinian state in the very limited scheme of local autonomy. For his part, Arafat was reviled by some Palestinians as a traitor who had sold out for less than he should; familiar accusations, on either side, in comparable compromises like the partition of Ireland.

What was also curiously familiar from other national conflicts, from Ireland to Bosnia to South Africa, was that not only did either side see itself in the right, but each side saw itself as the victim. This sense was skilfully and even ruthlessly played upon by those Israelis who disliked the settlement. It had previously been a loose convention that the Israeli government of the day would be supported abroad – or at least not undermined – by its Israeli opponents. This convention was now broken by Likud under its new leader Benjamin Netanyahu, a capable and plausible man, who looked good on television, spoke fluent American, and enjoyed the reflected glory of the Entebbe raid in which his brother Jonathan had died heroically. In England, the argument was chewed over at length in the columns of the *Jewish Chronicle*, where Chaim Bermant was a voice of gently mocking, ironic dissent from the move towards regressive Jewish chauvinism.

But Jewish-American opinion remained more important than the rest of the Dispersion put together, because of its size and social and economic weight, and because it exerted that weight in a country whose policy was crucial to Israel. Many American Jews backed Rabin, instinctively sharing his own appreciation of the case in which Israel found itself. Curiously enough, this was understood by all sides, whatever conclusions they drew. The truth was that by the 1990s Israel was in *Zugzwang*. That is the name in chess for the point where a player has no good move. Though not checkmated, or in check, or even with a piece under threat, he finds that every possible move must lead to a deterioration of his position. *Zugzwang* is literally 'compulsion to move' under the rules of chess. Under no such formal compulsion, Israeli governments tried to do nothing and postpone the evil day, but doing nothing was in its own way a bad move: the Arab population increased and became more intractable, while the question of whether Israel could remain both Jewish and democratic became ever more acute. And that applied to Likud as much as to Labour. Rabin himself was no dove by nature, as his record showed. He had been a fierce fighter of Arab armies, and a brutal suppressor of the Intifada. But he knew that something now had to be done. What he agreed to had perhaps the makings of the Jewish-Arab binational state which Magnes and others had so forlornly advocated half a century before. Or it might have been an amalgam of Jabotinsky's spirit and Magnes's: force, and then compromise. It certainly followed what Hannah Arendt had said, that a binational state was no answer in itself, since in itself it was a solution which could only be achieved as part of a solution.

Above all, the agreement of 1993 was a rejection of the spirit which had imbued Zionism and Israel for so long, indeed more and more since 1967. Even well-disposed observers had noticed the change

coming over Israel in those decades, a new hardening and intransi-
gence. Some compared this increasingly and inevitably militarised
country with a new Sparta or Prussia. Conor Cruise O'Brien found the
last comparison absurd: how could such a nation of quarrelsome
individuals be called Prussians? That missed the point about Prussia,
which had been characterised not merely by regimentation and
discipline, but by a desperate keying up of effort to fight beyond its
weight in the great game of nations, and in turn by a tenor of hysteria
and immoderation. Even Bismarck, the greatest of Prussians, had often
trembled on the brink of rage, given to violent outbursts and smashing
of jugs. That was echoed in Israel where, as one of Philip Roth's
characters said, everyone shouts. They shouted not least in the Knesset
and, by all accounts in Cabinet meetings. Shouting as they did, they
could not always hear their own voices. Nor had they for so long
listened to the voices of restraint, even from Prussia itself. In a calmer
moment, Bismarck had once said that 'Nothing could be more
dangerous for Germany than to play the part of a man who has just
come into money and now throws his weight around', advice which
itself was almost a variation on Goethe's line, '*In der Begrenzung zeigt sich
erst der Meister.*'

Rabin was now acting on that precept: mastery is knowing when to
stop, the very lesson Israel had for so long unconsciously ignored – or
even consciously. In a hallowed Israeli story, Moshe Dayan used to
instruct classes at the staff college where, after outlining a problem, he
would add, 'And I want no Jewish solutions here.' What he meant was
that he wanted his battles, in the field or on the sand table, won
through daring, dash and ferocity, rather than through the traditional
Jewish virtues of subtlety, cunning and patience. Nearly a century after
Herzl had adumbrated it, and nearly fifty years after its creation, the
Jewish state found itself groping towards a Jewish solution.

That was just what some feared. After the White House handshake,
Likud representatives went to Washington to 'quietly set in motion', as
Sidney Blumenthal saw it, 'a coalition of American-Jewish conservatives, Christian rightists, and under-employed ex-cold warriors' to
frustrate the Rabin plan. They found a receptive audience in some
quarters. Norman Podhoretz had criticised the peace process since it
first began to proceed after Rabin's election in 1992, and now quoted
Jeremiah's ominous lines, 'Peace, peace; when there is no peace'. In
turn, American liberals like Arthur Hertzberg were incensed by this
politicking. Hertzberg had refused to testify against the Likud

government's settlements policy before the Senate Foreign Relations Committee: 'I didn't feel it was cricket for American Jews to use the US government as a weapon against the elected Israeli government.' And now 'these guys are doing all these things against the elected government of Israel'.

Some went further than jeremiads or bad sportsmanship. From its early days Zionism had been a secular movement, and Israel was a secular state though one whose relationship with Jewish Orthodoxy had been increasingly tense and awkward. On the other side were the Orthodox themselves, many of whom had opposed Zionism on religious grounds, some of whom rejected Israel as an impious anticipation of God's will, and a few of whom saw Auschwitz itself as divine punishment of that impiety and colluded with Palestinian nationalists. But another strain had developed in apposition: militant religious Zionism. It affected only a small minority of American or other western Jews, but it flourished vigorously among its faithful followers in Brooklyn, and they fed their colleagues in Israel, the most fervent of whom were settlers on the West Bank. Their mood was brilliantly caught in fictional highlight by Roth in his novel *The Counterlife*. The Judaean settler Lippman screams at the very name 'Left Bank', regards the Arabs with undisguised hatred, and feels for quavering American Jews scarcely less contempt. He is there to stay, on 'our land' (not even God's land, as Chaim Bermant pointed out); the Palestinians have no right to be there; their resentment of Jewish settlement means only one thing: 'I will stand here with my people, *until the Arabs stop throwing stones at the Jew* ... They are throwing stones at Jews. *Every stone is an antisemitic stone.*'

Five months after the White House meeting, nature imitated art but in hideous parody. A settler called Baruch Goldstein went into a Hebron mosque firing a sub-machine-gun, killing twenty-nine worshippers before he was killed himself. Although there was outrage and horror in Israel, it also became clear that, both on the West Bank where he lived and in Brooklyn where he came from, there were not a few Jews who sympathised with Goldstein and regarded him as a martyr. Worse still was to come, worse in terms of the rent soul of Jewry. Rabin continued his engagement with the Palestinians, using sticks and carrots, kicks and kisses. Some of the kicks were brutal: Rabin barely concealed either his glee at the assassination of one Islamic leader and enemy of Israel in late 1995, or the fact that it was the work of Israeli agents. Then in November the Prime Minister spoke at a large rally in Tel Aviv in support of the Peace Settlement. As he was leaving it, he was shot by another fanatic opposed to compromise, Yemeni-born in this case.

The death of Rabin caused a profounder shock than almost any event since the foundation of Israel, it caused intense grief, and it caused bitter recrimination. Before his death, Rabin had been subjected to a campaign of vilification extreme even by the robust standards of Israeli politics. Amos Oz had lamented the 'Nazification' of Israel by her more savage critics, who had compared her to the Third Reich, and there had indeed been caricatures of Begin in SS uniform. But it was not European leftists who had put up posters of Rabin in that same uniform, it had been Israeli rightists. Some were ready, Rabin's widow among them, to blame Likud for encouraging a climate in which such murderers could breed. Likud and its American supporters could only indignantly reject the charge as an unfair smear. The one thing by which all were united was a sense of shame and anger. Within weeks, Rabin's assassination had led to almost as many conspiracy theories as President Kennedy's thirty-two years earlier, and with more prima facie evidence. The Israeli secret service had been at best grotesquely incompetent; at worst there were dark rumours of collusion between its members and the assassin.

When the news was telephoned to the head of the internal secret service, who was abroad at the time, he blurted out the words, 'It's a Jew.' This did not suggest sinister foreknowledge of a plot although there was evidence that some officials may have had some such foreknowledge, only an instinctive, and dreadful, recognition of who was the most likely murderer. Rabin's successor was his old adversary Shimon Peres, who vowed to continue his work, to continue the peace process, to continue the search for a 'Jewish solution'. But the assassination all the same came as a frightful way to mark the centenary of *The Jewish State*. A great scheme meant not only to rescue Jewry but to unite it had caused terrible schisms in its heart. They were scarcely healed by the hair's-breadth victory of Netanyahu in the 1996 elections, and the mixture of bluster and conciliation he adopted as his policy. Later that year, a poll found more than 40 per cent of Israelis apprehensive about civil war – among Jews, not with the Arabs. Israel had not yet answered Sharett's question, 'Which of these two biblical souls will win over the other in this People?', or even decided to continue with the search for a 'Jewish solution'.

Epilogue

1996

When the Lord turned again the captivity of Sion:
then we were like unto them that dream.

Ps.cxxvi.1

Did the dream come true? In the most literal sense it plainly did. A hundred years after Herzl published his outline for a Jewish state, such a state exists and approaches its fiftieth birthday. Just as Ashley had hoped in 1840, God's chosen people have returned, many of them, to the land of their fathers. 'If you want, it's no fairy-tale,' Herzl had said, and, coming from a dandyish literary journalist as he offered such a fanciful plan, his words almost protested too much. Today, Israel is no fairy-tale; it is a reality in many ways beyond the wildest imagination of the Zionist pioneers. Against all odds, and as it turned out in the shadow of the greatest and most horrible of catastrophes, a country was born, lives, and is home to more than four million Jews, although also – something whose implications the early Zionists neither foresaw nor anticipated – a non-Jewish population of nearly two and a half millions: almost a million Palestinian Arabs, both Muslim and Christian, along with Druze, in pre-1967 Israel, and another almost million and a half Arabs in the Territories. From any perspective, that is the most intractable problem facing the Jewish state, for all that Herzl and so many of his successors tried to ignore it or wish it away.

His movement may still claim an astonishing list of achievements to its credit. There is the personal achievement of so many earlier settlers who gave their lives to the thankless and exhausting labour of tilling land and breaking rock, of those who dedicated themselves with monastic zeal to the ideal they believed in, of those who laid down their lives fighting for their land and their people in a succession of wars. Self-sacrifice in any cause moves the spirit, and a cause which inspired so much sacrifice might have been wrong, but could not have been trivial.

There is the broader social achievement of taking Jews from many different backgrounds and transferring them to another social and economic situation (in the case of European immigrants very often a lower one). Israel is in many ways quite unlike what those who first dreamed of it had envisaged. It does not much resemble the elegant Viennese café culture Herzl hoped for, while other aspects of its bustling consumer life would not have pleased Ahad Ha-am or A. D. Gordon. And yet there has been accomplished the great feat of turning the Jews from a class into a society. Chesterton sneeringly complained that he knew of Jewish financiers and musicians, but no Jewish ploughmen and ditchers. If he could revisit the Holy Land after seventy-five years he would find just those, along with Jewish farmers, engineers and street-cleaners. It is true that most menial jobs in Israel are performed by Oriental Jews or Arabs (as they are by comparable groups in most western countries), but the dream of a country 'where even the policemen will be Jewish' exists, along with the Jewish crooks and whores those policemen have to arrest, just as Ben-Gurion sardonically hoped.

There is the political achievement of creating a free and open democracy from scratch. That democracy has many blemishes. 'Free and open' cannot possibly be used of the Territories, and it is no excuse (though true enough) to say that Arabs have often been ruled less brutally by Israel than by most adjacent countries. That has not persuaded the Palestinians. All imperial rulers, even the more enlightened ones, have throughout this century continually been forced to face the puzzling truth that subject peoples prefer self-rule to good rule. And yet, when the worst is said about Israel by its critics, the very fact that so many abuses have been exposed by journalists, and that the injustices of the early years of the state have been remorselessly examined by scholars, testifies in itself most eloquently to an openness which most certainly is not found elsewhere in the neighbourhood.

Critics of Israel have no shortage of grievances, but they always come across this stumbling block. They can call Israel a colonial settlement, the last Crusader kingdom, an offshoot of Europe. All of which is in some degree true: Israel is the western rampart which Herzl foresaw, a new empire of Outremer. In some practical ways it may be becoming more Asiatic, but in others it remains distinctly European. Significantly enough, Israel belongs to the European Broadcasting Union, competes in the dread Eurovision Song Contest, plays bridge in European tournaments, all of which would seem absurd in the case of any of its neighbours. The Jewish state justifies Jabotinsky's uncompromising, and today painfully unfashionable, assertion that the Jews belong to Europe and for two thousand years have helped create the culture of the West. Perhaps that explains why it is a unique island of constitutional government in the Levant, not to say anywhere between Europe and India (itself another European creation). The literary critic Edward Said is Palestinian by birth but long American by residence and, more than he may realise, by outlook. He has been a doughty champion of his people's cause, with much authentic injustice to complain of. But although he rages against Israeli leaders, not only despising Shamir but bitterly denouncing Rabin within days of his death, he can scarcely hold up Assad of Syria or Saddam of Irak, as higher types of national leader. He has to admit bafflement at the 'consistently futile, wasteful and tragic' Arab world. What has led to its 'almost total absence of democracy and accountability? . . . What is it about Arab society that allows dangerously inept and quixotic rulers to go on ruling without a civil society?' What indeed? Perhaps it is no accident, as Marxists used to say, that the one patently occidental state in the region is its one open society.

There has been the cultural achievement, of creating not only a new nation and people but a new culture and language. This may be the most astonishing of all Zionism's feats, especially when compared with similar endeavours. Modern Hebrew was created in the heyday of linguistic nationalism and revivalism, but its rebirth was more extraordinary than any other. Literary nationalists in European countries sometimes concocted alleged odes or epics in the national tongue to demonstrate its former glories, but those tongues were in fact spoken every day by the Finns, or the Czechs, or the Romanians. Although modern literary Greek is largely an artificial construct, there had been a continuous tradition of Greek dialects spoken by ordinary people from Antiquity until today.

More poignant has been the story of Irish Gaelic. A language spoken by millions at the end of the eighteenth century was terribly ravaged, along with the people who spoke it, by famine and emigration, but it was still spoken by hundreds of thousands at the end of the nineteenth century, when enthusiasts proclaimed its official revival. Douglas Hyde began the Gaelic League on his slogan 'the necessity of de-anglicising Ireland' in 1893, not long after the Hebrew revival had begun in earnest. His programme was adopted by the advanced nationalists of We

Ourselves ('Sinn Fein'), and then became the official policy of the independent Irish state born in 1922. The Irish constitution declared Gaelic 'the first national language' of the country, and for generations its resuscitation was the great project of the state, with the language taught through draconian compulsion to all children, with all official institutions, functionaries, and political parties named in Gaelic, and with proficiency in it an essential qualification for public appointments. A hundred years on, the Gaelic revival has been a total and abject failure. Irish is now spoken as their everyday tongue by fewer than 20,000 people, the number who might attend a moderately important football match; the population of a small town; or a fraction of 1 per cent of the population of the Irish Republic, a country which is in no true sense bilingual and whose culture is in many ways more anglicised than ever.

By extreme contrast, the Hebrew revival has been a success almost unimaginable to its earliest proponents. Though scarcely spoken since the Babylonian captivity, the language was kept in suspended animation by divines and poets throughout the Third Exile. Of course any language which is read and written can be spoken. Although Latin has not been a vernacular language since around the seventh century, there has never been a time since when it was not spoken as well as written and read by learned men. Not only was it the language of intercourse as well as liturgy in the Roman Catholic church, there were as late as the nineteenth century such esoteric survivals as the use of Latin as the language of debate in the Hungarian diet, the language of instruction at Louvain university, and the language of official correspondence by the Polish post office. But no one has ever envisaged its revival as a demotic tongue, which would be as amazing as the revival of Hebrew.

Modern Hebrew was unknown two centuries ago and spoken by very few a hundred years ago. It may bear even less relationship to the language of the Psalms than does modern Greek to the language of Pericles. But it is a fact, a reality, the everyday tongue of more than four million people, more people than the population of the Irish Republic; not to say that more Arabs speak Hebrew daily than Irish speak Irish. The Irish prime minister Eamon de Valera used to speak with awe and envy of the 'miraculous' rebirth of Hebrew, but it was no miracle, only a product of human will which other nations could have emulated if they had wanted. And this language has produced a culture of its own, from newspapers of great vulgarity to novels and poetry of great delicacy, with even the high literature rooted (again, all unlike the poetry which is still being written, however well, in Gaelic) in the living language of the people. It is a breath-taking accomplishment.

And there is finally the psychological achievement of Zionism, adumbrated as long ago as Hess and plainly stated by Pinsker, Herzl and Ahad Ha-am, of making a new Jew. All Zionists implicitly accepted that there was something wrong with the Jews. In their humiliating exile they had become 'Yids', as Jabotinsky put it. They were a race of traders, of shnorrers, of parasites even, just as the antisemites said. They were physically feeble and unattractive, puny and unmanly. Zionism wanted to make men of the Jews. Gordon and the Labour Zionists wanted the Jew to become a farmer and an artisan, Jabotinsky and the Revisionists wanted the Jew to become a soldier. Those projects have succeeded almost to a fault – the latter more than the former. The heroism among the descendants of the Maccabees of which Macaulay spoke in 1833 has been seen on a scale he could not have dreamt of.

The days of pioneering Zionism were closely bound up with collectivist socialism, epitomised by the kibbutz, and Israel in its early years had a socialist economy and a corporative society to a degree unknown in any free country, the state interwoven in intimate embrace with welfare services, collectivised agriculture and business, and the ruling Labour party. In the end, the Israeli brand of socialism has been at very best a partial success, but then socialism had been no more than a partial success wherever and in whatever form it has been tried. There have been bitter historical and personal antagonisms between the two broad streams in Israeli politics, Labour and Likud, but also a profound difference about the political economy. That argument the Likud can claim to have won experimentally in favour of the free market (even if the Likudniks' *laissez-faire* rhetoric might sound even more impressive had they had not been as addicted to outside subvention as Labour). Israel has provided the most dramatic evidence in the old argument about heredity and environment, inherited and acquired character, whether individual or national. For centuries in Christendom the Jews were despised for being cowardly weaklings; now there is a Jewish state, whose army is for its size the most formidable on earth. For centuries in Christendom, the Jews were hated and envied for being clever with money; now there is a Jewish state, whose economy was for long a disaster. The case for nurture over nature can be rested.

All of those achievements are remarkable and irreducible, for all the great weight of hostility bearing upon Israel, for all her foes' grievances, real or imaginary. And yet, having listed the achievements of Zionism a hundred years after its conception, we are left with not so much a parallel list of failures as a bewildering web of paradoxes.

The first is the simplest: although most Jews have acquired through circumstances a strong emotional identification with the Jewish state, most have not chosen to join it physically. Most Jews on earth today do not live in Israel, and do not have any serious intention of going to live there. Equally, many, and it may be most, Israelis are, or are descended from, people who would not have left their homelands through choice; or, if they had had a free choice, would not have gone to the Holy Land. The concept of aliyah or 'ascent' implied a degree of volition, an act of will. That was true of the earliest Ascents before 1914, composed as they were of enthusiasts dedicated to building a Jewish homeland. But even they were enormously outnumbered at the time by those Jews who left eastern Europe for the West. After 1918, Palestine and then Israel became a refuge for numbers of Jews. Jewish homeland or Jewish state did not, tragically and appallingly, provide an answer to Jabotinsky's 'objective Jewish Question', the persecution of European Jews, who perished in far greater numbers. But many Jews escaped from Europe, and then from Arab countries in the 1950s, Ethiopia in the 1970s, Russia in the 1980s and 1990s. Not only were most of these forced involuntarily to emigrate, they were also forced involuntarily to immigrate: had every frontier been open, they might have gone elsewhere.

Since the early days of Israel, many other frontiers have indeed opened, and Israelis have been free to move again. The result is that, by the 1980s more Jews were emigrating from Israel every year than were immigrating to it. At least half a million Israelis, an eighth of all citizens, now live abroad; and the fourth largest Israeli city by population is Los Angeles. Rabin once called these *yordim* – those who descend rather than ascend – 'the dregs of Israeli society'. He later apologised (to an *émigré* newspaper in Los Angeles, not surprisingly), but the continuing net drain still rankles. Israeli patriots are angry, both at the *yordim* and at the far more numerous Jews who admire Israel but do not want to live there. And yet this anger, tension and bitter recrimination, for all that it is voiced by self-proclaimed Zionists, reflects in itself a failure on the part of Zionism. The Israeli journalist Matti Golan has written a short sharp polemic, *With Friends Like You* [1], to explain 'what Israelis really think about American Jews'. Some of his hits are palpable, aimed not at the marginal

---

[1] Though published in Hebrew with the alarmingly different title *Money in Exchange for Blood.*

western Jew so much as at 'someone with what's known as a "deep personal commitment to Israel"'. You do all the right things. You give to the United Jewish Appeal. You visit Israel every couple of years and never forget to bring a souvenir from the Wailing Wall and a painting from the artists' colony in Safed.' To Golan this western Jew, who claims to be a friend and a partner, is neither, but 'my enemy. A more harmful and dangerous one than the PLO.' Not only had the whole world turned its back on Israel, Golan says, Dispersion Jewry had lost its ardour when the going got tough, and he quotes as evidence Philip Klutznik, who had said in the immediate aftermath of the 1973 war that American Jews 'must be aware of the danger of being too preoccupied with Israel'. Golan is particularly contemptuous of Jewish-American liberals like Michael Lerner, the editor of *Tikkun*, who have suggested that aid to Israel should have political strings attached, and of the faint-hearted squeamishness of Dispersion liberals in general who were so shocked by the means used to repress the Intifada, or rather by the attendant publicity which sullied the cherished image of purity.

Above all, Golan uses the old charge that Jewish life in the West is disintegrating, and that there is an 'Unmentionable Choice for American Jews: Assimilate or Emigrate'. But in truth the choice is not unmentionable at all, and Golan is making what lawyers call a bad point. He knows, as everyone knows, that there is not the smallest prospect of most western Jews' going to live in Israel voluntarily. If the only choice is between emigration and assimilation, even to the point of losing their Jewish identity, then they are, in fact, going to take the latter as the more rational and attractive choice. Admiring Israel from afar as they do, the Jews of America have also more practically endorsed Henry Morgenthau's words: they have found America to be their Zion. Golan can argue, plausibly in his own terms, that philosemitism is a more insidious danger for Dispersion Jewry than antisemitism, acceptance more corrupting than persecution. But if followed to its logical conclusion, that leaves him actively longing for recrudescent antisemitism as the last hope of Zionism. That was just the conclusion Meir Kahane did reach before his assassination in New York in 1990: he not only welcomed the hostility which drove Russian Jews to flee for Israel, but looked forward eagerly to another rebirth of Jew-hatred and harassment in America which would leave no choice, unmentionable or otherwise, for American Jews. They would be forced to 'ascend' whether they wanted to or not. To which Jewish-Americans might reply in Judah Magnes's words, woe betide

Zionism if the world be such as to have an America one of whose ruling forces is antisemitism.

When neo-Zionists like Matti Golan say that philosemitism and not antisemitism is threatening western Jews, they are also saying that the 'Jewish problem' has been entirely reversed since the nineteenth century. Hess and Herzl should have been so lucky as to be stifled by the embrace of a society in which Jews could assimilate as much as they choose and prosper as much as they are able. If Zionism means what some of its Israeli advocates now say, then it has reinvented itself in diametrical opposition to the original scheme. In one way, the most vehement predictions or lurid warnings of Jewish anti-Zionists in the late nineteenth and early twentieth centuries have been falsified. Zionism has not endangered so many Jewish interests as Moritz Benedikt said it would; nor has it, despite the warning of Claude Montefiore (though also despite the best efforts of the rulers of the former Soviet empire), stamped the Jews everywhere as strangers in their native lands. If dual loyalty has not been the intolerable difficulty some feared that it would be, that has been because of a common-sense recognition that all but totalitarians or simpletons have mixed, multiple or ambiguous loyalties; and that allegiance, like the truth, is rarely pure and never simple. But it is also true that for the millions of Jews of the Dispersion, the existence of a Jewish state has affected their position, requiring them for long, in a just phrase, to have a different foreign policy than their compatriots of other religions or origins. Herzl thought that a Jewish state would resolve the Jewish Question for those Jews who, as he foresaw, remained in the West, by easing their position. Instead, they have many of them found their 'Jewish Question' complicated rather than simply wiped away.

Polemics like *With Friends Like You* are problematic in another way. Although the accusation that Zionism is a form of racism was spiteful and malevolent, wounding and intending to wound, a detached observer might wonder why someone like Matti Golan objects to it. His Zionism has fiercely rejected not only the Galut, but also Judaism. He insists that it is unnecessary to have any connection with previous Jewish tradition, or any religious faith, to be Jewish, saying a trifle cutely that 'I respect God too much to believe in Him', and asking, 'who says that Jewishness is a matter of going to synagogue and not eating pork? I don't need to go to synagogue to feel Jewish. I don't have to spend Yom Kippur fasting and praying, because Yom Kippur and Rosh Hashanah and all the other Jewish holidays are national days of rest not just religious occasions.' This makes the High Holy Days of the Jewish faith sound like Christmas and

Easter in the increasingly secularised West, mere opportunities for merriment emptied of any sacred significance; or like the Fourth of July, purely secular national holidays. But those comparisons raise other and painful paradoxes. For all the spite of the Zionism-is-racism resolutions, a Zionist like Golan does define his nationalism in precisely racial terms. Ambiguous as the German word *Judentum* is, its ambiguity had a point, since being Jewish has always implied a mixture of religion, ethnic descent, and common culture and characteristics. Zionists like Golan have abandoned religion and traditional culture, and are left with nothing but a variation on Disraeli's 'race is all'. An Israeli is a Jew, who is defined purely by birth, which manages to present a challenge both to religious and to secular Jews in the West.

Devout Jews like Jonathan Sacks, the British Chief Rabbi, are understandably anxious about the dwindling of western Jewry. Western Jews have not only existentially rejected Zionism by not making aliyah but have largely rejected Judaism by secularism and even Jewishness by intermarriage. The last is a peculiarly sensitive subject. In west European countries, intermarriage increases all the time. By 1996, the *Jewish Chronicle* reported that 39 per cent of Jewish men in England who were married (or cohabiting, another sign of the times) had non-Jewish wives (or consorts), the figure rising to 44 per cent for men under forty. In the United States, the figure had already passed half: in the lustrum 1985–1990, 52 per cent of American Jews had married gentiles, overtaking the rate of intermarriage in Germany before Hitler. It is more and more heard that marriage is doing to the Jews what persecution failed to do: an accusation made by Philip Roth's fictional Lippmann – 'in America they are bringing about a second Holocaust . . . What Hitler couldn't achieve with Auschwitz, American Jews are doing to themselves in the bedroom' – and the factual Golan. It was made in brutal pictorial form by a cartoon which Mordecai Richler came across reading an Israeli newspaper one sleepless night. Two boxes showed, on the one hand, the huddled inmates of a death camp, on the other, a Jewish bride being married in front of a Christian altar. The caption read 'Final Solutions'. Richler decided not to wake his sleeping gentile wife to show her this cartoon. And yet intermarriage is the supreme example of that assimilation for which so many Jews longed, the ultimate demonstration of their arrival in a free and open society. It can even be argued, as by the French writer Alain Finkielkraut, that intermarriage has a positive side: it 'doesn't mean one is abandoning one's tradition. On the contrary, it demonstrates a desire to disseminate the message throughout the world.' Many mixed couples bring up their children to be conscious of their Jewish inheritance. And, anyway, where is someone like Sacks left? Does he look to Israel as the last true Jewish bastion? Does he, a pious Jew who deplores mixed marriage even if some of its offspring may consider themselves more or less Jewish, pin his hopes on a land of racially pure atheist Hebrews? That is truly paradoxical.

For less devout Jews, there is another awkward paradox. Up to, and especially in, this century the Jews have been the greatest of all victims of racism and nationalism. Zionism reacted by proposing a nationalism of its own, purer than the European nationalisms on which it was modelled, because even more exclusive. In the consequence, this has been made more troublous by what might be called Hitler's revenge. His own mad and murderous career discredited not only Jew-hatred (to the point that a member of the Cambridge New Right is supposed to have complained that Hitler had made intellectually respectable antisemitism impossible) but all theories of racial superiority, or at least of European racial superiority; and Israel is inescapably both a European colony on Asian soil, and an extreme demonstration of the principles of the nineteenth-century European nationalism.

'America' is likewise a European colony, in origin and invention, from its discovery by one Italian adventurer and its naming after another onwards. But the United States became a colony with a difference: a country founded not on a people but on a proposition. Both when they were uninterested in or frankly hostile to Zionism, for most of the first half of the twentieth century, and then when they became passionate sentimental if not practical Zionists in the second half, American Jews evaded a thorny problem. Not only do they prefer living in the United States to Israel, but, as Hans Kohn pointed out years ago, their own country is inspired by entirely contrary principles to the Jewish state's. For all its intermittent history of slavery, nativism, racism and, not least, antisemitism, the American republic was non-ethnic, in theory and sometimes in practice. It rejected European nationalism just at the time when that nationalism was emerging fully-fledged, and in the most practical ways. As Ronald Reagan used to say in a corny but touching set-piece speech, you cannot become an Englishman simply by going to live in England or a Frenchman by going to live in France, but 'anyone can become an American'.

Anyone cannot become an Israeli. A. M. Rosenthal, columnist and sometime editor of the *New York Times*, writes often and movingly about the ugly lingering nativist spirit among Americans which wants to exclude immigrants, as it did early in this century, sometimes on barely disguised racist grounds. Rosenthal is also a passionate defender of Israel, a country with the most distinctive of immigration policies: bring me your poor, your huddled masses, yearning to breathe free, but only if they are Jews. Israel has a 'Law of Return' for those who have never lived on its soil, but not for many who once did; and even the hundreds of thousands of non-Jews who live as Israeli citizens do not enjoy the full rights of citizenship taken for granted in most western countries. The 'Who is a Jew?' controversy aroused much anger in the Dispersion, but because of its practice rather than its theory. Few American or British Jews stopped to ask themselves how they might feel if immigration to their own countries were determined by 'Americanness' or 'Englishness', while those qualities were themselves adjudged by monsignors or archdeacons. Admiring the Israeli achievement as they do, western and especially American Jews have not asked themselves whether they would care to live in a country where only Christians could own much of the country's land. Within living memory there were large numbers of houses in American cities and suburbs which, through restrictive clauses against sale to 'Hebrews', only gentiles could buy; today, there are vast acreages in Israel which only Jews can buy.

In Israel there are other ominous overtones besides. One of the pregnant words of the 1990s has been 'separation': to make life tolerable, Jew and Arab must be kept physically apart. But there is barely a shade of difference between 'separation' and 'segregation'; or 'apartness', which is translated into Afrikaans as '*apartheid*'. This is bitter for many liberal Jews in the West; and it has made some of them think again about what Zionism has done – of necessity rather than malice aforethought – to the old Jewish humanitarian tradition. In the case of American Jews especially, they must know that it is the very absence of the kind of ethnic nationalism and cultural homogeneity exemplified by Israel which has made possible their own triumphant story.

The dissonance between Israel and Dispersion goes further still. European and American Jews have taken sides over what might be called, in Neville Chamberlain's unjustly abused words, a struggle in a faraway country among people of whom we know nothing. Or very little: the extent of detachment between the two communities may be judged by another statistical curiosity, that Hebrew is now spoken by more Arabs than Jewish-Americans. Perhaps the critical word should be Americans. Israel keeps everyday links with Europe, bridge and broadcasting apart, that it does not with America. This is partly a reflection of American insularity. Take the activity in which twentieth-century man (and sometimes woman) invests so much emotional (and sometimes physical) energy: organised sport. The Americans play a 'World Series' in a sport no one else in the world plays; they do not play the sport whose World Cup unites the rest of mankind. That goes for Jewish America. There are hundreds of thousands of Jewish-Americans who know the names of the Yankees' pitchers and the Dodgers' outfielders; how many Jewish-Americans can name a single member of the Israeli national soccer team?

As the hundredth anniversary of *The Jewish State* arrived, the tensions between Israel and Dispersion have in some ways become sharper. The Israeli politician Yossi Beilen had already caused a stir by telling Jewish charitable audiences in the West that Israel was now self-sufficient and in no need of hand-outs, before the World Jewish Congress meeting in Jerusalem in January 1996, where the eminent Israeli novelist A. B. Yehoshua rounded on the Dispersion in terms rarely heard before. Not only could it keep its money, it could keep its Jews: 'We don't need you any more. We don't need either the money . . . or the political support.' Israel was now a prosperous self-sufficient state. And, to tell the truth, 'most of the population doesn't want any more aliyah . . . it's almost overcrowded here', though at least the indigenous population spoke Hebrew, and from now on 'we don't want to talk to you in broken English or French. We're going to talk to you only in Hebrew.' Apart from implicitly admitting what others had plainly said, that traditional Zionism was dead, this blew an icy blast of candour over the supposedly warm relations between Israel and western Jewry. Yehoshua may be near the knuckle when he says that the Dispersion secretly preferred Israel 'in distress and at war', since it gave world Jewry an identity and purpose, though a country which says it needs no money from outside, after having received as much as Israel has, is open to the charge of ingratitude, or at least of chutzpah.

Dissonance and detachment have political implications. A further skein of paradoxes concerns Israel's strength: at one time or another, the country has been portrayed as vulnerable, or invincible. This is a contradiction which might seem fair enough in the light of her curious history. No doubt the two-sided portrait has been convenient for Israel, but her enemies can scarcely complain. For half a century, Araby has used grandiose language about destroying the Zionist entity, and should not be indignant if that rhetoric is sometimes taken seriously. But Israel herself is confused. Is she great or is she tiny? Is she independent or reliant? Is she strong or weak? The confusion is illustrated by an Israeli joke. Two men discuss their country's disastrous economic condition. One has a brainwave. They should go to war with the United States. Subsequently the victorious Americans will rebuild the Israeli economy as they did the German and Japanese economies after 1945. The second man ponders this idea, and says, 'But what if we should win?'

Behind this humour lies what has haunted Israel's relationship with Washington and New York, with the American administration and with American Jewry. Zionism was meant to make the Jews free men, in charge of their own destiny. Although Israel has often behaved as if this were literally true, she has in practice depended on American goodwill and generosity. Consciousness of this may have affected what can sometimes be the self-righteous and paranoid tone of Israeli discourse. A song endlessly popular in Israel says that 'The Whole World is Against Us'. The whole world is not, in fact, against them, but this idea of embattlement *contra mundam* has become an essential part of Israel's self-image, even if once more mercifully tempered by traditional Jewish irony. In one cartoon in an Israeli newspaper, a mighty IDF armoured column pushes far into the Arabian desert, empty except for one little old woman shaking her fist at the Hebrew warriors. One trooper says to another: 'You see. Antisemitism even here.'

There had been another paradox earlier. Zionism had among its purposes a repudiation of the age-old Jewish tradition of passivity and defeat. Namier was obliquely expressing this Zionist spirit when he said that there was no modern Jewish history, 'only a Jewish martyrology, and that is not amusing enough for me'. Israel was to be modern Jewish history incarnate, amusing or otherwise. And yet, this is a country, as Glenn Frankel puts it, whose 'unifying historical myths were the twin traumas of Masada and the Holocaust': a country which has been psychically on the defensive since its inception, almost, in some dim recess of its national consciousness, awaiting another catastrophe. It would not be surprising that this mixture of self-confidence and self-doubt had often produced neurotic symptoms.

The Zionist attempt to replace Jewish martyrology with Jewish success in the eyes of the world has been thwarted in a peculiarly paradoxical way. The very years of Israel's unmistakable fall from world-wide grace were also the years when the Final Solution – the ill-named 'Holocaust' – became an unmistakable world-wide obsession. Not everyone welcomed this. Diana Pinto has rightly said that 'five thousand years of life cannot be reduced to twelve years of horror', and Jonathan Sacks has said that, while understanding the obsession with that catastrophe of those who survived it, and who in some cases devoted the rest of their lives to pursuing those responsible for it, he admires more those who turned their backs on the past, determined to build a new Jewish life. His predecessor as British Chief Rabbi, Lord Jakobovits, has also warned against 'the sanctification of the holocaust as a cardinal doctrine in contemporary Jewish thought and teaching,' wondered whether it can be accepted as authentically Jewish and as conducive to healing the wounded morale of the Jewish people, and regretted 'a holocaust mentality of morose despondency among our people'.

These warnings have not been widely heeded. 'The Holocaust' has become the twentieth century's defining event, but one open to all sorts of interpretations, uses and abuses. The German-Jewish critic Theodor Adorno said that there could be no lyric poetry after Auschwitz; others set out to prove him wrong, some with more success than others. Paul Celan, a Jewish survivor of the catastrophe, showed himself one of the great poets of his age before admitting some private defeat and killing himself in 1970, yet another in the line of Jewish suicides. The last and almost the saddest of all came in 1987. Primo Levi was an Italian Jew who had been deported to Auschwitz but survived to write the masterpiece *Se Quest' è un Uomo* (*If This Be a Man*[2]). After more than forty years in which he seemed to have come to terms with what had happened, he ended his life, to the dismay of many. It was impertinent to criticise him or to speculate about his motives, but a suspicion was inevitable that he could no longer bear the burden.

Levi earned his living as an industrial chemist and had never made a career out of the death camps. Others were less scrupulous. The Final Solution has been used, and misused, loaded with an intellectual and emotional freight it could not carry. Always there has been an attempt to discover hidden meaning. How, it is asked, could the commandant of Auschwitz have spent his evenings listening to Schubert after a hard day's work killing Jews? What did it mean? But perhaps it had no meaning; perhaps the man just liked music; perhaps the conjunction of the names of Schubert and the commandant proves nothing at all, except to illustrate with unusual vividness Pascal's saying that mankind is the glory and the shame of Creation; and perhaps the answer to an unanswerable question remains what the camp guard said to Primo Levi's 'Why?': '*Hier ist kein warum*' – 'Here is no why'.

[2] Though published in New York under the bathetically thick-skinned title *Survivor from Auschwitz*.

But too many will not take no why for an answer. The death camps have become an image continually cheapened by over-use. The minor poet and feminist heroine Sylvia Plath was one of the earliest, grotesquely comparing her father to the Germans and herself driven off 'like a Jew A Jew to Dachau, Auschwitz, Belsen. I began to talk like a Jew. I think I may well be a Jew.' Anyone can share in the event. The inappropriate word 'holocaust', having been invested with its new sense, is then borrowed for other contexts, often even more inappropriate: AIDS is 'a new Holocaust', so are sectarian massacres in Bosnia. Both popular and esoteric culture have got in on the act. Instead of being the subject of calm reflection, the death camps have been turned into Holocaust memorialism, or into what one critic harshly called Manhattan Holocaust chic, even into Holocaust kitsch or, in another harsh phrase, 'Shoah business', to the point where a Parisian fashion designer can show clothes 'inspired' by the camp inmates' uniform. In 1978, a lamentable lowbrow television series called *Holocaust* made a stir, if not quite with the intended effect: a survey of American schoolchildren at the time found a large number who believed that the 'Holocaust' was a Jewish festival. In 1991 the highbrow English novelist Martin Amis wrote an experimental novel about the death camps, *Time's Arrow*. And in 1994 the middlebrow American director Steven Spielberg made a film, *Schindler's List*, just as stylish, and just as unapt a match of form and content. It may be that the most skilful artists are those least fitted (if anyone is) to the subject. '*Pour juger les hautes et grandes choses il faut un coeur de même*': if Montaigne was right, cleverness and skill are not enough. Or it may just have been that the twentieth century is a tragic age which cannot understand tragedy.

Israel has inevitably made her own use of the event, with an annual day of commemoration, and a museum near Jerusalem devoted to the extermination of the European Jews. Years passed before anyone thought of following this example, but then, in the late 1980s, another fashion began. One monument was put up in Drancy outside Paris, to commemorate the 100,000 French Jews who were assembled there for deportation to the death camps, which was fitting enough in view of the record France needed to atone for. Harder to explain was the rash of Holocaust museums in the United States, above all 'the' Holocaust Museum in Washington, a monument to something, though not necessarily what was intended; not so much a museum as a shrine and, as Ian Buruma puts it, 'a rather-too-pretty shrine at that', with cattle trucks arranged as installation art, piles of victims' shoes as tastefully lit as in a

modern art gallery, and the visitor invited to 'take on the identity' of a
victim with a card at the entrance.

In terms of numbers of visitors at least, this museum is a roaring
success. Other attempts to keep alive the memory have been more
divisive. In more than one country, 'Holocaust denial' laws have been
passed decades after the event, in response to a small but noisy group,
some of them with faint scholarly pretensions, who claim that the
extermination of the Jews had not happened or had been exaggerated.
Such a law has been passed in Canada and Germany, though not in the
United States, where it would be a constitutional infringement of the First
Amendment, and where in any case there are enough people who
understand that the answer to lies is not to imprison the liars but to tell the
truth. England has no such law either, but it has enacted a War Crimes
Act amid bitter controversy: after the Bill had been passed in the House of
Commons with only a minority of MPs voting either way, it was rejected
by the House of Lords, and was then passed into law by the invocation of
the Parliament Act for only the fourth time in ninety years. In the words
of the Hungarian-Jewish-born peer, Lord Bauer, the Bill was a further
erosion of the rule of law, thanks to its patently retroactive character. But
then its purpose was not in the usual sense legal, deterrent or even
punitive. As an Israeli official said during the trial of an alleged murderer
who turned out to have been wrongly identified, and as an Australian
lawyer said who was concerned with the passing of a similar law in his
own country, the object of such laws and trials is to keep alive the memory
of an appalling event. 'Holocaust denial' laws and war crimes laws were
both intended to help stem the age-old virus of Jew-hatred.

So was Zionism, but its success here has been mixed. In the last decade
of the century antisemitism has quickened its pulse, quite apart from the
opportunities for Jew-hatred in the new guise of anti-Zionism. In Russia,
the most potent nativist demagogue to emerge after the collapse of the
Soviet Union has been Vladimir Zhirnovsky, whose flagrant playing of
the antisemitic card despite his own Jewish ancestry suggests a man not
only with no sense of decency but no sense of the ridiculous. Antisemitism
is clearly audible also in newly independent Hungary and Poland.
Surveys in Austria show that a substantial part of the population admit to
a dislike of Jews and think that there are too many in Austria (despite so
many Austrians' efforts once), and there are manifestations of antisemitism in other central European countries also. H. G. Wells once said in a
none-too-veiled way that 'There is room for some very serious research
into the question why antisemitism emerges in every country the Jews

reside in'. There is room for more serious research into why antisemitism persists in countries the Jews do not reside in. Weirdest of all is Japan, a country with almost no Jewish inhabitants at all, but where a series of books reached the best-seller lists in the 1980s and 1990s about the Jewish plot for world domination, and where in 1995 a large-circulation glossy magazine filled with the usual consumer ads ran a long article entitled 'There were no Nazi Gas Chambers'.

Even in the West, there are ugly recrudescences. In France, the National Front has enjoyed considerable electoral success while its leader dismissed the Final Solution as a 'mere detail' of twentieth-century history and insulted the primate of France, Cardinal Lustiger, a Jewish-born survivor of that detail (the unfortunate cardinal has also been cold-shouldered in Israel, as a Jewish apostate). In the tropical countries of the misnamed Third World, anti-Zionism again and again elides into antisemitism, and vice versa. An official of the African National Congress in South Africa has said that 'Hitler should have killed the Jews', showing a shaky grasp on history; Robert Mugabe, the Zimbabwean leader, calls white farmers 'so hard-hearted they could be Jews'; while state-controlled television and radio in Harare in the 1980s invariably referred to no-good countries by conventional epithets: 'racist South Africa',[3] 'expansionist Morocco' and 'Zionist Israel'. The first was a fair enough description of the apartheid regime (though whither or why Morocco was expanding, who could say?), but 'Zionist Israel', apart from pleonasm, demonstrated something more alarming. Herzl had wanted to escape from the sort of antisemitism which used the very word 'Jew' as a taunt. He might have understood a Michael Jackson song whose lyrics used 'Jew me' in a derogatory sense; he would have been dismayed to find, a hundred years on, that 'Zionist' had also become a term of abuse or a sneer.

He would have been puzzled also by other persistent symptoms of antisemitism: by an increasingly bitter black movement in the United States, where Farrakhan calls Jews 'bloodsuckers', or by the reaction to *Schindler's List*. On the one hand it enjoyed an enormous success in the West, notably in Germany, for the wrong reasons, giving as it did a falsely comforting version based on an ambiguous and unrepresentative figure; on the other hand the movie was banned in Muslim countries like Malaysia and Indonesia on the ground that it was too sympathetic to the Jews.

---

[3] As in the authentic case of a weather forecast: 'Storm clouds are moving north across racist South Africa.'

And here is the final and greatest paradox of all. 'You and I belong to a race which can do everything but fail,' Disraeli once said to Leonard Montefiore. In so many ways, Zionism has not failed. Its justification has been simple enough in the eyes of Israelis like Yeshayahu Leibowitz and Amos Oz. These writers have not 'talked Zionism', in the Hebrew phrase, meaning to prate high-sounding nothings. They share the contempt of another Israeli novelist, David Grossman, for the 'empty clichés full of baseless arrogance ("We must move the ship of Zionism forward")' characteristic of some zealots, notably those settled in the Territories. Those who speak such phrases are talking Zionism as much as American journalists who see Israel 'fulfilling the warrant of King David'. For Oz, the question is much less rhetorical and more practical. To be a Jew 'means to feel that whenever a Jew is persecuted for being a Jew – that means you'; and to be a Zionist means not wanting 'to exist as a fragment of a symbol in the consciousness of others'. Leibowitz was even more down-to-earth: the purpose of Zionism has been 'to free the Jews from their ancient political subordination to the Gentiles – little more, certainly no less'.

Maimonides had seen this emancipation coming with the Messianic redemption in which rather few Israelis now believe, but it had not been the only, or even the chief, purpose of Zionism at its inception: Herzl's first purpose had been to find 'the solution to the Jewish Question'. A hundred years on, the achievement of that goal has been much more ambiguous. In the summer of 1967 the dream seemed to have been fulfilled. A Jewish state had been established in the aftermath of the greatest of Jewish catastrophes, had united Jews everywhere, not at first, but at one moment when another catastrophe seemed imminent but, in contrast to a quarter-century earlier, had been saved by a new spirit of resistance and toughness. After that astonishing victory, Israel was admired throughout the world, and Jews everywhere were bonded in awe and exhilaration. If only time could have stood still. As it was, for Israel, Zionism and Jewry, the summer of 1967 was the moment Goethe speaks of which, once lost, eternity will never give back. Over the ensuing decades, the plot lost its thread.

Measured in blunt statistical terms, the Jews of the West are dwindling, even to the point of a *Vanishing Diaspora* in the title of Bernard Wasserstein's book. In Europe especially, the Jewish population is shrinking, through intermarriage but also through something else Jews are doing or not doing in their bedrooms: whereas east European Jewry was once extremely fertile, with very large families, and Orthodox Jews

still are, assimilated Jews, notably in England, now have a birth-rate well
below the level of stable replacement. Other Jewish writers have agonised
over *The Future of the Jews*, foreseen the *Fin du peuple juif*, or even asked *Why
Should Jews Survive?* and Wasserstein concludes elegiacally that in Europe
they will not. We are 'witnessing the disappearance of the European
Diaspora as a population group, as a cultural entity and as a significant
force in European society and in the Jewish world . . . Slowly but surely,
they are fading away. Soon nothing will be left but a disembodied
memory.' But even if this is not in itself too pessimistic a prognosis (and it
may be), it has coincided, in one more paradox, with Jewish triumph in
the West. It would be tedious or neurotic to list the number of Jewish
names eminent in politics, literature, music, science, journalism, publishing, television and radio, finance and commerce in the western world as
the second Christian millennium closes, but everyone knows that the list
is huge.

In America the triumph is greatest of all. At little more than 2.5 per
cent of the American population, Jews enjoy astonishingly disproportionate success in all the fields where they have been allowed to exert
themselves. In a magazine article which caused some unease among his
fellow Jews in 1996, Philip Weiss pointed out that sixteen of the forty
richest men in the United States, 26 per cent of reporters, editors and
executives in the most important print and broadcast media, 40 per cent
of partners in leading New York and Washington law firms, and 59 per
cent of writers, producers and directors of the most successful Hollywood
movies were Jewish. Weiss wryly noted that when he had been at
Harvard and an editor on the *Crimson*, the college paper, a half century
after the bigoted Lowell had tried to keep Jews out of Harvard with the
cringing Lippmann's approval, a woman student from a poor Irish-
American family had complained to him that the *Crimson* was a Jewish
men's club. The hundreth anniversary of *The Jewish State* found a Jewish
State; but it also found two Jews representing the great trading blocs,
United States and European Union, in their negotiations; and two others
as Home Secretary and Foreign Secretary[4] of the country where Inglis
had once said that the Jews must ever remain a separate nation and
whence Carlyle had hoped to see them driven to Palestine. Is all of that so
much less of a Jewish achievement than Israel?

---

[1] Mickey Kantor, Sir Leon Brittan; Michael Howard, Malcolm Rifkind. Howard
and Rifkind were not in fact unprecedented: for the first few months of the
National Government in 1931, Sir Herbert Samuel was Home Secretary and
Lord Reading, Foreign Secretary.

Just as the Jews of the West may be facing steep or even terminal demographic decline, the *Verjudung* of which their foes once complained has come true: western culture is permeated by Jewishness. To the extent that it has not been black, American popular culture in the twentieth century has been Jewish, from Hollywood to Broadway, from show songs to mordant humour. And that popular culture is America's greatest gift to the world. It is arguably as much of a gift as the huge contribution to high European culture which the Jews made between emancipation and destruction. It is also arguably a greater gift than the cultural attainments of Israel in its first half-century. To adjudicate between Gershwin, Mahler and Joseph Tal would be invidious, or to judge among Bellow and Roth, Svevo and Kafka, Oz and Grossman. But Jewish creativity sometimes seems to have gone a little flat in the Jewish state, much as Irish creativity does in the independent Irish state: not negligible in its achievement, unless compared with the literary record of Ireland from Swift, Goldsmith and Burke to Wilde, Yeats and Joyce.

What is for certain is that Hebrew Israel and Jewish Dispersion are different and that Zionist polemics only serve to emphasise these differences. An explanation for the rage of Hillel Halkin or Matti Golan is not far to seek. It stems from frustration. American journalists have spotted what has happened, why the very successes of Israel have dulled the edge of practical Zionism for Jews outside Israel. The establishment of Israel had given 'something crucial' to American Jews, as Glenn Frankel of the *Washington Post* says: 'a way of preserving their Jewish identity even while participating in the freewheeling assimilationist American culture . . . Israel, which was supposed to rescue Jews from the Diaspora, instead made it easier and more attractive for Jews in America to remain where they were.' Or as Arthur Hertzberg puts it, Israel remains a centre of Jewish loyalty for most Jewish Americans, 'but not in the way that the Israelis imagine. For many American Jews, Israel is not only a cause to be supported but a place whose existence helps to make them more comfortable and secure in America.'

Besides which, the identification of western Jewry with Israel inevitably fluctuated as circumstances changed. It was tepid in the early years, intense in 1967, dwindled to the point where Irving Howe could write after the 1973 war that many were prepared to contemplate the disappearance of Israel. Finally, and by yet another paradox, it was the undoubted success of Israel in safeguarding her own position which weakened her ties with the Dispersion. If the dwindling of antisemitism in the West represented one 'danger' to Zionism, Israel's progress towards compromise and peace with the Arabs represented another. As Amy Dockser Marcus of the *Wall Street Journal* has written, peace makes both Israelis and western Jews 'realise that, once Israel's future is assured, both sides no longer share a common agenda'.

Both inside Israel and outside, the slow coming of peace has meant that a more relaxed and honest attitude can be taken to Zionism and its history. In any case, Israelis have always tended to be more relaxed and honest in this respect. Doubtless a disingenuous propaganda campaign was waged in the early years of the state about how the Arabs had fled unprovoked, but this was mainly for export consumption. In her book *Since Time Immemorial* the American journalist Joan Peters comforted Israel's western supporters by arguing in effect that Palestine really had been a land without people for a people without land; that not only had the Holy Land been wretchedly misgoverned by the Ottomans (an undeniable proposition), and not only had no 'Palestine' existed in terms of national consciousness in the nineteenth century (unarguable also), but that most 'Palestinian' Arabs had immigrated to the land after the Zionist settlements began and that their descendants had no right of residence. This was an argument few Israelis would ever have made with a straight face. In fact, the most succinct 'review' Peters's book ever received came from Moshe Dayan, before she published it: 'Jewish villages were built in the place of Arab villages . . . There is not one single place built in this country that did not have a former Arab population.' But then the Israelis could afford to be more candid with themselves. Like any other country, Israel has its 'beautiful national legends' and its hypocrisies. Chiefest of these has been the endless angry condemnation of Palestinian terrorism by a state which was patently founded on terrorism, among other things, and which has continued unashamedly to bomb refugee camps and assassinate its enemies, one of them disposed of to Rabin's satisfaction shortly before his own death at an assassin's hand. But there is all the same an honesty within Israel which its distant enthusiasts have not found it easy to share.

Not all have remained starry-eyed, however. Among the minority of western Jews who have looked hard at Israel, some have grown not so much disenchanted as distanced. Some are struck by the increased stridency and narrowness of public life. Two British Jews have complained about this: the Labour politician Gerald Kaufman, oppressed in general terms by chauvinistic regression, and the musician Hans Keller, angered in particular by the chauvinistic philistinism which still prevents the public performance of Wagner in Israel. Two north

American novelists observed the same stridency in private life also. One of Philip Roth's characters notices how everyone in Israel shouts the whole time, while Mordecai Richler finds Israeli hotel staff 'unique. They are unobliging at best and, given any opportunity, downright rude.' These vague disquiets were part of a larger pattern, easy to detect however much repressed. Western Jews have not only grown more detached from Israel; some of those who have stopped to think about it have found themselves almost forced to disassociate themselves from the Zionist project. Back in the late 1940s, Richler had been an ardent member of the socialist Zionist group Habonim, and had at least thought about making aliyah, while the radical American journalist I. F. Stone had travelled *Underground to Palestine* in the company of illegal immigrants from displaced persons camps in Europe. Both illustrated how western Jews were caught up in the exalted mood of the time. As Stone had seen it, 'The Jews were besieged by hostile Arab armies on every side but one, the Mediterranean . . . Israel seems doomed by diplomatic duplicity and Arab ambush . . . It was typical of the Jewish community that the first ceremonial act in the newly recognised "Jewish National Home" was the laying of foundation stones for the Hebrew university . . . the Jews had proven that Arabs could not crush them by infiltration and Guerrilla warfare . . .'

Thirty years on, his understanding had changed. In 1975, Stone wrote a preface to Fouzi El-Asmar's book *To Be an Arab in Israel.* He accepted the author's charge: 'You have done to my people what others did to you.' He recalled the early days of 1948, and quoted a gloating Arab leader of that time who had said that the Arab-Israeli War would lead to a bloodbath of Jews: 'Had the Arabs won, the guilt would lie on them; we won, so the guilt lies on us.' And he grasped that Zionism had involved a psychological act of denial along with a physical act of displacement: 'Jewish life went on *as if the Arabs weren't there.* In a profound sense, the yishuv, the Jewish community, had to pretend the Arabs weren't there, or confront ethical problems too painful to be faced . . . What were the rights and wrongs implicit in the movement to recreate a Jewish state in the homeland of two thousand years before? Could the Jews deny that it was an Arab homeland too?' And Richler, too, revisited Israel in the 1990s, more than forty years after he had thought of migrating there, saw the huge Jewish accomplishment in Israel; 'but much of it was achieved on land where another people, however unambitious, was rooted. Their failure to cultivate their gardens does not justify their displacement by a stiff-necked people turning up and saying, "This is the turf God Almighty promised me and mine thousands of years ago. We took it by force of arms in the first place . . . Now we're back, what's left of us, so move over or get out."'

Others have been increasingly perturbed both by what Zionism has done to the Arabs and by what it has done to the Jews. There are sceptical, mocking voices like the English novelist Howard Jacobsen, saying that Jews are not meant to live in a desert, or more earnest voices like the American historian Paul Breines, musing in his book *Tough Jews* on how fantasies of power triumphing over powerlessness had excited Jews from Freud onwards (he might have gone back to 1840, and said from Lassalle onwards), and how the glorification of physical force had become such a theme of Revisionist (and not only Revisionist) Zionism. Under Begin and Shamir, Israel had been ruled by men who were themselves exponents of force, heirs to Jabotinsky with his belief that 'it is the highest achievement of a multitude of free human beings to be able to act together with the absolute precision of a machine'. For a time, the Dispersion was excited by this very toughness. One of Philip Roth's characters notices the kicks which western Jewry gets from Israel: 'The American Jews get a big thrill from the guns. They see Jews walking around with guns and they think they're in paradise. Reasonable people with a civilised repugnance for violence and blood, they come on tour from America, and they see the guns and they see the beards, and they take leave of their senses. The beards to remind them of saintly Yiddish weakness and the guns to reassure them of heroic Hebrew force.'

Clearly there has been in this an element of compensation. With all the difficulties of their lives, the Israelis are living out history in a way in which Jews ensconced comfortably in Long Island, north London or southern California are not. Identifying at a distance with Israel has made up for obscure feelings of guilt not only about the fate of the European Jews but about their own prosperity and security; but this was part of the psychological exercise which needed to be, but could not be, suspended in time. The further the memory of 1967 receded, the less intense the identification between Israel and Dispersion has inevitably become, and the polemics of Halkin and Golan are in this sense self-defeating. The more they try to embarrass western Jews about their failure to come to Israel, the more they remind western Jews not only how different their interests may have become but how different the two communities are.

Sometimes the two seem to fit the joke about Berlin and Vienna a hundred years ago: in Israel, the situation is serious but not hopeless, in the Dispersion, the situation is hopeless but not serious. The Dispersion is incorrigible. Although the Jews have emerged from powerlessness, they have retained so much of the old spirit bred in the ghetto, the use of irony and wit as forms of defiance. This is true of western Jewry in general but of its largest group in particular. Jewish America is profoundly different in many ways from central and east European Jewry from which it sprung. Hans Keller was fascinated by Jewish sociology, but based his observation on Vienna where he grew up and London where he spent his adult life. He used to remark by way of exampling Jewish distinctiveness that both homosexuality and alcoholism were almost unknown among Jews; he meant in Döbling or Hampstead; he could not possibly have said that if he had known New York or Los Angeles in the last quarter of the twentieth century. But if it is different from the old Jewish Europe, Jewish America is also profoundly different from the Jewish state. In 1948, Delmore Schwartz had said that within six months Israel would change its name to Irving. His joke backfired. Zionism became Israel, Jewish America became Irving: the Jewish America of *Portnoy's Complaint*, of Woody Allen's films, of the comedian Lenny Bruce,[5] of a Country and Western band called Kinky Friedman and the Texan Jewboys singing, 'They ain't makin' Jews like Jesus any more'. Only in America . . .

Western Jewry may still have its anxieties. Some are concerned about identity, seduced into a no longer hostile society, undone by 'the problems of success', though this was the very reverse of the problem which Hess and Herzl addressed. At the same time, Jews must everywhere be constantly, if dimly, conscious of the possibility of renewed antisemitism, like a mother taking her child's temperature. This is why almost no Jews are indifferent to Israel, or want her to fail. For all the dwindling of Jewry and Jewish consciousness, that consciousness will always be kept alive by the possibility of persecution; there will always be those – will in fact be more and more – who, like Arthur Miller puts it, would not regard themselves as Jewish if it were not for antisemitism. And as long as that consciousness exists, all those who share it will be inclined to have some emotional affinity with Israel. Not that Israel's future is now in serious doubt. As Yehoshua irritably says, and as events have shown, Israel is capable of looking after itself, militarily if not

---

[5] With his skit about Jewish Christ-killers: 'we did this about two thousand years ago – two thousand years of Polack kids whacking the shit out of us coming home from school . . . All right, I'll clear the air once and for all, and confess. Yes, we did it. I did it, my family . . . we killed him because he didn't want to become a doctor.' Cf. the New Yorker who said, 'Okay so we killed him. But only *for three days*.'

economically. Although the PLO has not, by early 1996, renounced its original charter refusing to recognise the Jewish state and calling for its complete destruction, the charter is a dead letter, inspiring only a few zealots on either side who affect to take it seriously. In reality, almost everyone, Arab or Jew, now understands what Macaulay wrote about the Protestant settlements in Ireland: 'Whether, in the great transfer of estates, injustice had or had not been committed, was immaterial. That transfer, just or unjust, had taken place so long ago, that to reverse it would be to unfix the foundations of society. There must be a time of limitation to all rights.'

And few outside the Levant seriously call for a reversal of the original Zionist project. In an early Hebrew novel, Feinberg's *Le'an* (*Whither*), it is left to a madman to advocate the Zionist idea. In Philip Roth's novel, *Operation Shylock*, published in the same year that Rabin and Arafat met on the White House lawn, the novelist was haunted by another madman, a look-alike calling himself 'Philip Roth', who had come to Israel to preach 'Diasporism: the Only Solution to the Jewish Problem'. This 'ardent Diasporist' stands Zionism on its head, arguing that 'the so-called normalization of the Jew was a tragic illusion from the start', and that a Jewish state in the heart of Islam is not so much tragic as suicidal. 'The time has come to return to the Europe that was for centuries, and remains to this day, the most authentic Jewish homeland there has ever been, the birthplace of rabbinic Judaism, Hasidic Judaism, Jewish secularism – and so on. The birthplace, of course, of Zionism too. But Zionism has outlived its historical function. The time has come to renew in the European Diaspora our pre-eminent spiritual and cultural role.'

This project is little more fanciful than Zionism seemed when Herzl first advocated it, but is not likely to catch on. And yet western Jews have demonstrated their own Diasporism simply by staying put, and no longer apologise for it. More and more, if they are honest, feel like Mordecai Richler: not so much in his misgivings about Israel but in his reaction when he told an aggressive Israeli that 'I'm not only Jewish but Canadian, and Montreal just happens to be my home'. Not very long after he said this, the local nationalism in that home town took on once more an ugly tone, when a Quebec politician complained that the narrow 1995 vote against political separation had been distorted by the 'ethnic' vote. But it is a fair guess that if Richler or other 'ethnics' ever felt that they had to leave Montreal it would not be for Jerusalem but for New York or London or Los Angeles, a choice already made by numbers of South African and Argentine Jews in the past decade.

What the Jews of the Dispersion have come to recognise is not only that Israel, however much they admire it, is not their home, but that the Israelis, however much they admire them, are no longer their people. Jabotinsky had said that the Jews had become Yids and that they should become Hebrews again; and this has happened to four million Israelis, to the extent that they are like nothing quite seen before in Jewish history, maybe even the 'Hebrew-speaking gentiles' of Georges Friedmann's phrase. There are also millions more Jews in the world who have ceased to be Yids, but who do not want to become Hebrews, either. Their motives are not ignoble. They may never have heard of Lucy Dawidowicz, Hans Kohn or Ruth Wisse. But they might know what Dawidowicz had meant when she regretted the way in which Zionism had come to loathe the Dispersion, 'the good and the bad without distinction'; and they silently resent this loathing. Were all the qualities of the Galut really so bad, the patience, the gentleness, the humanity, the world-citizenship, the irony? They might even wonder whether there might not have been a connection between 'the bad' Diasporic qualities – the anxiety, the repression, the neurosis – and the extraordinary creativity which flourished in the Dispersion between the Jews' emergence from one form of isolation in the ghetto and the return of them to another in Israel. They might understand what Kohn had meant when he quoted Goethe's saying that the Jews had been dispersed through the world 'in order fully to develop all that is good in them for the benefit of mankind'. And, although they might understand Wisse's citing the great Jewish sage Hillel's words, 'If I am not for myself, who is for me?' in a Zionist sense, they might also be tempted to complete the quotation: 'And if I am for myself alone, what then am I?'

The final paradox might be that Zionism has succeeded in everything but its ostensible purpose: to resolve the Jewish Question by normalising the Jewish people and ending their chosenness. That had been the aim of the early Zionists, and it became an obsession after Hitler. In the shadow of the death camps, the Yiddish poet Kadia Molodowsky bitterly asked, 'O God of Mercy | For the time being | Choose another people.' And yet the Jews remain in some manner chosen, even in their own land, in a way they cannot escape from; normality has not arrived. Staunch western defenders of Israel like Norman Podhoretz and Alan Dershowitz insist that, in the former's words, 'Criticism of Israel based on a double standard deserves to be called antisemitic.' But even if this proposition were logically impeccable, and even allowing that much criticism of Israel is unfair, this in itself also represents a failure on the part of

Zionism. Long before the horror of Rabin's assassination, a war of words was being fought among western Jews, no longer, as earlier in the century, over the desirability of a Jewish state but over what its future should be. An Austrian antisemite in the 1890s thought that culture was what one Jew cribbed from another; in the 1990s, in London, Paris, Washington or New York, he might have thought that political debate was one Jew arguing with another, the *Jewish Polemics* of the title of Arthur Hertzberg's book, the fierce renewed controversy of Zion over the Jewish state which could not exist if that state did not itself exist. As for normalisation, over the past thirty years the affairs of the Holy Land and its fewer than seven million inhabitants have attracted more coverage simply in terms of newspaper column inches and television footage than all of tropical Africa with its several hundred millions, or India with its 850 millions. That is a curious kind of normality.

Criticism of Israel may often be unfair, and the accusation of dual loyalty against Dispersion Jews unjust. But the very fierceness of that criticism, and at the same time the heat of the continuing tensions and debates over Israel among western Jews, show that, despite the Balfour Declaration, and never mind the rights of the existing non-Jewish communities in Palestine, the rights and political status enjoyed by Jews in any other country have indeed in some degree been affected by the creation of a Jewish state. Even in emotional terms, the earlier appearance of Jewish solidarity which Israel seemed to have achieved in 1967 had faded. A century ago, assimilated if maybe self-hating Jews like Karl Kraus felt not only a lack of affinity with but almost an aversion from the caftaned *Ostjuden*. Having acquired as they thought an affinity with the tough open-shirted Israelis, many western Jews now feel a revulsion from the skull-capped zealots who claim to represent the Jewish people, who claim all of Judaea and Samaria as the Land of Israel, and who claim to be doing the Lord's work when they massacre Muslims at worship or assassinate Israeli statesmen. In the shadow of those dreadful events, 'in blood and fire' once more, what has been in some ways an emotionally false relationship between Israel and Dispersion may yet be resolved, each going its own way in friendship but neither depending on the other.

In the end, those original goals of resolving the Jewish Question and normalising the Jewish people were perhaps always unattainable; or perhaps the pioneers of Zionism did not understand the law of unintended consequences. At the time Israel was born, Arthur Hertzberg had wryly quoted Oscar Wilde: there are two tragedies in life; one is not getting what you want, the other is getting it. On the face of things,

Zionism got what it wanted. The outcome, if not tragic, was not as it was meant to be. A century ago Ahad Ha-am warned the seemingly emancipated Jews of the West that in their desperate desire to be like the gentiles they were in reality debasing themselves, that they had found 'slavery in freedom'. Zionism was meant to end that subtle slavery as well as the more obvious subjection of downtrodden and persecuted Jews, but it created another form of enslavement. Or so it may seem, consciously or unconsciously, to those Jews who have not chosen to join the Jewish national movement, even if they also recognise that Jewish life will not for ever continue in the Dispersion, certainly not as traditionally known.

But then tragedy has many layers of meaning. When that old Zionist who later changed his mind, I. F. Stone, was once asininely asked how he as an American radical could admire the notorious slave-owner Thomas Jefferson, he gave the admirable reply, 'Because history is a tragedy and not a melodrama.' Again, as Amos Oz points out by way of recommending a compromise with the Palestinians, there are two kinds of tragedy. There is the Shakespearian, where everyone ends up gloriously dead, and there is the Chekhovian, where everyone ends up puzzled and disappointed, but alive. Jewish history has seen too much of Shakespearian tragedy; and Zionism, with its contempt for 'Diaspora cleverness' and Jewish solutions, all unwittingly saw itself in tragic and heroic, even in melodramatic, light. Succeeding in so many ways, it failed to understand the true tragic nature of history; it failed to end the Jewish drama by winding it up as a sub-plot on the stage of history. Extraordinary though it has been, Zionism has surely been but one episode in a much greater story.

To: james.ron@mcgill.ca
From: CHARLIE READE <bookman3@mindspring.com>
Subject: Re: Sold -- ship now! 705C The Controversy of Zion : Jewish Nationalism, the Jewish
State, and the...
Cc:
Bcc:
Attached:

Dr. Martha Ron
PO Box 940
Wellfleet, MA 02667

Thank you for your order. Your package has been sent via US PS Media Rate.
Media rate takes from 10 - 14 business days.

BEST,

CHARLIE READE
bookman3@mindspring.com
COMPUTER BOOK WORKS
78 READE STREET

Bibliography

(Place of publication is London unless otherwise specified.)

Prologue

There are numerous histories of the Jews. Heinrich Graetz, *History of the Jews* (6 vols, 1891–2) is still important, and has not been brought up to date. More digestible recent volumes include Howard M. Sachar, *The Course of Modern Jewish History* (1958), which has a useful bibliography, Paul Johnson, *A History of the Jews* (1987), and the idiosyncratic Norman Cantor, *The Golden Chain* (1995). Leon Poliakov's *History of Antisemitism* has been translated in 4 vols (1965–85). The *Encyclopedia Judaica* is indispensable.

For general nineteenth-century background, see E. J. Hobsbawm's great trilogy, *The Age of Revolution 1789–1815* (1975), *The Age of Capital 1848–1875* (1962) and *The Age of Empire 1875–1914* (1987). Raphael Mahler, *A History of Modern Jewry 1780–1815* (1971) has much useful material. The Revolutionary debates and Napleon's appeal to the Jews were dealt with in an excellent programme on Radio 3, *How to Make the Jews Happy*, written by Matthew Reisz, in 1990. Luther and the tradition of German antisemitism are covered learnedly in Paul Lawrence Rose, *Revolutionary Antisemitism in Germany from Kant to Wagner* (Princeton 1991).

1 The Jewish Question

Alex Bein, *The Jewish Question*, Trans. H. Zohn (New York, London and Toronto 1983) is less a narrative than a fascinating compilation, particularly valuable for several hundred pages of Notes and Excurses. For Heine, apart from standard biographies, see S. S. Prawer, *Heine's Jewish Comedy* (1983); John Gross's study of *Shylock* (1992) is absorbing for both Börne and Heine; Isaiah Berlin's essay on 'Benjamin Disraeli, Karl Marx and the Search for Identity', in *Transactions of the Jewish Historical Society of England*, XXII (1970), is equally valuable. So is Robert S. Wistrich, *Revolutionary Jews from Marx to Trotsky* (1976). Robert Blake, *Disraeli* (1966) is the best single-volume life, condensing Moneypenny and Buckle's multi-volume monster.

2 People or nation?

As an introduction, there is E. J. Hobsbawm's brilliant essay *Nations and Nationalism Since 1780* (2nd Edn. Cambridge 1992). See also Elie Kedourie, *Nationalism* (1960 and subsequent edns) and Ernest Gellner, *Nations and Nationalism* (1983). In the vast literature on Wagner, Cosima Wagner's *Diaries* (Trans. Geoffrey Skelton, 2 vols, 1978–80) are essential. Rudolph Sabor, *The Real Wagner* (1987) is eccentric but absorbing. *Das Judentum in der Musik* has been translated several times, and is discussed in Bryan Magee's penetrating essay *Aspects of Wagner* (1972). See also the documentary compilation Manfred Eger, *Wagner und die Juden: Fakten und Hintergründe* (Bayreuth 1985).

The best accessible anthology of Zionist writing is *The Zionist Idea*, Ed. and Introduced Arthur Hertzberg (1959 and paperback editions). This gives extracts from Alkalai, Kalischer, Hess, Smolenskin, Pinsker, Herzl, Nordau, Ahad Ha-am, Gordon, Buber and others, with historical commentaries. Although, as has been said, all quotation is by definition selective, some of the excisions are severe, and there may be a hint of partisanship: Magnes and Jabotinsky are very skimpily represented. Mose Hess, *Rom und Jerusalem* has been translated more than once, e.g. by Maurice J. Bloom (New York 1958). See also Isaiah Berlin, *The Life and Opinions of Moses Hess* (Cambridge 1959).

3 At home in Europe

Robert S. Wistrich, *The Jews of Vienna in the Age of Franz Joseph* (Oxford 1990) is a masterly book, inadequately described by its title: it is more intellectual than social history, but it illuminates far beyond its apparent compass. So does Fritz Stern's splendid *Gold and Iron: Bismarck, Bleichröder and the Building of the German Empire* (1977). See also P. G. J. Pulzer, *The Rise of Political Antisemitism in Germany and Austria* (1964).

4 I have the solution

For Dreyfus, Jean-Denis Bredin, *The Affair*, Trans. J. Mehlman (1986).
Theodor Herzl's *Gesämmelte Zionistische Werke* are in 5 vols (Berlin 1934),
his *Briefe und Tagebücher* in 4 (Frankfurt 1983–90), his *Complete Diaries*
Trans. H. Zohn, Ed. R. Patai (New York 1960); there is a shorter
selection of the Diaries Ed. and Trans. M. Lowenthal (1958). *The Jewish
State* is available in several editions (extracts in Hertzberg), *Altneuland
(Old-Newland)* in fewer (e.g. New York 1940).

There are many histories of Zionism, most of them (in defiance of
Hobsbawm, see p. xiii) by commited Zionists. In single volumes are
Walter Laqueur, *A History of Zionism* (1972), marred for anyone with a
more serious interest by inadequate references, and Conor Cruise
O'Brien, *The Siege: The Saga of Zionism and Israel* (1986), unashamedly
personal and partisan as well as entertaining. David Vital has written
three volumes on *The Origins of Zionism* (1975), *Zionism: The Formative
Years* (1982) and *Zionism: The Crucial Phase* (1987). Still best for the early
years is Adolf Böhm, *Die Zionistiche Bewegung* (2 vols. Tel Aviv 1935–7).

5 Mauscheln

Karl Kraus's collected *Werke* were edited by Heinrich Fischer (14 vols.
Munich 1952–67), regrettably with no critical apparatus at all, leaving
many occasional pieces without explanatory context. This edition does
not include his early writings, among them *Eine Kröne für Zion*, which is
found in the *Frühe Schriften*, Ed. J. J. Braakenberg (2 vols. Munich 1979).
Worth consulting also is Edward Timms, *Karl Kraus: Apocalyptic Satirist*
(New Haven and London 1986). Arthur Schnitzler's *Der Weg ins Freie*
(1907) was translated, very well, by Horace Samuel as *The Road to the
Open* (1913), and his *My Youth in Vienna* has also been translated, by
Catherine Hutter (New York 1970). They deserve to be in print, as
does Henry Wickham Steed, *The Hapsburg Monarchy* (1913), a fine
example of the foreign correspondent's craft, with its riveting if
ambiguous passage on the Jews. Arthur Ruppin, *The Jews of Today*,
Trans. M. Bentwich (1913) is still worth reading.

Theodor Lessing, *Der jüdische Selbsthass* (Berlin 1930) does not appear
to have been translated, unlike Houston Stewart Chamberlain, *Die
Grundlagen des neunzehnten Jahrhunderts* (2 vols. Munich 1899–1900): *The
Foundations of the Nineteenth Century* (1911), and Otto Weininger, *Geschlect
und Charakter* (Vienna 1903): *Sex and Character* (London and New York
1906). George Clare, *Last Waltz in Vienna* (1981) is much better than its

title suggests, a poignant account of 'the destruction of a family 1842–1942'.

6 Englishmen of Hebrew faith

Cecil Roth, *A History of the Jews in England* (Oxford 1941) needs to be brought up to date. David Feldman, *Englishmen and Jews: Social Relations and Political Culture 1840–1914* (New Haven and London 1994) is a valuable academic study. Frances Stevenson wrote *The Marconi Scandal* (1962), Katherine Frank told the story of Matthew Nathan in *The Voyager Out: The Life of Mary Kingsley* (1986). *An English Jew: The Life and Writings of Claude Montefiore*, Selected and Ed. Edward Kessler (1989), is useful but does not include Montefiore's most pungent attacks on Zionism.

7 'America is our Zion'

The six-volume History of the Jewish People in America is almost uniformly good (as well as handsomely printed), despite the rather arch names of the volumes: Eli Faber, *A Time for Planting, The First Migration 1654–1820*; Hasia R. Diner, *A Time for Gathering, The Second Migration 1820–1880*; Gerald Sorin, *A Time for Building, The Third Migration 1880–1920*; Henry L. Feingold, *A Time for Searching 1920–1945*; Edward S. Shapiro, *A Time for Healing: American Jewry since World War II* (Baltimore and London 1992).

For the great migration, Irving Howe, *The Immigrant Jews of New York 1881 to the Present* (1976) is a wonderful book, humane as well as learned. Edward Bernard Glick, *The Triangular Connection: America, Israel and American Jews* (1982) is mentioned here because it is useful for the early part of the story as well as after the foundation of Israel.

8 A national home

There is a biography of *Ahad Ha-am* by Leon Simon (London and New York 1960) as well as *Nationalism and the Jewish Ethic: Basic Writings of Aham Ha-am*, Ed. Hans Kohn (New York 1960), though this does not include 'Truth from the land of Israel'. He is treated helpfully in Shlomo Avneri, *The Making of Modern Zionism* (New York 1981), as are several others including Jabotinsky. Martin Buber, *Israel and Palestine* (1952) gives a short introduction to this writer's work. See also Hermann Cohen, *Religion und Zionismus* (Crefeld 1916).

English anti-Zionist polemics include Laurie Magnus, *Zion and the Neo-Zionists* (1917), Philip Magnus, *Jewish Action and Jewish Ideals* (1917), Claude Montefiore, *The Dangers of Zionism* (1917). Bernard Wasserstein, *Herbert Samuel* (1992) is an absolutely first-class biography, as well-written as it is scholarly. Leonard Stein, *The Balfour Declaration* (1961) remains the standard study. See also two biographies of Balfour, by Kenneth Young (1961) and Max Egremont (1980).

9 A Seventh Dominion

Dissenter in Zion: From the Writings of Judah L. Magnes Ed. and with Introduction by Arthur A. Goren (Cambridge, Mass. and London 1982) gives an excellently edited conspectus of this neglected and admirable man's thought. G. K. Chesterton, *The New Jerusalem* (1920) and Hilaire Belloc, *The Jews* (1922), are both long out of print and likely to reman so. Isaiah Berlin's essay on 'L. B. Namier' is in *Personal Impressions* (Oxford 1980), Namier's own essay on 'Zionism', in *Skyscrapers* (1931). See also Norman Rose, *Lewis Namier and Zionism* (Oxford 1980).

10 Blood and fire

For the Roman Catholic Church and for Italy respectively, see Sergio I. Minerbi, *The Vatican and Zionism: Conflict in the Holy land 1895–1925* (Oxford and New York 1990), and Meir Michaelis, *Mussolini and the Jews: German-Italian Relations and the Jewish Question in Italy 1922–1945* (Oxford 1978). Joseph B. Schechtman, *The Jabotinsky Story* is a partisan biography by a colleague in 2 vols, *Rebel and Statesman 1880–1923* (New York 1956) and *Fighter and Prophet 1923–1940* (New York 1961). A detached life of this extraordinary figure would be very useful, though not easy to write; apart from its subject's remaining acutely controversial, the biographer would need Jabotinsky's own command of more than half a dozen languages from Russian to Italian to Hebrew. He is also treated in Avneri, *Making of Modern Zionism.*

Some of Einstein's writings on the subject are in Albert Einstein, *About Zionism* Trans. and Ed. Leon Simon (1930). There is an inadequate biography of Arthur Koestler by Iain Hamilton (1982). Apart from his didactic novel *Thieves in the Night*, Koestler wrote *Promise and Fulfilment: Palestine 1917–49* (1949).

11 Fulfilling the American dream

See Feingold, *A Time for Searching* for Jewish America between the wars, including the story of Harvard and the quotas. Ronald Steel sardonically recounts *Walter Lippmann and the American Century* (1981), Neal Gabler tells the story of *An Empire of their Own: How the Jews Invented Hollywood* (New York 1988).

A good introduction to the Russian story is the collection of essays, *The Jews in Soviet Russia Since 1917* Ed. Lionel Kochan (1970 and subsequent edns). The antisemitism in Malcolm Muggeridge, *Winter in Moscow* (1934) has been discussed.

12 To the gates of Hell

The literature on the Final Solution now exceeds 20,000 books. A good single volume on this unbearable subject is Lucy Dawidowicz, *The War against the Jews 1933–45* (1975). The Italian army's story is told in Jonathan Steinberg, *All or Nothing: the Axis and the Holocaust 1941–43* (1990).

Joseph Roth's *Werke* are published in 4 vols (Cologne 1975–6); *The Radetzky March* is translated by Eva Tucker (1984), Sefan Zweig's attractive and poignant memoirs *The World of Yesterday* were published after his suicide (1943). Chaim Weizmann gave his side of his dealings with Ben Gurion in his memoirs, *Trial and Error* (1949). The sorry story of British Palestine in its final years is excellently told in Nicholas Bethell, *The Palestine Triangle: The struggle between the British, the Jews and the Arabs 1935–48* (1979). Isaac Kramnick and Barry Sherman, *Harold Laski: A Life on the Left* (1993), tells incidentally the story of one British Jew's conversion to Zionism. Menachem Begin gave his own revealing account in *The Revolt* (New York 1951).

13 Victors, not victims

English accounts of early Israel include Woodrow Wyatt, *The Jews at Home*, published as a *Tribune* pamphlet (1950) and two acute articles by Hugh Trevor-Roper, 'Searchlight on Israel', *Sunday Times*, 4 and 11 April 1951. For postwar Jewish America see Shapiro, *A Time for Healing*. Hannah Arendt's article 'Zionism Reconsidered' is in the *Menorah Journal*, Vol. 33. No. 2., Autumn 1945; Arthur Hertzberg's 'American Zionism at an Impasse' is in *Commentary*, October 1949. The files of both these journals (successively edited by Eliot Cohen) are fascinating in themselves, illustrating how equivocal towards Jewish nationalism the liberal Dispersion remained until the 1960s.

Sharett's journals were published in Israel and in Hebrew, despite the opposition of the Likud government, in 1978. They have not been translated, but extracts are given in Livia Rokach, *Israel's Sacred Terrorism* (Belmont, Mass. 1980). Alfred M. Lillienthal, *What Price Israel?* (Chicago 1953) is an impassioned account by an American Jew who became a full-time anti-Zionist activist.

14 They and we

Numerous books deal with the relations between Israel and western, especially American, Jewry. See Peter Grose, *Israel in the Mind of America* (New York 1983), Melvin I. Urofsky, *We are One! American Jewry and Israel* (1978), Charles Liebman, *The Ambivalent American Jew* (Philadelphia 1973) and Stephen D. Isaacs, *Jews and American Politics* (New York 1974); also two polemical works critical of the Israeli lobby, Paul Findley, *They Dare to Speak Out* (Chicago 1985), and George W. Ball and Douglas B. Ball, *The Passionate Attachment: America's involvement with Israel 1947 to the present* (New York and London 1992). Most useful of all is Edward Tivnan, *The Lobby* (New York 1987), a thoroughly documented account of what became the most formidable lobby in American politics, to the point where it could scarcely be controlled by its creators.

The controversy over Hannah Arendt, *Eichmann in Jerusalem* (1963) was told, strongly from her side, in Dwight Macdonald, 'Hannah Arendt and the Jewish Establishment', *Partisan Review*, Spring 1964, reprinted in his *Discriminations* (1974). Bernard Levin, 'Am I a Jew?', *New Statesman*, 23 July 1965, is reprinted in *Harold's Years 1964–1976: Impressions from the 'New Statesman' and the 'Spectator'*, Ed. Kingsley Amis (1977). Isaac Deutscher, *The Non-Jewish Jew* (1968) gives the Marxist version, Philip Klutznick, *No Easy Answers* (New York 1961), a Jewish-American leader's surprisingly ambivalent reflections. More thoughtful still is Jakob. J. Petuchowski, *Zion Reconsidered* (1966).

15 Hebrews and Jews

Raymond Aron, *De Gaulle, Israël et les Juifs* (Paris 1968) was translated, *De Gaulle, Israel and the Jews* (1969). For more on the American Jews see Charles E. Silberman, *A Certain People: American Jews and their Lives Today* (New York 1985). For the estrangement of Jews from liberalism, see Arthur Liebman, *Jews and the Left* (New York 1979). Meir Kahane's story is told in Robert I. Friedman, *The False Prophet* (1990).

Three contrasting phillipics are Uri Avnery, *Israel Without Zionists: A*

Plea for Peace in the Middle East (New York and London 1968), Hillel Halkin, *Letter to a Jewish American Friend: A Zionist Polemic* (Philadelphia 1977), and Ruth R. Wisse, *If I Am Not for Myself* (New York 1992). Israel Shahak is the subject of a long article by Christopher Hitchens, 'Holy Land Heretic', *Raritan*, Spring 1987, reprinted in *Prepared for the Worst* (1989).

16 Fractured friendships

The story of American-Israeli relations from the 1970s to the 1990s is told in Tivnan, *The Lobby*, and in Glenn Frankel, *Beyond the Promised Land* (New York 1994). Newspapers and magazines are indispensable for this period. The *Jewish Chronicle* of London, the most distinguished weekly of its kind in English, has supported Israel far from uncritically. So has the strongly pro-Israeli *New Republic* of Washington, and the *New York Review of Books*, where several writers expressed the anguish of liberal Jewish-America at the course Israel was taking. Two such were Arthur Hertzberg, who collected his occasional pieces in *Jewish Polemics* (New York 1922), and Bernard Avishai, who went to Israel, returned, and wrote *The Tragedy of Zionism* (New York 1985). A former editor of the *New Republic* also collected his interesting thoughts in Michael Kinsley, *Curse of the Giant Muffins* (1987). See also Amnon Rubinstein's *The Zionist Dream Revisited* (New York 1984). Norman Podhoretz published *Making It* in 1967, *Breaking Ranks* in 1979. Alan M. Dershowitz's *Chutzpah* (Boston and London 1991) caused much, largely derisive comment. For the Pollard case, see Wolf Blizer, *Territory of Lies: The Exclusive Story of Jonathan Jay Pollard* (New York 1989).

Jewish-American, and Canadian, novelists deserve detailed treatment of their own. See the works of Saul Bellow, Mordecai Richler, Philip Roth and Joseph Heller, but especially Roth's *Portnoy's Complaint* (1969), bitterly denounced by some Jews, *The Counterlife* (1987), and *Operation Shylock* (1993); and Heller's *Good as Gold* (1979). For a sub-genre of Jewish fiction, see Paul Breines, *Tough Jews: Political Fantasies and the Moral Dilemma of American Jewry* (New York 1990).

Epilogue 1996

Several Israeli writers have ruminated on Zionism and the Jewish future. Apart from their distinguished novels, Amos Oz has written *The Slopes of Lebanon*, Trans. M. G. Bartura (1990), *Under this Blazing Light* Trans. Nicholas de Lange (Cambridge 1995), David Grossman, *The*

Yellow Wind (1988) and *Sleeping on a Wire: Conversations with Palestinians in Israel* (1993). Matti Golan's *With Friends Like You*, Trans. Hillel Halkin (New York 1992), claims to tell 'What Israelis *really* think about American Jews'. Bernard Wasserstein describes the *Vanishing Diaspora: The Jews in Europe Since 1945* (1996).

There are many other books which I have consulted, with or without profit. Some worth mentioning in random order are David Vital, *The Future of the Jews* (Cambridge, Mass. and London 1990), Lucy C. Dawidowicz, *What is the Use of Jewish History?* (New York 1992), Boas Evron, *Jewish State or Israeli Nation?* (Bloomington 1995), Michael Goldberg, *Why Should Jews Survive?* (Oxford and New York 1995), Amos Elon, *The Israelis: Founders and Sons* (New York 1971), Yehuda Bauer, *The Jewish Emergence from Powerlessness* (1980), Roberta Strauss Feuerlich, *The Fate of the Jews: A People Torn between Israeli Power and Jewish Ethics* (1983), Bernard Lewis, *Semites and Anti-Semites* (1986), and Michael Lerner, *Jewish Renewal* (New York 1994).

References

Preface

xi *Some people like Jews* quot. N. Rose, 'Churchill and Zionism', in Ed. R. Blake and Wm. R. Louis, *Churchill* (Oxford 1993), p. 147

xiii *to be a Fenian* E. J. Hobsbawm, *Nations and Nationalism since 1780* (Cambridge 1990), p. 13
where every character, E. Gibbon, *Memoirs, vide* Buriton, 26 July 1762
stained in every page E. Gibbon, *The Decline and Fall of the Roman Empire,* Ch. xxxv, 452 A.D. n.

xiv *You have observed* Gibbon, *Memoirs, vide* 18 March 1776
No one in 1880 F. Stern, *Gold and Iron: Bismarck, Bleichröder, and the Building of the German Empire* (New York 1977), p. 497

xv *For it is the day* Isa. xxxiv. 8

Prologue: 1840

1 *been chosen by God* E. Hodder, The Life and Times of the Seventh Earl of Shaftesbury (London 1886), vol. i, pp. 310–11
universal syllabub D.N.B. *s.v.* Carlyle

5 *Jews, Turks, Infidels* Book of Common Prayer: Collect for Good Friday

5n *If the Jews had not* B. Disraeli, *Life of Lord George Bentinck* (4th Edn, London 1852), p. 488

6 *They are our masters* quot. Paul Lawrence Rose, *Revolutionary Antisemitism in Germany from Kant to Wagner* (Princeton 1990), p. 7

8 *this nation is* Voltaire, *Dictionnaire philosophique, s.v.* 'Juif'
not really a religion et seq. quot. Rose, op. cit. p. 93–4

9 *by freeing the Jews* A. J. P. Taylor, *The Habsburg Monarchy* (London 1948), p. 17

10 *How can we make* quot. *Making the Jews Happy* BBC Radio 3 programme by Matthew Reisz
their misery is a ibid.

if someone wanted to ibid.

the vices of the National Assembly debate 23 Dec. 1789, ibid.

11 *We must grant everything* ibid.

Thousands of years of 1er Floreal (20 Apr) 1799, quot. F. Kobler, 'Napoleon and the restoration of the Jews to Palestine' in *The New Judaea*, Sept. 1940, p. 190 (the authenticity of this proclamation has been disputed, although Napoleon planned an appeal to the Jews of the Levant)

It was as a Catholic quot. H. M. Sachar, *The Course of Modern Jewish History* (1958), p. 60

12 *unless the fundamentals* Spinoza, *Tractatus Theologico-Politicus, Opera* vol.i (The Hague 1890), p. 396

13 *they would cover* quot. R. Mahler, *A History of Modern Jewry 1780–1815* (London 1971), p. 633

13 *without complaint* quot. Mahler, p. 621

15 *he breeds his children* D.N.B. *s.v.* Gideon

the Jews are strangers quot H. S. Ashton, *The Jew at Bay* (London 1933), p. 155

16 *degenerated from the qualities* et seq. Parliamentary Debates, 17 Apr. 1833

17 *How can a real Jew* quot. A. Berry, 'The Historian who changed Europe's fate', *Sunday Telegraph*, 4 June 1995

18 *Even the Christians marvel Ferdinand Lassalles Tagesbuch* Ed. Paul Landau (Breslau 1891), pp. 160–1 quot. R. Wistrich, *Revolutionary Jews from Marx to Trotsky* (1976)

1 The Jewish Question

21 *There is a sense* I. Berlin, *Personal Impressions* (Oxford 1980), p. 40

23 *Yes. I was* version in L. D. Dawidowicz, *The Golden Tradition* (1967), p. 338

24 *had no liking for Judaism* A. J. Ayer, *Part of My Life* (Oxford 1977), p. 13

despised, downtrodden race et seq. 'Der Jude Shylock im Kaufman von Venedig' in L. Börne *Samlichte Schriften* (Dusseldorf 1964), vol. i, pp. 49–504

25 *Money is the God* quot. S. S. Prawer *Heine's Jewish Comedy* (Oxford 1983)

a hospital for poor, sick et seq. H. Heine, 'Das neue israelitische Hospital zu Hamburg'

26 *He was always making* Lady G. Cecil, *Life of Robert Marquess of Salisbury* (London 1921) vol. i, p. 218

it is really nonsense George Duke of Argyll, *Autobiography and Memoirs* (London 1906), vol. i, p. 280

I am the blank paper R. Blake, *Disraeli* (London 1966), p. 504

the persecution of the Disraeli, *Bentinck*, p. 499
27 *living and most striking* Disraeli, *Bentinck*, p. 496
28 *Christianity is incomprehensible* B. Disraeli, *Sybil*, Bk. ii, Ch. 12
the word [juif] is taken here quot. L. Wieseltier, 'Washington Diary', *New Republic*, 15 May 1995
29 *Money is the jealous God* K. Marx, *Zur Judenfrage*, in *Marx-Engels Werke* (Berlin 1964), vol. i, p. 374, quot. R. W. Wistrich, *Revolutionary Jews from Marx to Trotsky* (1976), p. 35
We should send this quot. Johnson, p. 349
the emancipation of mankind quot. ibid. p. 351
every tyrant is backed by a Jew K. Marx, 'The Russian Loan', quot. in E. Silberner, *Historica Judaica* (1949), p. 35
30 *it is revolting . . . He is as greasy . . . from the Negroes* quot. Johnson, p. 350
31 *is the centuries-long* I. Berlin, 'Benjamin Disraeli, Karl Marx and the search for identity', in *Transactions of the Jewish Historical Society of England*, xxii, 68–9, p. 18
All is race B. Disraeli, *Tancred* vol. ii, ch. 14
32 *How limited is human* quot. ibid. p. 13
no opinion of his own quot. ibid. pp. 12–13
33 *an end to the servility* quot. Sachar, p. 262

2 People or nation?

36 *who has shown us* R. Wagner, *Jewry in Music*
of necessity what ibid.
37 *all Jews ought to burn* C. Wagner, *Diaries*, 19 Dec. 1881
the Jews were, after all C. Wagner, *Diaries*, 2 July 1878
38 *Whatever our religions König Ludwig II. und Richard Wagner Briefwechsel*, Ed. O. Strobel (Karlsruhe 1936–9) 11 Oct. 1881
Wagner is the best 13 Apr. 1882, quot. R. Sabor, *The Real Wagner* (1987), p. 285
39 *Are you English or Russian?* T. Zeldin, *France 1848–1945* (Oxford 1977) vol. ii, p. 3
even if it lacked the A. Oz, *Under This Blazing Light* (Cambridge 1995), p. 44
41 *we, as a people* et seq. Alkalai, 'The Third Redemption' quot. *The Zionist Idea*, Ed. A. Hertzberg (New York 1959), pp. 105–7
without such a settlement Kalischer, *Seeking Zion* quot. ibid. pp. 111–14
42 *the only true philosopher* I. Berlin, 'The Life and Opinion of Moses Hess' (Cambridge 1959), p. 20
feeble echo of French quot. ibid. p. 23
44 *the head of Goethe* quot. ibid. p. 24
here I stand again Rom und Jerusalem, First Letter

45 *one of the first victims* Taylor, *Habsburg Monarchy*, p. 77
 Ever since Innocent III Rom und Jerusalem, Foreword
 The liberation of ibid.
47 *The really dishonourable Jew* quot. Hertzberg, p. 121
 the Germans hate the religion ibid. p. 120
 The holy spirit, the creative ibid. p. 134
 we, therefore, need not . . . when we speak ibid. p. 138
50 *happily one does not* W. Raabe, *Der Hungerpastor* (1864), ch. 36
51 *It is the first time* Stern, *Gold and Iron*, p. 168
 the fiscal and quot. G. A. Craig *Germany 1866–1945* (Oxford 1978),
 p. 84
52 *Stoecker and Treitschke* Craig, p. 154
53 *more worthy of the* Hertzberg, *Zionist Idea*, p. 180
54 *a spiritual nation* Smolenskin, *It is Time to Plant* (1875–7), in Hertzberg,
 Zionist Idea, p. 145
 a national sentiment which ibid. pp. 145–6
 quite different and quite Smolenskin, *The Haskalah of Berlin* (1883) in
 Hertzberg, *Zionist Idea*, p. 154
 The proper and the Pinsker, ibid. p. 198
55 *the world will gain* G. Eliot, *Daniel Deronda*, ch. 42
 distinctive national character, Pinsker, loc. cit. p. 183
56 *it is not the Jews* A. Jellinek, *Aus der Zeit: Tagesfragen und
 Tagesbegebenheiten*
 (Budapest 1886) quot. R. W. Wistrich, *The Jews of Vienna in the Age of
 Francis Joseph* (Oxford 1990), p. 243
 a nation as highly quot. ibid. p. 245
 a small state like quot. ibid. p. 244
 We are at home quot. ibid. pp. 243–4
58 *people who are leaving . . . if the wave of emigration* Smolenskin, *Let Us
 Search Our Ways*, in Hertzberg, *Zionist Idea*, p. 151
 We have adopted the quot. *Making the Jews Happy*

4 'I have the solution'

63 *to have a few foreigners* et seq. M. Proust, *Du côté de chez Guermantes*,
 ch. 1
64 *The Jew who tries to* quot. Wistrich, p. 442
66 *in no other land in* quot. ibid. p. 424
 state within a state quot. ibid. p. 283
 an honest peace with quot. ibid. p. 425
67 *the moral earnestness with* quot. ibid. p. 283
 increase still further quot. ibid.
 if one could constitute quot. Wistrich, p. 270
68 *Exactly the same thing . . . Who created the Liberal* A. Schnitzler, *The Road
 to the Open (Der Weg ins Freie)* Trans. H. Samuel (1913), p. 78

the most ardent representatives quot. Wistrich, p. 203
our antisemitism is not quot. ibid. p. 213
69 *almost devoid of* quot. G. Wheatcroft, *The Randlords* (1985), p. 205n.
the financial Jew operating . . . being led by the nose quot. ibid. p. 206
the modern Anglo-Jewish plutocracy D.N.B. s.v. Belloc
70 *the Jews were in* H. Wickham Steed, *The Hapsburg Monarchy* (1913),
p. 176
71 *My only relaxation in* T. Herzl, *Briefe und Tagebücher* (4 vols, Frankfurt
1983–90) vol. i, p. 14
gloomy ghetto . . . like a quot. Wistrich, p. 241
72 *still rigidly confined to . . . a ghetto we must clear . . . My brethren, they won't
. . . want to . . . get . . .* T. Herzl, *The New Ghetto*, Trans. H. Norden
(New York 1955)
at twelve o'clock The Diaries of Theodor Herzl Ed. M. Lowenthal (1958),
p. 7
73 *a Secret Society* Wheatcroft, *Randlords*, p. 141
No, no, no et seq. *Diaries of Theodor Herzl*, 2 June 1895
74 *I have the solution* Hertzberg, *Zionist Idea*, p. 203
No one can deny Herzl, *The Jewish State*, ch. 2
We are a people ibid. ch. 1, Introduction
Palestine is our unforgettable ibid. ch. 2, 'Palestine or the Argentine?'
75 *a wondrous breed of* ibid. Conclusion
Our adversaries may be T. Herzl, First Congress Address, in Hertzberg,
Zionist Idea, p. 266
because is afflicts the M. Nordau, Speech at First Congress, in
Hertzberg, *Zionist Idea*, p. 239
our excessive production Herzl, *Jewish State*, ch. 2, 'Causes of
Antisemitism'
76 *the most important* et seq. Herzl, *Diaries*, 24 Nov. 1895
77 *will be our most* quot. H. Arendt, 'Zionism Reconsidered', *Menorah
Journal* vol.33, No. 2 (Autumn 1945), p. 180
had nothing to do H. Kohn, 'The Jewish National Idea', *Menorah
Journal*, vol. 46, Nos. 1 & 2 (Autumn-Winter 1958), p. 23
une analogie frappante! T. Mann, *The Magic Mountain*, ch. 37
We shall know how quot. J. J. Petuchowski, *Zion Reconsidered* (New York
1966), p. 24

5 **Mauscheln**

82 *the Jewish people has been* A. D. Gordon, *People and labour*, in
Hertzberg, *Zionist Idea*, p. 372
the gradual improvement A. Oz, 'A.D. Gordon Today', in *Under This
Blazing Light* (Cambridge 1995), p. 117
83 *I never know whether* quot. Wistrich, *Jews of Vienna*, p. 422

setting an avalanche in motion Herzl, *Diaries*, 4 Feb. 1896
a powerful machine-gun ibid. p. 70
we shall no longer have ibid. 4 Feb. 1896
84 *We are committing* quot. C. Glass, 'Whose Country is it?', *Spectator*, 2 Mar. 1985, p. 22
take up the white R. Kipling, 'The White Man's Burden'
had achieved the A. J. P. Taylor, *The Troublemakers* (1957) p. 90
85 *I shall transport over there . . . have nothing, however* Herzl, *Diaries*, 9 June 1895
87 *a parochial retreat.* Wistrich, p. 459
evil craving . . . to remould quot. ibid. p. 459n.
from many directions, religious ibid.
88 *nobody else was* A. Schnitzler, *My Youth in Vienna* (New York 1970), pp. 6–7
I myself have only Schnitzler, *Road to the Open*, p. 69
89 *which is known as* et seq. *Eine Kröne für Zion*, in K. Kraus, *Frühe Schriften*, Ed. J. J. Braakenberg (2 vols., Munich), vol. ii, p. 298
some clear-sighted Jews Steed, *Hapsburg Monarchy*, p. 182
90 *one of the gentlemen . . . new theory that the* Kraus, ibid. p. 298
Many Christians say themselves ibid. p. 304
What common bond ought ibid. p. 308
91 *it is almost unimaginable* ibid. p. 314
92 *frequently discernible . . . their easy knack* Steed, *Hapsburg Monarchy*. p. 193
a Viennese product ibid. p. 192
oriental enclaves in European Fackel, No. 11, July 1899
93 *when Jewish figures* G. Clare, *Last Waltz in Vienna: The Destruction of a Family 1842–1842* (1981), p. 87
Mauschel is an anti-Zionist T. Herzl, 'Mauschel', in *Zionistische Werke* vol. i. p. 209
94 *Away with you Jews* Kraus, *Kröne*, p. 312
heard a brook ibid. p. 313
I feel with the overwhelming . . . I go along with the 'Er ist doch e Jud' in K. Kraus, *Untergang der Welt durch schwarze Magie*, Ed. H. Fischer (Munich 1960), p. 333
96 *battens so upon the* Steed, *Hapsburg Monarchy*, p. 169

6 Englishmen of Hebrew faith

98 *the campaign's centre* Herzl, *Diaries*, 18 Nov. 1895
There is only one country Nordau, 'Speech at First Congress', Hertzberg, p. 237
99 *before the days of Hitler* G. Orwell, 'Antisemitism in Britain', in *The Collected Essays, Journalism and Letters of George Orwell*, vol. 3, *As I Please* (1970), p. 385

101 *We sympathise with you* quot. M. Sachar, *Course of Modern Jewish History* (1958), p. 495
the German Jew extraction has become in Africa quot. Wheatcroft, *Randlords*, p. 206
Johannesburg is essentially quot. ibid. p. 205
102 *the little empty homes* H. Belloc, 'Verses to a Lord'
the modern Anglo-Judaic D.N.B. s.v. Belloc
104 *it would not be* B. Wasserstein, *Herbert Samuel: A Political Life* (Oxford 1992), p. 136
105 *The number of Jews The Crawford Papers: The Journals of David Lindsay, 27th Earl of Crawford etc.*, Ed. J. Vincent (Manchester 1984), p. 82
Although I loathe antisemitism H. Nicolson, *Diaries and Letters 1939–45* (1967), 13 June 1945
106 *I have read none of his* Herzl, *Diaries*, 21 Nov. 1895
a smart officer, Captain ibid. 24 Nov. 1895
107 *directed itself towards . . . the organisation of Jews . . . would heartily support* ibid. p. 387
they are in such . . . that they look patriotically ibid. p. 389
otherwise we should have . . . Of late their situation ibid. p. 390
108 *Vous prêchez à un converti . . . there is less talk* ibid.
Is it opportunism or cowardice . . . is a baptised Jew ibid. 7 Aug. 1903
if it were possible ibid. 11 Aug. 1903
109 *But we do give . . . it would create alarm . . . This is less intolerable as Your Excellency rightly* ibid.
111 *should be provided by* quot. Wasserstein, *Samuel*, p. 131
112 *I dote on the . . . their dreamy minds . . . a cheerful person who* quot. K. Frank, *A Voyager Out: The Life of Mary Kingsley* (1987), p. 265
I shall keep that, quot. ibid. p. 269
113 *her open soul* quot. ibid. p. 271
That is the idea Herzl, *Diaries*, 25 Nov, 1895
an egregious blunder ibid. p. 442
114 *an Englishman of . . . (or 'Englishmen of the Jewish faith'),* vide *An English Jew: The Life and Writings of Claude Montefiore*, Ed. E. Kessler (1989), p. 141
a most living religion ibid. p. 12
115 *though antisemitism Encyclopaedia Britannica*, Eleventh Edition, s.v. 'Antisemitism'

7 America is our Zion

120 *But there was gold* A. Cooke, *Alistair Cooke's America* (1973), p. 285
121 *the short-sighted policy . . . in today's free* quot. I. Howe, *The Immigrant Jews of New York* (1976), p. 320
a small and feeble quot. ibid. p. 205

fool yourselves quot. ibid. p. 206

122 *It was in America* A. Einstein, *About Zionism* (1930), p. 34
*Oh my name is . . . You bet my life . . . Sadie Salome Go Home . . . Yiddle on
Your Fiddle . . . Where's the percentage in . . . Oy, oy, oy, those* quot. Howe,
ibid. p. 122

123 *Hundreds of thousands of* ibid. 207
We Jews shall be able J. Magnes, *Dissenter in Zion: from the Writings of
Judah L. Magnes*, Ed. A. A. Goren (Cambridge, Mass. and London
1982), p. 68
Why can we not ibid. p. 68

124 *Let us Americans* A. B. Glick, *The triangular Connection: America, Israel, and
American Jews* (1982), p. 45
the Pilgrim's inspiration Howe, *Immigrant Jews*, p. 208

125 *My approach to Zionism . . . In time, practical experience* Glick, ibid.
p. 46

126 *the place is made ready.* quot. Howe, ibid.

128 *that such a memorial . . . that so many Jewish . . . we modern Jews do
not* quot. Glick, op. cit. p. 36
a pretty good joke quot. ibid. p. 39
the entire Jewish press . . . a little State in Palestine quot. ibid.
flavour of the Stock Exchange quot. ibid. p. 41
the Zionist scheme that has New York Times, 11 Aug. 1897, quot. ibid.
p. 41

129 *small, weak state* quot. ibid. p. 42
A Jewish State Impossible New York Times, 10 Sept. 1897, quot. ibid.
Speaking as an American quot. ibid. p. 44
America is our Zion. Howe, op. cit. p. 129

8 A national home

131 *the very existence* Aha Ha-am, *The Jewish state and the Jewish Problem*, in
Hertzberg, *Zionist Idea*, p. 265
one of the great E. Waugh, 'The American epoch in the Catholic
Church', in *The Essays, Articles and Reviews of Evelyn Waugh*, Ed. D.
Gallagher (1983), p. 384

132 *A comparison between Palestine . . . There two facts make* Ahad Ha-am, op.
cit. p. 269

133 *we tend to believe abroad* et seq. quot. S. Avneri, *The Making of Modern
Zionism* (New York 1981), p. 123

134 *do not read Faust* quot. W. Laqueur, *A History of Zionism* (1972),
p. 395
Aha, so now the quot. I. Berlin, *Personal Impressions* (Oxford 1982),
p. 46n.

135 *those who have no* C. Montefiore, 'The Dangers of Zionism' in *Papers
for Jewish People*, 1918, p. 5

136 *You know, you have* et seq. quot. Wasserstein, *Herbert Samuel*, p. 198
137 *where the Jews can.* ibid. p. 199
    How is it practicable? Daily Chronicle 25 Feb. 1896, quot. Wasserstein,
    p. 206
    the noble-hearted Herzl The Times, 8 Dec. 1905
138 *perhaps by that time* quot. Wasserstein, p. 203
    But now conditions are quot. ibid. p. 206
    an ambitious and grasping quot. ibid. p. 204
139 *the ultimate destiny . . . very keen to see* ibid. p. 206
    A stirring among et seq. ibid. p. 208
140 *a spiritual and intellectual* ibid. p. 209
    reads almost like a quot. ibid. p. 210
141 *long, hot and pompous dinner* K. Young, *Arthur James Balfour* (1963)
    p. 139
    an immense body of quot. ibid. p. 257
    shared many of her quot. ibid.
    the Zionist organisation quot. C. C. O'Brien, *The Siege* (1988), p. 124
142 *the Jews seem to* D. Vital, Zionism: The Crucial Phase (1987), p. 219
    in which the idea H. Moscowitz, 'Zionism no Remedy', *New York
    Times*, 10 June 1917
    the time has not P. Magnus, *Jewish Action and Jewish Ideals* (1917), p. 9
143 *we used to hear about* et seq. L. Magnus, *Zion and the Neo-Zionists* (1917),
    p. 11
    to invest the Jewish, et seq. *The Times*, 14 May 1917
    I deprecate the expression . . . quot. L. Stein, *The Balfour Declaration* (1961),
    p. 525
144 *to bolster up German* quot. Laqueur, *History of Zionism*, p. 145
145 *a worse bondage* D. Gilmour, *Curzon* (1994), p. 481
146 *Lloyd George and Balfour* A. J. P. Taylor, *English History 1914–1945*
    (Oxford 1965), p. 98n.

9 A Seventh Dominion

152 *borders were revised* J. J. Lee, *Ireland 1912–1985* (Cambridge 1989),
    p. 46
153 *Not that I have Magnes,* Dissenter, p. 184
    is a paradox worthy . . . made 'Jewish' by the . . . Conceived and born in. ibid.
    p. 186
    with its complex 'Jewish ibid. p. 184
154 *be it right or wrong* quot. Gilmour, *Curzon*, p. 482
    he is out for something quot. ibid. p. 521
    a denial of almost. I too, believe in Magnes, p. 187
    helping the Jewish people ibid. p. 196

155 *talking Hebrew – vocabulary limited* ibid. p. 25
the more I see of quot. Wasserstein, *Samuel,* p. 243
156 *received from Major . . . Errors and omissions* quot. ibid. p. 247
first Jewish ruler in ibid. p. 248
might have chosen America O'Brien, *Siege* p. 168
157 *it is good . . . forty brave lads* A. Elon, *The Israelis: Founders and Sons*
(1983), p. 137n.
Jews and blood Ahad Ha-am, *Nationalism and the Jewish Ethic* Ed. H.
Kohn (New York 1962), p. 26
158 *where everybody . . . the Jews shall continue* G. K. Chesterton, *The New
Jerusalem* (1920), p. vi
friction between . . . what he wanted was H. Belloc, *The Jews* (1922),
p. 17
159 *an anonymous Press* ibid. p. 47
can only be charged ibid. p. 78
the countries where Jewish ibid. p. 237
I would like to add Jewish Chronicle 2 Nov. 1917
the strange selection made Belloc, op. cit. p. 245
160 *a flat and violent contradiction* Chesterton, op. cit. p. 141
where is Sir Herbert ibid. p. 242
Jews are Jews ibid. p. 264
it was always called ibid.
we have not known personally ibid. p. 284
the Jews in it are ibid. p. 293
a combination of intellectual I. Berlin, 'L. B. Namier' in *Personal
Impressions* (Oxford 1982), p. 63
161 *had abandoned the traditional* ibid.
are the more unhappy N. Rose, *Lewis Namier and Zionism* (Oxford 1980),
p. 2
to assume protective colouring Berlin, loc. cit. p. 69
162 *an intolerable bore unless* A. J. P. Taylor, *Personal History* (n.d.) p. 111
Orthodoxy is a melting L. B. Namier, 'Zionism', in *Skyscrapers* (1931),
p. 129
with the loss of ibid. p. 133
treat him to a terrifying Berlin, op. cit. pp. 72–3
he didn't basically like quot. Rose, p. 5
There is no modern Jewish Berlin. op. cit. p. 72
163 *What more can we* quot. Rose, p. 33
164 *if it be Imperialism* J. Wedgwood, *The Seventh Dominion* (1928), p. 4
fear of Signor Mussolini ibid. p. 32
Jerusalem seems populated ibid. p. 12
165 *this transplanting of peoples* ibid. p. 90
Zionism will give peace ibid. p. 128

Wir Juden und Berlin, op. cit. p. 72
Mr Levy, can you et seq. ibid.

10 Blood and Fire

166 *everything is open to them* Herzl, *Diaries*, 23 Jan. 1904
167 *were to all intents* C. Weizmann, *Trial and Error* (1949), p. 35
    that Jerusalem would quot. S. I. Minerbi, *The Vatican and Zionism: Conflict in the Holy Land 1895–1925* (Oxford 1990), p. 96
168 *The return of the Jews* quot. ibid. p. 97
    or else they will go there quot. ibid. p. 100
    the Holy Church is apostolic quot. ibid. p. 101
    The undefined British quot. ibid. p. 119
    the efforts of Our predecessors . . . that non-Catholic foreigners quot. ibid. p. 131
169 *will the pillaging* quot. M. Michaelis, *Mussolini and the Jews* (Oxford 1978), p. 12
    that a Jew should lead quot. ibid. p. 16
170 *right here, in this* quot ibid. p. 13
    faire le jeu d'Angleterre quot. ibid. p. 25
    the Jewish problem does not quot. ibid. p. 28
171 *Because the Yid* quot. A. Rubinstein, *The Zionist Dream Revisited: From Herzl to Gush Emuninim and Back* (New York 1984), p. 4
172 *I am a Zionist, because* quot. Avneri, *Making of Modern Zionism*, p. 62
174 *It is the highest* quot. ibid. p. 172
175 *the Muslims are kin* quot. Laqueur, *History of Zionism*, p. 228n.
    the inner life of Jewry Weizmann, *Trial and Error*, p. 63
176 *The Arabs are and will* quot. Laqueur, p. 176
177 *I have no understanding* quot. Laqueur, p. 348
    when the Arab claim Jabotinsky, Evidence to Royal Commission (1937), in Hertzberg, *Zionist Idea*, p. 562
179 *away from the larger . . . if it were physically possible* Magnes, *Dissenter*, p. 208
    because without it Simon, Introduction to Einstein, *About Zionism*, p. 18
    The German Jew who ibid. p. 37
180 *repeat the old mistake* ibid. pp. 44–6
    Zionism is not a movement Einstein, op. cit. p. 58
182 *this country gradually* S. Webb, 'The Decline of the Birth Rate', Fabian Tract No. 13 (1907)
    that everyone who has quot. M. Richler, *This Year in Jerusalem* (1994), p. 23
    there was irreconcilable Taylor, *English History*, p. 277
    rigid and intolerant et. seq. quot. I. Kramnick and B. Sherman, *Harold*

Laski: A Life on the Left (1993) p. 279
183 *My views on Zionism* quot. ibid. p. 278
the whole world Elon, *The Israelis*, p. 179
185 *the sign of the Covenant* A. Koestler, *Thieves in the Night* (1946), p. 75
impossible English women . . . One of my daughters C. Mackenzie, *My Life and Times: Octave Eight 1939–46* (1969) p. 47
these Hebrew Tarzans . . . In other words Koestler, *Thieves*, p. 151
186 *Why should our endeavour* Shakespeare, *Troilus and Cressida*, V.x.36

11 Fulfilling the American dream

189 *it would be a misfortune* quot. H. L. Feingold, *A Time for Searching: Entering the Mainstream 1920–1945* (Baltimore and London 1992), p. 189
methods for more efficiently quot. ibid. p. 16
Jews and Christians quot. ibid. p. 17
190 *One of the saddest* quot. ibid. p. 18
not yet American Jew quot. ibid.
at Harvard class distinction quot. R. Steel, *Walter Lippmann and the American Century* (1981), p. 13
seriously challenge ibid. p. 29
191 *bad for the immigrant Jews . . . I do not regard the* quot. ibid. pp. 193–4
192 *fairly distinct in their . . . sharp trading and blatant . . . the rich and vulgar and* quot. ibid. pp. 191–2
by satisfying the lust . . . hysteria and animal passions . . . the authentic voice of . . . the Jews by their parvenus . . . something inside of me quot. ibid. pp. 330–2
193 *Jew-bating produced* quot. ibid. p. 189
I am obviously one of . . . other-worldliness of a . . . the extra-Palestinian Jew is . . . It is a splendid thing quot. ibid. p. 190
194 *there are more Jews* quot. Kramnick and Sheerman, op. cit., p. 277
there are now about quot. Howe, *Immigrant Jews*, p. 213
195 *Your five-to-two is* E. Waugh, *The Loved One*, ch. 1
a Jewish holiday quot. N. Gabler, *An Empire of Their Own* (19), p. 2
196 *twixt Sarah's son* R. Kipling, 'The Burden of Jerusalem', quot. C. Hitchens, *Blood, Class and Nostalgia* (1990), pp. 86–8
197 *While you was being* quot. Gabler, op. cit. p. 336
Hitler and Hitlerism will quot. ibid. p. 33
Although I had never B. Hecht, *A Child of the Century* (New York 1955). p. 106
198 *social, political* ibid. p. 483
the international Jews et seq. quot. in Rose, 'Churchill and Zionism', p. 150
199 *petty Jewish Foreign Office* M. Muggeridge, *Winter in Moscow* (1934), p. ix

Supposing two or three et seq. ibid. p. 234
the autonomous Jewish territory C. Abramsky, 'The Biro-Bidzhan Project'
in *The Jews in Soviet Russia Since 1917* (Oxford 1978), p. 71

12 To the gates of Hell

204 *the one thing in* A. J. P. Taylor, *The Origins of the Second World War*
(2nd. Edn. 1963), Foreword: Second Thoughts, p. 11
205 *the unpleasant spectacle Fackel*, No. 11, July 1899
Mir fällt zu Hitler K. Kraus, *Die dritte Walpurgisnacht*
207 *a disaster of historic . . . the antisemitism of men* Jabotinsky, Evidence, loc.
cit. p. 560
208 *A corner of Palestine . . . Tell the Arabs the truth* ibid. p. 569
211 *The environment was* D. Macdonald, 'The Responsibility of Peoples', in
Memoirs of a Revolutionist (Cleveland 1958), p. 39
these wailing Jews quot. B. Wasserstein, *Britain and the Jews of Europe
1939–45* (Oxford 1979), p. 351
212 *It is hard to think* F. W. Maitland, *Memoranda de parliamento* (1893),
lxxxiii-iv
would have aroused the quot. Orwell, *Collected Essays etc.* vol iv, *In Front
of Your Nose*, p. 133
213 *the composure and behaviour* et seq. H. Keller, 'Vienna 1938' in *1975
(1984 minus 9)* (1975), p. 37
214 *Even the parsons are . . . each nation will* J. Roth, *The Radetzky March*
(1984), p. 129
no road other than quot. Wistrich, p. 663
nine-tenths of what S. Zweig, *The World of Yesterday* (1943), p. 22
experienced the slightest ibid. p. 25
as an emotional prison. quot. Wistrich, p. 649
the dangerous dream quot. ibid. p. 652
215 *the world of my own* Zweig, *World of Yesterday*, p. 328
The New Italian is organised quot. Avneri, *Makings of Modern Zionism*,
p. 163
216 *the goodwill of . . . establishment of the* quot. 'Berlin's mandate for
Palestine', in C. Hitchens, *For the Sake of Argument* (1993), p. 256
217 *the authorities may rest . . .*
If our dream for Zionism House of Commons, 17 Nov. 1944, quot. N.
Bethell, *The Palestine Triangle* (1979), p. 183
218 *acted like court Jews* N. Cantor, *The Sacred Chain* (1995), p. 395
219 *a problem of at least . . . a moral need and postulate . . .*
the problem of Jewish . . . that the gates of Palestine quot. Laqueur, p. 546
220 *a declaration of war* Magnes, *Dissenter*, p. 382
221 *that the Revisionist programme . . . the choice between emigration* H. Arendt,

'Zionism Reconsidered' in *Menorah Journal*, vol. 33. No. 2 (Autumn 1945), p. 162

in all human history Magnes, Opening Address of the Academic year at the Hebrew University, in *Dissenter*, p. 410

222 *Is it possible that this* ibid.

224 *there appears to have* quot. Bethell, *Palestine Triangle*, p. 207

and consequently must abandon paraphrase in I. Berlin, 'Chaim Weizmann', in *Personal Impressions*, p. 57

the very idea of compromise New York Times, 17 Feb. 1945, Magnes, *Dissenter*, p. 423

225 *all it will do* ibid. p. 424

one could see how far Magnes, *Dissenter*, p. 434

226 *the idea of the Jewish . . . The prophets of Zionism.* Laqueur pp. 560–1

a surrender by quot. Kramnick and Sheerman, op. cit. p. 357

any more than quot. ibid. p. 556.

227 *Let the Arabs be encouraged* quot. B. Pimlott, *Hugh Dalton* (1985), p. 389

strongly committed to support . . . the Palestine issue is G. Orwell, London Letter in *Partisan Review* Fall 1945, in *Collected Essays*, vol. iii, p. 450

this is a Protestant quot, J. Beatty, *The Rascal King: The Life and Times of James Michael Curley* (New York 1992), p. 449

228 *to play on racial* quot. Kramnick and Sheerman, op. cit. p. 554

In song, in prose quot. Richler, *This Year*, p. vii

229 *My dear friends* et seq. Hecht, *A Child*, p. 229

231 *the Jewish vote in New York* Magnes, *Dissenter*, p. 445

setting up two tiny ibid. p. 446

the rift between the ibid. p. 442

out of evil good . . . quot. O'Brien, *The Siege*, p. 282

13 Victors, not victims

235 *with unconscious irony* Hugh Trevor-Roper, 'Searchlight on Israel', *Sunday Times*, 4 Apr. 1951

236 *terrorist, right-wing . . . closely akin New York Times*, 4 Dec, 1948

237 *Like other nations* quot. T. Rahe, *Frühzionismus und Judentum* (Frankfurt 1988), p. 1

And the Reich begat G. Steiner, *The Portage to San Cristobal of AH* (1982), p. 129

239 *Whatever happens, we have* H. Belloc, *The Modern Traveller*

240 *only a small minority* R. Crossman, *Paletine Mission* (1947), p. 211

Because it is a socialist ibid.

the greatest danger of all W. Wyatt, *The Jews at Home* (1950), p. 9

Both Jerusalems are full E. Waugh *The Letters of Evelyn Waugh*, Ed. M Amory (1980), 7 Feb. 1951, p. 345

241 *The Act by which* quot. R. F. Foster *Modern Ireland 1600–1972* (1988),
     p. 257
     What an extraordinary phenomenon et seq. Trevor-Roper, loc. cit.
242 *much to the surprise.* E. S. Shapiro, *A Time for Healing: American Jews
     Since World War II* (Baltimore and London 1992), p. 34
244 *Hank and Bess were winners* quot. ibid. p. 15
245 *I doubt whether it would* Orwell, *Collected Essays*, vol. iv, pp. 510–11
     the socialist revolution J.-P. Sartre, *Portrait of the Anti-Semite* (1949), p. 126
     there is no black ibid., p. 127
246 *a group of people* Arendt, 'Zionism Reconsidered',
     even a transfer of all p. 164
     is no solution since p. 171
     a startling unanimity et seq. A. Hertzberg, 'American Zionism at an
     Impasse', in *Commentary*, Oct. 1949, pp. 340–5
247 *would allow no interference* ibid. p. 342
249 *exposed us in front* quot. E. Tivnan, *The Lobby* (New York 1987), p. 46
     for calculated cold-blooded quot. ibid. p. 45
     what the Gentile will say quot. ibid. p. 47
250 *When are you Americans* Hertzberg, 'American Zionism', p. 344
     the greater part of the ibid.
     the Jews of the United States quot. Shapiro, *Time for Healing*, p. 205
     to American Jews, America quot. Tivnan, p. 32
251 *that his unwavering* Berlin, 'Namier', p. 76
     an act of apostasy for ibid. p. 78
     In the eighteenth century ibid. p. 77
     a Jew or an Englishman quot. Kramnick and Sheerman, *Harold Laski*,
     p. 559
252 *Jews can be antisemitic* A. M. Lilienthal, *What Price Israel?* (Chicago
     1953), p. 137
     a terrible personal blunder . . . The better your case ibid. p. 146

14 They and we

255 *for the first time* quot. Tivnan, pp. 48–9
256 *that Israel's power* quot. ibid. p. 49
     going to get a goddamn thing quot. ibid. p. 50
257 *am aware how almost* quot. G. W. Ball and D. B. Ball, *The Passionate
     Attachment: America's Involvement with Israel 1947 to the Present* (New York
     and London 1992), p. 47
258 *Nowhere have Jews felt* et seq. H. Kohn, 'Zion and Jewish National
     Idea', *Menorah Journal*, vol. 46, Nos. 1 & 2 (Autumn 1958), pp. 17–46
259 *a passionate summary* quot. Tivnan, p. 51
261 *through Social Democratic Vienna* G. D. H. Cole, *An Intelligent Man's Guide*

to the Postwar World (1947), p. 787

262 *I never like this expression* G. Poli and G. Colcagno, *Echi di una voce perduta: incontri, intervisti e conversazioni con Primo Levi* (Milan 1992), p. 204
Why the misprision J. P. Stern, 'Is this right?', *London Review of Books*, 19 Apr. 1990, p. 14
The word shoah falsifies Oz, *Under This Blazing Light*, p. 81
if it would give greater quot. P. Johnson, *History of the Jews*, p. 558

263 *self-hating Jewess Intermountain Jewish News*, 12 Apr. 1963
comes off so much better . . . the only one who . . . in place of the monstrous quot. 'Hannah Arendt and the Jewish Establishment', *Partisan Review*, Spring 1964, in D. Macdonald, *Discriminations* (New York 1974), p. 309

264 *too much meaning is being Times Lit. Supp.* 30 July 1993, p. 5

265 *if the Jewish people* quot. Macdonald, op. cit. p. 313
in the Jewish tradition quot. ibid. p. 316
a paean of transcendence quot. 'Judges in Israel', in J. Sparrow, *Controversial Essays*, (1966), p. 10

266 *It is one of the horrors of . . . that it has thrust upon* Sparrow, ibid. p. 12
I know perfectly well et seq. B. Levin, 'Am I a Jew?' *New Statesman*, 23 July 1965

267 *Everything which society* I. Deutscher, *The Non-Jewish Jew* (London 1968), p. 57
As an unrepentant Marxist ibid. p. 5

269 *if you plan to run for* Tivnan, p. 53
the values and hopes ibid.
I don't know whether P. Klutznick, *No Easy Answers* (New York 1961), p. 123
even the crimes are ibid. p. 131

270 *become his sheltering umbrella* ibid. p. 126
I know I was elected quot. Tivnan, p. 56
a more serious danger quot. ibid. p. 58

271 *lost a great friend* quot. Tivnan, p. 59
had come to my Washington quot. ibid. p. 60
an admirable experiment Commentary, April 1961
The Jewish policeman J. J. Petuchowski, *Zion Reconsidered* (New York 1966), p. 15

272 *an undesirable limitation and . . . My brothers are being* ibid. p. 91
then it was likewise ibid. p. 114

273 *Sing ye to the Lord* Ex. xv. 21
You Hebes really taught quot. C. E. Silberman, *A Certain People: American Jews and their Lives Today* (New York 1985), p. 202
Two weeks ago Village Voice, 15 June 1967

15 Hebrew and Jewish

274 *After the Six-Day New York Review of Books*, 23 Nov. 1989
275 *a three-sided dilemma* G. Frankel, *Beyond the Promised Land* (1994), p. 33
Some even feared R. Aron, *De Gaulle, Israël et les Juifs* (Paris 1968), p. 14
276 *as much as possible* R. Aron, *Memoirs* (1990), p. 341
I have felt myself quot. Laqueur, pp. 35–6
provoked no emotion Aron, *Memoirs*, p. 336
a Jew of French culture ibid. p. 337
277 *in a democratic regime* ibid. p. 395
Jews and French, yes ibid. p. 348
278 *it is important that New Left Notes*, 19 June 1967, quot. A. Liebman, *Jews and the Left* (New York 1979), p. 569
between pro-Israel cold Sol Stern, *Ramparts*, August 1971
the New Left today D. Balch, *New York Times*, 6 July 1975
was dead as a political Cantor, *Sacred Chain*, p. 408
280 *Hey, Jew boy, with* quot. R. I. Friedman, *The False Prophet* (1990), p. 92
288 *Reasonable people The Times*, 27 June 1975
289 *criticism of any other* G. K. Chesterton, *A Selection from his nonfictional prose* Selected by W. H. Auden (1970), Foreword, p. 11
few Jews, including anti-Zionists D. Selbourne, *The Spirit of the Age* (1993), p. 186
290 *the trade unions and ... was effectively* 'Holy Land Heretic', *Raritan*, Spring 1897, in C. Hitchens, *prepared for the Worst* (1989), p. 37
The first was the dishonesty ibid. p. 34
291 *he has a mental perversion ... What shall we do ...* ibid.
of course, a specific U. Avnery, *Israel Without Zionists: A Plea for Peace in the Middle East* (New York and London 1968), p. 47
it transferred people from ibid. p. 37
292 *The fact is that since* ibid. p. 147
unmistakably and irrevocably ... it does not include a ibid. p. 155
decision not to live H. Halkin, *Letters to Jewish American Friend: A Zionist Polemic* (Philadelphia 1977), p. 30
I am not sure ibid. p. 18
so that if anything happens ibid. p. 11
293 *can all be slaughtered* ibid.
I am convinced, is doomed ibid. p. 25
Bar Mitzvah, two ibid. p. 57
they are no more ibid. p. 57
not because it is ibid. p. 68
Looked at closely M. Richler, *This year in Jerusalem* (1995), p. 260

16 Fractured friendships

296 *the historical pattern* E. Sprinzak, 'When Gush Comes to Shove', *New Republic*, 23 Mar. 1992, p. 33

297 *The only thing that* quot. Tivnan, *Lobby*, p. 123
People thought they ibid. p. 104

298 *Fuck the Jews, they* quot. Cantor, *Sacred Chain*, p. 402
Are we going to quot. Tivnan, p. 157
if I get back in quot. A. and L. Cockburn, *Dangerous Liaisons: The Inside Story of the US-Israeli Covert Relationship* (1992), p. 313

299 *We just beat his* quot. Tivnan, p. 159

300 *Were American interests* ibid. p. 158

301 *No one has a right to . . . the man has not* quot. ibid. p. 169
in East Beirut people quot. E. Steen, 'British Jews and the "Big Lie" ', *Sunday Telegraph*, 11 July 1982

302 *but not for making . . . find it difficult to . . . Paradoxically I feel more . . .* ibid.
Goyim kill goyim or 'Gentiles kill gentiles and the Jews are blamed': A. Hertzberg, *Jewish Polemics* (1992), p. 14
am not in the dissenting quot. Tivnan, p. 173

304 *the whole wretched* P. Foot, 'A shoddy little fantasy', *Spectator*, 9 May 1981
when we began to J. Treglown, *Roald Dahl: A Tale of the Unexpected Daily Mail*, 18 Feb 1994; this is as Dahl wrote his article; it appeared in the *Literary Review* (Aug. 1983) changed at the editor's insistence to 'the Israelis'

306 *what Brandeis was* Shapiro, *Time for Healing*, p. 73

308 *This real world is rife* quot. 'Still Chosen', *New Republic*, 3 Dec. 1984, in M. Kinsley, *Curse of the Giant Muffins* (1987), p. 81
but that case is ibid.

309 *the continuing war* ibid. p. 82
the demographic crises G. Steiner, 'Why Israel mut accept double standards', *Sunday Times*, 2 Jan. 1983

310 *We came to conquer . . . am telling you, what . . . I say what you think* quot. Sprinzak, loc. cit.

311 *to the United States* et seq. G. Vidal, 'The empire lovers strike back', *Nation*, 22 Mar. 1986
a new branch grafted A. Rubinstein, *The Zionist Dream Revisited* (New York 1984), p. 30
and real blood ibid. p. xix
Labour Zionism is B. Avishai, *The Tragedy of Zionism* (New York 1985), p. 10
the revolutionary institution ibid. p. 9
okay, put me down quot. M. Golan, *With Friends Like You* (New York 1992), p. 57

313 *nervousness, insecurity* quot. A. M. Dershowitz, *Chutzpah* (Boston and London 1991), p. 7
was virtually Judenrein ibid. p. 65
shed our second-class status . . . before the bureaucratic quot. L. Wieseltier, 'Washington Diary', *New Republic*, 29 July 1991
314 *Derschowitz's Jewishness* ibid.
315 *It's not our being* Golan, *With Friends Like You*, p. 39
Immigrants from every 'An open letter . . .' in *The Collected Essays, Articles and Reviews of Evelyn Waugh*, p. 498
but Jewish status was Avishai, *Tragedy*, p. 262
317 *only two groups that are . . . kids with names like . . . Kissinger, Krauthammer, Rosenthal* quot. X. Smiley, 'Gulf splits Roman Catholics and Jews', *Sunday Telegraph*, 23 Sept. 1990
318 *American men and women* quot. G. Frankel, *Beyond the Promised Land* (1994), p. 304
315 *clobbered the Jewish community* quot. ibid. p. 305
For the first time ibid. p. 307
322 *quietly set in motion* S. Blumenthal, 'The Western Front', *New Yorker*, 5 June 1995
323 *I didn't feel it was* quot. ibid.
I will stand here P. Roth, *The Counterlife* (1987), pp. 125–6

Epilogue 1996

330 *the dregs of Israeli* quot. Golan, *With Friends Like You*, p. 9
331 *someone with what's known* ibid. p. 6
my enemy. A more ibid. p. 12
I respect God too much p. 128
who says that Jewishness p. 110
333 *in America they are* Roth, *Counterlife*, p. 107
doesn't mean one quot. B. Wasserstein, *Vanishing Diaspora* (1996) p. 336
We don't need you quot. *Jewish Chronicle*, 26 Jan. 1996
337 *five thousand years of life* D. Pinto, 'L'identité juive a l'aube du prochain millenaire', paper at 1995 Annual Conference of Academie Hillel
339 *like a Jew* S. Plath, 'Daddy', in *Ariel* (1965)
a rather-too-pretty shrine I. Buruma, 'Passports to the suffering club', *Independent on Sunday*, 3 July 1995
340 *There is room for some* quot. C. Lees, 'The darker side of H.G. Wells', *Sunday Times*, 22 Nov 1992
341 *so hard-hearted they Daily Telegraph*, 23 July 1992
You and I belong quot. Stein, *Balfour Declaration*, p. 494

342 *empty clichés full* D. Grossman, *The Yellow Wind*, Trans. H. Watzman (1988), p. 45
    means to feel that whenever Oz, *Under this Blazing Light*, p. 80
    I am a Zionist because ibid. p. 81
343 *witnessing the disappearance* Wasserstein, *Vanishing Diaspora*, p. 290
    P. Weiss article, *New York*, 29 Jan. 1996
344 *something crucial . . . a way of preserving* Frankel, op. cit. p. 218
    realise that, once Israel's quot. W. Raspberry, 'Adjustment to the loss of an enemy', *International Herald Tribune*, 29 Sept. 1994
345 *Jewish villages were* quot. L. Tal, 'Premissed land', *Times Lit. Supp.*, 4 June 1993
345 *unique. They are unobliging . . .* Richler, *This Year*, p. 231.
346 *You have done to my . . . Had the Arabs won . . . Jewish life went on . . .* I.F. Stone, Foreword to Fouzi El-Asmar, *To Be an Arab in Israel* (1975), p. 1
347 *The American Jews get* Roth, *Counterlife*, p. 79
349 *Whether, in the great* T. B. Macaulay, *History of England*, ch. 7
    the so-called normalization P. Roth, *Operation Shylock* (1993), p. 32
    I'm not only Jewish but . . . Richler, *This Year*, p. 167
350 *the good and the* quot. Howe, *Immigrant Jews*, p. 17
    O God of Mercy quot. ibid. p. 453

Index

Abel, Lionel 263
Abyssinia 170
Action Français 64
Adams, John 10
Adler, Dr Hermann 113
Adler, Viktor 68, 113
Adorno, Theodor 338
Africa: antisemitism 341; apartheid 284–5, 285–7, 341; East 110; Ethiopia 312; states 284; *see also* South Africa; Uganda
African National Congress 341
agnosticism xiii
Ahad Ha-am (Asher Zvi Ginsburg) 130–3, 157, 326, 329, 351
Ahram, Al 174
aid: US to Israel 247–8, 300–1, 311, 319, 331, 336; loan guarantee 317–19
Akademischer Verein Kadimah fraternity 70
Albia fraternity 70
Albu, George 101
Alexander II, Tsar 49; assassination 53
Alexander III, Tsar 53, 108
Alexander, David 143
Alexander, Lucie 138
Alexandria 3, 18
Aliens Bill, 1905 (British) 109, 141
aliyah ('ascent'; migrations to Israel) 96, 126, 250, 318, 330; 1st 58, 119, 330; 2nd 82–3, 119; 3rd and 4th 156
Alkalai, Yehudah 40–1
Allenby, Gen. Sir Edmund 151
Allegemeine Zeitung des Judentums 51
Alliance Israélite Unvierselle 17–18
Altelena 236
America 9–10; *see also* United States of America *and entries below*
American Council for Judaism 220
American Hebrew 121, 128
American Indians 10

American Israeli Public Affairs Committee (AIPAC) 257, 298, 313
American Jewish Committee 250
American Zionist council for Public Affairs 257
American Zionists 124–5, 126, 193, 218–20, 221
Amin, Idi 284–5
Amis, Martin: *Time's Arrow* 339
Andrewes, Lancelot, bishop of Chichester 7
Anglo-Jewish Association 110, 143
Anglo-Saxon Chronicle 13
Anschluss 68
anti-colonialism 278, 284
Anti-Defamation League 252
Antisemitic Congress, *1882* 66
antisemitism 267; *16–18C.* 5–9; *19C.* 51–3, 57, 68–70; after WWI 157–60, 166; *1980s* 303–4; *1990s* 340–1; and colour 278–80; and communism 198–200; in England 98–103, 157–60, 185, 223–4, 244; in Germany 51–3, 57, 68–9, 203–6, 207–12; Hungary 66; racist 68–70; Sartre on 245–6; Soviet 198–200, 243; US 59, 188–90, 223, 225, 226, 227–8, 242, 243–4, 268–9; and Zionism 88–9, 177, 290–1
Antonius, George 208
apartheid 284–5, 286–7, 335, 341
Aqaba, Gulf of 272–3
Arab countries: nationalism 298; war with Israel *1948* 235–6, 346; summit, *1978* 295; *see also* Islam; Territories; *names of countries*
Arab Revolt, *1936* 208, 217
Arabs, Palestinian xii, xiii, 83–4, 86, 132–3, 139, 153, 154, 163, 164, 165, 173–4, 175, 176, 177–8, 179, 182, 307, 208, 219, 226, 258, 259, 345, 346–7;

WWI 152–3; after 156; hostilities and terrorism 156, 157, 180–1, 216–18, 228–9, 231, 248–9, 285; exiles/refugees 231, 247, 269, 270, (and Saudi Arabia 298), (camps 302, 303); Intifade 314–15, 321, 331; statistics 325; *see also* Palestine Liberation Organisation
Arafat, Yassir 320
Arendt, Hannah 14, 77, 214, 221, 236, 321; *Eichmann in Jerusalem* 263–6; 'Zionism Reconsidered' 245–6
Argentine 73, 74, 110, 117, 209
Argyll, George Douglas, 8th Duke 26, 28n, 32
Arlozorov, Chaim 184
army, Jewish proposed 175–6
Aron, Raymond 275–7, 305
Ashkenazim 44, 239
Ashley Cooper, Anthony, 7th Earl of Shaftesbury 1–2,7, 17, 18, 40, 325
Asquith, Herbert Henry 140–1, 144
Assad, Hafez al- 327
Assembly of Jewish Notables, *1806* 11
Attlee, Clement 224, 261
Auden, W. H. 289, 303
Auschwitz 211, 261, 267, 323, 338
Australia 340; immigration policy 209; imperialism 164; Labour movement 201
Austria: *18C.* 9, 10; *19C.* 44, 45, 51, 67–8, 69–70, 89, 214, 350; Mayerling 73n; *1900* 88; *1920–30s* 203, 205; *Anschluss* 68; WWII 212; after 261; *1990s* 340; *see also* Vienna
Austro-Hungarian Empire 65–8, 152
Austro-Prussian War 151
Avineri, Shlomo 313
Avis, Joseph 99
Avishai, Bernard 307, 311–12, 315
Avnery, Uri 291–2
AWACS sale 297–8, 299–300
Ayer, A.J. 24
Azzam Pasha 225

Baader-Meinhof gang 307
Babeuf, François 42
Badeni (Austrian prime minister) 91n
Baghdad Pact 254
Baker, James 298–9
Balabanoff, Angelica 169
Balfour, A. J.: Aliens Bill 109, 141; meets Weizmann 135, 141; PM 140–1; Foreign Secretary 141, 142; afterwards 154
Balfour Declaration xii, 126, 143, 145–7, 152–3, 154, 168
Balliol College, Oxford 114, 137, 161
Bank of Israel 287
Barker, Gen. 223

Barnato, Barney 101
Baron Hirsch Fund 73
Baruch, Löb (Ludwig Börne) 22–3, 24, 25, 28, 30
Bauer, Bruno: *Die Judenfrage* 21, 29
Bauer, Peter, Lord, 300, 340
Bayreuth 94, 141
Becker, Nikolaus 43
Beer, Amalie 14
Beerbohm, Max 104
Begin, Menachem 324; in WWII 216; with Irgun 218; 229, 231; opposition leader 249, 272; Likud 282; PM 288, 294–5, 296–7, 300, 302–3
Beilen, Yossi 336
Beirut, 216, 301, 302, 307
Beit, Alfred 101
Belgium 22, 55
Belloc, Hilaire 69, 102, 158–9, 239, 268; *The Jews* 158
Bellow, Saul 36n, 245
Ben Avi, Ittamar 170
Ben-Aharon, Yossi 319
Ben-Gurion, David: early life 81, 82, 83; and Jabotinsky 175, 185–6, 208; *1940s* 218, 219–20; PM of Israel 236–8, 249, 250; retires 248; PM again 254, 255–6, 269, 270
Benedict XV, Pope 168
Benedikt, Moritz 83, 89, 93, 332
Benjamin, Walter 213, 214
Bentinck, Lord George 25
Bentwich, Norman 183
Berg, Alban 93n; *Lulu* 93n
Bergelson, Dovid 243
Berit Shalom 180
Berlin, Germany: *1840* 18; *19C.* 22, 24, 28, 51, 52, 57, 123; *1920s* 203
Berlin, Irving 122, 317
Berlin, Sir Isaiah 21, 31, 160, 162, 251, 316
Bermant, Chaim 321, 323
Bernadotte, Count Folke 236, 303
Bernsztajn, Ludwik *see* Namier
Betar youth movement 171, 176, 183
Bevin, Ernest 224, 227, 228, 229, 230
Bible: translated 134
Billroth, Theodor 52
Biltmore programme, *1942* 218–20, 226
Birkenau 221
Biobidzhan 200
Bismarck, Otto von 30, 68, 134, 151, 183, 298, 322
Black Panthers 280
blacks 60, 268, 278–80; apartheid 284–5, 286–7, 335, 341; Ethiopian Jews 312; in South Africa 285–6
Blake, William 7
Blaustein, Jacob 250

Bleichröder, Gershon 50, 51
Bloch, Dr Joseph 67
Bloch, Marc 276
'blood libel' 17–18, 66
Blum, Léon 276
Blumenthal, Sidney 322
B'nai B'rith, League of 265, 269
Board of Deputies of British Jews 143
Boer War 102, 260
Bohemia 3, 86, 283
Bols, Sir Louis 156
Bolshevism 169–70, 198, 199, 200
Bonn, Germany 42
Börne, Ludwig (Löb Baruch) 22–3, 24, 25, 28, 30
Bradlee, Benjamin 299
Brandels, Louis: American Zionist leader 124–6, 176, 183, 251; meets Balfour 142; resigns, *1921* 193; *1929* 183; US Supreme Court appointment 124, 191, 192
Brazil 209, 215
Breines, Paul: *Tough Jews* 347
Brichto, Sidney 301–2
British Army 111; Jewish units in 157, 171, 173, 175–6, 216; enter Jerusalem 151
Brod, Max 92
Brosch, Hermann 96
Bruce, Lenny 348
Brzezinski, Zbigniew 296
Buber, Martin 133–5, 214
Buchanan, Patrick 317
Buckley, William 317
Budapest 65
Bulgaria 52
Bund, the 199
Burns, John 69, 101–2, 105n
Buruma, Ian 264, 339
Bush, Frank 122
Bush, George 298, 318–19, 320
Byrd, William 7

Campbell, James 280
Canada: in British Commonwealth 164; Holocaust denial law 340; Jews in 349
Canning, George 24
Cantor, Eddie 122
Cantor, Norman 278
Caran d'Ache 63
Carlyle, Thomas 2, 17, 343
Carmichael, Stokely 279
Carpenter, Edward 69
Carter, James 295, 296, 297, 299, 304
Catholic Church *see* Roman Catholic Church
Cecil, Lady Gwendolen 26

Cecil, Lord Robert 146
Celan, Paul 338
Cezanne, Paul 63
Chamberlain, Houston Stewart 94–5; *Die Grundlagen des Neunzehnten Jahrhunderts* 94
Chamberlain, Joseph 109
Chamberlain, Neville 335
Chateaubriand, Vicomte de 13
Chatilla camp 302, 303
Chemirsky, Alexander 200
Chesterton, G. K. 102, 158, 159–60, 289, 326; *The New Jerusalem* 158
Chicago, Illinois 128
Chicago Israelite 128
Chlowson, Daniel 28
Christian Socialism 69, 71, 100, 203, 205
Christian X, King of Denmark 211, 215
Christianity 4, 5, 6–7, 8, 28, 88, 115; *see also* Church of England; Protestantism; Roman Catholic Church
Church of England 15, 23, 101
Churchill, Sir Winston xi, 146, 154, 196, 198–9, 217, 237
civil rights 279
Civiltà Cattolica 167
Clare (Klaar), George 92–3
Clemenceau, Georges 63
Clermont-Tonnerre, comte de 11
Clinton, William 320
Cobden, Richard 46
Cohen, Ellen 113
Cohen, Elliot 306
Cohen, Hermann 134–5
Cohn, Harry 195, 196
Cole, G. D. H. 261
colonialism 84–5; anti- 278, 284; *see also* imperialism
colour (racial) 227, 284; *see also* apartheid; blacks; racism
Columbia university, New York 189
Commentary 243, 263, 271, 306, 307, 311
Communism: early 87; *1920s* 163; Koestler 184; US 196–200, 242–3; Israeli 241–2, 277; *1960s* 277; *1980s* 307–8
concentration camps 260–1; Auschwitz 211, 261, 267, 323, 338
Conference of Presidents of Major American Jewish Organisations 257, 269, 302, 313
Constantinople 173
conversions: from Catholicism 23n; from Judaism 5–6; (*18–19C.*, England 15, 23–5, 28, 104), (Kraus 91); Marranos 5–6, 15; *see also* intermarriage
Coughlin, Father Charles 188
Courts of Aldermen 15
Cranbourne, Lord 217n
Crawford and Balcarres, David Lindsay, 27th Earl 105

Cremieux, Isaac Adolph 17–18
Crete 178
Cromwell, Oliver 6, 99
Crossman, Richard 239–40
Crusades 13, 85
culture 36, 203, 327, 344, 350–1
Curzon, George, Marquis 145, 146, 154, 179
Czechs 3, 86, 91, 152, 282

Dahl, Roald 304
Daily Graphic 115
Dalton, Hugh 227
Damascus: *1840* 17–18, 41, 43
Davar 248
Dawidowicz, Lucy 243, 350
Day 243
Dayan, Moshe 345; early career 223, 292–2; chief of staff, Israeli troops 248, 322; defence minister 272, 273; resigns 287
de Gaulle, Charles 275, 276, 277
de Valera, Eamon 178, 328
Dearborn Independent 188
Decter, Midge 310–11
Deir Yassin massacre 231, 236–7
del Val, Cardinal Merry 168
Denmark, 22, 211, 215
Dershowitz, Alan 350; *Chutzpah* 313–14
Deutsch, Emmanuel 55
Deutscher, Isaac 44, 266, 267–8
Deutsches Volksblatt 90
Diamand, Hermann 88
Diaspora, the (Dispersion; Galut) 3–4, 9, 41, 55, 76, 293
Dickens, Charles 99; *Hard Times* 27
Dillon, John 101
Disraeli, Benjamin, 1st Earl of Beaconsfield 5n, 52, 305, 341; character 26–7, 31–2, 33, 50; *Alroy* 33; *Coningsby* 27, 31; *Tancred* 27–8, 32–3
D'Israeli, Isaac 23–4, 28
Dizengoff, Meir 170
Dominican Republic 209
Dor, Lea Ben 291
Dostoievsky, Fyodor 157, 264
Drancy monument, France 339
Dreyfus, Alfred 61–4, 71, 313
Dreyfus, Mathieu 62
Drumont, Edouard 61, 64, 277
Druze 325
Dryden, John 7
duelling 70
Dugdale, Blanche 163–4
Dühring, Eugen: *Die Judenfrage* 52–3
Dulles, John Foster 247–8, 255–6, 257

Dutch Republic 6
Dutton, Frederick G. 299

Eban, Abba 255, 256, 271, 286
Eden, Sir Anthony 258
Edward VII, King 104
Egypt: ancient 2, 30–1; *18C.* 11; Nordau in 84; *1944* 217; *1948* 235; *1967* Six Days war 272–3; *1973*, Yom Kippur attack 181–2; *1977* 295; peace treaty, *1978* 295
Eichmann, Adolf 216, 264; trial 262–3
Eilat, straits 248
Einstein, Albert 122, 179–80, 180–1, 206–7, 236, 294
Eisenhower, Dwight D. 247, 256, 257
Eisenmenger, Johann Andreas: *Entdecktes Judenthum* 8
El-Asmar, Fouzi: To *Be an Arab in Israel* 346
Elibank, Master of 103
Eliot, George 55, 99: *Daniel Deronda* 55, 113
Ellmann, Richard 244
Encyclopaedia Britannica 115
Engels, Friedrich 28, 30, 42
England: Jews in (*17C.* 6–7, 9, 98, 99), (*19C.* 15, 40, 50, 60, 76, 98–106, 109–16), (*20C.* 135, 185), (in literature 24, 55, 99–100); antisemitism 98–103, 157–60, 185, 223–4, 244; *see also* Britain; Church of England; London
English Reform Judaism 114
Enlightenment 7–8
Entebbe, *1976* 287
Epstein, Jason 271
Erasmus 6
espionage 312–13
Ethiopian Jews 312
Europe: Jews in, *18C.* 9; *19C.* 39–40; *20C.* Israeli links with 326–7, 334, 335, 343, 349; *see also* names *of countries*
European Broadcasting Union 237
European Union 343
Evian, France, conference 209
Exodus (film) 259
Exodus 1947 (steamer) 229

Fabians 138, 181–2
Fackel, Die 89, 92, 94, 204n
Falwell, Jerry 308
Farouk, King of Egypt 235, 238, 254
Farrakhan, Louis 279, 309, 341
fascism 166, 168–70, 184
Fatah 255
Federation of American Zionists 121
Feinberg: *Le'an* 349
femininity 95

Fiddler on the Roof (musical) 268
films 194–6, 259, 339, 341
Final Solution: Hitler imposes 210–13,
 221–3; in Italy 215–16; Western attitude
 221–3, 223–4, 260–7, 337–40; *see also*
 Holocaust
Fineberg, Rabbi S. Andhill 243
Finkielkraut, Alain 333
Fitzgerald, F. Scott 195
Fitzgibbon, John, Lord Clare 241
flag, Zionist 75
Flanagan, Bud 123n
Foot, Michael 239, 304
Foot, Paul 304
Ford, Gerald 299
Ford, Henry 188
Fortas, Abe 271
Forward 121, 194, 243
Fox, William 195
France: revolutionary xii, 10–11; *18–19C.*
 11–12, 38–9, 45, 60, 61–4; WWI 142,
 151, 152; and Final Solution 276, 339;
 Suez affair 255; French Jews 275–7;
 1990s 341
France Juive, La 61
Francis I, emperor 67
Francis II, emperor 12
Frankel, Glenn 275, 337, 344
Frankfurter, Felix 192–3
Franklin, Benjamin 10
Freeman, Edward 52
Freemasonry 159, 168
French Revolution 5, 10–11, 69
Freud, Sigmund 43, 89
Frewing, Mrs: *The Inheritance of Evil* 27n
Friedjung, Heinrich 68
Friedmann, Georges 350
friendship 37–8
Furtado, Abraham 12

Gaelic language 39, 53–4, 122, 327–8, 329
Gaelic League 53–4, 327–8
Galicia, Austria 56, 87, 92, 133–4
Gandhi, Mahatma 207, 212
Gaza *1955* 248; *1967* 274; *1987* 315
genius 35–6, 47, 95
German language 29n, 85, 92, 205
German Nationalist Party 68
Germany: *16C.* 6; *18C.* 22–3; *19C.* 14–15,
 18, 22, 41–3, 51, 57, 86; early *20C.* 134;
 universities 118, 134; WWI 135, 152,
 169, 204; Weimar republic 202–3, 213;
 1920s 162, 169, 203; *1930s* 165, 169, 192,
 204–7, 216; WWII 210–12, 301n, *see also*
 Final Solution; *see also* Berlin; National
 Socialism
Gestapo 213

ghettos 4, 10, 212, 213, 279n, 280
Gibbon, Edward xiii–xiv
Gildersleeve, Virginia 225
Ginsburg, Asher Zvi *see* Ahad Ha-am
Giolitti, Giovanni 44
Gladstone, William Ewart 32, 52, 113, 137
Glazunov, Alexander 191, 306
Goethe, Wolfgang von 350
Gogol, Nikolai 156
Golan, Matti 315, 344, 347; *With Friends
 Like You* 330–3
Golan Heights 273, 274
Goldsmid, Col. Albert 112–13
Goldsmid, Francis 50
Goldsmid, Maj-Gen. Sir Frederic 112
Goldstein, Baruch 323
Gordon, A. D. 82, 160, 326, 329
Gordonia Labour Youth group 246
Gorky, Maxim 179
Gramsci, Antonio 167
'Great Britain: Jewish population 135;
 immigration control 109, 141; *1914*
 136–40; WWI 135, 260; Mandate in
 Palestine 151–65, 208–9, 217, 223, 224,
 229–31, (end 231–2); *1918–20s* 157–64,
 260; Labour movement 201; WWII 211,
 223–4; Suez crisis 254–5, 258; *1980s*
 305–6; terrorism against 229; *see also*
 England; imperialism; Labour party,
 British; *and entries below*
Greece 165, 178: Salonika 222
Greek language 327, 328
Greenberg, Hank 244
Greene, Graham 99
Grey, Sir Edward 138
Grossman, David 342
Gruenbaum, Yizhak 172
Grund (journalist) 108
Gryn, Rabbi Hugo 303
Gulf of Aqaba 272–3
Gulf war 316–17
Gunpowder Plot 7
Gush Emunim (Block of the Faithful) 296
Gwynne, H. A. 198

Ha'aretz 157, 296
Habonim group 228, 346
Haganah (Defence Force) 176, 207, 218,
 223, 236, 237
Haig, Alexander 301
Halévy, Fromental 35, 36, 37
Halkin, Hillel, 344, 347; *Letters to a Jewish
 American Friend* 292–3, 310
Hamas Islamic movement 295–6
Hambro family 267
Hamburg 22, 25
Hamilton, Sir George 158

Handel, George Frederick 7
Hannukkah 2–3
Ha'olem Hazeh 291
Hard Times (Dickens) 27
Harden, Maximilian 203–4
Harvard 189–90, 191, 313, 343
Hashahar 53
Hashomer Hazair (Young Guard) 246
Hasidic movement 14, 134
Haskalah 54
Hatzfeldt, Countess 30
Hearst, William Randolph 197
Hebrew Labour *see* Labour Zionists
Hebrew language 4, 53–4, 155, 171, 179,
    292, 327, 328–9, 335, 336
Hebrew Union College, Cincinnati 123,
    190
Hebrew University, Jerusalem 155, 165,
    180, 183, 221, 346
Hebron massacre 323
Hecht, Ben 197–8, 228–9, 236; *A Flag is
    Born* 228; 'Letter to the Terrorists of
    Palestine' 229
Heine, Heinrich 24–5, 26–7, 30, 100, 205
Henry, Commandant 61
Hentoff, Nat 271
'Hep! Hep!' riots 14
Herder, Johann 8, 94
Hertzberg, Arthur: early life 246–7; in
    Israel 250; journalism 302–3; *quoted* 273,
    274, 322–3, 344, 351; *Jewish Polemics* 351
Herz, Henriette 14, 22
Herzl, Theodor 44, 70–8, 332; early life
    65–7; at university 70–1; with Hirsch
    73–4; journalism 53, 62, 64, 71–6, 83,
    90, 91, 93; *1896* xi–xii; at 1st Zionist
    congress 75–6, 98–9; propounds
    Zionism 77–8, 81–2, 83–4, 85–7, 110,
    115; in England 76, 105–6, 110–13, 116;
    in Italy 166, 167–8; in Russia 106–9;
    death 137; *Altneuland* 84; *Das neue Ghetto*
    72, 76; *Der Judenstaat* 70–1, 74, 75–7, 83,
    88, 128–9, 324, 325; criticism of 97, 131;
    children of 213
Herzog, Chaim 282, 320
Hess, Moses 166, 215; early life 42; and
    Buber 43; and G. Eliot 55; and Marx
    42–3, 44; *Rom and Jerusalem* 44–5, 46–8,
    48, 125–6
Hibbat Zion 56, 82
hijackings 281, 287
Hillel 350
Hillquist, Morris 121
Hilton, Judge 59
Hirsch, Rabbi Emil E. 12
Hirsch, Baron Maurice de 73–4
Hitler, Adolf xiv; early career 203; *1930s*
    169, 170, 192, 204–9; WWII 210–11;

Final Solution 210–12, 217, 218, 221–2,
    223, 226; effects 237–8, 264, 267, 334;
    Mein Kampf 203
Hobsbawm, E. J. xiii, 36n
Hobson, J. A. 69, 102; *Imperialism* 163
Hoeflich, Eugen (M. Ben Gavriel) 174
Hofstein, Dovid 243
Holland 22
Hollywood 194–8, 259
holocaust 261–3, 264, 338–9; denial laws
    340; monuments and museums 339–40;
    see also Final Solution
Holocaust (novel) 299
Holocaust (tv series) 339
Holy Land 3n, 12–13, 40–1, 47–8, 66, 74;
    first settlements in 87; *see also* aliyot;
    Israel; Jerusalem; Palestine
Hook, Sidney 236
horse-racing 50, 73
Horthy, Admiral 211
Hovevei Zion Association 106, 110–11, 113,
    137
Howe, Irving 123, 306, 344
Hungary: *19C.* 65–7, 86; after WWI 152;
    1944 262; *1956* 277; *1990s* 340; Austro-
    Hungarian Empire 65–8, 152
Hussein, Sherif, Emir of Mecca 153
Hyde, Douglas 327

Idelson, Avraham 172
identity, Jewish 266–8, 275–6, 283–4,
    315–16, 333, 335, 348
Ihud Association 255–6
imperialism 103, 118, 278; *19C.* 84–5; *1920s*
    163–4
India: British 85, 112, 224; partition 230–1;
    racism 284
Inglis, Sir Robert 15
Innocent III, Pope 45
intermarriage 162, 251, 283, 316, 333–4
Intermountain Jewish News 252
Intifada 314–15, 321, 331
Irak 235, 255, 297, 316–17
Iran (Persia): *1980* revolution 295
Ireland 349; *17–18C.* 3, 7, 85, 178, 241;
    19C. 39, 81, 86; *1916* 111; *1917* 127; *1920*
    Government of Ireland Act 146; *1922*
    328; emigration to US 122, 127; Fenians
    191; Free State/ Republic 164, 328;
    nationalism 26, 86; Oranmore 23n;
    partition 146, 152, 178; religion 7, 86,
    131–2, 178; Sinn Fein 216, 327–8; *see also*
    Gaelic language
Irgun Zvei Leumi force 217, 218, 223,
    228–30, 231, 236, 259
Isaacs, Godfrey 103
Isaacs, Rufus 103–4

Islam 4, 5, 9, 118, 239; Hamas 295–6; 'Revolt of' 295–6
Israel: in *Daniel Deronda* 55; state established, *1948* 235–8, 243, 247, 346; *1949–59* 238–9, 240–1, 243, 247–53; (Suez crisis 254–6); Six-Day war, *1967* 272–3, 274; *1970s* 294–7, (*1973* war 257, 281–2), (*1979* peace treaty 295); *1980s* 309–10. (wars with Lebanon 295, 301–2), 311–17, (Operation Moses 312), (Intifada *1987* 314–15, 321, 331); *1990s* (Gulf war 316–17), 317–24, 325–7, 329–30, 346; European affiliation 326–7; immigration and emigration statistics 250, 330; irrigation 247; Law of Return 238, 284, 315, 335; political system 287n, 315, 329; US aid 247–8, 300–1, 311, 319, 331, 336, (loan guarantee 317–19); relations with US 255–7, 268–73, 277–80, 292–3, 296–301, 302, 304–5, 306–14, 316–23, 330–1, 334–7, 343–5, 347–8; Gulf war 316–17; *see also* aliyot; Holy Land; Palestine
Israel Defence Forces 236
Israeli Peace Now 302
Israeli-Egyption peace treaty, *1978* 295
Istóczy, Gyözö von 66, 88
Italy: *19C.* 33, 39, 44–5, 86, 166–8; WWI 152; fascist 164, 166, 168–70, 225n; WWII 211, 215–216; nationalism 215–15

Jabotinsky, Vladimir 165, 183, 278, 279, 327, 347; character 175, 180; early life 170, 172; WWI 173; and army 171, 173, 175–6; and Italy 215–16; journalism 172, 173, 181; and Koestler 184; and nationalism 174–5, 215–16; on Yids 171–2, 329, 349–50; views of Zionism 171–3, 174–7, 179, 185–6, 207–8, 301, 309; death 215
Jackson, Jesse 309
Jacobsen, Howard 306, 347
Jakobovits, Lord 338
Janner, Greville 301
Japan 340–1
Jaurés, Jean 62
Javits, Jacob 248
Jazz Singer, The (film) 195
Jefferson, Thomas 10, 352
Jellinek, Adolf 56–8, 125, 158
Jerome, V. J. 196
Jerusalem: Holy City 12, 153; under Romans 3; Destruction of Temple 3; *19C.* 13; *1917* British take 151; Holy Places 109, 140, 168, 180; King David hotel 229; Hebrew University 155, 165, 180, 183, 221, 346; *see also* Holy Land;

Palestine
Jerusalem Post 291
Jessel, Sir George 50
Jesus Christ, 5, 115
Jeune Turc 173
Jewish Chronicle 106, 301, 316, 320, 321, 333
Jewish Colonisation Association 73
Jewish Councils 212, 265
Jewish Defence League 279–80
Jewish Press 279
Jewish Religious Union 114
Jewishness 266–8, 275–6, 283–4, 315–16, 333, 335, 348
Jockey Club 50, 104
Johannesburg 102, 163
Johnson, Lyndon 256, 269, 271
Jones, Leroi 279
Jordan 238, 273, 296; *see also* West Bank
Joseph, Sir Keith 305
Joseph II, emperor of Austria 9, 67
Jowett, Benjamin 114
Judaism (religion) 2–3, 4, 6–7, 8, 40–1; Holy Days 2, 332–3; *see also* conversions; Orthodox Jews and Judaism; Reform Judaism

Kahane, Rabbi Charles 279
Kahane, Rabbi Meir 279; Jewish Defence League 279–80; and Russian Jews 281; and Likud 282; in Knesset 309–10; death 331
Kaim, Isidore 51
Kalinin, Michael 199
Kalischer, Zvi Hirsch 41
Kant, Immanuel 8
Kaufman, Gerald 345
Kautsky, Karl 68
Kazin, Alfred 244
Keller, Hans 92n, 213, 345, 348
Kennedy, John F. 269, 270, 271, 299
Kennedy, Robert 299
Keynes, J. M. 224
Khazar tribe 10
Khomeni, Ayatollah 295
Khrushchev, Nikita 200
Kibbutzim 81, 219, 241, 291
Kibya, Jordan 248, 249
Kingsley, Mary 112
Kinsley, Michael 308–9, 319
Kipling, Rudyard 84; 'The Burden of Jerusalem' 196; 'Gehazi' 103
Kishinev, Russia 106, 110
Kissinger, Henry 305
Klutznick, Philip 255, 269–70, 331
Knowland, William 257
Koestler, Arthur 184–5, 200; *Thieves in the Night* 184–5

Kohn, Hans 77, 258–9, 334, 350
Kohn, Leo 170
Kopkind, Andrew 244–5
Koran Club 251
Kramer, Victor 189
Kraus, Karl 44, 65, 89–97, 121, 204, 290, 351; early life 89; *1930s* 205–6; conversion 91; on Hitler 205–6; *Die letzen Tage der manschheit* 93; *Fackel* 89, 92, 94, 204; *Eine Krone für Zion* 88–9, 90–1, 93–4, 121, 205, 206; 'Er ist doch e Jud' 95; translations of Shakespeare 205
Kristol, Irving 308
Kuwait 316–17

Labour Herald 304
Labour movement, international 201
Labour party, British 304; *1929* government 181–3; *1945* government 223–4, 226–7, 239–40; *1950s* 258, 305; Jewish members 305–6
Labour party, Israeli *see* Mapai
Labour Zionists (Hebrew Labour; Poale Zion) 82, 83, 171, 176, 184, 200–1, 311–12; Haganah 176, 207, 218, 223, 236
Ladino language 4–5, 222
Laemmle, Carl 195, 196, 197
Laharanne, Ernest: *La nouvelle question d'Orient* 46
languages 4–5, 29n, 36, 85, 171, 327–8; *see also* Gaelic; Hebrew; Ladino; Yiddish
Lansdowne, Henry Petty-Fitzmaurice, 5th Marquis of 110
Laqueur, Walter 130, 226
Lasker, Eduard 51
Laski, Harold 183–3, 194, 226–7, 251
Laski, Nathan 182, 226
Lassalle, Ferdinand 18, 30–1, 33, 44, 174
Latin 328
Lavon, Pinchas 248
Law of Registration of Inhabitants 316
Law of Return 238, 284, 315, 335
Lawrence family 267
Lawrence, T. E. 142
Lazaron, Rabbi Morris 225
League of Justice 225
League of Nations 153
Lebanon: *1978* attack 295; *1981* 297; *1982* war 301–4, 307n
Leeds 157
Left and Right 68–9, 304–8; New Left 277–8
Lehi terrorist group 216–18
Lehman, Herbert 225
Leibowitz, Yeshayahu 303, 342
Leipzig 134
Lenin, V. I. 163

Lerner, Michael 331
Lessing, Gottfried 9
Lessing, Theodor 91: *Der jüdische Selbsthass* 91
Levi, Hermann 37–8
Levi, Primo 222, 262, 338; *Se Quest'é un Uumo* 338
Levi, Sylvain 155
Levin, Bernard 266–7, 277
Levin, Rahel 14
Levy, David 318
Lewes, George Henry 55
Libre Parole 61, 63
Lichtheim, Richard 176
Liebermann, Hermann 88
Ligue Antisémite 64
Likud coalition 282, 288, 290, 303, 309, 315, 321, 322–3, 324, 329
Lilienblum 132
Lilienthal, Alfred M. 252, 257
Lindsay, John 280
Lippmann, Walter 190–3, 197, 310, 343
Lissauer, Ernst 206
literature, Jews in: English 24, 55, 99–100, 184–5
Lithuania 9, 10, 23, 218
Livingstone, Ken 304
Lloyd George, David 136, 140–1; Marconi scandal 103–4; and Samuel 138–9; *1917* 144; and Ireland 146
London, England: *17C.* 99; *18C.* 15; *19C.* 18, 76, 101, 104, 105–6, 110–12, 113, 116; *20C.* 130; Reform Service 114
London, Meyer 121
London School of Economics 182–3
Londonderry, Circe, Lady 185
Los Angeles 280, 330
Lovers of Zion Association 113
Lowell, Abbott L. 189–90, 191, 343
Lozère 38–9
Lubentschik, Naftalli 216
Ludwig II, King of Bavaria 38
Lueger, Karl 69–70, 203
Lurie, Hayyim 41
Lustiger, Cardinal 341
Luther, Martin 6
Luxemburg, Rosa 203
Luzzatti, Luigi 167
Luzzatto, Moses Chaim 33
Luzzatto, Samuel David 33

Macaulay, Thomas Babington 16–17, 85, 140, 329, 349
Maccabeans club 111, 116
Maccabees 75, 171, 329
Macdonald, Dwight 210–11, 265, 310
MacDonald, Ramsay 183

Machover, Mosche 302
Mackenzie, Compton, 185
Magnes, Judah: early life 123–4; in New
    York 124, 153, 154; *1918* 153–5; in
    Palestine 155, 157, 179, 180, 181, 220,
    231; *1944* address 221–2; and Weizmann
    179, 180, 181; writes to *NYT* 224–5
Magnus, Laurie 143, 206
Magnus, Sir Philip 139, 142
Maidanek camp 260
Maimonides 34, 342
Maitland, F. W. xiv, 212
Malcolm X 279
Manchester, England 82, 135, 182
Manchester Guardian 102, 136
Mann, Thomas: *Doctor Faustus* 77
Mapai (Labour party, Israeli) 287–8, 296,
    315–16, 329
Mapam party 242, 277
Marconi Company 102–3, 111
Marcus, Amy Dockser 344
Margoulioth, Ezekiel 23
Markish, Perez 243
Marr, Wilhelm 51
Marranos 5–6, 15
marriage 162, 251, 283, 316, 333–4
Marshall, Louis 189, 190, 257
Marx, Karl 32, 33, 69, 198, 246; early life
    28; Jewishness 28–30; relations with
    contemporaries 30–1; and Hess 42–3,
    44; views of imperialism 85 marxism
    69, 167, 199; Marxist Social Democracy
    69, 91; *see also* Bolshevism; communism;
    socialism
Masada 3, 337
Maskilim 14, 81
Maurras, Charles 313
mauscheln 93
Maxwell, Robert 319–20
Mayer, Louis B. 195, 196, 197
McCarthy, Joseph 242, 307
McCarthy, Mary 265
McMahon, Sir Henry 153
Meir, Golda 287, 295, 302
Mellor, David 314–15
Mendel, Rabbi 13
Mendelssohn, Moses 14
Mendelssohn-Bartholdy, Felix 36–7
Mendizábal, Juan 15
Menorah Journal 193, 258
Menorah Monthly 128
Merchant of Venice, The (Shakespeare) 24, 99
Meyerbeer, Giacomo 35, 36
Midstream 271
migrations of population 164–5, 178–9; *see
    also* aliyot
Miller, Arthur 267, 348
Minton, John 240

Mitterrand, François 276
Moledet party 310
Molodowsky, Kadia 350
Mommsen, Theodor 202
Moncrieff, Algernon 103
Mondale, Walter 304–5
Monet, Claude 63
Montagu, Edwin 113, 138; in Cabinet
    144–5, 146
Montagu, Sir Samuel, Lord Swaythling
    106, 112; career 113–14; in Holy Land
    137; writes to *Times* 137–8
Montaigne, Michel de 34
Montefiore, Claude 106, 332; early life
    114; lay preacher 114–15; statement in
    Times 143; on Balfour Declaration 145,
    205; 'The Dangers of Zionism' 135–6
Montefiore, Leonard 341
Montefiore, Sir Moses 18, 114
Montreal 349
Moral Majority 308
More, Sir Thomas 13
Morgenstern, Julian 190
Morgenthau, Henry 129, 331
Morning Post 198
Morocco 341
Moskowitz, Henry 142
Moyne, Lord 217–18, 288, 303
Mugabe, Robert 341
Muggeridge, Malcolm 199; *Winter in
    Moscow* 199
Müller, Wilhelm 94
music 34–5, 36
Musil, Robert 96
Mussolini, Benito 164, 168–70, 211, 215
Myerson, Bess 244

Namier, Lewis B. 45, 222, 278, 337; early
    life 160–1; character 161–2; and Oxford
    University 161, 251; anti-German 165;
    marriage 251; and Weizmann 251; and
    Jerusalem University 165
Napolelon Bonaparte 11–12, 14, 22, 45
Napoleon III 45
Nasser, Gamal Abdul 254, 272
Nathan, Mathew 111–12
Nation 310
National Religious Party 316
National Socialism 23, 96; early rise 203;
    1930s 170, 184, 192, 197, 208, 279; Final
    Solution 210, 211, 216, 265
nationalism: *18C.* 8–9, 12, 38; *19C.* 14,
    38–9, 44, 76–7, 86, 134, 151; WWI 142,
    151–2; *20C.* 258–9; and racism 283, 334;
    Arab 298; Canada 349; German 86,
    134; Hungary 86; Irish 26, 86; Italian
    44–5, 86; Jewish *see* Zionism

Nazi and Nazi Collaborators (Punishment) Act 263
Netanyahu, Benjamin 321
Netanyahu, Jonathan 321
Neue Freie Presse 62, 71, 83, 89, 91
Neumann, Angelo 37
Neumann, Sigismund 101, 104
Neuzeit 64
New Amsterdam 9
New Left Notes 278
New Liberalism 138
New Republic 191, 310
New York: *17C.* 9; *18C.* 59; *1880s–1920* 119–22, 124; *1920s* 188–90; *1930s*, 194, 198; *1940s* 218, 227–8, 229; blacks in 279–80; schools 280; terrorist activity in 281; Temple Emanu-El 124, 190; universities 189
New York Review of Books 311
New York Times 317, 334; late *19C.* 128–9; *1917* 142; *1944* 224; *1948* 236; *1958* 259; *1975* 278; *1982* 302
New Zealand 164
Newfoundland 164
Nicolson, Harold 105
Nixon, Richard 257
Nobel Peace Prize 295
Nordau, Max 75, 84, 88, 98, 99, 117, 132, 175
Novy, James 271
Nuremberg Laws 206

O'Brien, Conor Cruise 254, 307n, 322
Observer 307n
Occupied Territories *see* Territories
Ochs, Adolph 128–9
O'Connor, Cardinal 317
Odessa 53, 54, 171
Of Thee I Sing (Gershwin) 189)
Ofer, Avraham 287
Operation Moses 312
Orthodox Jews and Judaism 46, 87, 114, 127, 323; in Final Solution 213; in Israel 290, 315, 316
Orwell, George 99, 227, 245, 277–8, 284
Ottolenghi, Gen. 167
Ottoman empire 345; early 13; *19C.* 17, 46; early *20C.* 118, 173; Young Turks 173; WWI 136, 138, 142; after 154, 178
Oxford University 15, 113, 251; Balliol 114, 137, 161
Oz, Amos 39–40, 82, 262, 324, 342, 352

Pale of Settlement 49, 53, 120, 130
Palestine: ancient 2–3, 13; under Romans 3; *18C.* 11; *19C.* 11, 74, (Hess's proposal 46–8), (Ah-had's 131–3); early *20C.*, 58,

82; British proposal, *1914* 136–40; 1st Aliyah 58, 119, 330; 2nd 82–3, 119; 3rd 156; 4th 156; Yishuv 83, 155, 180, 201, 216, 219, 226, 229; *1918* population 156; Balfour Declaration xii, 126, 143, 145–7, 152–3, 154, 168; British Mandate 151–65, 208–9, 217, 223, 239–40; Labour movement in 200–1, 311–12; *1930s* immigration restrictions 182, 209; WWII 216–20; after 223, 224–32; terrorism in 216–18, 228–9; partition 219, 230–2; *1942* Biltmore programme 219–20; after WWII 223, 224–32, 235, 239; federation proposed 291; *1948* onwards *see* Israel; *see also* Arabs, Palestinian; Jerusalem; Yishuv
Palestine Liberation Organisation (PLO) 255, 282; Entebbe airport 287; *1982* attack on 301–2; *1993* agreement 320–2; *1996* 348
Palestine Post 217
Palmerston, Henry Temple, 3rd Viscount 1–2, 16, 18
Paris, France 34–5
Parliament, Houses of: *18C.* 15; *19C.* 15, 17, 25, 100; Rothschild in 50; Belloc in 69, 102; Marconi scandal 102–3; *1923* 158; *1941* 217; *1950–60s* 305; War Crimes Act 340
Parsons, William 189
partition 231; of India 230–1; of Ireland 146, 152, 178; for Palestine 219, 230–2
Passfield, Sidney Webb, Baron 181–2; White Paper 182, 194
Passover 2, 7, 17–18
Peace for the Holy Land 225
Peel Commission 209, 219, 230
Peres, Shimon 287, 315, 316, 324
Perlman, Eliezer (Ben-Yehudah) 53
Perlmutter, Nathan and Ruth Ann 308
Persia (Iran): *1980* revolution 295
Peters, Joan: *Since Time Immemorial* 345
Petliura 175
Petuchowski, Jakob J. 271, 272
Phalangists 302
Picquart, Col. Georges 62
Piedmont 22
Pinsker, Leo 54–6, 57, 130
Pinto, Diana 337
Pius X, Pope 166, 167, 168
Plath, Sylvia 338–9
Plehve, V. K. 106–7, 109
Poale Zion 82; *see also* Labour Zionists
Pobedonostsev, Constantin Petrovich 53
Podhoretz, Norman 265, 322, 350; Vidal criticises 310–11; *Breaking Ranks* 307; *Commentary* 243, 263, 271, 306, 307, 311; *Making It* 306–7

pogroms: *19C*. 53, 54, 58; Kishiev 106; Odessa 171
Poland: *18C*. 9, 10; *19C*. 12; *1863* rebellion 49; after WWI 156, 330; *1930s* 204; WWII 210; *1990s* 340; *see also* Warsaw
Pollard, Anne and Jonathan 312–14
Porges, Heinrich 37
Protestantism and Protestants 8, 95, 140; Reformation 6; in Ireland 7, 86, 178; 'Jerusalem' (Blake) 7; US 49, 187
'Protocols of the Elders of Zion' 198
Proudhon, Pierre-Joseph 29
Proust, Marcel 63–4, 313
Prussia 322; *18C*. 10; *19C*. 51
Psalms 6, 12
psychology 95
Punch 100, 157
Purim 2, 7

Rabin, Yitzhak: early career 287; PM 287, 314, 321, 322, 323 4, 330, 345; death 324
racism: and antisemitism 68–70; and Labour movement 201; in South Africa 341; US 268, 278–80; Zionism as 282–4, 332–3, 334; *see also* apartheid
Ramparts 278
Rathenau, Walther 169, 203
Read, Herbert: *The Green Child* 33
Reade, Charles 99
Reader's Digest 252
Reagan, Ronald 297–300, 304–5, 334
Reform Advocate 128
Reform Judaism 87; American 127–8, 129; English 114; Hebrew Union College 123, 190; New Liberalism 238
Reformation 5, 6
refugee camps: Arab 302, 303
Reinach, Joseph 206
Renaissance, the 5–6
Renan, Ernst 56
Rerum novarum (encyclical) 69
Revisionism 176–7, 184, 198, 220–1, 249, 279, 312, 347; Betar youth movement 171, 176, 183
Rhineland 4
Rhodes, Cecil 73
Rhodes, Greece 13
Ricardo, David 15n
Richler, Mordecai 333, 345–6, 349
Robespierre, Maximilien de 10–11
Rom und Jerusalem (Hess) 44–5, 46–7, 48
Roman Catholic church: coversions 5; Dublin 131–2; language 328; mixed marriage 283; Pope 166, 167; US 122
Romania 18, 152, 166, 238
Rome and Romans: ancient 2, 3; *19C*. 44, 45, 171

Roosevelt, Franklin D. 125, 196, 209, 211, 218, 227, 256, 257
Rosebery, Archibald Primrose, 5th Earl of 50, 105
Rosenberg, Julius and Ethel 242–3
Rosenthal, A. M. 310, 317, 334
Rosenweig, Franz 134
Rossini, Gioacchino 7
Roth, Joseph 213; *Radetzkymarsch* 213–14
Roth, Philip 185, 322; *The Counterlife* 323, 333, 345, 347; *Operation Shylock* 349; *Portnoy's Complaint* 348
Rothbard, Murray 307
Rothschild family 50–1, 100, 104, 267
Rothschild, Alfred 105
Rothschild, Edmond, Baron de 58, 93
Rothschild, Hannah 50, 105
Rothschild, Lionel, Baron de 50, 52
Rothschild, Lionel Walter, 2nd Baron 51, 139, 144
Rothschild, Victor, 3rd Baron 288
Rothschild, Meyer, Baron de 50
Rothschild, Nathan, 1st Baron 104, 108, 117, 144
Royal Commission on Palestine 172, 207–8
Royal Engineers 111
Rubinstein, Amnon, 291, 311
Rubinstein, Joseph 37
Rudolf, Crown Prince of Austria 73
Ruppin, Arthur 118, 180, 183–4
Ruskin, John 82
Russia: *18C*. 10; *19C*. 23, 49, 53, 54–7, 58; *1900* 81; revolutionary movement 87; *1905* revolution 118–19; WWI 135; *1917* revolutions 142, 198; Herzl visits 106–9; *1930s* 199–200; *1948* 235, 237; *1950s* 243, 254; *1960s* 272, 281; *1970s* 281; *1980–90s*, emigration 317–18; antisemitism 198–200, 340

Sabbath 114–15, 119
Sabra camp 302, 303
Sacks, Dr Jonathan 316, 333, 337
Sadat, Anwar 295, 297
Saddam Hussein 316, 327
Safire, William 310
Said, Edward 278, 327
Salomons, Sir David 50
Salonika, Greece 222
Salvador, Joseph: *Paris, Rome, Jerusalem* 45–6
Samaria 275, 288, 294, 296, 310; *see also* West Bank of Jordan
Sampson, Gideon 15
Samuel, Sir Herbert, Lord: career 136, 138; religion 137, 138; Marconi affair

103–4, 159; *1914* Cabinet memo 138–40;
  1917 144; and Weizmann 136–7; *1931*
  343n; British proconsul in Palestine
  155–6, 158, 159–60, 176
Samuel, Montagu *see* Montagu, Sir
  Samuel
San Remo conference 153–4
Sanhedrin 11–12
Sarfatti, Margherita 169
Sargent, John Singer 105
Sartre, Jean-Paul 245–6, 275–6
Sassoon, Reuben 141
Saudi Arabia 297, 298
Schanzer, Carlo 169
Schapiro, Leonard 199n
Schiff, Jacob H. 129
Schindler, Alexander 302
Schindler's List (film) 339, 341
Schneider, Ernest 90
Schnitzler, Arthur: *Der Weg ins Freie* 67–8,
  88
Schoenberg, Arnold 93n, 94, 96, 203
Schönerer, Georg von 68, 69, 91n
Schulberg, Budd: *What Makes Sammy
  Run?*' 197
Schultz, Rabbi Benjamin 242
Schwartz, Delmore 245, 348
Schwarzenberg, Felix 45
Scott, C. P. 136
Scott, Sir Walter: *Ivanhoe* 259n
Seipel, Monseignor. 203
Selbourne, David 289, 303–4
Seligman, Joseph 59
Sephardim 4, 9, 222
Serbia 40
Shaftesbury, Anthony Ashley Cooper, 1st
  Earl of 7
Shaftesbury, Anthony Ashley Cooper, 7th
  Earl of 1–2, 7, 17, 18
Shahak, Israel 290–1
Shakespeare, William 352; *The Merchant of
  Venice* 24, 99
Shalit, Ann and Benjamin 315–16
Shamir, Yitzhak (Yezernitsky) 216, 217,
  229, 303, 310, 316, 318–19; early career
  303
Shanker, Albert 280
Sharett, Moshe 247, 248–9, 324
Sharon, Ariel 248, 297
Shertock, Moshe 170, 183; *see also* Sharett
Shinwell, Emanuel 158
Sholem, Gershon 265
Siberia 200
Sicily 39
Silver, Rabbi Abba Hillel 252, 255–6
Simon, Leon 179; *Studies in Jewish
  Nationalism* 193
Sims, Dewey 269

Sinai 272–3, 274
Six-Day war, *1967* 272–3, 274
Smith, Gerald L. K. 242
Smolenskin, Peretz 53, 54, 58
Smyrna 178
socialism 69, 85, 87–8, 91, 168–9, 200,
  277, 329; Christian 69, 71, 100, 203,
  205; Jewish Social Democratic Party 88;
  Mapon party 242, 277; Marxist Social
  Democracy 69, 91; *see also* Communism;
  National Socialism
Sokolov, Nahum 174
Sonnino, Sidney 167
South Africa: blacks in 285–6; Boer war
  102, 163; gold mining 101, 201;
  imperialism 164; racism 341
Soviet Union *see* Russia
Spain: *15C.* 4, 5–6; Inquisition 9; *19C.* 15
Sparrow, John 266
Spectator 251
Spinoza, Baruch 12–13, 34
sport 335–6
Sprinzak, Ehud 296
Squadron, Howard 302
Stalin, Josef 195, 200, 210, 235, 264, 307
Stanley, Venetia 140, 144
Stavsky, Abraham 184, 236
Steed, Wickham 89, 92
Stein, Edith 23
Steiner, George 237, 309, 34
Stern, Fritz xiv
Stern, J. P. 262
Stevenson, Adlai 299
Stoecker, Adolf 51, 52, 57n
Stone, I. F. 352; *Underground to Palestine*
  231, 346
Strindberg, Johan August 94
Strousberg, Baron Bethel 51
Students for a Democratic Society 278
Suez canal 50, 254–6, 258
suicide 3, 96, 212–15, 221, 306, 338
Sulzberger, Arthur Hays 225
Sykes, Sir Mark 145
Syria 142, 216, 247, 254, 272, 273, 301
Syrkin, Marie 263

Taaffe, Eduard von 52
Tancred (Disraeli) 27–8, 31–3
Tausig, Carl 37
Taylor, A. J. P. 9, 45, 84–5, 146, 161, 162,
  182
Tedeschi, Corrado 170
Tel Aviv 184, 236, 271
Tempo 168
Territorialist movement 110, 117
Territories, West Bank *1967* 274–5, 318;
  Arabs in 325; Jewish settlements in 288,

296, 326; *see also* Gaza; West Bank of Jordan
terrorists, dealing with 217
Tevere 170
Thackeray, William Makepeace 99, 100
Thalberg, Irving 197
Thatcher, Margaret 305
Third World 277, 341
Tikkun 331
Time 297
Times, The: *1840* 1; *1882* 70; *1899* 89; *1903* 106; *1905* 137; *1917* 143, 144; *1920* 198; *1975* 288
Tisch, Laurence 296–7
Tisza-Eszlar case 66
Titus, emperor 3
Tivnan, Edward 258, 269, 300
Tnuat Haherut (Freedom Party) 236–7
Tolstoy, Leo 82, 132, 238
Toussenel: *Les juifs rois de l'époque* 28
Trans-Jordan 176, 235
Treblinka camp 260
Trevor-Roper, H. R. 241
Trilling, Lionel 244
Trotsky, Leon (Bronstein) 198, 200, 267, 304
Truman, Harry S. 224, 227–8, 235, 256, 257
Trumpeldor, Joseph 156–7
Tucholsky, Kurt 213
Turkey *19C.* 17, 85, 132; early *20C.* 107; in WWI 173, 175; after WWI 151, 152–3, 165, 178; Young Turks 17

Uganda 284–5, 286; Entebbe airport 287
Uganda Offer 110, 117
Ukraine 10, 130, 156
Ulster 146, 178
unions, Labour 201
United Jewish Appeal 248
United Nations: General Assembly, *1947* 231; *1973/5* resolution 282–4; Special Committee on Palestine 225, 230; *1948* 236; *1978* 295
United States of America: Jewish immigration, *19C.*, 49, 58–60, 119; early *20C.* 119–29; WWI 135, 141–2, 152, 271; between wars 187–201; WWII 218, 219–21, 223, 271; *1940s* 220–1, 222, 226, 227, 247; *1950s* 242, 247–8, 249–8, 249–53; Suez affair 255–6; Gulf war 316–17; relations with Israel 255–7, 268–73, 277–80, 292–3, 296–301, 302, 304–5, 306–14, 316–23, 330–1, 334–7, 343–5, 347–8; aid to Israel 247–8, 300–1, 311, 319, 331, 336, (loan guarantee 317–19); antisemitism 59,

188–90, 268–9, 308–9, 313–14, 331; AWACS sale 297–8, 299–300; Conference of Presidents of Major American Jewish Organisations 257, 302, 313; Holocaust museum 339–40; Jewish immigration restrictions 187–8, 194, 209, 211, 228; petition to President 128; presidential elections 256–7, 269; *see also* New York
universities: *19C.* European 52, 70, 82; Oxford 15, 113, 251, (Balliol 114, 137, 161); *20C.* US 189
Uris, Leon: *Exodus* 259
usury 12

Vallat, Xavier 276
Vance, Cyrus 296
Venice 4, 45
Verdi, Giuseppe 7
Vergani, Ernst 90
Verjudung 6, 24
Victoria, Queen 18, 26
Vidal, Gore 310–11
Vienna: *19C.* 52–3, 56, 58, 59, 64, 65, 67, 69, 71–2, 73, 86, 214; *1900* 88; Kraus in 89, 91; Hitler in 203; *1930s* 171; after WWII 261; *Bürgertum* 83; University 70
Village Voice 273
Vilna 171, 172
Vogelstine, Rabbi 206
Voltaire, François de: *Dictionnaire philosophique* 8
von Treitschke, Heinrich 52
Vorwärts see Forward

Wagner, Cosima 35, 37, 141
Wagner, Eva 94
Wagner, Richard 34–8, 70–1, 92n, 95, 261, 345; *Das Judentum in der Musik* 35–7, 38
Wales 139
Walker, Jimmy 194
Wall Street Journal 344
Wannsee conference, Berlin 215
War Crimes Act 340
Warburg, Felix 155
Warfield, David 122
Warner Brothers 195
Warsaw 49, 107, 212, 307
Washington: Holocaust Museum 339
Wasserstein, Bernard: *Vanishing Diaspora* 342–3
Waugh, Evelyn 99, 131, 240–1
Webb, Beatrice 181–2
Webb, Sidney, Baron Passfield 181–2; White Paper 182, 194
Weber, Nancy 273

396

Webern, Anton von 93n
Wedekind, Frank 94
Wedgwood, Josiah 163–5; *The Seventh
    Dominion* 163–5
Weidenfeld, George, Lord, 185
Weininger, Otto 95–6, 213; *Geschlecht und
    Charakter* 95
Weiss, Philip 343
Weiss, Rabbi Avi 313
Weizmann, Chaim 74, 124, 133, 134; early
    life 812; in Britain 82, 135, 136–7, 141,
    144, 145, 154; in Italy 170; and
    Jabotinsky 175, 176, 177, 179; and
    Magnes 179, 180, 181; and Namier 251;
    1930 181; *1940s* 219, 220, 223; *1944* 218;
    1948 250
Wells, H. G. 181–2, 340
Welt, Die 83, 93, 134
Werfel, Franz 94
Wertheim, Maurice 225
Wertheimer, Josef von 67
West Bank of Jordan 274–5, 288, 294–5,
    296, 303, 312, 323
'Whole World is Against Us, The' (song)
    337
Wieseltier, Leon 314
William, King of Prussia 51
Wilson, Harold 304
Wilson, Woodrow 126, 152
Wise, Rabbi Isaac Mayer 129, 206
Wistrich, Robert 87
Witte (Russian finance minister) 108–9
Wittgenstein, Ludwig 95
Wolf, Lucien 106, 115–16, 117, 135, 141–2
Wolffsohn, David 75, 118
World Jewish Congress 336
World War I 124, 126–7, 135, 136, 138,
    151–2, 204, 260; profiteering 157;
    postwar settlements 152–4
World War II 210–11; bombing 301n;
    Final Solution 210–13, 215–16, 221–3;

end 223–4
World Zionist Organisation 220
Wouk, Herman 252
Wright, Richard 245
Wyatt, Woodrow 239, 240

Yadlin, Asher 287
Yehoshua, A. B. 336, 348
Yezierska, Anzia: 'How I Found America'
    120
Yiddish language 4–5, 10, 37, 93, 94, 171,
    222
Yids 171–2, 329, 349–50
Yishuv in Palestine 83, 155, 180, 201, 216,
    219, 226, 229, 311
Yom Kippur 281–2, 332

Zangwill, Israel 106, 117, 189; *The Melting
    Pot* 120
Zanuck, Darryl 196
Zealots 3
Zeff, Joseph 121
Zetterbaum, Max 88
Zhirnovsky, Vladimir 340
Zionism xi, xii–xiii; initiated 65, 75–8,
    84–5; 1st Congress 75–6, 90, 98–9, 106,
    113, 131, 167; 2nd 82; 4th 81; 6th 110;
    7th 117; *1913* Congress 83; 4th 81; 6th
    110; 7th 117; *1913* Congress 83; and
    anti-semitism 88–9, 177, 290–1
Zionist Action Committee: *1905* 118; *1942*
    220
Zionist General Council 177, 181, 235
Zionist Organisation of America 181, 193,
    201
American Zionists 124–5, 126, 193, 218–20,
    221
Zola, Émile 63
Zukor, Adolph 195
Zweig, Stefan 213, 214–15